Decision-Making

FOR

DUMMIES®

A Wiley Brand

by Dawna Jones

FOR

DUMMIES®

A Wiley Brand

Decision-Making For Dummies®

Published by: **John Wiley & Sons, Inc.,** 111 River Street, Hoboken, NJ 07030-5774, www.wiley.com

Copyright © 2014 by John Wiley & Sons, Inc., Hoboken, New Jersey

Published simultaneously in Canada

No part of this publication may be reproduced, stored in a retrieval system or transmitted in any form or by any means, electronic, mechanical, photocopying, recording, scanning or otherwise, except as permitted under Sections 107 or 108 of the 1976 United States Copyright Act, without the prior written permission of the Publisher. Requests to the Publisher for permission should be addressed to the Permissions Department, John Wiley & Sons, Inc., 111 River Street, Hoboken, NJ 07030, (201) 748-6011, fax (201) 748-6008, or online at http://www.wiley.com/go/permissions.

Trademarks: Wiley, For Dummies, the Dummies Man logo, Dummies.com, Making Everything Easier, and related trade dress are trademarks or registered trademarks of John Wiley & Sons, Inc., and may not be used without written permission. All other trademarks are the property of their respective owners. John Wiley & Sons, Inc., is not associated with any product or vendor mentioned in this book.

LIMIT OF LIABILITY/DISCLAIMER OF WARRANTY: WHILE THE PUBLISHER AND AUTHOR HAVE USED THEIR BEST EFFORTS IN PREPARING THIS BOOK, THEY MAKE NO REPRESENTATIONS OR WARRAN-TIES WITH RESPECT TO THE ACCURACY OR COMPLETENESS OF THE CONTENTS OF THIS BOOK AND SPECIFICALLY DISCLAIM ANY IMPLIED WARRANTIES OF MERCHANTABILITY OR FITNESS FOR A PARTICULAR PURPOSE. NO WARRANTY MAY BE CREATED OR EXTENDED BY SALES REPRESEN-TATIVES OR WRITTEN SALES MATERIALS. THE ADVISE AND STRATEGIES CONTAINED HEREIN MAY NOT BE SUITABLE FOR YOUR SITUATION. YOU SHOULD CONSULT WITH A PROFESSIONAL WHERE APPROPRIATE. NEITHER THE PUBLISHER NOR THE AUTHOR SHALL BE LIABLE FOR DAMAGES ARISING HEREFROM.

For general information on our other products and services, please contact our Customer Care Department within the U.S. at 877-762-2974, outside the U.S. at 317-572-3993, or fax 317-572-4002. For technical support, please visit www.wiley.com/techsupport.

Wiley publishes in a variety of print and electronic formats and by print-on-demand. Some material included with standard print versions of this book may not be included in e-books or in print-on-demand. If this book refers to media such as a CD or DVD that is not included in the version you purchased, you may download this material at http://booksupport.wiley.com. For more information about Wiley products, visit www.wiley.com.

Library of Congress Control Number: 2013956849

ISBN 978-1-118-83366-7 (pbk); ISBN 978-1-118-84749-7 (ebk); ISBN 978-1-118-84753-4 (ebk)

Manufactured in the United States of America

10 9 8 7 6 5 4 3 2 1

Table of Contents

Introduction

· ·

*T*ake a look at any company's results, and you see the effectiveness of its decision-making. One needs only to witness our global issues — such as diminishing biodiversity and lack of employee engagement — to recognize the consequences of past decisions. Expanding decision-making proficiency requires evolving deep perception together with higher awareness at a personal and organizational level. Without being able to see the big picture, decision-makers can't leverage the invisible forces to achieve prosperity.

As the business environment has changed from being predictable to being uncertain and from being simple to being complex, a transformation is required in how decisions are made, both individually and within organizations. As it redefines its role in society, business must restore trust with its employees and its customers. Personally, professionally, and organizationally, it's time to gain access to all your creative resources and intelligences so that you can make the decisions you need to, to prime your company for success in this ever-changing world.

In this book, in addition to insights into intuition — a key but often overlooked component of good decision-making — are thoughts and ideas from inspirational business owners, stories of innovative start-ups, and conventional and collaborative tools. Mostly you discover how you can participate in designing both a fresh, rejuvenated world of work and world at large.

About This Book

Day-to-day decision-makers wrestle with information overwhelm and priority setting in dynamic conditions. To top it off, humans are complex beings with lots of hidden and unnoticed biases. Decision-making is clearly both an art and a science.

In *Decision-Making For Dummies,* I provide both traditional and very innovative approaches to decision-making. I demystify some of the mysteries about intuition, bias, and rational decision-making, while showing you how to take a more intelligent approach to decision-making. For example, probably no other topic generates more diversity of opinion than decision-making, especially when it comes to the role of intuition. Top business schools teach rational decision-making despite research showing it's not that effective and even though real-world entrepreneurs rely on their intuition backed up by data. You can discover how to use intuition to improve your capacity to perceive situations more accurately and make decisions in dynamic environments and to handle complexity and uncertainty with confidence.

The tools, skills, and perspectives in this book offer ways for decision-makers like you to evolve your decision-making. In so doing, you'll gain greater confidence in who you are and what you bring to the decision-making process. And if you're overly confident as a decision-maker, I hope you'll gain some humility so that you can embrace diverse, seemingly opposing ideas, to become more flexible in your approach.

Nothing in this book is about *either-or* thinking, and the information I include serves each person differently. Not only will you find information that will help you address the particular decision-making challenges you face in the moment, but you'll also find information that helps you grow as a decision-maker.

Like all *For Dummies* books, the material is organized in an easy-to-access structure. Sidebars and paragraphs that accompany a Technical Stuff icon offer tangential information that enriches but isn't essential to understanding.

I've also established a few conventions. First, I differentiate between the brain's intelligence (its mental/intellectual fitness) and the heart's intelligence, an idea common in eastern traditions, which holds that the heart's intelligence is the path to innate knowledge. Second, I use the word *intuition* to denote your higher intelligence. It is not a mystical power; it is a powerful tool. In this book, I show you the science and the value of intuition.

Finally, you may note that some web addresses break across two lines of text. If you're reading this book in print and want to visit one of these web pages, simply key in the web address exactly as it appears in the text, pretending as though the line break doesn't exist. If you're reading this as an e-book, you've got it easy — just click the web address to be taken directly to the web page.

Foolish Assumptions

The biggest assumption I made while I wrote this book is that you want to know how to become a better decision-maker. Some other assumptions I made include the following:

✔ You've noticed that the results of current decisions come at a high cost, and you want to minimize the negative consequences of decisions.

✔ You recognize the value of self growth and may also yearn for something more than repeating the same cycles over and over.

✔ You're either in business or you fervently care about the role business plays in society and in shaping the world we live in.

✔ You feel that your workplace is stymying your or your team's ability to make good decisions, and you want strategies you can use to create an environment that promotes sound decision-making.

Icons Used in This Book

Just like signposts on a road, *For Dummies* books use icons to point to certain kinds of information. Keep an eye open for these symbols.

This icon points to advice, words of wisdom, and tips that help you choose with greater discretion what is right for your situation.

This signal helps you know what to focus on. It highlights specific and important points to keep in mind.

This icon points out information that, although interesting and insightful, isn't absolutely necessary to know to become a better decision-maker. Feel free to skip these bits.

Not surprisingly, this icon indicates potential pitfalls, unanticipated dynamics, or responses you might have to deal with during the decision-making process.

I use this icon to highlight the experiences of real companies. Some serve as inspiration; some as lessons in what not to do.

Beyond the Book

In addition to the material in the print or e-book you're reading right now, this product also comes with some access-anywhere content on the web. Check out the free Cheat Sheet at www.dummies.com/cheatsheet/decisionmaking for advice on how to communicate a decision, pointers for sorting through a sea of data to get the information that can help you make a good decision, and more. In addition, I've provided lots of bonus material at http://www.dummies.com/webextras/decisionmaking that goes beyond the content in both the print and e-books.

Where to Go from Here

The beauty about a _For Dummies_ book is that it is completely intuitive. Head to the pages you need when you need them and trust your instincts to guide you. Take a look at the Table of Contents for general topics or the index for more specific content. Head to a chapter that appeals to you (maybe you're curious how to communicate a decision you think will be unpopular), and then find a chapter that includes information you're skeptical about (intuition and decision-making — aren't those two things mutually exclusive?). Why take this approach? For two reasons: First, sticking to familiarity is the enemy of sound decision-making; this give you a chance to jolt your own thinking voluntarily. Second, whatever you read, you'll find detailed information that you can apply to your decision-making today.

Apply what you read and see what happens. Becoming a better, more effective decision-maker starts one decision at a time, as does transforming your business to meet the needs of the new, interconnected world we all live in.

You can also find more information in a few other _For Dummies_ business books, including _Leading Business Change For Dummies,_ by Christina Tangora Schlachter and Terry Hildebrandt; _Leadership For Dummies,_ by John Marrin; _Emotional Intelligence For Dummies,_ by Steven Stein; and _The Leadership Brain For Dummies,_ by Marilee Sprenger — all published by John Wiley & Sons, Inc. None of these books is required, but all offer supplemental tools, skills, and views that can promote your growth as a decision-maker.

Find me on LinkedIn (http://ca.linkedin.com/in/dawnahjones/) or register at http://www.frominsighttoaction.com/decision-making-for-dummies/ to gain access to decision-making support.

Part I
Getting Started with Decision-Making

getting started with

decision-making

In this part . . .

- ✔ Find out how global and societal shifts are changing the way decisions are made, resulting in seemingly simple decisions being infinitely more complex than you may have previously thought

- ✔ Differentiate between strategic, tactical, and operational decisions

- ✔ Improve your decision-making by developing higher levels of personal and organizational awareness

- ✔ Learn how workplace environment and company structure affect decisions

- ✔ Foster an environment that leads to high-quality decisions

Chapter 1

Big-Picture Pressures on Decision-Makers

Decisions are being made all the time, every minute of every day, and most of them are made automatically, without much intentional thought. Subtle yet pervasive forces influence the accuracy of every decision. Most decision-makers aren't aware of these forces, yet their impact has huge consequences on company fortunes and people's lives. With each decision, small or big, that you and I make, we shape the experience of life and, more boldly, the design of the world.

In this chapter, I show you how big-picture pressures are forcing business decision-makers to engage in higher-order thinking, to see things from multiple perspectives, and to embrace rather than fear uncertainty and complexity. More importantly, you discover how adapting to these changes lets you become a leader who is purpose-driven — someone who leads by example, inspires confidence in his or her employees, and creates a working environment that is healthier and gets everyone working together toward success.

Making Decisions in an Ever-Changing World

Although believing that your situation or your company's fortunes are beyond your control may be easier than facing the alternative, the truth is that experiences — yours or your company's — are shaped by the moment-to-moment decisions. Unfortunately, in business, many of those decisions are made under duress because the fires you have to fight every day can distract you from seeing the situation from a different perspective. When you're under pressure, routines — even inefficient ones — can feel like a lifeline.

To move forward, you need to step back from those routine patterns so that you can gain insight and see the opportunities you've been overlooking.

The ground shifting beneath your feet

Your beliefs guide what questions you ask when you assess a new situation and how you view the information you uncover. They also act as a filter for the ideas that inform your reality. In business and in life, dismissing what doesn't fit is natural. But in the end, it also makes you resistant to change. After all, you can't change what you can't see.

In this section, I outline the big-picture trends impacting businesses today, explain how traditional beliefs about how business is done collide with today's reality, and show you what it means to you as a decision-maker so that you can select which beliefs to keep and which to change.

The reliance on intelligence rather than force

The first big shift is the growing reliance on intelligence (engaging in a higher-order thinking) rather than force (surviving at any cost) when working with natural resources and human potential. According to the old mindset, resources are unlimited, and waste is considered acceptable, despite the inefficiencies. Because nature's contribution to the economy is difficult to count, the best solution is to leave it out or dismiss it as an externality. The new mindset says that nature's resources can't be counted, but they do count.

The error of the old way of thinking is becoming more evident. One 1997 estimate calculated nature's annual contribution to the economy at $33 USD trillion!

Companies that value nature's contribution are far more profitable than those that do not. A fast-growing number of start-ups and private and semi-private companies in many sectors — even beyond the more obvious sectors like clean technology — readily grasp this concept and are growing rapidly. Global companies such as Novo Nordisk (http://www.novonordisk.com), Canon (http://www.canon.com), and Unilever (http://www.unilever.com) are examples. Non-profit B-Lab (http://www.bcorporation.net/what-are-b-corps/the-non-profit-behind-b-corps) has certified over 1,000 companies as B-Corps in 33 countries. B-Corps must pass rigorous social and environmental performance standards to provide consumers with transparent reporting. You'll find those companies listed at http://www.bcorporation.net.

The rise of professional networks within and beyond a company's borders

The second big shift affects how employees are viewed. Today, business performance is powered by professional networks that exist both within and beyond a company's boundaries. These professional networks, which are engaged in achieving a shared goal, extend well beyond the control of internal management and, as a result, require a shift in management style. With technology as a major disruptor of how work gets done, work between colleagues around the globe can now easily take place collaboratively in a flash via a Google hangout, a Skype call, or a custom app on your mobile device.

The old belief that employees are replaceable and have to be constantly told what to do is giving way to the belief that people are knowledgeable and want to contribute their talent. The growing movement for creating great work environments — places that tap people's potential and creativity, invite and honor their contributions, respect and value them as people, and count social and environmental health as essential — is a natural outcome of the understanding that good decisions and great work comes from engaged employees who work well together and feel good about their accomplishments. Ethical decisions are a natural result of a healthy workplace. Double bonus!

When workplace and management conditions make it difficult, if not impossible, for employees to contribute meaningfully, their talent is repressed as they are forced to fit into preconceived roles, a situation that creates stress-related illnesses that cost companies in the U.S. $300 billion annually. Unfortunately, workplaces have been slow to adjust, as employee disengagement statistics show. Yet as leadership skills become deeper and more universal (Chapter 13 tells you how to develop these skills), workplace health and — ultimately — workplace decisions will improve.

The changing perception of business's role

The third big shift is the changing perception of business's role. The traditional view has been that business's sole purpose is to be an economic engine, to make money. The new perspective is that business is an integral part of society and a subset of the larger ecological system and that it can be a force for good. This purpose can be achieved when companies engage their employees in a higher purpose, one that goes beyond mere profit.

This shift has occurred largely due to the size of the issues demanding solutions, coupled with a deep yearning for meaning and purpose. Addressing these issues demands imagination, collaboration, and the highest level of inspired innovation ever achieved by humanity. In this climate, business as usual isn't an option.

The old way of doing things promotes "either/or" thinking: *either* profit *or* doing good (service); *either* the environment *or* the economy. This kind of mindset limits companies' capacity to spot opportunities to adapt to the emerging new realities. So don't think in "either/or" terms. Instead, insert the word *and:* profit *and* doing good; the environment *and* the economy. See how this little tweak enables you to broaden your thinking?

Companies that recognize they are part of society and have, in addition to their money-making role, a responsibility to the environment, their communities, and so on, are more profitable. Their relationships with employees and customers is genuine and trustworthy; they look after the environment because it is the right and smart thing to do, and they find creative ways to embed social and environmental responsibility into profit-making endeavors. Their comfort with working in unpredictable, complex situations gives them the edge.

The rise of social media

A change in the way people communicate and access information brings us to the fourth big shift. Social media and mobile technology is changing how consumers and employees acquire information and make their career or consumer purchases. In short, current technology makes it extremely easy to get information quickly across political and geographic boundaries. The effect is to broaden perspective.

Before social media and modern technology, businesses followed a model in which they produced products (or services) and then coerced customers to buy. The goal was to do whatever it took to compete and win. Today, however, social media and global connectivity enable the consumer to quickly hold companies accountable for the consequences of their decisions.

In this way, consumers are now change agents. They select which companies to support, using apps, like Buycott (`http://www.buycott.com`), which allow them to buy products that reflect their principles, and they give their loyalty to companies whose ethics and values align with their own. (Buycott is pretty neat: To use the app, you scan a product, and the app tells you which company is behind the brand and cross references this information with causes you've identified as important.)

It's not likely that social media or technology will save civilization, but business owners can use it as a tool to restore transparency and trust in business practices and decisions. You can use it to connect with your customers and employees, build and burnish your brand reputation, and promote customer service by providing meaningful customer interactions and responses to customer comments.

Businesses aren't the only ones who need to be careful about the reach of social media. Aspiring employees need to be aware, too. Recruiters and prospective employers often take a look at Facebook pages to see who their applicants really are. Status reports announcing how you blew off an appointment because the sun was shining, as one person did, get you blacklisted by top recruiters.

The need of employees to do work that matters

The fifth big shift in the business environment is away from doing work solely to achieve financial security to doing work that matters. This shift challenges the old idea that employees are an asset not much different from other line items on the budget and will do what you tell them out of fear of losing their jobs.

Instead, employees (and customers) today want to be agents for change. They're no longer trapped in workplaces that don't work; they can work anywhere and do rewarding work they love. They move jobs, change careers, and start their own businesses. Younger generations in particular easily adapt, inherently believing that they can accomplish any goal; they want a job that will enable them to be true to their values and to be able to, as one put it, "take my whole self to work." Companies that acknowledge this shift seek to engage employees and remove built-in corporate cultural barriers that obstruct collaboration or innovation.

A 2013 survey conducted by Aspire, a company that provides executive coaching and development for women, found that 78 percent of female corporate professionals are not setting their sights on the boardroom; instead, they're considering leaving their current positions to start their own companies.

Assessing what these changes mean to you

As the preceding sections make clear, the business decision-making environment has changed. Adhering to a "business as usual" model won't get you the results it used to. If your company is to adapt to a new business climate, how you make decisions must change to reflect the new realities. Consider the following:

- **Making changes in the supervisory role:** The role of managers is moving from a model in which the boss controls individual and team performance to a model in which the boss's role is to enable and support teams that self-organize to achieve a shared goal. In this new world, bosses must display a higher level of leadership: You must know how and when to step back, you must stay curious and be able to foster curiosity and creativity in your employees, and you must be committed to removing procedures and processes that block teamwork.

✔ **Changing the way you work with employees:** Decision-makers must embrace a collaborative style of working with employees. Collaboration frees up knowledge and talent in a way that facilitates creativity and problem-solving. When presented with a goal or a problem, for example, collaborative teams aren't hemmed in by a rigid process; instead, they can adapt and adjust, as necessary, to dynamic situations.

Embracing a collaborative work style requires a change in mindset regarding your relationship with your employees and how power should be used. Rather than wielding power and control over your employees, you'll work *with* them. You'll also place more trust in yourself and others, based on a genuine conviction that people want to bring their best selves to life, and it's your job to bring out the best in them. In doing so, you will also discover hidden talents and achieve personal fulfillment as well.

✔ **Improving the way you manage risk:** Those making the switch away from traditional management roles are better able to manage risk exposure. Being aware that bigger forces are at work gives you the edge and ability to adjust.

If you rely on a command-and-control management style, you can easily become complacent. After all, someone who thinks he's in control usually doesn't know when he's lost it. Market trends and upstart companies with different approaches can fundamentally change the business environment and leave you and your company foundering.

A great resource for ways to integrate smart practices into every aspect of your company is the book *Embedded Sustainability: The Next Big Competitive Advantage,* by Chris Laszlo and Nadya Zhexembayeva (Stanford Business Books).

Embracing Uncertainty and Unpredictability

Humans tend to be apprehensive about — and some outright fear — uncertainty. Yet uncertainty is often the catalyst that lets you expand your leadership skills, broaden your business thinking, and improve your decision-making. Whether you embrace uncertainty or try to hide from it, one thing is for sure: The business decision-making environment has changed. It is more complex, unpredictable, and ambiguous than ever before. In this section, I share a few things you can do to make dealing with uncertainty easier.

The acronym *VUCA* encapsulates the new operating conditions for life and business: **v**olatility, **u**ncertainty, **c**omplexity, and **a**mbiguity. Accepting this different reality gives you your edge. Rather than avoiding change, you can stretch into higher potential.

Increase integrity and truth-telling

Combine changing societal values with the connectivity made possible by social media, and consumers and customers are able to hold you and your company accountable in ways that were nearly impossible just 25 years ago. As a result, businesses must be honest, come clean when mistakes are made, and work to earn the trust of not only their customers but also the communities in which they do business.

Notice what is happening on the innovative edges

Being in business today means being on your toes all the time! If you're feeling content and pretty secure, chances are you're looking for threats in familiar places — and not where they truly exist. Innovative start-ups — not your traditional competitors — are the ones who can change the terrain overnight.

If you're looking for innovative approaches to management or information on bossless organizations, check out the following:

- **The Self-Management Institute (www.self-managementinstitute. org):** It has practical tools for running flat (that is, no management layers), self-organizing companies.

- **Cocoon Projects in Italy (http://www.cocoonprojects.com):** It has come up with an innovative way to account for value created by each contributor (there are no job interviews) and to calculate value-added among peers. Cofounder Stelio Verzera's article, which describes Cocoon Projects' philosophy, was awarded the Digital Freedom Award by the Management Innovation exchange (http://www.mixprize.org/ hack/liquid-organizations-realizing-next-evolutionary-stage-anti-fragility?challenge=18606). To learn more about Liquid Organizations, see http://www.liquidorganization.info.

Don't limit planning to an annual task

Annual planning worked when business environments were more predictable. Today, committing to a year-long plan that ignores changing conditions in the meantime is a fairly high-risk strategy. If your decision-making process is based on old business beliefs, you'll feel stressed out and under pressure right now. Unless your business beliefs have undergone a radical tune up in the last six months, you're behind. One option, for example, is to adopt a Lean/Agile (software development) principled approach to change, which uses client/customer feedback and responds to changing circumstances.

Make your decision-making process values-based

Upgrade your decision-making process so that it is value-based. In this model, your company must be clear about what its values are and then make every decision in alignment with those values. Values used for decision-making aren't the glossy ones from the poster pinned to the wall. They declare what is important enough to guide your decision-making and direct how things get done. To discover the difference between belief-based and values-based decision-making, head to Chapter 5.

Cultivate learning and curiosity

Organizations that cultivate learning and curiosity as core skills tend to exhibit these characteristics:

- ✔ **They're flexible.** Learning organizations aren't fixed on concrete thinking, which is a sure-fire way to prevent better decision-making.

- ✔ **They recognize that mistakes are part of the learning process.** Instead of fear-based decision-making, in which judgments tend to center on what someone should have or could have done, the focus is forward-looking.

- ✔ **They use curiosity to open doors to new ideas.** Curiosity is a critical core skill in a complex decision-making environment because the complexities don't show up until the problem you thought you'd solved returns with a vengeance! In companies that don't embrace curiosity, employees and teams tend to dismiss inconsistencies, even though inconsistencies actually point to things that should be explored to find out what is happening.

Invest in your personal and professional growth

You are the most important part of the equation. The difference between a successful business, one that can adapt to emerging new realities, and an unsuccessful one is your leadership. Do you want to have 12 years of experience, or 1 year of experience 12 times? The beauty of personal growth is that, when facing adverse conditions, you can become more creative.

Developing yourself as a decision-maker gives you increased capacity to regulate and use your emotions as information, to make better decisions under pressure, to understand how your intuition operates and to use it to your advantage, and to expand your thinking so that you can anticipate unintended consequences early on.

Raising the Integrity and Ethics of Business Decisions

Although many companies know their markets, care about their customers, and pay attention to doing what is right for all, a few companies have lost the public trust because of their reckless decision-making governed by self-interest. Often the difference between good companies and bad ones comes down to *ethics,* the moral code of conduct that underpins ethical decision-making.

The public has very little tolerance for unethical behavior: corporate decisions and actions that do more harm than good; that place self-interest over the interests of the communities in which they operate, the environment, or their employees; and that unfairly skew the distribution of wealth. Ultimately, running a company unethically leads to unhealthy workplaces, seriously compromised decision-making, lower profits, and failure.

Ethical companies, on the other hand — those that serve communities, care about their workers, care for the environment, and don't succumb to narrow and short-sighted thinking — will ultimately supplant their unethical competitors. Restoring trust with employees, customers, and society as a whole starts with recognizing the wisdom behind using business as a force for good. In this section, I explain what ethical decision-making is and why it's good for business. Chapter 19 delves into the topic in more detail.

Overcoming factors that lead to unethical decisions

Although some business decision-makers are unscrupulous, most don't start out with the intention to make unethical decisions, but they make them none-theless. So if the problem isn't intent, what is it? As I explain in this section, unethical decisions can be a consequence of skewed or narrow thinking, on-the-job pressures, and other factors that you probably don't realize set the stage for ethical transgressions. Read on to discover what factors often lead to unethical decisions and what you can do about them.

Having too narrow a focus

When the focus is too narrow, you pay more attention to the short term rather than the long term, or you're more committed to meeting financial goals than delighting your customers.

Seeing the big picture is an integral part of making ethical decisions. When you step back, you gain new and wider perspective that can reveal patterns that you may not have noticed before. This broader perspective enables you to see connections between what before may have seemed to be unrelated enti-ties and, as a result, consider the far-reaching implications of your decisions. You can also see familiar patterns that may indicate that your decision-making is going around in circles and not really producing the change or benefit you were hoping for.

Not linking your decisions to your values

Ethical decision-making is rooted in the capacity to anchor decision-making to your values. Doing so lets you know what's important when things seem uncertain, and it gives you a standard by which to judge the outcome of the decisions you make. Values-based decision-making is different from decision-making based on beliefs or assumptions, a topic I discuss in more detail in Chapter 5.

Succumbing to workplace pressures

When intense pressure to achieve targets exists, people are tempted to take shortcuts that can compromise standards. To counter this, step back to dis-cover the source of the pressure and identify where knee-jerk reactions to demands have hijacked a more intentional approach to decision-making. Also try to balance short-term thinking with long-term vision and goals. When you include the long term in your decision-making, you tend to make better deci-sions because you're applying a broader perspective to the problem.

Making assumptions

When the information underpinning the decision is too limited, you find your-self making assumptions. To counter this tendency, engage customers and employees as active participants in your company's decision-making. Doing so broadens the information available for decision-making. As a bonus, it also bolsters your company's value because of the loyal and committed relation-ships you develop. In addition, making information available and transparent within the company reduces the inclination to make assumptions or act on speculation.

A great way to gain insight is to give airtime to employee ideas that don't fit the norm. Gary Klein, author of *Seeing What Others Don't: The Remarkable Ways We Gain Insights* (PublicAffairs), calls these *outlier beliefs:* They're impor-tant beliefs that are not firmly supported by current thinking.

Using the wrong metrics to judge success

The criteria you use to evaluate success has a direct bearing on what you and your employees pay attention to. Yet as important as it is to measure the right things, many managers and companies unwittingly use metrics that measure the wrong things, are at odds with the company's stated mission, and, in the worst cases, foster unethical behavior. If, for example, you reward employees only for making budget targets, they may postpone or avoid doing things like updating equipment for safety — a decision that could lead to inju-ries or death.

To determine whether the metrics you've put in place are creating an envi-ronment that promotes breaches of ethics, monitor the consequences of decisions. One way is to map key decisions so that you can see the results and consequences. By taking this step proactively, you'll be able to correct a course of action before it's too late. In Chapter 19, I share how to set ethi-cal standards and create an environment that brings out the best in your employees.

Designing a healthy decision-making environment

If you look back on the best and worst decisions you've ever made, you'll prob-ably discover the same thing I did: People don't make the best decisions in stressful circumstances. But stressful conditions happen all the time, you say.

There's a difference between a stressful event that must be addressed or resolved (equipment breakdown on your production line is jeopardizing your being able to complete or ship a big order to an important customer, for example) and the stress caused by being in a work environment — often characterized by unreasonable workloads, unsupportive managers, excessively long work days, and so on — that puts employees on high alert 24/7 with no end in sight.

In this type of workplace environment, the stage is set for poor decision-making. Inherent to making good decisions is designing the workplace that supports better decision-making. This means converting unhealthy workplaces into healthy ones. Healthy decision-making environments have common characteristics. Here are a few of them:

- ✔ They instill a sense of belonging and community among coworkers.

- ✔ The relationships are professional, and the company's purpose is front and center.

- ✔ Shared values underpin what is important to the company and its employees, and these values anchor decision-making in both good and tough times.

- ✔ Leaders exist at every level, decision-making is decentralized, and decision-making processes are in place. Employees at every level take personal responsibility for making decisions and accepting the consequences.

- ✔ Communication is open and honest, even when the news isn't good, and any issues are brought forward through informal and formal feedback loops so that adjustments can be made without delay.

- ✔ Learning — even learning from mistakes — is valued, which, in addition to strengthening the organization's decision-making, makes it more adaptive and resilient in uncertain and changing conditions.

- ✔ Complexity and uncertainty are valued, and decision-making isn't driven by the fear of losing control. Instead, decision-makers engage their and others' creativity to actively respond to new challenges.

A company with a healthy decision-making environment is the kind of company that creates value through its relationships with employees, customers, suppliers, and stakeholders. Rather than being too big to fail, it is too valuable to fail. In Chapter 2, I show you how to set up a company for effective decision-making. In Chapter 12, I show you how to strengthen internal and external relationships, and in Chapter 19 I explain how to upgrade your company's culture to support ethical decision-making. Restoring trust and ethical integrity in business is the way in which your business can do business more intelligently and intuitively and become a force for good.

Chapter 2

The Key Ingredients for Effective Decisions

Decision-making is rarely logical, despite assertions that it's based on rational thinking. Different ideas don't have a chance when they fail to fit into what decision-makers believe will or won't work. Just ask anyone who has ever put together a perfectly good proposal on how to increase profitability only to have the proposal shot down. Nor can innovation take place when decision-makers are unaware of how thinking influences perspective or risk perception.

Knowing what is going on under the surface drives results and gives you a chance to improve and adjust. In this chapter, I introduce you to decision-making styles and discuss what the rational mind can't see when it comes to risk perception. I also show you the three key elements that make decisions effective: a common language, the workplace culture, and your self-knowledge.

Distinguishing the Different Kinds of Decisions

The kinds of decisions you face fall anywhere on a spectrum from strategic to operational/frontline. If you're a small business owner — until you add staff and distribute responsibility, that is — you make decisions across the full spectrum. If you're in a medium-sized to large company, the kinds of decisions you face depend on how your organization distributes decision-making authority and responsibility: centralized at the top or decentralized through all levels, for example. In addition, the type of decisions you're responsible for depends on your role in the company. In this section, I describe the different kinds of business decisions. Each kind of decision calls for a different kind of thinking and decision-making style.

Traditionally, big companies are organized hierarchically, with authority allocated at each level of management down to the front line. In theory, direction comes from the top and moves down through the company for implementation. The speed and complexity of the business environment challenges this way of assigning decision-making power because it is slow. Still, this is the prevalent organizational style; even medium-sized companies lean toward using the combination of hierarchy and authority. For that reason, in this section, I lay out ways that decisions are typically thought or talked about. Different organizational structures and sources may use different terminology.

Strategic decisions

Strategic decisions are executive-level decisions. Strategic decisions are made in every area, from IT (information technology), HR (human resources), finance, and CRM (customer relations), for example. Strategic decisions look ahead to the longer term and direct the company to its destiny. They tend to be high risk and high stakes. They are complex and rely on intuition supported by information based on analysis and experience. When you face a strategic decision, you may have time to consider options reinforced by the gathered information, or you may have moments to decide.

To make good strategic-level decisions, you need to be comfortable working with a lot of information and have the ability to see the interrelationships among the company and its employees, clients, suppliers, and the communities it reaches. You need to be collaborative, in touch with what is going on, open-minded, and flexible without being wishy-washy. You can read more about the decision-making process for strategic decisions in Chapter 10 and more about what you rely on as a decision-maker in Chapter 13.

Yahoo's CEO Marissa Mayer created a strategic plan to foster the company's renewal: Knowing that each was interrelated, Mayer focused on people, then product, then site traffic, and then revenue. She began by hiring great people and taking steps to stop talented Yahoo employees from going to other companies. She then bought companies to strengthen the Yahoo product, knowing that a strong product keeps employees, builds traffic, and generates revenue.

Tactical decisions

Tactical decisions translate strategic decisions into action. Tactical decisions are more straightforward and less complex than strategic-level decisions. When they are in alignment with your company's core values or its overall mission, tactical decisions add even more value to the outcomes of the implementation. Conversely, if tactical decisions become detached from the company's direction, you and your employees end up expending a lot of effort on tasks that don't help the company achieve its goals or vision.

Tactical decisions fall in the scope of middle management. Middle managers are the proverbial meat in the sandwich; they make things happen. In vertically organized hierarchies, middle managers translate top-level decisions into goals that can be operationalized. You can read more about making decisions as a manager in Chapter 14.

Operational and frontline decisions

Operational and frontline decisions are made daily. Many operational decisions are guided by company procedures and processes, which help new employees get up to speed and serve as a backdrop for more experienced employees, who, having mastered the current procedures and processes, can detect and rapidly collate additional information, like cues, patterns, and sensory data, that aren't covered by the procedures. Take mechanics, for example: A master mechanic is able to apply procedures and specifications to fix a problem, and his accumulated experiences (and intuition) strengthen his troubleshooting abilities. Detecting subtleties is an intuitive intelligence. The effect is faster and more accurate diagnosis or assessment of a particular situation.

 Because conditions are more concrete and predictable, operational and frontline decisions as a rule hold less risk strategically and tend to follow a more routine pattern. But therein lies the danger: They can hold more risk for health and safety for the simple reason that complacency sets in, and people become less alert.

Identifying the Different Decision-Making Styles

What kind of decision-maker are you? To help you find out, I explain the different styles of decision-making. These styles are conveniently labeled, but how you apply them depends on each situation you're in and the people you're with (a topic I discuss in detail in Part IV). The following is a list of decision-making styles, which I've drawn from the work of Kenneth Brousseau, CEO of Decision Dynamics:

- ✔ **Decisive:** With decisive decision-makers, time is of the essence. Their mantra is "Get things done quickly and consistently, and stick to the plan." This decision-making style applies one course of action, using relatively little information. Being decisive comes in handy in emergency situations or when you have to clearly communicate operational-level health and safety decisions.

- ✔ **Flexible:** Flexible decision-makers are focused on speed and adaptability. They acquire just enough data to decide what to do next and are willing to change course if needed. This decision-making style works with several options that can change or be replaced as new information becomes available. Being flexible comes in handy when you have to make decisions in dynamic, uncertain situations. Flexible decision-making is relevant to all levels of decision-making.

- ✔ **Hierarchic:** Hierarchic decision-makers analyze a lot of information and seek input from others. They like to challenge differing views or approaches and value making decisions that will withstand scrutiny. Once their minds are made up, their decisions are final. This decision-making style incorporates lots of information to produce one option. This characteristic can be handy, depending on the application; financial forecasting and capital procurement decisions come to mind.

- ✔ **Integrative:** Integrative decision-makers take into account multiple elements and work with lots of input. They cultivate a wider perspective of the situation and invite a wide range of views (even ones they don't agree with). They flex as changes arise until time is up and a decision must be made. This decision-making style uses lots of information and produces lots of options. It's handy for executive-level or managerial decision-making in fast-moving, dynamic conditions where the decision has a big impact on people or resources.

If you don't feel like you fit into any one of the decision-making characteristics I list here, rest assured. First, you bring more than what is described here to the business decision-making process. Second, these styles are not exclusive: You may use characteristics of more than one style, or you may use different styles in different situations. To understand more about personal decision-making styles and the similarity to a company's style, see Chapter 5.

Your approach to decision-making must change as you move into different levels of responsibility and into new decision-making territory. What works at the operational level, for example, is a disaster at the strategic level. To change your mindset as a decision-maker, you must be willing to increase your flexibility and flex your brain muscles. You must let go of what you're comfortable with to enter different decision-making territory, which will expand your decision-making skill.

Recognizing the Workplace Environment and Culture as a Force

Workplace health and effective decision-making are linked. I'll spare you the details (are you relieved?). Suffice it to say that the workplace environment directly guides your decisions. This was a key point in Malcolm Gladwell's book *Blink: The Power of Thinking without Thinking* (Back Bay Books), in which he explains what he calls the *power of context.* In a nutshell, the simple question "Am I safe or unsafe?" can trigger growth (when you feel safe) or protection and risk aversion (when you feel unsafe).

One of the biggest mistakes companies make is not paying attention to how workplace environment and cultural assumptions and beliefs influence decision-making. Fortunately, more and more are becoming aware that healthy cultures and environments that are both emotionally and physically safe produce better decisions. In this section, I show you how growth impacts decision-making and workplace health and explain how the design of the organization affects how decisions get made.

Mapping your company on the innovation curve

A company's culture is revealed in the quality of the workplace relationships (I cover this in Chapter 12) and how well the company treats change or handles the unexpected. One way to find out whether your company embraces or fears change is to determine where it falls on the innovation curve. In this section, I tell you what the innovation curve is and what it can reveal about you and your company.

Introducing the innovation curve

A company's position on the innovation curve indicates how it thinks about, embraces, or adapts to change. On one end of the innovation curve are Innovators; on the other end are Laggards:

- **Innovators:** A very small percentage (2.5 percent) of companies and decision-makers fall into this category. They break the rules because, as far as they're concerned, there are no rules. They instigate *disruptive technologies,* technologies that change how people live and see the world. Innovators brought us downloadable music, Google maps, and social networking. Innovators are incubators for start-up companies that thrive on the edge of uncertainty and boldly lead where no other company has gone before.

Question for you: How long did it take you to experiment with social media in your business? When did your business get its Facebook page or start monitoring customer feedback on Yelp.com? The longer you took to explore the effects of new technology on your business, the further behind you become, exposing your company to greater uncertainty.

- **Early Adopters:** Early Adopters are people and companies who are quick to grasp a good idea when they see one. They prefer to lead, not follow, and they aren't afraid to invent or adopt different ways of doing things if doing so gives them an edge. About 13.5 percent of people and businesses fall into this category. They are risk takers.

- **Early Majority:** People and companies that fall into this category are open to change as long as it doesn't rock the boat too much. They operate in the zone between the Early Adopters and the Late Majority folks, veering back and forth between the two. They want innovation, but only after the bugs have been ironed out. Their business culture can be in transformation for several reasons, one of which is that they are moving from a command-and-control structure to a more adaptive and flexible culture.

- **Late Majority:** People in this group, which constitutes 34 percent of people and companies, prefer to wait until they feel absolutely certain about what is going on. Results have to be consistent before they feel comfortable introducing new ideas into their culture. When it's no longer practical to resist, they'll transplant an idea from elsewhere but will do so without adapting it to fit. If this quick fix fails, which is highly probable, they blame the idea rather than examine how the implementation process may have sabotaged their success. Late Majority companies prefer to avoid risk and prevent mistakes, value perfectionism and predictability, and don't like surprises. They have a low level of trust in their employees' abilities and insert tons of controls to ensure that no one colors outside the lines. (Note that some of these characteristics also apply to Early Majority companies that still have one foot stuck in old habits.)

- **Laggards:** The Laggards are the real old-timers who prefer to use a rotary phone, still fax messages, and don't know how to turn on a computer. Get the picture? About 16 percent of people and companies fall into this category.

Companies that don't manage their cultures can unintentionally punish or block the creativity and innovation they expect employees to deliver. In the next section, I tell you how to avoid creating this issue.

Building a culture that values innovation

Over-controlling cultures block innovation, which is a product of flexible thinking and a company's mindset (which you can read more about in Chapter 3), as well as the ability to spot insights.

An unexpected event or a disruption to the routine can be an opportunity to take a serious look at processes that stymie progress, to reinvent how things get done, and to open the door to creative solutions. Answering the following questions can shed light on how tightly you control situations and data rather than allow intuition or insight to prevail:

- ✔ **Do you have excessive procedures and processes in place to control how things get done?** If you or your company put too many controls in place, you foster an environment that isn't conducive to innovation.

- ✔ **Do you listen to or ignore information that doesn't fit the norm or red flags that an employee may raise?** If you ignore information that doesn't fit your or your company's beliefs or business culture, you are missing the moment to adapt, check for ethical issues, or discover a totally different approach to routine situations.

- ✔ **To what extent do you trust your employees to do what is required to achieve a goal?** Put simply, in low-trust workplace cultures, employees become conditioned to not take initiative or innovate. Conversely, high-trust workplaces foster employee initiative; they trust their employees to get the job done.

- ✔ **Do you punish mistakes or use failures to learn?** Trust and the ability to learn from failure are all part of an Innovator's tool kit; they are also key indicators of whether your organization has the capacity for flexibility.

Perfectionism can undermine your company's ability to adapt. Companies that seek perfection squelch creativity and insight. To avoid this trap, try to cultivate a culture that instills higher levels of trust in individuals. This, combined with the organization's collective talent, can counterbalance fear of mistakes.

When you move closer to the Innovator category, you shift perspective. Instead of seeing a mistake as a failure, you treat it as another step in the experimentation process. Had 3M been locked into perfection, the Post-It Note wouldn't exist. Post-It Notes came about when a glue that was being formulated wasn't sticky enough — a happy accident born out of a production mistake. Similarly, Thomas Edison, who was told he was too stupid to learn anything, viewed his 1,000 attempts to invent the light bulb as 1,000 steps rather than failures. When you become an Innovator, you adopt the spirit of patience and perseverance by staying focused on the goal.

Accounting for company organizational structures

The number of employees impacts a company's organizational structure. When companies are small, working relationships and roles are more transparent to everyone. Making decisions is a matter of agreeing on what tool will be used in relation to the importance of the decision. As the number of employees increases, decision-makers recognize a need to organize how work gets done, yet unless an intentional decision is made to choose how to organize, companies tend to fall back on a hierarchical decision-making structure that distributes decision-making to different levels of authority. The problem with command-and-control structures is that, as a company continues to grow, such structures are too slow to make or implement decisions in fast-changing situations.

At the point where a company feels the need to organize working relationships, it can choose a different structure, one in which everyone is responsible and accountable for achieving the mission of the company. This option is one that many companies are exploring.

Organizational challenges and company size

For effective and participatory decision-making, relationships must be stable and people must know who to go to — and this is where size comes into play. In theory, at a certain point, an organization just becomes too large to accommodate those kinds of relationships. So what's the tipping point? According to Robin Dunbar, a British anthropologist, it's about 150. In fact, there seem to be two points at which companies alter how work gets done: when they grow beyond 50 employees and when they grow beyond 150 employees. In the following list, I outline the organizational challenges businesses of different sizes face:

- **From 1 to 50 employees:** Companies of this size can take two approaches to organization: They can implement an organizational structure right at the beginning by agreeing on how decisions will be made and what kind of organization would work effectively, and by selecting the clientele profile they want to work with. Or they can wait until things get so dysfunctional that the business is at risk of failure and they're forced to put systems in place.

- **From 50 to 150 employees:** If you haven't made clear decisions on how you'll decide or who you'll engage in different kinds of decisions, you must do so now. Consider this your company's awkward teenage stage. By putting in place systems and processes, you help your company graduate from winging it to being more organized. Gaining employee engagement in gathering or relaying market intelligence keeps a company current with new developments. Similarly, supplier relations become an integral part of reputation-building, so making sure your employees have shared commitment to quality and customers reduces risk as your company continues to grow.

- **More than 150 employees:** At this stage in a company's growth, whatever decisions a company has made about how it gets things done stabilize and settle. Dunbar's rule, noted earlier, states that in groups with more than 150 members, relationships destabilize. One solution, used by W. L. Gore, a sportswear manufacturing company with 10,000 employees, is to work in units of 150. This structure enables the company to gain flexibility without sacrificing growth.

Not all companies run into the 150 rule. Companies that use a self-management model organize around how work gets done. They set up clearly defined roles and accountabilities long before they reach the 150 employee stage. Self-managing companies, like the world's largest tomato processing company, Morning Star (400 employees), has strong processes and agreements in place that allow them to grow while maintaining clear guidelines for internal relationships and decision-making.

Reviewing the organizational options for small and medium-sized companies

Basically, you can organize people by their relationship and expertise to a specific function, or you can organize how work gets done. The distinction separates a traditional structure, which aims to manage people, from one that organizes how each person contributes to the achievement of the overall mission of the company. Autonomy and self-managing are built in to a governance approach that centers on individual and collective achievement of a mission.

Organizations are made of relationships, so you have options around how to arrange the relationships in your company so that decision-making is participatory and effective. If you run a company that has fewer than 150 employees, you have several organizational options; which of these options will work best for your company depends on what you hope to achieve for employees and customers:

- ✔ **Establish a self-management structure.** This self-managed approach brings in more structure, not around who has power but around how each person contributes to the mission.

   Follow the lead of Morning Star, which has worked out the agreements and accountabilities necessary to operate with 400 employees. You'll find sample contracts on http://www.self-managementinstitute.org.

- ✔ **Create job titles to designate areas of responsibility, and then decentralize the decision-making, using clearly defined participatory decision-making processes.** The functional lead accepts accountability but works as a peer with his or her team to bring value to the company and customer. Remaining open to hearing feedback from employees and customers keeps your decision-making in stride with emerging requirements. You can read more in Chapter 12 about the importance of remaining open to hearing inconvenient truths delivered by staff and customers.

- ✔ **Designate job titles, areas of responsibility, and accountability, and then delegate specific levels of decision-making authority to each level of management.** This is the organizational structure that most businesses are accustomed to. It centers on an organization in which a manager exercises control over people in order to get work done.

At the very least, give some thought to your decision-making structure. If you don't make the decision intentionally, then the traditional hierarchical business structure (the one where decision-making resides at top echelons and is handed down from on high) becomes the default decision-making structure. In this situation, areas of responsibility, like marketing or human resources, are often assigned to a lead. Competitive silos and groups of power can form, distracting attention away from performance goals.

Choosing a structure conducive to fast growth

The traditional approach in pyramid-style company organizations is to assign decision-making authority to each level of command and to mandate that each lower level must ferry the decision up to the next before approval is granted. This structure is too slow to be effective when change is occurring quickly.

To combat this, some growing companies purposely select a decision-making process that fits their values: They either decentralize or use participatory decision-making processes in which the final decision rests with the lead person. These approaches, which promote making decisions as a community, give a company greater flexibility and match company growth with company values. This kind of structure works well for small companies and, if done well, it can also work well in medium-sized companies that prefer the flexibility that comes with self-organizing and the autonomy that comes with personal responsibility.

Morning Star is a pioneer of the flat organizational approach. (You can read more about the flat organizational approach at http://www.self-managementinstitute.org.) Another innovative company is gaming company Valve, which employs a self-organizing structure based on the *wisdom of crowds,* the idea that the many are collectively smarter than the few. Valve has turned this concept into a uniquely creative approach to customer and employee relationships and decision-making. To read more about this theory, check out James Surowiecki's book *The Wisdom of Crowds* (Anchor).

The strongest innovators are found in the technology sector and come from young entrepreneurs who haven't gotten locked into a conventional way of thinking. If you're looking for new ways of thinking that also seem to scale nicely, explore what companies like Cocoon Projects in Italy are doing, for instance. For more information visit http://cocoonprojects.com/en/ or http://LiquidOrganization.info.

Putting together your decision-making structure

The best organizational structure is one that offers clarity, flexibility, solid processes, and agreements about how decisions are made; clear communication regarding goals; and ways to monitor and provide feedback. Such structures create the stable framework upon which working relationships can function effectively.

The methods you put in place must be clear, thoughtful, and intentional, and you must be willing to adjust as your company's relationships evolve. To agree on the decision-making process you want to work with internally, follow these steps:

1. **List all the decisions you typically make in a day, week, month, or quarter.**

2. **Identify who is best positioned to make the decisions you list in Step 1, based on speed, access to information, or other key criteria.**

3. **For each type of decision, create guidelines for who to include, which process to use, and which shared company values apply to the decision-making process.**

   Include the following kinds of information in your guidelines:

   • **The decision-making tools to be used:** Select and apply your own principles to fit your business. If a decision-making tool like dot voting, described in Chapter 11, will work, then use it. If you need something more sophisticated, then select a tool that fits the importance of the decision and the need for employee input. Cocoon Projects, for example, applies the principle of using the smallest tool possible to get the job done. (I cover decision-making tools in Chapters 11 and 17.)

   By matching the decision-making tool to the kind of decision, you replace random decision-making with a process that ideally ensures employee contribution, resolves issues quickly, and is relevant to the situation. In short, you gain speed and accuracy.

   • **The amount of time allocated for each level of decision:** This timeline marks the time available from input through to the final decision. Some decisions, depending on their magnitude, may take no more than a few minutes; others may take weeks or months.

   • **Guidelines regarding employee involvement:** This would cover how long and in what capacity employees participate in the decision-making process.

As you create your process, keep these suggestions in mind:

✔ Decentralize decision-making so that the people with real-time information are the ones making the decisions.

✔ Use technology to ensure that internal information flows openly.

✔ Let go of decisions that are better made elsewhere. Doing so frees your desk of decisions that frontline employees are better qualified to make. If you find it difficult to give away control, read the upcoming section "Developing the Decision-Maker: To Grow or Not" or hop on over to Chapter 4.

Assessing the health of the workplace

A company is a community of people, each having unlimited potential, who agree to work with others. The quality of the interactions and relationships within the workplace dictates what gets done and how well. So when the workplace isn't healthy, neither is the company. An unhealthy company is not an environment conducive to sound decision-making. Therefore, it's important to monitor the health of your company. Here are a couple of key indicators:

- **Stress-related illness:** Frequent incidences of stress-related illness suggest that a company's workplace is unhealthy. This doesn't mean that a small business should panic if someone calls in sick. But if the employee repeatedly calls in sick, take the time to look more deeply.

- **Ethical decision-making:** The business culture can reinforce ethical behavior or encourage unethical behavior. The following conditions influence the likelihood of ethical decision-making:

  - **A person's well-being and sense of security:** Do employees feel valued? Are they part of an important endeavor? Companies that demonstrate care and compassion for employees emphasize well-being and sustain an environment for ethical decisions. I discuss the role of stress in decision-making in Chapters 3 and 4.

  - **Workplace conditions:** How well do your employees relate to one another? The healthier the workplace, the higher the probability of ethical decisions. Companies that don't pay attention to the workplace environment set themselves up for poor decisions at every level but more likely at the top.

  - **How power is used:** How much influence do employees have on the company's direction and relationships?

In the next chapter, I go into more detail about how business culture and workplace health set the context for decision-making, for better or for worse. Head to Chapter 19 to find out how to create an environment that promotes ethical behaviors and decisions.

Developing the Decision-Maker: To Grow or Not?

Today, the lines between private and public life and between work and personal time are blurred, and it's easy to lose touch with what is important to you and to what you want from life. Beliefs you're unaware of also get in the way of your changing course, even when you want to. They can also prevent you from recognizing changes that are going on around you, putting you and your company in a vulnerable position.

To counter these forces so that you can become the manager and leader you want to be and so that you can effectively manage in diverse environments, decision-making today demands that you expand your self-awareness and become more flexible in your thinking.

Knowing thyself

All the tools and techniques in the world don't make you a better decision-maker or communicator. To become a better decision-maker, you must know yourself. Consider that you play the most important role in effective decision-making for these simple reasons:

- ✔ You take yourself with you wherever you go. In other words, whether you make a decision through a knee-jerk reaction (who hasn't?) or take a more deliberate approach, the information you receive is interpreted through filters that you use to make sense of reality. You must know what those filters are because you can't get away from yourself when you're making decisions. This is why knowing yourself — being aware of your triggers, your beliefs (both conscious and unconscious), your assumptions, your preferences, and so on — is so important to *your* being able to make effective decisions.

- ✔ Your communication skills and style dictate how effective you are in your interaction and relationships with your colleagues or subordinates.

I show you more about expanding self- and organizational awareness in Chapters 4 and 5.

Avoiding temptations that obstruct sound decisions

Company performance and achievement of goals get traded off when key decision-makers — often in executive, management, or supervisory roles — give into one or more temptations, such as the following:

- ✔ **Putting career aspirations ahead of the company's success:** When you succumb to this temptation, your priority is to protect your career status or reputation. Examples include taking credit for someone else's idea or failing to recognize another's contribution. Although people who engage in this behavior say that this is just how business gets done, it's unethical, and the consequence is that lousy decisions get made. Turf wars result, and any attempts to improve the situation result in defensiveness. The opportunity you have is to help others succeed, which helps you succeed as well. If the company culture doesn't reward achievement of goals, a leadership and cultural overhaul may be in order.

✔ **Insisting on absolutely correct decisions in order to achieve certainty:** When management yields to this temptation, there is no tolerance for error, especially human error. The result? Employees feel set up for failure. There is never enough information to finally decide (100 percent certainty is an unattainable goal), and confusing directions to employees combined with the desire to make the right decision can result in procrastination and delay. Ultimately, companies that succumb to this temptation lose out to more agile and flexible companies. The cure for this temptation is to trust in yourself and your team to creatively achieve results, which involves learning from mistakes. In Chapter 12, I explain how to tap into your and your team's creativity.

✔ **Letting the desire for peace and harmony in the workplace result in avoiding conflict and being uncomfortable with delivering unexpected news:** The problems? First, the harmony you're so intent on preserving is fake. Relationships seem friendly on the surface, but people will release their frustrations in nonproductive ways, like backstabbing around the water cooler. Second, this environment is conducive to poor decision-making simply because good decisions need diverse views and perspectives to be out in the open for discussion. When no one wants to talk about the big issues, decision-making is severely compromised.

To cure this temptation, flip the perspective on conflict. Don't see it as bad; see it simply as a way to look at things from a different perspective. Allow your decision-making conversations to air diverse perspectives on the issue, and have a zero-tolerance policy for personal attacks or the belittling of others' ideas — behaviors that are distracting and destructive when you want to gain value from the different thinking in the room. In Chapter 4, I tell you how to use conflict to engage creativity, and in Chapter 9, I explain how to use different perspectives to generate options for consideration.

Courage is needed to grow as a decision-maker. To read a fable on how these temptations show up in business environments, see *The Five Temptations of a CEO: A Leadership Fable,* by Patrick Lencioni (Jossey-Bass).

Chapter 3

Company Culture and Decision-Making

*O*ver a decade ago, I was facilitating a change initiative in an organization. In a single moment, I felt forward motion roll back, as if there were an undertow resisting movement. An unseen force in the company was counteracting good intentions. I had to know what was causing the underlying resistance besides some fairly entrenched beliefs about how things worked. Turns out it was the workplace culture.

Workplace culture carries so much power because it operates largely beneath awareness. In the same way your beliefs create your reality, a company's culture creates its results. A workplace culture can be conducive or corrosive to innovation, growth, adaptability, engaged employees, and so on.

Luckily, if you're a small company, workplace culture is pretty straightforward. People trust what you do, so what you say has credibility and inspires confidence. You lead by your actions and by how you engage others in decision-making. As your company grows, however, things get slightly more complicated. In this chapter, I show you how a company's mentality, addictions, attention to workplace health, and approach to risk impact decision-making — and provide pointers on how you can overcome the challenges that undermine good decision-making.

Recognizing the Importance of Company Culture

Business culture is relevant to day-to-day activities in the workplace. Roughly 85 percent of employee effectiveness is driven by the systems, processes, and underlying assumptions in the workplace culture. Only 15 percent of employee effectiveness is driven by employee skills.

Think about what that means: Your company's culture has a greater impact on employee success than your employees' talents do. So changing behavior isn't the best place to start if you want to make the changes stick. In this section, I help you uncover the hidden forces behind your company's culture, show you the value in assessing your company's mindset, and point out common cultural addictions that may be holding your company back.

Paying attention to invisible forces

How does a company with a lot of potential fail? When deeply rooted beliefs or assumptions drive business results, resistance arises when you consciously try to change direction.

A business has two minds, just as a human does. Think about it. When you are a new driver, you consciously pay attention to everything: You look ahead, look in the rearview and side mirrors, check your speed, pay attention to your distance from the curb, count the number of seconds between you and the car ahead, consciously decide when to activate the turn signal, place your hands on the wheel just so, and so on. All your attention is focused on how to drive.

After you've been driving for awhile, however, most of those actions are second nature. Think of the times you've driven to a destination but, because you were engrossed in conversation or thinking deep thoughts, didn't actually remember the trip there. This happens because the human mind stores details in your subconscious so that you can do certain things without consciously thinking about them. It's energy efficient!

Business cultures work pretty much the same way as driving does. So does business decision-making. After you have the workplace culture or the decision-making dynamics firmly established, the business virtually steers itself. As helpful as this phenomenon is most of the time (it lets our brains concentrate on things that need our attention), there is a downside: Your busy mind stops paying attention to whether the habits you've formed are good ones or not. It takes a crisis to get your attention. In a car, it may be an accident or a near miss; in business, it may be that you're overwhelmed and stressed out. You're under pressure but can't see what to change.

The point and purpose is to observe how the business culture creates the character of the company, which in turn influences the character of its leaders and, subsequently, its decision-making. Here are some ways you can target your observations:

- ✔ **Look closely at how you reward effort or inspire contribution, and include metrics.** Doing so lets you see whether the processes and procedures are helping or hindering what you hope to achieve. Do you reward inside targets over customer-centered actions? Are you measuring time spent on a project or actual results? Ask staff and your customers. They'll know.

- ✔ **Observe how mistakes are handled.** Doing so gives you insight on your company's relationship with risk: Is it something to be avoided or viewed as an opportunity to learn? Is the company asking for innovation but then punishing mistakes?

- ✔ **Watch for patterns in decision-making.** When you notice definite patterns, find out why your company does things the way it does. If the answer is, "That is the way things are done around here," you know that the invisible beliefs are running the show unchallenged. Asking "Why?" also lets you explore how effectively the relevant assumptions fit the current conditions. Then, after you see the consequences of those assumptions, you can update the underlying belief.

A young sales representative working for a U.S. bank was top salesperson in her region in three months. In spite of her success, she was looking for a new job because she noticed that, at the end of each month, low performers were fired. This top sales rep wanted to work for a company that wouldn't throw her under the bus if she had a tough month. What she was observing was the company's underlying belief that employees are expendable and easily replaced. In this case, the company didn't take the time to manage its culture; it was too busy making money. Meanwhile, it was losing talent — which has a cost.

Many companies don't take the time to learn how they are creating issues that result in the loss of talent or impaired decision-making. To avoid joining their ranks, step back to observe your company from a higher vantage point. Look at your company with fresh eyes, as though you knew nothing about it. Or observe it through your customer's perception: How would a customer describe your company's character? When you try to observe your company from a different perspective, think of the company's culture as its personality and then ask yourself whether you would enter into a relationship with this company and or trust this company when dealing with it.

Assessing your company's mindset

Companies think in different ways. How they think is a reflection of their cultures, combined with their leadership awareness and their commitment to learning. Generally companies fall roughly into one of three categories:

- ✔ **High-performance companies:** These companies anchor decisions to values centered on caring about employees and customers and preserving or enhancing social and environmental value. They are typically comfortable with uncertainty, make ethical decisions innately, and are agile. Highly networked and collaborative, they build value through relationships and partnerships within the local community and with their customers and suppliers. Informal learning is promoted, and decision-making is decentralized. Employees are highly engaged and accept personal responsibility and accountability. A shared and strong sense of purpose drives financial security.

One such high-performance company is the innovative, fast-growing start-up Hubspot. This inbound marketing company has a high-performance mindset, stays flexible and open-minded, and willingly tolerates a fair amount of ambiguity. Hubspot also monitors its culture constantly to address issues that could undermine performance before they become problems. Hubspot describes its culture code in a slide deck that you can see at `http://www.slideshare.net/HubSpot/the-hubspot-culture-code-creating-a-company-we-love`. Check it out!

- ✔ **Companies in transition:** These companies are adapting to changing market, social, and environmental conditions. Their transition is from a traditional way of thinking and seeing the business economic role to a more flexible, bigger picture view that embraces more variables and, therefore, has greater opportunity. Focused on profit, they may also have embraced sustainability, social responsibility, or community outreach programs. Employee engagement depends on management style and how consistently it is practiced in every corner of the company. Decision-making is a mix of centralized and decentralized, using participative and authority-based (boss) approaches. Risk exposure to unethical decision-making is the consequence of what management behavior and company metrics reinforce as acceptable.

When the cultural DNA is undergoing an overhaul, it can feel like a mash-up and be confusing, causing fear in certain segments of the workplace. Open and honest communication that keeps everyone up-to-date helps offset fear of uncertainty. When companies in transition don't stick to their long-term vision, they can join the ranks of the next category: desperate companies hanging on by a thread.

- ✔ **Companies that are hanging on by a thread and are willing to do anything to survive:** In companies like this, decision-making authority and hierarchy are inseparable and centralized. Information is used to gain internal political advantage, and employees are trained to be passive and are punished if they push innovative ideas or contrarian views forward. The workplace environment may be toxic, and, as you'd expect, employee engagement is lower, levels of fear are higher, and a lot of creative energy is wasted due to a no-tolerance for uncertainty mindset (a characteristic of companies addicted to perfection). High levels of stress mean low levels of intuition, resulting in compromised decision-making. A company like this may or may not be able to adjust to changing conditions in the business environment or to changing customer values.

Can you identify which of the previous categories your company falls into? Armed with this knowledge, you can begin to make intentional decisions that will take your business where you want it to go. The alternative? Defaulting to the subconscious cultural assumptions that may be undermining your full success.

Interestingly, which of these mindsets a company falls into isn't necessarily governed by how long it's been in business or its stage of growth. The key is the company's willingness and ability to stay in tune with what is going on both internally and externally. When decision-makers stay tuned to changing conditions internally (changes in culture and employee engagement) and externally (what's going on with customers), they quickly adapt. Companies attached to deeper, outdated habits, on the other hand, fail to notice the part culture plays and so they resist change, both intellectually and through standards set in workplace expectations.

Spotting addictions in company culture

Companies, like people, have addictions that make it hard to see alternative and better ways of doing things. As a result, decision-makers and company cultures repeat the same old responses, even when those responses don't yield the results that were hoped for. Here are some addictions to watch out for in your company:

- ✔ **Addiction to perfection:** Perfection doesn't allow any mistake, any exposure to risk, or any kind of vulnerability. Ironically, the fear of making a mistake actually creates a situation in which the a company and its decision-makers are even *more* exposed and vulnerable to risk. (I tell you how to handle risk in the section "Assessing Risk and Its Impact on Decision-Making."

- ✔ **Addiction to certainty and predictability:** Companies that need certainty and predictability exhibit little or no tolerance for surprises and unexpected events. They repress the exact insights that would propel them into higher performance. To maintain such predictability, companies go to extreme levels to control information, issues, and people — a situation that heightens the risk of employee creativity and the workplace culture imploding due to lack of trust.

To convert the addiction to certainty into a healthier strategy for running your business, you need a complete shift in mindset. The ship (company) has to push away from the shore so that its passengers (employees) can make new discoveries. Radically innovative learning experiences can crack the pattern open enough to offer a vision and build confidence in taking a different tack.

Creating High Performance Workplaces for Decision-Making

The workplace atmosphere — whether it is an emotionally safe place for decision-making or an environment where every decision feels like a choice between a slow death or a fast one — influences decision-making. For that reason, you want to create a workplace that facilitates sound, informed, and timely decisions, rather than decisions made out of fear or ignorance or made too late. In this section, I explain the importance of finding a balance between long- and short-term focus, discuss how the physical environment can accelerate (or impede) the decision-making process, and share why good workplace relationships are vital to good decision-making.

Paying attention to long- and short-term focus

To be successful in business, you need to focus on both the short term and the long term. You give short-term focus to issues that are concrete, immediate, and predictable. Quarterly reports place focus on the short term, for example. Long-term focus relates to issues that are more vague, uncertain, and perhaps visionary. Long-term vision gives your company direction.

Avoiding short-termism

Many businesses exhibit what I call *short-termism,* the tendency to focus on the short term and ignore (or largely overlook) the long term. The plague of short-termism in business is seductive because it deals with practical concerns rather than big-picture issues that don't appear to have a direct effect on the bottom line or short-term profitability.

Short-termism can undermine your company's success. If your internal reports focus on tracking revenue targets achieved over a 90-day period, for example, you may miss key indicators that are only apparent when you take a longer view. Unless someone keeps an eye on the longer term, no one has a reason to look up and, therefore, will not see the bigger picture or recognize important changes in the business and global environment. This lack of awareness makes your company vulnerable and likely to be taken by surprise. The solution is to balance your long- and short-term focus. Doing so is essential for your business's financial success and its sustainability.

Highly successful companies balance short-term and long-term views. Consider the newly emerging social enterprises that use a very wide lens, one that integrates what is going on with the planet and society with their business goals. Their view that everything is interconnected compels them to tackle larger environmental and social issues that impact the economy as a whole because they understand that those larger forces also impact their businesses! This view gives companies a serious leadership edge.

Taking the long view

As a leader and decision-maker, you must consciously work with short- and long-term focus simultaneously. Doing so helps ensure that you are prepared for the future as it unfolds, often in a way that you cannot imagine. If you and other decision-makers are focused on the short term, you must integrate long-term focus to balance your insight. Here are a couple of ways you can instill long-term focus:

- **Determine your company's strengths and how your company can contribute in a larger sense.** For example, many companies make serving society and protecting the environment a key part of their focus. Finding out the strengths of your company leads to a vision of serving a higher purpose, which inspires employees beyond measure.

- **Find out which practices are impeding your company's ability to pay attention to both the short term and the long term.** Examples of practices that commonly stifle your ability to focus on both long- and short-term issues include focusing solely on market share or on building the bottom line, or operating in constant crisis mode without examining whether the crisis is real or is simply an adrenaline hook.

Engage your staff to share their insights and ideas. Doing so can clear the path for collaboration. Involving employees in deciding what the longer-term vision looks like, for example, is a great way to both inspire your workforce and to come up with a meaningful vision. (You can find more information on vision in Chapter 10.) Employee engagement is a vital ingredient to successful decision-making.

Using smart design to speed up decision-making

Slow decisions are costly, and the inability to get real-time information is frustrating to staff. Anything that slows down the information exchange or cooperation from team members affects the speed and accuracy of the decision.

One of the simplest ways to accelerate decision-making is to pay attention to the design of the workspace. Workspaces designed for decision-making support health and interaction.

Chances are you've worked in a company in which the workspace was a large room filled with cubicles organized into clusters and separated by walls. In traditional companies, where authority designates power and status, senior personnel get first dibs on the coveted corner office with windows. But when it comes to decision-making and employee interaction, this design just doesn't work. Cubicles and corner offices restrict contact and open communication.

To accelerate decision-making by cleverly using available space, try the following:

- **Remove physical barriers.** Rethinking the whole cubicle design is one way to remove physical barriers, but paying attention to how people move through the space is important, too. Ever noticed how people make their own paths when the sidewalks don't take them where they want to go? It's a matter of following the flow of movement. Employees need to lead the design because they'll know what's needed to facilitate information exchange and social interaction — two key ingredients for more informed and faster decision-making. Follow the path they naturally use to work with their peers.

- **Think about lighting.** Some people are highly sensitive to the electromagnetic fields put out by lighting; for some, it can even impair their functionality, including their decision-making capacity. Some evidence also indicates that fluorescent lights block the alpha brainwave state, which is required for creativity.

- **Consider the role of color in creating mood.** Try to match the mood to the function of the space. For instance, green is relaxing, allowing employees to shift from hyper stress into a more creative state. Include a color design expert on the design team to match the color with the purpose of the space. For ideas, take a look at the use of color in the design of a co-working office in London, England, at `http://www.azuremagazine.com/article/a-brilliant-co-working-space-in-london`.

- **Think about ambient sound and proximity to nature.** Both are ways to reduce stress and support better well-being and decision-making. The right kind of music can calm emotions and reduce stress. One business office was located beside a pasture with horses. Employees visited the horses during their lunch break, returning to the office much more relaxed.

Tear down these walls (and add a touch of casual)!

One company discovered that decision-making improves when you take the walls down — literally. A large pharmaceutical company, GlaxoSmith Kline, discovered that only 35 percent of work took place in cubicles but that 85 percent of the space was allocated to them. Removing the walls and cubicles created an open environment and led to a 45-percent improvement in the speed of decisions! Employees were happy, and decisions were made more quickly.

Another example of a workplace design that's conducive to collaboration and decision-making is Skype's office in Tallin, Estonia. This thoughtful arrangement includes small rooms for idea exchange, a casual space (complete with chandelier) to kick back in, a café where people can sit down to eat (although most of the food is eaten on the run), and desk décor that employees can customize as they like.

If you're looking for ideas on how you can revamp your workspace, try these suggestions:

- ✔ **Ask your staff.** Ask employees for ideas on what changes would make sharing information and making decisions easier. You may be surprised by the answers you get. Stand up desks! Why not?

- ✔ **Consult with a designer specializing in workplace design.** Professional designers know how to match the design with the purpose and intention of the space. Engaging a savvy designer who incorporates the kind of activity and interaction desired will produce a more productive and inviting environment.

- ✔ **Check out websites offering design advice.** You can find a lot of information online about design trends, design principles, examples of good and bad designs, and so on. Just enter "workplace design trends" into your browser's search feature. Also, for tips on workplace design, check out `http://www.hok.com/thought-leadership/workplace-strategies-that-enhance-human-performance-health-and-wellness/`.

Co-workspaces

Co-workspaces, like HUB Amsterdam or HUB L.A., are gaining in popularity. These spaces are designed for collaboration; they connect solopreneurs who share a vision or values and provide a place where colleagues are around to test and share ideas with. Created for socially conscious solopreneurs who work alone but desire community, the workspaces are characterized by open and unusual configurations, and they often include a kitchen and common eating area.

Mum's the word: Withholding info in hierarchies

In companies based on traditional hierarchies, information is used to advance up the ranks. As a result, withholding information is a way to promote self-interest. Also, when employees use information to gain power, decision-making slows down; sometimes it comes to a grinding halt. In working environments where information is used to gain influence and power, you'll notice the following:

✔ The decision-maker has the difficult task of finding out, on his own, what is happening. Because information isn't shared easily (if at all), the decision-maker makes assumptions, which reduce the accuracy of his or her decisions.

✔ The decision-maker can't always trust the accuracy of the information he or she receives. It may be incomplete, skewed (deliberately or not), or false.

✔ The decision-maker can't be entirely sure who to trust in the organization. Some people are genuinely there to serve the organization's interests. Others are there to advance their own agendas while appearing to be collaborative and trustworthy. The result is that employees wind up watching their backs and guarding information or, worse, end up burning out.

Oddly, those who believe that withholding information gives them more power often don't realize that most of this information is on Twitter. Although the smartphone has reduced person-to-person communication, it has changed transparency for the better.

Paying attention to working relationships

If working relationships are healthy and strong, so are decisions. In healthy, strong working relationships, people embrace diverse views, work together toward a common goal, invent ways to work around obstacles and barriers, share ideas without needing to take (or steal) credit, are curious, and explore inconsistencies in a direct but non-threatening way. Healthy working relationships produce goal-oriented decisions. Effort is focused on attaining the goal.

In contrast, unhealthy relationships produce fear-based decisions. Employees focus their efforts on staying safe or advancing their self-interest over the company's goals. Blame, judging, knee-jerk conclusions, power grabs, bullying, outbursts, and intimidation — all characteristics of unhealthy working environments — create a cover-your-butt mentality. (Emotion in and of itself isn't a bad thing. In Chapters 4 and 17, I show you how you can use emotion to make better decisions.)

Good working relationships are imperative for a healthy workplace in which things get done in a spirit of collaboration. Generally, working relationships succeed when

> ✔ The lines of communication are open, and accurate information flows freely.
>
> ✔ Employees are empowered to make decisions without looking over their shoulders.
>
> ✔ A high level of mutual trust exists, as does a sense of belonging.

When you foster successful working relationships, you get fast and accurate decisions.

Assessing Risk and Its Impact on Decision-Making

Successful companies are ones that recognize and deal effectively with risk. Whether risk works for or against effective decision-making depends on how you work with it. After all, risk is a matter of perception, and people perceive risk differently. Consider the businessman who was also a mountain-bike rider. He took his fiancée mountain biking for the first time. At the end of the ride, he asked her how she'd liked it. She said, "How can you do it? Riding along the edge of the cliff like that?" His reply: "What cliff?"

In this section, I show you how human beings perceive risk and then explain the three tacks you can take in regards to risk: work with it, avoid it, or embrace it.

How does your company deal with risk? To find out, check out the discussion on the innovation curve, which I introduce in Chapter 2. Where you fall on the innovation curve indicates whether your company works with risk well or considers it a threat to your success.

Understanding how humans perceive risk

A great deal of how you perceive risk is based on factors outside your conscious awareness. The point? All the rational data in the world won't save a decision-maker from how humans think. In this section, I outline how people (and businesses) tend to view risk and how these perceptions distort what you rely on for decision-making. (Plenty more mental traps exist in the minds of decision-makers, including prejudices and biases, which I cover in Chapter 4.)

People place more weight on potential losses than on gains

People in their personal lives and in business weigh — either consciously or subconsciously — the risk of loss over the potential gain. They weigh the risk of losing all they've built or acquired against the likelihood of a future reward that is intangible and uncertain, and often opt to protect what they have over going for the uncertain future benefit.

This tendency has value for two reasons: One, you can observe when the risk of losing leads to risk aversion (which I explain in the next section), enabling you to intentionally decide whether to override fear of losing to make a bold decision. Second, by recognizing that employees will be listening for what they'll lose rather than what they'll gain, you can tailor your message when you communicate changes.

When communicating decisions on a new change initiative, don't simply sell them on the benefits of the change. Doing so doesn't meet the emotional need to know how the change impacts what they have, know, and are comfortable with now. Instead, explaining how their experience and expertise will build value or contribute to the change helps employees feel more comfortable.

The more people have, the more risk averse they become

In personal life, you've worked hard to build up your lifestyle, acquire possessions, and live the way you want. You're not going to be that interested in losing it all by taking a risk, even when you know changing is the smart thing to do. Similarly, the longer a company is in existence, the more it has to lose when presented with an opportunity that is accompanied by high risk.

Fear of losing market share results in a higher level of risk aversion and jeopardizes the company's ability to stay nimble in the face of coming changes. A risk-averse company becomes protective and, as a result, stagnates. Decision-making leans toward meeting internal goals rather than customer needs or employee values. Even though the pressure to change is evident and obvious, fear of losing what's been gained so far will be in conflict with taking the risk to change.

When people have no control over the risk they're being asked to accept, they perceive the risk as greater

If employees don't feel that they have any control or say in the matter, they tend to view the situation as highly stressful and saturated with risk. They may go through the motions to implement a plan or directive, but no one's heart is in it. Consider the difference between deciding you want to learn how to ski versus being pushed down the mountain.

You make life easier for everyone by engaging employees as the true architects of the change. People do not resist change, but they do fight change that is imposed upon them or that feels unfair. If you haven't genuinely involved them, at least communicate the decision about impending change by explaining how past and current practices connect to the direction. That way you can help your employees see how their past experience and expertise fit into what lies ahead.

People prefer a path of least resistance

Continuing to do what you've been doing is easier than venturing into new territory. The path of least resistance is defined by predictability and certainty. Maintaining the status quo seems preferable to taking an active stance toward adapting or stretching into new terrain. This approach lasts until a crisis leaves no other choice. Uncertainty, while often feared, is the juice for creative exploration and experimentation; it allows a decision-maker to do something different, exciting, and exhilarating.

If your organization has created passive employees who wait to be told what to do, then those employees will do what they've always done because taking the initiative in a command-and-control setting can have career-limiting consequences and be emotionally unsafe. To help transition passive employees into ones who are more active and involved, ask questions that elicit solutions from them. If they don't respond right away, stick with the line of questioning and be patient. Remember, your company's culture and management style has trained employees to be risk averse and passive.

Rebuilding confidence takes time. For more information on how to get employees involved in decision-making, head to Chapter 13. You can also read David Marquet's book *Turn the Ship Around! A True Story of Turning Followers into Leaders* (Portfolio Hardcover). You can also find more of Mr. Marquet's wisdom in his video *Turn the Ship Around! How to Create Leaders at Every Level*, at https://www.youtube.com/watch?v=iiwUqnvY1l0.

The further into the future you go, the less certain things appear

Human beings are short-sighted. The farther we look into the future, the less certain everything appears. As a result, we tend to discount future risk because it isn't concrete, viewing it as just a fuzzy possibility that may or may not happen. (This tendency explains why taking action to mitigate climate change was stalled in the mid-1980s and why people still eat too much fried food!)

Additionally, when risk is described in clinical terms that use mind-numbing numbers, it's even easier to discount. But translate that risk into more specific terms, and the image gets much sharper. The more specific the risk, the more real it seems, regardless of how likely it is to take place. Chances you're more inclined to buy travel insurance that covers a terrorist attack than to buy it "just in case."

To counter these tendencies, work with your employees to generate scenarios that feature the possible risks and then treat them as if they are real. Doing so fosters better decisions. I show you more about scenario-building and risk in Chapter 9.

Working with risk in a complex world

Do you see risk as something to fear? Do you use it as a lens for assessing potential health and safety issues? Does being on the risky edge inspire you to dive deeply into bold innovation? In this section, I show you how to use risk to invent or reinvent.

When you focus on something, that thing tends to suddenly appear everywhere. When you focus on risk, for example, everything looks risky. Therefore, be mindful of what you pay attention to. Obviously, you don't want to ignore risk — I for one like to know that the aircraft mechanic is watching for what could go wrong with the airplane's engine — just be very aware of the influence.

Being risk averse: Looking at the good and the bad

The traditional definition of risk focuses on loss, injury, and destruction. No wonder being risk averse sounds like a solid plan . . . and it is when applied to health and safety decisions. Not putting people in danger is a very good thing.

To address health and safety issues, you can deliberately seek out potential risks to your employees' or customers' health and safety. Be aware of pressures to take shortcuts in order to deal with budget restraints or to meet production or sales targets, for example. By preventing risks to health and safety, you become more aware of places where management pressure hijacks the sensibility of decisions. In this case, risk aversion helps you make a better decision.

But you can be too risk averse. If the conditions around your company change but your thinking doesn't, you'll fall into the trap of relying on tried and trusted principles that no longer fit the current reality. Being afraid to make a mistake is a form of risk aversion that, in a climate of rapid and unpredictable change, is exceptionally risky and puts your company at the very back of the innovation curve (which I describe in Chapter 2).

Using risk as a threshold for bold moves

Consider using risk as an opportunity to make a radical leap of trust. Companies often wait for a crisis before changing, yet doing so narrows options and ultimately pushes the company to panic rather than to come up with a creative solution. Although a crisis can be the impetus for making a radical transformation, you don't have to wait for a crisis before you make a bold move. What is the risk of not acting? Answering that question puts things in perspective.

Two conditions must be in place for you to take full advantage of using risk to innovate:

- ✔ You know that what you've relied on before isn't working, and you recognize that persistently relying on what doesn't work puts you and others under enormous pressure.

- ✔ You can focus on what you want to achieve in the future and have the courage to pursue it.

Risk can be a wonderful tool for innovation and change. To work with risk as an accelerator for innovation, do the following:

- ✔ **Nail down your higher purpose as a company.** The higher purpose is inspirational and should viscerally engage employees. (It alone won't serve as the accelerator, but it is one of the pillars for stability when your company enters a period of change.) Head to Chapter 8 for information on how to articulate your company's higher purpose.

- ✔ **With active participation from your employees, create a vision for the contribution the company aspires to make to society and the environment.** A vision alone won't help unless it is used as the basis for making decisions on direction and creative strategy. You'll find more on vision in Chapter 10.

  The Values Center (`http://www.valuescenter.com`) assessment is one way for a company to identify what employees value and how close the company is to fulfilling aspirations. With an assessment, you'll gain a baseline for where you are now and can choose what to change in order to close the gap between what is current reality and what is desired. Use an assessment to help you understand why potential productivity is being wasted in competitive turf wars or on activities that really waste the value of the talent you're employing.

- ✔ **Act on insights.** Listen to the employee who comes up with an off-base suggestion that doesn't fit anything you've ever done before. Ideas that merit further consideration should feel simultaneously risky and exciting and align with your company's purpose and vision.

  Ideas that come out of left field get compromised or lost when crammed into logical-analytical thinking too soon. To avoid shooting down ideas that don't match past practices, don't use what you did in the past as the standard by which you evaluate the new idea's merits. Instead, look ahead to the goal and place more emphasis on whether the idea *feels* right at a gut level. Apply logical thinking later, when you're moving toward implementation.

✔ **Pay attention to dreams that offer insights.** I can hear you laugh! Some of the most inspired innovations have been adapted from ideas presented in dreams. Dreams can offer warnings or insights that help a company reinvent itself in a moment of crisis. To use dreams to solve problems and spawn ideas, do the following:

- **Before you drift off to sleep, state a need and follow this with a question you're struggling to answer.** For example, "How can I resolve this issue?" By actively planting the seed, you — and your intuition — will be clear on the problem. By asking the question, you activate deeper creative knowledge.

- **Pay attention to the details of the dream.** You'll find the answer symbolically conveyed. Make notes in the middle of the night or first thing in the morning. Even if you don't get the answer in a dream, you've primed the pump for your intuition, so you may find that the answer comes later, as a blinding flash of insight when you least expect it!

Dreams are richly symbolic, so don't expect step-by-step instructions. When interpreting a dream, be prepared to do some adaptation. For example, water often refers to emotion, which could suggest that, if your dream has water in it, it's a signal to pay attention to the emotions — yours or others. By the way, dreams are one dial on your intuition channel, although they're not reliable or predictable. You can find more about intuitive decision-making in Chapter 7.

I have a dream . . .

Dreams can bring answers to a particular need. Jack Nicklaus improved his golf swing from a dream, and we might not have the sewing needle if an inventor hadn't listened to his dream. Another person whose dream influenced her corporate empire was entrepreneur, philanthropist, and social activist Madame C. J. Walker (1867–1919). Walker founded and built a highly successful African-American cosmetic company that made her the first female self-made millionaire.

Walker's success began with a problem. She suffered from a scalp infection that caused her to lose most of her hair. To remedy the problem, she began experimenting with patented medicines and hair-care products. One night, she had a dream in which "a big, black man appeared to me and told me what to mix up in my hair. Some of the remedy was grown in Africa, but I sent for it, mixed it, put it on my scalp, and in a few weeks, my hair was coming in faster than it had ever fallen out. I tried it on my friends; it helped them. I made up my mind to begin to sell it."

Walker was an inspiration and a success. Her rise from a poor childhood in the American South to the head of an international, multi-million dollar corporation was made by taking one risk after another while serving others who shared a similar condition.

Part II

… Growing Yourself
…ision-Maker

M1A-299907
4BQIX1006FER
Title DECISION MAKING FOR DUMMIES
Condition Good
Location Aisle 26 Section 3 Shelf 4 Item 991
Description This item shows signs of wear from consistent use, but it remains in good condition and works perfectly. All pages and cover are intact , but may have aesthetic issues such as small tears, bends, scratches, and scuffs. Spine may also show signs of wear. Pages may include some notes and highlighting. May include "From the library of" labels. Satisfaction Guaranteed.
ASIN 111883366X
Employee 1468
If anything is incorrect, please contact us immediately at orders@jensononline.com and we will make it right.
Thank you again for your purchase and please leave feedback online!

…d *Decision-Makers Do*

…ur emotional state gives you access to your intui-
…ep breathing to reach the inner calm.

…ul questions helps you illuminate what you're
…uestions like, "Why are we doing this?" and "If a
…n would she make?" Powerful questions always
… answer.

…pressed can deepen your understanding of the
…ion.

…back gives decision-makers the capacity to link

…**wth:** Such growth converts what you don't
…vantage. When you ask, "What can I learn from
…forward?" you turn your experience into knowl-
… be useful later on.

web extras

Learn why your ego is a key factor in your decision-making and how to use it to your advantage at `http://www.dummies.com/extras/decisionmaking`.

In this part . . .

✔ Find out how fear and failure build character and provide experience you can use to grow as a decision-maker

✔ Learn how to improve your relationship with yourself and others for more accurate interpretation and better communication

✔ Discover how to apply the principles related to your personal growth to your company so that you can expand your organization's capacity for sound judgment and stronger results

✔ Tap into your heart's intelligence to make intuitive and intelligent decisions

✔ Understand how to work with unintended consequences and use mistakes to strengthen decision-making

Chapter 4

Growing Your Business by Growing Yourself

*W*ho you are matters to your employees and your customers, and it affects your decisions. In this chapter, I show you how your personal growth impacts your leadership and the decisions your company makes. Head to Chapter 5 to find out how personal growth applies to business.

The future is created one decision at a time. The consequences of each pivotal decision you or your company makes cumulatively add up to shape your world and the world we all share. Business is in a position to accept a major leadership role by tackling the large issues that threaten human survival, including addressing the effects of global climate change and addressing poverty, as well as food and energy security, for instance. Doing so begins with attaining greater awareness, and this awareness starts with you.

Connecting Personal Growth to Effective Decision-Making

In a fundamental shift that is underway, the business world is transitioning away from operating purely out of self-interest. The move is accompanied by a wave of social change, environmental awareness, and public unrest that companies ignore at their own peril. More and more businesses are coming to recognize that the economy is dependent on the ecological resources needed to sustain all life on the planet and on the human resources that both make and use their products. As a result, they're looking for and finding progressive solutions to perplexing problems, like how to revitalize their organizations while both decreasing operational costs and tackling social or environmental issues. Unilever is one company that is building social goals into their brand strategy, for example.

All companies can join this movement, and it starts with you. You are the force behind the positive change in your life. You're the person behind working relationships in your company. And you're the one who decides whether you grow and adapt or not. In this section, I show you the ins and outs of how your personal growth is vital for sound decision-making.

American psycho: The profile of a CEO

Disconnected from emotion, no capacity for guilt, no compassion, and no concern about the consequences of their actions — these characteristics define a psychopathic personality. Sadly, they are also the characteristics many would list when describing CEOs. Interestingly, this popular perception of CEOs has some basis in fact. Four percent of CEOs actually fit the profile of psychopath (only 1 percent of those in the general public fits this profile).

Charming and smooth-talking, psychopathic CEOs ruthlessly pursue self-gratification, self-interest, and their own goals over the needs and goals of their firms. Here are some of the classic traits of a psychopath:

- He is insincere, unreliable, and can't remember the truth.

- He is superficial, charming, and of average intelligence.

- He has no remorse, guilt, or shame.

- He won't hesitate to be a jerk and fails to notice when he is.

- He has poor judgment and fails to learn from experience.

- He is egocentric and incapable of love.

- He lacks insight.

- His sex life is impersonal and trivialized (I had to include that!).

And yet . . . CEOs fitting this profile have made a lot of money (mostly off of other people's lives).

Business opinion wavers on whether having a psychopath for a CEO is a good or bad thing. The short answer seems to be that it depends on what you're trying to achieve. As business leads itself away from acting out of pure self-interest to working collaboratively, the psychopath isn't a winning character profile. The good news is that 96 percent of CEOs don't fit the psychopath profile and, therefore, have the potential to restore public and employee trust in business.

Exploring vulnerability as a leadership quality

Vulnerability — the willingness to be changed and to let the walls down — can be a strength in business leaders. Without it, you can't lead, learn, or do anything other than what you've already been doing. Lack of vulnerability creates an exceptionally threatening world, in which those at the top defend their companies and themselves from risk, from information, and from meaningful relationships.

In a business context, being vulnerable means embracing these underlying principles: openness, transparency, and a willingness to admit that you know nothing — all of which enable you to be curious and receptive to new ideas. Add in a dose of compassion, and you access your heart's intelligence, a topic I cover in greater depth in Chapter 5. Being vulnerable enables you to see and receive information currently being ignored or beyond sight.

How do you practice vulnerability in business or, for that matter, life? Let me count the ways:

- **Examine problems from as many different perspectives as possible without engaging one iota of defensiveness.** When you do this, you see a whole lot more than you're currently taking into account. Viewing issues from multiple perspectives protects you from thinking narrowly and missing critical information. It also reduces the chance that you'll jump to conclusions and increases inquisitiveness, which leaves you open to insights.

- **Uncover assumptions.** Ask yourself, "What am I taking for granted here?" Constantly solicit uncensored feedback so that you learn not to be threatened by uncomfortable information that is essential for sound decision-making. (I discuss assumptions in more detail in Chapter 9.) When you uncover assumptions, you build integrity, credibility, and reliability through your willingness to hear both good and bad news.

- **Approach each situation with a sense of curiosity and complete lack of certainty.** A sense of curiosity combined with a lack of certainty means your mind isn't made up or, if it is, you're open to adjusting to new information. When decision-makers fail to practice curiosity and fixate on being certain, they create silos in thinking, a situation that leads to internal turf wars where employees channel their efforts into protecting their territory.

- **Have compassion and care.** Both are part of *empathy,* the capacity to see and feel from another's viewpoint. Without empathy, access to intuition — a vital component of sound decision-making — is blocked.

Having compassion for the ego

When decisions don't go as planned or teams don't perform as well as they could, egos are often involved, particularly as you move higher up the chain of command. I recall one businessman defending his right to be egotistical, saying he couldn't be ambitious without it. Maybe. Maybe not.

The fact is that the ego gets blamed for a lot of poor decisions. Fair enough. When the boss is critical or puts an employee down in order to feel more important himself, blaming the ego makes sense. But is the ego really to blame? In this section, I explore the role of the ego and tell you how to ensure that it doesn't highjack your decisions.

Looking at the ego's role

The ego's job is to make sure you feel safe and secure in the world. It looks after your physical, emotional, and social well-being. Most of these physical, emotional, and social needs become beliefs that are stored in your subconscious. If they are not met, these needs can derail decisions as your ego — your subconscious protector — takes charge instead of you.

Three categories of needs exist:

- **Basic survival:** These are the physical needs. Unmet ego-based decisions come from fear or anxiety about not being safe or not having enough . . . money, clothes, or whatever makes you feel safe and secure. (Now you know why people and companies who obviously have a lot of money still don't feel they have enough.) Blaming and judgment are behaviors expressing an underlying survival fear or insecurity.

- **Recognition, gratitude, acceptance, and validation:** These are the social needs. Unmet ego-based decisions in this category come from anxiety about not belonging, feeling accepted, or being acknowledged. Decisions are motivated to compensate for lack of self-worth. In the workplace, blame-finding runs rampant, and the culture exhibits a deficiency of respect. Conversely, when a company's culture supports the emotional well-being of its employees, they feel they can safely bring more of their skills and abilities to the fore.

- **Self-esteem:** Self-esteem (feeling good enough) and self-worth (being respected for the value you bring to the world) are intertwined emotional needs. Self-confidence plays a part as well. Ego-based decisions in this realm aim to fill gaps in self-esteem or self-worth. People who want to feel better about themselves make decisions that meet their needs, and company goals fall to the bottom of the list. In fact, most of the senior level temptations, such as the desire for harmony over dealing with conflict or a focus on achieving a position of status over achieving results, can be triggered by the workplace culture, as discussed in Chapter 3, and aim to counterbalance deep emotional needs.

Getting ego under control

When ego gets in the way, it can be a strong deterrent to sound decision-making. To reverse the situation, try these tactics:

- **Instill a culture that supports employee well-being on every level, even the emotional and social levels, too.** When you instill a workplace culture that supports employees, you create a healthier decision-making environment that is oriented less toward self-interest and more toward achievement. Chapter 3 explains how to create a workplace environment conducive to decision-making, and Chapter 19 contains more information about how to instill an innate code of conduct through personal accountability and metrics that reward teamwork and reinforce trust.

- **Offer growth and development opportunities for employees at every level.** Both formal and informal learning opportunities give employees the autonomy to chart their own development. When you recognize that everyone leads, you'll have employees who are better leaders and decision-makers. Growth and development can partially substitute for traditional progression up the corporate ladder, particularly in companies where those opportunities are limited.

- **Instill a culture of genuine recognition and acknowledgement that goes far beyond the gold watch at retirement.** Say thanks without using a schedule. Build acknowledgement into the ethic of the company as a genuine expression of appreciation. Integrate simple acts of gratitude as a regular practice.

From a business standpoint, the simplest way to support employees is to take ego out of the equation. You do that by providing a healthy working environment and a consistent management style that recognizes and acknowledges the contributions of employees and demonstrates respect for all in the workplace. When the workplace supports and respects employee input, your employees can concentrate on giving their talent. In this way, care and compassion displayed by leaders and management inspire employee engagement beyond the intellect and support performance.

Tapping into emotions for effective decision-making

Traditional companies, born in the days when companies were managed like machines (a model that pervades today), ignore the value of emotions, viewing them as irrelevant to rational decision-making. This view assumes that people who operate like robots and don't allow feelings to cloud their intelligence make better decision-makers.

The problem with this approach is twofold: First, humans aren't robots, and emotional responses inform just about everything we do. Second, what you resist persists. If you push emotions down, they reemerge, often as undesirable behaviors: bullying, anger, intimidation, and my-way-or-the-highway attitudes that cloud everything. A better approach is to acknowledge that emotions are a type of information that *should* be considered in decision-making. In this section, I show you how unacknowledged emotions can take charge in decision-making and give you ways to work with emotions as data.

Understanding emotional responses

Your body detects, processes, and stores emotional data from your environment exceptionally fast. How fast? Different studies produce varying results, but all conclude that your subconscious processes information much faster than your conscious. (One study timed problem-solving processing speed of the conscious mind at 100 to 150 mph while the subconscious clocked in at 100,000 mph!) This suggests that there's a lot of information available to you when you make a decision that you might not be aware of. In addition, memories — gained from both pleasant and painful experiences — stay with you, stored in your subconscious. Together, your rational mind and your subconscious impact your responses to the situation and your decision-making.

What's interesting is that, although most people assume that the rational mind plays the bigger role in decision-making, the subconscious is really the captain of the decision-making ship. Your subconscious stores all your emotional data, as well as what it picks up from your environment. And emotional wounds from the past can hijack your decision-making. Unresolved emotional experiences hold a negative charge that interferes with how you interpret information. Think of a time when a subtle remark triggered an angry response, for example. Chances are you weren't reacting to the subtle remark but to the old wound that the remark triggered. In these situations, you want to convert the negative into neutral, which I explain in the next section.

Turning a painful experience into something useful

When you understand an emotion and the reasons behind it, it no longer has the baggage that can trip you up. Instead, it becomes knowledge that you can use to deepen your understanding of the situation or issue. Here's one method to transform a painful experience into something useful:

1. **Reflect on the situation where you originally experienced the painful emotion that was triggered.**

   Try to picture the situation in your mind's eye. Your goal is to see the interaction close up in order to know what triggered your response and emotions. Feel and accept the emotions you experience.

2. **Imagine the entire scenario again, this time from an emotionally detached point of view.**

   Be a fly on the wall. Observe your reaction to what is happening. Look for ways you could respond differently and more effectively. If someone else features in this memory, try to detect what motivated the entire incident from that person's point of view. Doing so helps you see what lies at the heart of the matter and enables you to hold empathy.

3. **Rewind and replay the scenario, but this time, insert a different response.**

   Watch how the scene plays out. Yes, you're using your imagination, but your subconscious experiences the event as though it's real. After reframing the incident to a much happier outcome, you should feel a sense of peace and resolution. If not, work with a few more different responses until you do.

Discovering the triggers to your emotional responses is useful for many reasons, but here are two: It strengthens your intuition (emotional baggage distorts the signal), and it helps you explore and examine your beliefs, which I cover in the next section.

Recognizing How Beliefs Influence Decision-Making

Everyone has beliefs. You've collected them since childhood. Through experiencing success and failures, more beliefs are added, until some run so deep that you may not even be consciously aware of them unless you take the time to examine why you do what you do. Beliefs help us make sense of experiences and serve as our moral foundation. Here's the kicker: Beliefs operate as if they are true, even though many are not. Beliefs set boundaries to what you perceive as possible and, therefore, shape how you think. Companies have beliefs as well and use them to make their decisions, just as you do.

Examining your beliefs: Do they limit your options?

Beliefs can limit or expand thinking. As Henry Ford said, "Whether you think you can or can't, you're right." In other words, your beliefs can limit your view of what is and is not possible. In this section, I help you take a look at your beliefs so that you can flush out the ones that are holding you or your business back.

Fred Smith, the founder of FedEx, submitted a paper presenting a proposal for overnight delivery of parcels to his Yale professor. His paper earned a C grade. The professor's feedback? "Great idea, Fred, but your ideas have to be feasible." To the professor, the idea of overnight delivery wasn't credible or believable; therefore, it wasn't feasible. To Fred Smith, it was.

Checking out limiting beliefs

Table 4-1 lists examples of limiting beliefs. In the left column are personal limiting beliefs; in the right, are the usual business limiting beliefs.

Table 4-1 Beliefs That Limit Your View of What's Possible	
Personal Limiting Belief	*Business Limiting Belief*
"I have to choose between making a living and making a difference. I can't have both."	"It's a battle. We have to fight to survive."
"I can't make money and do what I love to do. If I follow my passion, I have to sacrifice my lifestyle."	"If our product and service are brilliant, the customer will come."
"I have to take this job because another one might not come up."	"If you aren't in business solely to make a profit, you're anti-capitalist."
"Personal growth is a bunch of hooey. You have to be tough and force your way to success."	"How can we possibly learn anything about management from those people?"
"There is no need to change what I'm doing as long as everything is under control."	"Self-organizing doesn't work for us. We're different."

It's easy to miss how your thinking influences your decision-making. Beliefs aren't good or bad. They serve either to limit or empower. Sorting out what role your beliefs play in your life, your work, and your decisions gives you the power to decide which beliefs you keep and which you change.

Weeding out your own limiting beliefs

Innovation and radical breakthroughs are impossible without freeing up thinking. Inventors constantly meet up with limiting beliefs in reaction to their ideas. Being able to spot potential in offbeat ideas or unusual opportunities requires constant questioning to expose limiting beliefs. To understand how beliefs affect your thinking and your business, follow these steps:

1. **Make a list of what you believe to be true about your business.**

   These are your surface beliefs. They may sound like, "I don't believe that investing in leadership is important" or "We need to concentrate on what is practical and forget the rest." This list gives you an idea of what you use as a basis for your decisions or to rationalize them. If you can't name any, head to Step 2.

   None of the statements you write is bad or good, true or false. Identifying what is being said simply makes the thinking visible. So don't censor your list.

2. **Listen to your self-talk about what you can or can't do or what you do or don't believe to be true.**

   Self-talk refers to the hidden beliefs, like "I'm not good enough" or "self-managing doesn't work," that sit below your awareness. It includes thoughts running through your mind, as well as phrases that pop out uncensored in response to a situation. To identify your own self-talk, observe the language you use when you talk about yourself and your abilities, either inside your head or when you're talking to friends. As you uncover your own self-talk, add each item to your list. If you're having difficulty, ask someone you trust to help alert you to self-deprecating comments that repress your self-value and initiative.

   The purpose of this step is to gain insight, not punish or critique your thinking.

3. **Review your list and reflect on what the entries tell you.**

   For instance, an entry that says "Leadership is a soft skill and doesn't have anything to do with results" tells you that you don't see a connection between leadership and results. Somehow, for some reason, those two interconnected ideas have become separated. Use Step 4 to bring them back together again.

4. **Play "What If" with the beliefs you've uncovered.**

   Using the example entry in Step 3, for instance, what if you did see the connection? How would that change how you managed or made decisions? Everything is interconnected, so seeing two ideas or perspectives as two sides of the same coin helps you recognize potential opportunities and possibilities.

Busting your beliefs out into the open gives you the option to knowingly decide what you use as a basis for decision-making going forward.

Understanding how you perceive insight, intuition, and vision

Many of us fool ourselves that our perception of things is the only right way to see the situation. For decision-making, this mindset creates a blind spot. As a result, you can't see what's obvious to others. How you perceive reality depends on your mindset and the tools you use to perceive reality, which include the following:

- ✔ **Vision:** *Vision* is the capacity to see the world holistically, as an interconnected and interrelated web of relationships linked in patterns. Vision is what you see as possible for yourself and what you want in your life or for your company when you look ahead. In business, part of holistic thinking is contained in systems thinking, which is a way of mapping interrelationships in a process, for example.

- ✔ **Intuition:** *Intuition* is the ability to know without use of the rational mind. Intuition relies on learned patterns to rapidly isolate workable actions in rapidly changing circumstances. Intuition is so important to decision-making that I devote Chapter 7 to the topic, and I summarize your internal supercomputer's way of making decisions in Chapter 9.

- ✔ **Insight:** *Insight* is most aptly described by author Gary Klein as seeing what others don't. It's the capacity to discover new patterns in the everyday that lead to totally different ways of viewing the world. In the world of business, insight disrupts habitual thinking so something new can arise, or it serves as an advance warning sign. Insight is invaluable for finding the leverage points where a small amount of effort will go a long way.

These are the primary tools in your inner skills decision-making tool kit. Like all instruments, how finely attuned you are to each depends on how well you've reconciled past emotional issues, the extent to which you're aware of your beliefs, and how intentionally you make your decisions in each situation.

Acknowledging hidden bias or prejudice

Humans are complex beings, and that complicates decision-making. Welcome to the world of bias and prejudice, where, even when you think you're relying on rational thinking, there's a good chance you're not. Ingrained bias and prejudices override rational thinking. Table 4-2 shows examples of hidden biases and how they sneak into thinking.

Table 4-2	Common Ingrained Biases and Prejudices	
Ingrained Bias or Prejudice	*Why It's a Problem*	*Example*
Seeing yourself in an exceptionally positive light	You overestimate your abilities.	You always think you can get things done faster than you actually do, which can create problems with project schedules.
Taking credit for success but not for failures	If you don't use failure as an opportunity to learn, you are prone to repeating the same mistakes.	You're quick to accept credit but prefer to avoid acknowledging your failures. You might even accept credit where it's undeserved to bolster self-esteem and offset your perceived failures. Chapter 6 talks more about failures.
Using your own personal interests to decide what is fair or best for others.	Although you can easily see the effect of self-interest in others, it's harder to see its effects with your own decisions.	You can easily see how your colleagues are overloading their teams with work, but you don't see that you're doing the same thing.
Viewing members of a racial, ethnic, or stigmatized group as less than those in the "in" group	You don't recognize and, therefore, tend to deny incidents of racism or sexism, hurting all groups.	You accept a female colleague's ideas when they are endorsed by a male peer (a testimonial is required), but tend to reject them otherwise.
Failing to recognize hindsight as hindsight	You blame decision-makers for not predicting unpredictable events.	When a decision to invest in a company results in a huge loss, you point out where the decision-makers went wrong as though what is obvious now was as clear at the time of the decision. It wasn't.
Seeing others' behavior as a reflection of their character rather than the environment or situation	You blame the victim when things go badly and ignore valid concerns.	When whistleblowers report a company's fraudulent action, the company responds by vilifying the whistleblower rather than turning attention to how the fraud was allowed to occur.

Everyone has biases that impact the decisions he or she makes. To offset probable bias, whether you're aware of it or not, you deliberately remove the reasons that could prejudice your assessment. Note that I didn't say you need to give up your biases (some are so deep it would be impossible to do so): You just need to create a way to deal with implicit biases likely to distort the decision-making process.

Consider the hiring process: Each decision-maker has biases about a person's appearance, sex, race, or size, for example. These biases lead you to assume that you already know about a person's character or talent. Now suppose that you are hiring a new employee. One applicant is tattooed everywhere, and you don't like men or women with that many tattoos. Despite the fact that this applicant's track record is impeccable, you're not comfortable and don't see him as a viable candidate. But you're not the only decision-maker, so he advances to the short list.

To remove your bias against people with tattoos from the selection process, you decide to provide each prospective candidate with a work assignment typical of the assignments expected of someone in your employ. The submissions are intentionally submitted anonymously and then evaluated. Much to your surprise, your top choice was completed by the tattooed candidate. Your company hires him, and he goes on to add exceptionally high value to the company.

Gauging Personal Comfort with Conflict and Ambiguity

A lot of people are so afraid of conflict that they avoid it at all costs. It amounts to a fear of fear, but if the occurrences of violence in the workplace are any indication, conflict is not being used well. The truth of the matter is that conflict, when appropriately handled and channeled, can be a great way to open up ideas, uncover problems, and discover new and improved ways of doing things. In this section, I explain the important role conflict plays in upgrading a decision from mediocre to better and show you how, as your relationship to conflict changes, you can work with it more effectively in team or organizational settings.

Using conflict to your advantage

Conflict happens. What makes it valuable (or not) is how you use it. Conflict can be used to either accentuate differences or deepen understanding of what makes a person tick. The difference lies in asking the question, "What can I/we learn from this that adds to shaping a solution, achieving the goal, improving understanding, or promoting growth?"

Unfortunately, the typical approach to conflict asks the question, "How can I win or get my way?" This approach assumes that, in the case of opposing ideas, one person is right and the other is wrong and that the only way you can prevail is if the other person loses.

In addition, the conflicts you have with other people aren't the only conflicts that can stymy your progress or undermine your success. You can also be in conflict with yourself. When your expectations for what you thought, hoped, or wanted to happen don't materialize as you planned, you get mad at yourself, feel self-doubt or self-judgment, or blame someone else — and end up expending a lot of energy on being angry. Conflict can be detrimental. Therefore, it's important to know what can trigger conflict. Triggers for conflict include the following:

✔ **Differences in information and different interpretations of the same information:** The same information can be perceived in many different ways. If one person needs his or her interpretation to be the "right" interpretation, conflict can result. A better approach is to collect diverse perspectives to form a more complete picture.

Interpersonal conflict, for example, often results when two opposing views of what happened or what "should have" happened collide. Rather than fighting it out to see whose view wins, ask questions to discover what values or interests lie beneath the two views. This approach often leads to a better solution.

✔ **Differences in values due to dissimilar ways of thinking about what's important:** Companies and individuals often use beliefs to make their decisions. Beliefs are about what you think is true about how the world works. Values are about what is important. When a decision pops up that inspires a conversation about what's important, you've entered into a discussion about what values will hold sway when making the decision. The conflict creeps in when the participants have different values and beliefs about what is relevant and are not able to separate one from the other to gain objective clarity.

Use the difference of opinions creatively to explore what is important to each person and why. Engage in dialogue to find out the other person's views on the subject. In a business setting, if the company is clear about its values, aligning the decision to the values is a natural step.

✔ **Unmet expectations that create feelings of fear or lack of trust:** Fixed ideas on what should happen next or what you expect to happen is a surefire way to be disappointed when the outcome doesn't turn out exactly as you expected. The conflict arises from not trusting that what shows up has value to your life. A better approach is to be open to the outcome rather than trying to control it.

On a personal level, think of relationships that haven't worked out according to plan. In business, think of projects that went sideways. Analyze the unmet expectations to discover where you can replace fear or lack of trust with more trust in yourself. Discover what you can learn from projects that didn't turn out as planned.

Understanding classic responses to conflict

When conflicts surface, fear and doubt can commandeer any kind of rational thought, and before you know it, you've said something you regret or done something you wish you hadn't. The classic fear-based response is the fight or flight response — neither of which uses the moment wisely.

Looking at common responses to conflict

To better handle tense situations, you need to understand what conflict-resolution strategy you rely on in any given situation. Table 4-3 outlines the common responses. (Hint: The best response when dealing with complicated situations or decisions is to use conflict to collaborate or to flow into finding a solution.)

Table 4-3	Strategies for Dealing with Conflict	
Strategy	*Appropriate When...*	*Not Appropriate When...*
Avoiding conflict	The issue doesn't have a big impact or great importance to you. You wouldn't feel victimized if you walked away from the conversation.	The issue is a symptom of much bigger issues. If you don't step into the discussion, you'll feel victimized by subsequent actions.
Accommodating people	The issue matters more to them than it does to you. You want to show support or goodwill.	Your commitment is required. The solution presented violates your principles and values.

Strategy	Appropriate When . . .	Not Appropriate When . . .
Forcing the decision	Quick, decisive action is required to ensure you achieve your goals. The commitment of others is not required.	You simply want to get your way. Doing so breaks trust or damages relationships. The decision collides with team values.
Compromising results	Goals, concerns, needs are far apart, and you don't have the time to find common ground. Building the relationship is more important than completing the task.	No one is satisfied with an incomplete piece of the promising solution. You take this approach simply because you don't want to take the time to honestly collaborate.
Collaboration	You need to work through hard feelings to understand the diverse perspectives. Commitment to the solution is needed, and the relationship is important.	The issue is relatively unimportant to all parties. Neither side cares enough about the relationship.

Dealing with conflict collaboratively

To move from the fight or flight response to a collaborative approach, you need to be an astute and compassionate observer and then bring yourself back to a state of calm. Alternatively, you need to be self-aware enough to recognize you're emotionally compromised and then take a timeout before refocusing on the task. To prepare yourself to work positively with tension-filled situations, try one or more of the following:

✔ **Center yourself.** Restoring calm to your feelings and mind enable them to work together. When you are centered, you can see the situation with a clearer mind. Deep breathing (breathing from your diaphragm) is one way to silence the mental arguments. You can use deep breathing before you go into a tense situation and even while you're in the thick of things. For more information on using breathing and other techniques to work with conflict, check out *The Magic of Conflict: Turning a Life of Work into a Work of Art,* by Thomas Crum (Touchstone).

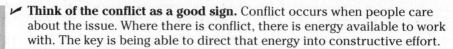

✔ **Think of the conflict as a good sign.** Conflict occurs when people care about the issue. Where there is conflict, there is energy available to work with. The key is being able to direct that energy into constructive effort.

If you view conflict in this way, you'll enter contentious situations with a forward-looking approach that enables everyone to discover the interests or concerns. You won't view conflict as something to fix, nor will you feel the need to judge which of the various viewpoints is right or wrong.

✔ **Listen carefully to understand the true intent of the person you are speaking with.** Often, when listening to one another, people tend to latch onto a sound bite, jump to conclusions, and then run off with the wrong idea. As you can imagine, the situation ends badly. Listening intently means letting go of preconceived notions and paying attention to the values and concerns underlying what is being said with the intention of understanding the situation.

When you listen intently, you gain insight into what lies at the heart of the matter for all. You'll walk away knowing whether the business culture is causing the situation or whether you're witnessing unintended consequences.

Trust that conflict can be utilized to benefit relationships and quality decisions. Being willing to change is a sign of strength, as long as the changes you make are in line with your values. In the next chapter, I show you how to raise both your self-awareness and your organization's awareness.

Chapter 5

Raising Self- and Organizational Awareness for Better Decisions

. . . .

In This Chapter

▶ Understanding how you process information and make decisions

▶ Discovering strategies for effective communication

▶ Tapping into your intuition and empathy

▶ Gaining tools to increase clarity and reduce stress

. . . .

*W*hen start-ups start up, their entire focus is on generating revenue and finding people who can leap tall buildings in a single bound, all while moving ideas forward. The emphasis is on faster-better-cheaper, and they run at warp speed and give little attention to running an effective organization. As the race to success continues, the processes used to look after things become habits that no one really pays much attention to until someone says, "Remind me: Why are we doing this?" That simple question marks a moment of opportunity, a chance to evaluate why you do what you do and to determine whether a different approach would be better. In short, it's a chance to adjust before a crisis gives you no other option.

Recognizing such opportunities when they occur and taking advantage of them require self- and organizational awareness. Becoming more self- and organizationally aware starts with a silent moment, a single question, and a step back — all of which benefit from *mindfulness,* the ability to be absolutely present in the moment. But just being aware doesn't change anything. The key is to use your reflection and understanding to select the best course of action. Over time, such experiences become knowledge — they're integrated into your thinking, one decision after another.

In this chapter, I show you how not all decisions are intentionally made and explain the intelligence of the heart, which can help you make better and clearer decisions. I also give you tools you can use to regulate emotions during decision-making, turning negative into positive and building internal strength through empathy.

Understanding How You Make Decisions

You make decisions constantly. You probably don't think much about what makes one decision effective and another ineffective until things don't go according to plan. So how do you (or I or anyone, for that matter) make all these small and large decisions every moment of every day? In this section, I list the typical decision-making processes people follow when they need to make decisions.

 Every person — and every company — uses each of these approaches. The key is to be aware of how you're making decisions so that you can handle uncertainty and unexpected events with greater confidence. You can also choose one form of decision-making as your select style and master it. Doing so helps you avoid being pulled in many directions by what is unseen and unobserved.

Instinctual decision-making

In instinctual decision-making, decision-makers don't reflect on the situation or on its meaning; instead they go straight to action. Instinctual decision-making kicks in when you feel you are in serious danger or are in survival mode. Instincts hijack any rational decision-making while simultaneously activating coping strategies that you've used successfully in the past. Your body tells your brain to go on high alert, and you feel like you have no options to choose from.

If you work for a company that uses fear, intimidation, and coercion as a management style, chances are you're in this mode and your decisions are compromised. Fear-based workplaces create a highly competitive, cover-your-butt mentality. To reclaim some sanity, use the tools I show you in the upcoming section "Reducing Stress to Make Better Decisions" or consider finding a better place to work.

Subconscious decision-making

In subconscious decision-making, you act first and think later, which makes it seem very similar to instinctual decision-making (see the preceding section); however, the cause is different. Rather than survival, as is the case in instinctual decision-making, you're reacting from past memories tucked away in your subconscious. Feelings like impatience, frustration, or anger show up when an event triggers an old memory and exposes an unresolved situation from the past. Conversely, positive emotions emerge when the situation or conversation touches a happy past memory.

Decisions driven by the subconscious are based on your personal life experiences added to the beliefs formed between birth and six years of age. During those early years, you download and store information from your emotional and social environment directly into your subconscious, creating the lens through which you view all subsequent interactions and experiences. Unless you invest in your personal growth, these subconscious beliefs will serve as the template for the rest of your life. To free up energy currently being used to store negative and energy-sucking emotions, refer to Chapter 4.

As I describe in Chapter 4, the majority of companies use beliefs to make their decisions — beliefs they usually don't remember to update over time. In unaware companies, everyone runs around, dealing with one crisis after another. Although this environment fuels adrenaline, turning work into an extreme sport minus the fun, it doesn't do much for decision-making. Decisions go around in circles, over and over again, yet always fail to ultimately address the issue or overcome the problem. This is especially true in a complex situation, where you may resolve one aspect of an issue but neglect to address other parts, which will eventually resurface. Why? Because in workplaces that run on speed, complexities get ignored as the company falls into a decision-making rut. Essentially, the company fails to step back and examine the situation from a wider view.

When you bottle up your emotions, your brain does its job and stores the pressure in your body so that you can keep functioning. Depression is one possible result. A better alternative is to learn how to regulate and manage your emotions instead of letting them manage you. You can find one method for doing so in the section "Comprehending the Value of a Deeper Intelligence," later in this chapter.

Belief-based decision-making

In belief-based decision-making, thoughts precede action, and you make a conscious choice. Basically, a pause occurs between what happens (the stimulus) and your response. During this pause, you have time to reflect and think logically, enabling you to make a deliberate choice. Your decisions are still based on past experience and the beliefs you've gathered over the years. However, because hidden emotional issues aren't hijacking you, you can work with others more effectively. As I explain in Chapter 1, most companies use a belief-based approach.

Both individual decision-makers' and companies' beliefs can send decision-making into repetitive loops, particularly if those beliefs are subconscious, as is the case in a company that is blind to the beliefs being used or isn't in tune with what is going on in the world. Additionally, companies that are running full speed ahead eliminate the pause period that allows them to think and insert logic. To offset this tendency, you can use the tools I discuss in the upcoming section "Reducing Stress to Make Better Decisions"; these tools apply equally to both individuals and to businesses.

The past beliefs on which this kind of decision-making are based may or may not be true. If the underlying beliefs that run the thinking and decision-making aren't reviewed and updated, change progresses slowly or not at all. Unless a radical change in mindset occurs, the best a company can expect is incremental change, even when faster change would be better.

Values-based decision-making

Value-based decision-making results when individuals or companies reflect on the values that are important and meet what they consider to be important needs. Because values are chosen or identified, you're in control of selecting the actions and behaviors that support your values. If you have identified trust as a value, for example, then you embed all the actions associated with trust into your decision-making and your behaviors. The question being asked is, "How does this decision align with my/our values?" The answer to this question reveals what's important and non-negotiable.

Achieving values-based decision-making at a personal level results from feeling emotionally or financially secure. I show you how to build a stronger sense of security in Chapter 4. You can find tips on managing your emotional state in the upcoming section "Comprehending the Value of a Deeper Intelligence."

Evolving to values-based decision-making at a company-wide level results from a shift in mindset. Instead of existing to survive, the mindset shifts to achieving financial security, which engages a different style of management as a way to serve a higher goal and purpose. Every decision is anchored by collectively agreeing upon values about what's important.

Values-driven decision-making

Values-driven decision-making is the choice for innovative companies that build self-organizing cultures from the get-go. Select public, private, and semiprivate companies that are clear about their contribution to society also employ values-driven decision-making. The company future is collaboratively designed by employees, customers, suppliers, and the community fan base.

Though it's tempting to take shortcuts when applying values to decision-making, there is a progression as decision-makers learn to distinguish between values-based decision-making (in which the decision aligns with what you deem important) and belief-based decision-making (in which the decision aligns with what you believe to be true). In essence, values-based decision-making is forward-thinking, whereas belief-based decision-making holds on to the past. With values-driven decision-making, greater clarity emerges, resulting in stronger efficacy.

Graduating to values-driven decision-making is the reward for achieving the internal transformation necessary to fully integrate knowledge gained by learning from past mistakes, paying attention to internal processes, and attending to workplace culture and relationships. Companies of all sizes can use values to make their decisions, and most companies run by young entrepreneurs start with and stick to values-driven decision-making. The processes, values, decisions, and so on that are used to achieve the result are connected, transparent, and trustworthy.

For more information on using values in making decisions, visit the Values Centre at `http://www.valuescentre.com`. Alternatively, watch Richard Barrett explain the difference here: `http://youtu.be/nldAsxCuIvM`.

Comprehending the Value of a Deeper Intelligence

Traditionally, business decisions have demanded cold, hard data, as in numbers that can be measured, arguments that can be rationally supported, and action going forward that leads to a predictable outcomes. What is missing — and often dismissed in business circles as irrelevant to intellectual performance — is the information you receive from your emotional and social environment — the workplace environment. In this section, I explain how your heart is a big part of the decision-making equation and what you can do to tap into its intelligence.

The link between your heart and your head in decision-making

Emotional and social data arising from interpersonal relationships and the degree of happiness or stress directly impact decision-making.

The heart performs an important role that goes beyond pumping blood. The heart's 40,000 neurons are a complex information-processing center, able to sense, regulate, and remember. Sensory data (blood pressure, heart rhythm, heart rate, and so on) is processed in the heart's neural system and transmitted to your brain by the vagus nerve and spinal cord. Of the fibers in the vagus nerve, 90 percent are dedicated to transmitting data from the body to the brain, and only 10 percent carry instructions from the brain to the body — the largest ratio of these ascending nerve fibers are from the heart and cardiovascular system.

The data that reaches the brain from the heart has been well documented to affect mental functions. When you are emotional or upset (frustrated, overwhelmed, and so on), the heart rhythms have a disordered pattern, which affects many important higher brain functions such as decision-making. The distorted signals that occur when you are feeling angry, upset, unhappy, or any other negative emotion impair your cognitive functioning and access to intuition. Conversely, when your heart is in a state of *coherence* — that is, when you are in a happy, calm, or peaceful state — your cognitive functions, including access to your intuition, are optimized.

The complex exchange of information between your subconscious (outside of awareness) and your conscious mind (what you're aware of) has a large role in priming and determining the types of decisions you make. The subconscious apparatus is always evaluating the inputs to the brain to determine whether you are in an unsafe environment or a safe one, where you can be creative and grow. Understanding this interplay between conscious and subconscious inputs helps you understand why healthy workplaces are so important to effective decision-making and higher functioning. You can find tools for staying functional while under stress in the sidebar "Tools for regulating emotions and expanding empathy."

Putting this knowledge to work

Understanding the heart's role in intuitive and cognitive functioning is relevant to business decision-making in two ways: First, higher functioning individuals mean higher functioning companies and higher functioning working relationships. Second, high-functioning companies with high-functioning working relationships lead to higher intellectual and intuitive abilities from employees.

Put another way, working environments that are emotionally stable and socially safe are better decision-making environments. In high-stress, high-pressure decision-making environments, the onus is on you, as a decision-maker, to gain mastery of your emotions and develop a stronger awareness of the effect the social environment (your key relationships and how you communicate) has. Doing so provides greater access to both intuitive and intellectual intelligence, enabling you and others to sense with greater accuracy — long before it appears in the pages of *Harvard Business Review* — what the future holds. The company, able to operate with full engagement emotionally as well as intellectually, gains an edge that puts it ahead of lower-functioning companies.

When you aren't managing your emotional state, a cascade of negative emotions like insecurity, anger, fear, frustration, or blame compromises your intuitive and intellectual intelligence. The result: You can't function optimally. To attain full access to your inner resources, your heart, mind, and emotions must be in a state of peace and alignment, a state of coherence. The trick is knowing how to attain that peaceful alignment when conditions are less than calm. In addition, the alignment, or coherence, among thought, emotion, and words is a core leadership and decision-making skill.

To understand how important coherence is, consider the effect of mixed messages. Chances are times have occurred when you've detected a mixed message: A person says one thing, but you sense a different message underneath, one that remains unspoken. The cause? What the messenger says is not in-line with his or her true feelings. Mixed messages work against trust and credibility.

Listening to your heart is the gateway for managing your emotions and establishing conditions for success. Companies that employ this knowledge adapt their workplaces to build trust, their leaders lead from the heart, and compassion and care are embedded into the DNA of the company's culture and thinking. Decision-making is optimized through well-being. Head to Chapter 7 to gain greater insight and understanding of how intuition works and how you can strengthen access to it when making decisions.

Reducing Stress to Make Better Decisions

Organizations are communities of people working together. When an organization is under pressure and/or stress and not doing well, the people in it are impacted. People under stress make poor decisions. It's not their fault. Stress occurs when high demands are combined with low levels of personal control over those demands. As you can guess, the more control employees have in responding to changing circumstances, the better. Yet companies that stick rigidly to the status quo without adjusting to changing circumstances unknowingly increase pressure on employees.

Companies that demand creativity and innovation while simultaneously ignoring unhealthy working environments compromise results. People can't create when they are barely coping.

The costs of not taking action to create better workplaces are high. In the U.S., the cost is estimated to be over $300 billion per year. In the U.K., the estimated annual cost is £13 billion. Steps taken to bring the workplace into a better state pay off in well-being for employees and reduced costs to business through productivity loss and direct savings in health benefits.

The mantra in business is that what gets measured gets managed. If you want to keep a better eye on the health of your workplace, measure the costs attributed to absenteeism, depression, aggression, and so on. The direct costs indicate the state of your company's health and the size of the problem. Indirect costs, which are harder to measure but have a high impact, include having employees who show up for work but function below their normal level of productivity. The costs to business from this source is estimated to be considerably higher than those attributed to stress. (Head to Chapter 12 for an explanation of the factors that contribute to stress and employee disengagement.)

To identify the degree to which performance is suffering, look for the following indicators:

- Poor performance
- Anxiety
- Fatigue
- Problems sleeping
- Headaches
- Digestion issues
- Substance abuse or other addictions

Every small step you take to increase care, mutual support, and sense of belonging is a big step toward improving conditions. I cover a few of these steps in this section, and you can find more in Chapter 12.

Manager, manage thyself

Having a grip on the methods and techniques you use when managing the troops and reacting to situations is important. Practically speaking, as a manager or a supervisor, you can do the following:

- **Notice how you respond to incoming demands.** Superiors who treat all incoming demands as top priority burn themselves and their staffs out. Are all the tasks and requests that come across your desk urgent? If you aren't sure, find out. Then set priorities based on the urgency of the task before assigning or presenting the demand to the team.

Try to select a response instead of simply reacting to demands. Add value to the process of allocating resources by understanding the requirement thoroughly. Don't just pass the urgency down the line.

✔ **Evaluate whether you've fallen into the trap of managing by crisis.** In other words, you've gotten sucked into the vortex of deliberate crazy-making, treating every event like an imminent threat to the organization, or, if no imminent threats are present, creating them. Too much crisis over a long period makes it too easy to blame others for what goes wrong and to take credit for what goes right. Besides, who can keep it up?

Notice whether you, or the organization, are addicted to the adrenaline of managing by crisis. If more crisis makes you feel more alive, that's a sure-fire recipe for little sleep and staying busy without having a clue where you're running to. The horizon, or longer term, is nowhere in sight.

✔ **Calm your mind and heart before making any important decisions.** Bringing calm to your heart and mind allows your heart, head, and emotions to work together for better decisions. There are several ways you can attain inner peace; one method I recommend for achieving inner calm is the HeartMath Quick Coherence technique, which I share in the nearby sidebar "Tools for regulating emotions and expanding empathy."

✔ **Build in breaks for yourself and staff.** Research suggests that peak performance is sustained in 90-minute spurts. Reflection time happens during breaks when your mind is distracted. Clarity and perspective are reclaimed.

Unless you must accommodate scheduling issues that require you to mandate break times, allow people to take their breaks when they need them. You'll know it's working when you and your staff have more get-up-and-go.

Managing the manager

To better manage what's expected of you and your workload, you need to clarify, with your manager, what the priorities are; otherwise, everything is urgent, and expectations are unrealistic. I once had a manager, for example, who communicated everything as urgent. After working nights and weekends to keep pace, I realized I was putting out more effort than was practical health-wise. Sure, I felt self-important, but I didn't have much of a life. So I went back to my manager with the list of the tasks I had been asked to perform and asked for priorities. The urgent items fell from all on the list to just two.

My point? Pushing up, respectfully, can help separate what's important from what's not. As you receive requests to complete more tasks, you can do the following:

✔ **Ask questions to understand the task's importance.** When a request lands on your desk, ask why it's a priority and how it serves the goal you're charged with.

✔ **Separate priority tasks from less important tasks.** Priority tasks are essential and should be the first tasks on the to-do list.

As you prioritize tasks, you're seeking to gain efficiencies. With this in mind, prioritize high-leverage tasks (those where a small effort achieves more than one goal) over low-leverage tasks.

✔ **Take breaks or go on a walk-about to gain perspective.** Progressive companies that realize the value of time out design a room or space for meditation or reflection so that their employees can reflect and see for themselves what's important. (And once you've identified what's important, validate your conclusion with your superior, if appropriate.)

Personal freedom and autonomy are critical to your health and well-being, so look for places to eradicate negativity and replace it with a focus on the positive. Optimism is energizing. Feeling victimized and helpless is draining. Take steps to stay connected to what matters to you and to what you want from life and from your career.

Practical ways to reduce stress in working relationships

Demands and expectations — and how those things are communicated — affect everyone in a company: clients, customers, coworkers, employees, and so on. In very tense settings, the pressure and ensuing stress can put people at risk, both emotionally and physically. When you notice that working relationships aren't heading in a positive direction, take action to reduce the pressure by lightening things up.

Lightening things up isn't the same as making light of the situation. Lightening things up always has a purpose. Here are a few things you can do to lighten up a stressful situation (note that doing these things proactively — that is, before stress gets too high — is even better):

✔ **Insert fun into the day-to-day workflow**. When you add fun to the equation, you gain detachment and the capacity to approach the situation from a totally different direction. Enjoying going to work is one aspect of incorporating fun into work; the other is injecting an appropriate dose of humor into tense situations to diffuse the tension (make sure the humor is at no one's expense).

I once worked with a team that was being hammered on by their clients for issues that were totally outside everyone's control. The stress was intolerable. So the team came up with a plan to brighten everyone's day, including their clients, and help everyone see the brighter side of the predicament. The strategy involved going to the joke shop and getting suitable props that gave the clients a laugh and diffused tension and anger. Taking this approach is not about making light of the client's predicament. Use humor to indirectly communicate that it's better to work cooperatively instead of yelling and screaming at the customer representative.

Comedy can turn a tough, boring, or stress-filled situation into a rejuvenating experience. But it works only if it doesn't target a person and includes everyone in the joke. A Southwest Airlines stewardess shows how it's done in this video: `https://www.youtube.com/watch?v=07LFBydGjaM`.

✔ **Take a break and get away from the workplace.** Doing so can quiet the mental noise and put you in a calmer state.

Getting outside into nature allows you to slow the pace, look after yourself, and reclaim perspective. So why not head to a park for lunch? Just remember to eat slowly so that you can slow the pace and reconnect to what is going on inside of you.

✔ **Provide space for meditation or yoga, or bring services into the company that can help instill a more relaxed state of mind.** If you can't do that, then provide access to services nearby so employees can find an oasis in the day. Instilling a sense of ease maintains commitment to the work because vitality is renewed. Better decisions result.

✔ **Take your meetings on a walk.** For one-on-one meetings, combine exercise with getting things done. Leave the personal distraction devices switched off so you can be present with the conversation. In larger meetings, when things get tense, take time out to walk about. In fact, take the whole conversation — or the whole meeting for that matter — on a walk . . . assuming it doesn't mean 20 people wandering down a trail. True, you won't all be talking about the same thing, but when you get back, you'll find more clarity has bubbled to the surface.

Implementing these and other techniques you come up with on your own can alleviate pressure for yourself and your peers and employees, and improve the workplace environment.

Stress-related illness has traditionally been seen as a sign of personal weakness. Underlying that assumption is the notion that the workplace environment and business culture have no effect on performance. We know now that this isn't the case. However, if you still believe stress-related illness reflects a weak constitution, it's a bias to manage. To uncover where that belief originated, ask yourself the question "Why?" You may have to ask it as many as five times to go deep enough to reveal the core belief at the heart of this assumption. When you do, however, you'll have gained greater compassion for yourself and your staff.

Tools for regulating emotions and expanding empathy

Have you ever noticed a retail space that has high turnover — no matter what business goes in, it fails? Or have you ever walked into a building or room and gotten a good feeling or, conversely, a bad feeling? What you were experiencing was the sum total of the emotional health of the interactions with the space. The health of working relationships defines the success of an organization. Looking after the health of working relationships is at the core of empathy building and, therefore, access to personal and organizational intuition.

The HeartMath Institute has developed techniques that individuals can use to gain calm under pressure and that companies can use to restore appreciation and empathy, which in turn gives access to intuition and to the heart's intelligence. In this sidebar, I share this tool.

HeartMath's Quick Coherence Technique: Gaining calm under pressure

HeartMath's Quick Coherence Technique is a wonderful way to come to grips when you're under a great deal of pressure. You can use this technique personally the next time the sky is falling or you're under pressure to make a decision and would prefer to make a good one. So if stress is what you're feeling, the Quick Coherence Technique is for you. This technique only takes a minute. No sweat! To gain quick coherence, follow these steps:

Step 1. Focus your attention in the area of the heart as you breathe a little slower and deeper than usual. Imagine your breath is flowing in and out of your heart or chest area.

Suggestion: Inhale 5 seconds, exhale 5 seconds (or whatever rhythm is comfortable).

Step 2. Make a sincere attempt to experience a regenerative feeling such as appreciation or care for someone or something in your life.

Suggestion: Try to re-experience the feeling you have for someone you love, a pet, a special place, an accomplishment, etc., or focus on a feeling of calm or ease.

Step 3. Recall a time when you felt good, at peace with the world. You can also think of a place where you feel at peace. Picture yourself in the moment. Feel the feelings. Thinking feelings won't help. You have to feel the emotions of love, appreciation, calm, and peace.

Once you feel a flood of warm, positive energy surround you, you're ready to take on that decision. For more information about this technique, visit this web page: `http://www.heartmath.com/personal-use/quick-coherence-technique.html`.

Chapter 6

Learning from Mistakes and Unintended Consequences

In This Chapter

▶ Using blind spots and past errors to improve future decisions

▶ Anticipating issues before they become problems

▶ Using failures to build character and credibility

*B*oth rational thinking and intuition can fail a decision-maker, and it's only in hindsight that you comprehend the flaws in the process. When you see and understand the source of decision errors, you gain the power to make better decisions. By learning how to work with failure, overcome mistakes, and deal with unintended consequences, you can transform difficult experiences into entrepreneurial wisdom.

In this chapter, I show you how to spot the blind spots that undermine the decision-making process, evaluate past decisions, and use mistakes — yours and others' — to improve your decision-making process and avoid similar mistakes in the future. This information will enable you to accurately access situations by observing and adjusting to dynamic circumstances. I hope it will also save you from blindly committing the same errors again and again.

Engaging in Reflective Learning

There are several ways to see whether the decisions you're making will ultimately lead to the results you'd hoped for. Fortunately, you don't necessarily have to crash and burn first (though crashing and burning tends to get some entrepreneurs' attention for the first time). Instead, you can step back and reflect, learning from the past in order to make better decisions in the future.

Identifying blind spots in the decision-making process

Unknown information and blind spots in the decision-making process can thwart the most skilled decision-maker. Blind spots are those instances in your decision-making where you can't see the underlying assumptions, beliefs, or routine patterns that are impacting the situation and that will divert direction to results you don't want instead of results you do. You can reveal blind spots by answering questions like the following:

- ✔ "Are the results that we are seeing the results that we were aiming for?"
- ✔ "Are customers paying on time?"
- ✔ "Are suppliers delivering what they promised when they said they would?"
- ✔ "Does our business attract loyal and repeat customers?"

Each question above has a simple "yes" or "no" answer that quickly shows you which areas need further exploration. The "no" answers reveal gaps between what you were originally aiming for and the results you're getting; they let you know that it's time to step back to examine why a difference exists. "Yes" answers indicate you're good to go forward. Keep in mind, however, that you must remain mindful to the risk of complacency.

When asked at periodic intervals, questions like these can help you to stay alert. You can also use questions to reflect on decisions that resulted in a set-back. Doing so helps you see ways to improve decision-making in the future.

Learning from decision errors and disasters

To learn from what's already happened, step back to check. The following steps guide you (you can also use these steps to verify that everything is on course):

1. **Verify the original aim of the decision.**

    Identifying the original aim clarifies whether it and the desired results were clear from the start.

    We live in a design-while-building-the-solutions world, and not everything will be totally clear from the beginning. If you're using these steps to determine whether a project or decision is on course, check whether the original goal is becoming more or less clear as it emerges during implementation.

2. **Observe the result and how well it aligns with the original goal.**

   Through careful observation, you can see how the results align with the original goal. In the case of evaluating a decision in progress, observe the results you are seeing at this point to see whether they're heading in the right direction and are consistent with the original aim.

3. **If the results are at odds with the original aim, review the information, actions, and so on that were made at each stage of the decision-making process to discover where you made assumptions that led the results astray.**

   Consider the following: the information your team relied on, the course of action you selected, how the decision was communicated and implemented, and how the implementation was monitored.

Breaking down the process in this way helps reveal where assumptions were made. You can see where information wasn't accessible and available to decision-makers in real-time; where actions were out of sync with the expectations of clients, customers, and/or other important stakeholders; where important factors were overlooked in the implementation of the decision; where communication broke down and risk was discounted; and where implementation failed to be monitored.

After you gain insight on why prior decisions didn't go according to plan, you need to apply that insight to future decisions. Consider what you can take away from these less-than-optimal experiences the next time you need to make a decision. You can also apply the lessons learned to make adjustments now to the processes you use to make similar decisions.

Turning Hindsight into Foresight

In general, mistakes are easy to see in hindsight. To avoid mistakes and avert disaster, the trick is to bring hindsight into foresight. In this section, you find strategies that may not turn you into a seer but will help you reduce mistakes and unintended consequences — unlike the unfortunate companies whose tales of woe I share.

Monitoring implementation and assessing risk

Many managers don't adequately assess risk and fail to monitor the implementation of their decisions — or they take these functions for granted, assuming that, as long as there is action, all is well. They focus on what lies ahead, not on what is happening in the wake of a decision. By monitoring the results of a decision, however, you gain the opportunity to discover unintended consequences and identify where ignoring risks leads to negative outcomes. In short, you'll know whether the decision is giving you the results you'd hoped for or moving in the opposite direction.

To ensure that you don't fall into the trap of rowing merrily toward shore while the boat deck burns behind you, do the following:

1. **Assess the probability and seriousness of a perceived risk *before* implementation.**

2. **Identify what could happen in the worst-case scenario and put a contingency plan in place to prevent an unintended consequence from accelerating into a disaster.**

3. **Closely monitor the situation after implementation to employ any safeguards that may become necessary.**

Knight Capital's software snafu

Knight Capital Group, Inc. (now merged with Getco Holding Co. under the new name KCG Holding, Inc.) is an American global finances company specializing in electronic execution of sales and stock trading. In 2012, the company installed a new program that inadvertently activated a dormant software application that began multiplying stock trades on the New York Stock Exchange. The result was a ridiculously high surge in accidental stock orders. It took 45 minutes (almost a lifetime in stock trading) to catch the error and shut trading down. The company suffered a $460-million trading loss and was later fined $12 million for trading violations and failure to put safeguards in place. Dramatic? Definitely!

Software issues are unpredictable and hold inherent risk, so the activation of dormant software was an unintended and unanticipated consequence. In the case of Knight Capital

Group's software rollout, advance thinking could have incorporated the following:

- ✔ Recognizing that a high possibility existed that a problem would occur, given the idiosyncrasies of software

- ✔ Assessing that the seriousness of the worst-case scenario would be very high

- ✔ Putting in place a contingency plan to address the risk, such as a kill switch to shut down the software the moment irregular trading activity was detected

If such steps had been taken, trading could have been stopped less than 1 minute after the dormant code was activated, not 45 minutes and 400 million orders later. Such hindsight can point to changes in how future decisions are made, using past disasters to build better decisions.

Foreseeing inadvertent effects of a decision

Sometimes a crystal ball would come in really handy for forecasting the results of a decision. In the absence of a crystal ball, the next best thing is to expand your thinking and broaden your perspective. The ability to see the entire landscape of possible outcomes and consequences — even ones that obscure possibilities — after a decision is implemented is a real skill and an advantage.

How can you see ahead and build in possible outcomes into your decision-making? Here are a few suggestions:

- **Explore the pros and cons of the decision.** Exploring the pros and cons gives you a heads-up on how the decision may play out either way. For example, hiring short-term or temporary employees is a convenient way to bring on resources when you need them, but the downside is a lack of loyalty on both sides.

- **Look for the relationship between a decision you're about to make and its wider impact on your reputation or what you are trying ultimately to achieve.** The key is to understand who the decision will affect and how. Figure out what the shareholders' vested interest in the result is and how they will feel about it.

  How your clients or employees or suppliers feel about a decision dictates their response. It's emotional. You can't argue against feelings with facts. Instead, consider their degree of support for your decision from the start. Your goal isn't to convince anyone; it's to understand how and why people care about the decision you're making. Do so, and you'll gain support for what you want to do, or you'll gain insight into why you won't get the support you're hoping for.

- **Map out scenarios.** Look into the future and examine what may happen if the decision is made and implemented. When you look at the different scenarios, you'll see options and alternatives where you previously thought none existed.

- **Intuit the future.** What's your gut feeling for where this decision will lead? Intuitive foresight is a quality of visionaries. Think of Walt Disney. See Chapter 7 to learn how to strengthen your intuitive decision-making.

- **Develop your ability to perceive the interconnectivity and interrelationships of all aspects of the decision, as well as the decision's direct and indirect consequences.** You can gain insight into interconnectivity and interrelationships by observing nature, the ultimate example of systems thinking. At every level in nature, from microenvironments to macroenvironments, things are connected in such a way that a change in one area produces ripple effects that spread throughout the system. When the natural ecosystem of both living (plants, animals, and micro-organisms) and nonliving (soil, water, air, and so on) factors isn't healthy, animals and plants die. Companies are ecosystems of living (employees) and nonliving (capital assets) elements working together. By seeing how one thing is connected to another, you can better recognize the inter-dependence of all the individual elements and, as a result, better antici-pate how decisions affect those interrelationships.

Listening to feedback from key suppliers and customers

Your company's success depends on how you treat key suppliers and cus-tomers. The most valuable relationships are ones in which open, honest com-munication facilitates mutual trust and shared ethics. When assessing your company's relationships with key accounts and customers, ask yourself these questions:

- ✔ **"How is the expertise of suppliers, buyers, and other parts of my com-pany's relationships network built into the information used for the company's decision-making?"** With the answer to this question, you discover where you're leaving valuable decision-making expertise out of the picture, enabling you to take steps to incorporate the views of your valued business partners at key decision-making points.

- ✔ **"Where have we intentionally incorporated feedback from clients and customers into the decision-making process?"** With the answer to this question, you recognize where you are building in client and customer feedback and where you can improve in order to make better real-time decisions.

- ✔ **"Can I trust a supplier's word, and can the supplier trust mine?"** The answer to this question reveals the degree to which your relationship is mutually trustworthy. If you were to characterize your relationship, would you describe it as one in which a handshake can seal the deal or one that relies exclusively on a legally binding agreement? (The question is about trust, not whether you would actually use either a handshake or a contract.) If something goes wrong, do you and this supplier have the kind of relationship that lets you cooperatively work out solutions?

Matt & Nat

Matt & Nat manufactures a vegan line of fashionable handbags. Some years ago, the company was approached by Holt Renfrew, a high-end Canadian retail company, to make Holt Renfrew the exclusive distributor of Matt & Nats vegan bags. Although the deal was such that most, but not all, retail outlets could continue to carry Matt & Nat products, there was one catch: The retail price would double.

One prominent retail buyer and distributor advised Matt & Nat not to double the price for no justifiable reason, but the company proceeded anyway. Retail outlets were unable to explain to customers why a bag that was $100 one week was being sold for $200 the next week, with no change to the product. The larger retail buyers, except for high-end Holt Renfrew, stopped carrying Matt & Nat bags, and competitors have since stepped in to offer a similar product at the price point originally held by Matt & Nat.

I was a Matt & Nat customer and understood it was a company that applied the principles of values-based decision-making; however, doubling the price didn't seem to be based on values. Although Matt & Nat landed a big fish, the company lost a lot of credibility and market share. It alienated many of the companies that distributed its product, and it made some customers, like me, question its values.

Regardless of Matt & Nat's fortunes today, this example points to the value of working with distributors and buyers as partners in your company's success. Incorporating their counsel into your information-gathering process can help you avoid a poor strategic decision.

Implementing other's ideas wisely

Often, managers and executives introduce new initiatives without the proper know-how. Almost every consultant on the planet has spent a lot of advance unbillable time with a prospect, explaining the merit of new ideas, only to have the prospect decide to do it all in-house. Other times, someone (usually a senior executive) reads the latest business book, grabs the idea, and transplants it into the workplace. In both scenarios, little or no consideration is given to what makes the idea work or how to apply it to different settings. When faced with such poorly executed initiatives, it's natural for employees to develop cynicism, especially as they witness the next "flavor of the month" idea march in, followed by more distracting but unproductive change.

Ideas superimposed into a company without the adjustments necessary to accommodate the workplace culture usually result in failure. Then the idea or the process (or worse, the employees) is held to blame. In addition, employees' productive energy is diverted to adjusting and adapting to internal changes that ultimately don't achieve the intent. They focus on internal dynamics, and customers can fall by the wayside. Organizations that act before thinking are prone to imposing an idea before truly understanding what mind-set or creative thinking is required to achieve the desired results.

Another problem related to using others' ideas is the tendency of companies to think that what works elsewhere can't work in their environment, even when those ideas and innovations could be beneficial. Without taking the steps to find out how an innovation in one business sector or company can seed or initiate original thinking in your own company, good ideas and exper-tise are left untouched and unexplored. The status quo is maintained.

To come up with internal innovations that fit the realities of your company's corporate culture, explore original ideas from other companies or other sec-tors and ask questions like, "What can we learn from this idea?"; "How might it apply to us?"; and "How could we better serve our customers if we adopt this approach?" Remember, curiosity precedes action. Inquiry gives you the chance to explore and tweak new ideas to better fit your situation.

Stopping to see the big picture

Most lousy decisions don't look or feel dumb in the moment. In fact, confi-dence and optimism often accompany crummy decisions. The reason boils down to *narrow cognition,* or narrow thinking. Here's why identifying narrow thinking is so hard: How can you tell when you're omitting a lot of relevant and important information that you can't actually see? The answer is that you have to broaden your view so that you see the big picture. You can widen perspective to see the bigger picture by doing the following:

1. **Clearly state the issue you're resolving.**

   For instance, you may say, "We want to cut costs while improving safety." This kind of statement gives you a clear picture of what informa-tion you need to gather.

2. **Gather information that builds your understanding of what must be considered.**

   Be sure to look at the issue from a wide perspective. In the example, for instance, don't restrict yourself to just the cutting costs portion. Instead, gather information on the costs (both direct and indirect) of maintain-ing the current practice, as well as on the savings that will be gained by implementing different approaches. You also need to learn what the safety issues are and what is causing them so that you can consider options that remove risk.

3. Ask your team for ideas.

You'll collectively identify better ways to solve the issue(s) identified in Step 1. You'll also be able to see which approach best accomplishes all parts of your objective. In the example, you would ask your team for ideas on how to gain efficiencies that go beyond cutting direct costs but are achieved by using a different approach. The solution results in lower cost and better safety practices.

Expanding thinking to see the bigger picture always results in better decisions, as long as you apply an open-minded approach.

Taking a wider view and gaining efficiencies

A senior manager of a large, successful house construction company was troubled by recurring accidents involving trade subcontractors falling off ladders from significant heights. In one particularly disturbing accident, a worker fell 16 feet (5 meters) and was impaled on a wooden stake. Although not fatal, the accident resulted in a long-term disability, a prosecution, and a significant fine. The senior manager approached his CEO to explore solutions, but the costs of renting or purchasing scaffolding was high. Instead, the CEO issued an edict requiring that the trade subcontractors purchase and erect scaffolding. Shifting the cost to the trade subcontractors resulted in many either disobeying the requirement (which, in most countries, was perfectly legal because they are independent) or purchasing cheap, substandard equipment (scaffolding is a significant investment). After another accident, the senior manager decided to try again to change the CEO's mind.

This time the senior manager calculated the cost of the fines, added associated legal costs, and included the value of the time spent arguing with and policing compliance, as well as the cost of time wasted shifting ladders from one place to another and the effect of schedule delays due to difficulty coordinating between the trades. Then he calculated the cost of renting and erecting scaffolding as part of the construction process itself. After documenting the efficiencies, he showed his calculations, which now included a broad array of areas, to the CEO.

After learning that scaffolding enabled several trades — roofers, guttering installers, window installers, bricklayers, painters, and even cleaners — to complete their work speedily, efficiently, and, more importantly, safely, the CEO changed his decision as his focus shifted from minimizing cost to gaining efficiency.

The senior manager's ability to imagine and calculate the broader implications of the decision helped the CEO expand his perspective. Whereas he originally looked solely at the costs of safety accidents, he now saw the bigger picture and recognized that a significant gain in operational efficiencies more than paid for the costs of the scaffolding. The end result had a positive impact on safety, operational efficiency, and on the construction company's reputation. The trade subcontractors appreciated it as well.

Overcoming persistent problems with procurement

Companies frequently deal with problems in the procurement process. These problems are often the result of building constraints into the procurement process or prioritizing money savings over employee health and safety. How goods or services are procured can also be a problem when procurement is driven by cost savings and omits quality — in either the services/products procured or the results — as a factor.

If you've sold goods or services to a medium-sized to large buyer, you've likely experienced times when your expertise is devalued or undervalued. The buyer isn't educated enough to know that the same criteria used to buy pencils doesn't apply to buying leadership development services, for example. More education is required so that the buyer can make a more informed decision. A reputation for quality and trust in the personal relationship are both ways that buyers gain assurance over the quality and depth of expertise they're investing in.

If you are a buyer or seller of services or products, the following considerations should inform your decision-making.

As a buyer, try the following:

- ✔ **Shift your thinking from fixing problems to understanding the situation and underlying causes.** To do so, try the following:

  - Look at the problem from different perspectives, from a spirit of genuine curiosity and interest.

  - Ask your suppliers or clients how your company is doing. The answer can give you valuable insight into what is going on.

Shifting your thinking so that you can learn from different points of view lets you see how your decision-making process and expectations either advance or undermine your ability to achieve what you're aiming for. When you incorporate asking, listening, and cooperatively coming up with solutions into your decision-making, you're promoting a win-win way of thinking.

- ✔ **Find out what thinking your financial wizards bring to the conversation.** Financial departments can help or hinder successful procurement. In less mature organizations, finance departments tend to make all the rules because they hold the purse strings. Ideally, however, you want your finance person or department to work as a team player. Therefore, when you're hiring your financial expertise, look for someone who can bring a strategic, more integrated outlook to the work and who recognizes that he is part of a team rather than in his own kingdom.

The ideal financial department is one that works with you, provides checks and balances, is able to see a decision from more than one perspective, and can give you the insight you need when you're making a higher-risk financial move.

If you're a seller who is having difficulty with your buyers, consider dropping problematic clients, those who use their buying power to control what you say or do, or who dictate standards that are far below your principles or ethical standards. To identify which clients you may want to consider giving the boot, each year go through your client list and identify the clients that fit these descriptions:

- Clients who haven't paid but have complained a lot about your services

- Clients who treat you as an inferior rather than as a respected team member

- Clients who aren't looking for a quality cooperative working relationship; instead, they're on a power trip

Although it's hard to say farewell to paying work, the stress of compromising your principles and ethics is even more costly. When you drop problem clients and recruit a better class of clients — ones who appreciate your company's services and pay on time — you gain better quality clients and better cash flow, experience less stress, and spend less time trying to get clients to pay and more time feeling absolutely fantastic about going to work. You'll also gain loyal, repeat clients and a relationship characterized by mutual respect.

Whether you're a buyer or seller, at the end of each project, ask questions like, "What went well?" and "What could be improved?" Make sure the conversation includes everyone involved — contractor, procurement manager, supplier, the individual accountable and responsible, and so on. Then end the discussion by asking, "What questions have we not asked?" and "What areas are we leaving out?" The answers to these questions ensure that you don't leave out key ideas or observations.

The cost of unwise frugality

The general manager of a local government department responsible for maintaining city roads, drainage, sewage, and water was repeatedly getting bad press for the apparent failings of his department. The failings caused considerable inconvenience for citizens due to breakdowns in mechanical infrastructure for water and sewage. The local council was taken to court for several cases of significant damage when insurance companies were unwilling to settle claims in a prompt and reasonable manner. Things got worse from there.

The general manager caught flack from all sides: press, residents, his superiors, elected officials, and so on, and his managers and staff were taking a lot of the heat. Then the general manager fell ill and took sick leave. While on sick leave, the manager reflected on his decisions and realized he largely based them on his repair know-how. When he returned to work, he made a list of the five most serious issues. His finance manager assisted by supplying data about the cost of the breakdowns, a list of the frequency of each type of breakdown, and a file of public complaint letters. After examining the data, the manager came up with a list of ten frequently repeated and serious problem areas. Maintenance quality and repair timeliness were at the root of six of the ten issues, and only two firms were involved.

One day, the general manager ran into an owner of one of the two problem firms. He asked the contractor to describe his business's relationship with the city council. The owner of the contracting firm said it was the worst business decision he had ever made, but because he needed the business, he felt powerless to change anything. He told the manager that the council penny-pinched his contract rates so low that he could

not recruit skilled managers or staff for the work. He shared that his equipment was also old and unreliable, which caused him to ignore safety requirements, buy cheaper products, and hire cheaper subcontractors — decisions that resulted in his company delivering repairs below the level required by the council. The contractor had complained frequently to the head of purchasing and supply for the municipal government, who told him the council wouldn't renegotiate because his firm was the cheapest and no one else would take the work at those rates. He was stuck.

The general manager was stunned. The fault did not lie with the contractors, but with the council's frugal ways. The council was getting exactly what it paid for. But the contractor was cheap! This was the insight he needed.

During his next meeting with the mayor, the general manager asked the mayor whether he wanted the problems, which had cost the council several million dollars in the past year, to continue or stop. He proposed that the smart way to deal with the problem would be to pay better rates and demand better service and quality in return. The mayor argued that doing so would mean raising taxpayer rates, but he listened to the manager's counter argument that the costs of poor service were being paid anyway.

In the end, contract rates were renegotiated, which resulted in an almost immediate improvement in response to breakdowns. The quality of repairs was also higher, which resulted in favorable press, much to the relief of the mayor, the general manager's boss, the general manager, taxpayers, contracting companies, and the staff.

Building Character and Credibility through Mistakes and Failure

As an entrepreneur or business owner, you know that failures go with the turf. Resiliency, the ability to bounce back and move forward from a personal failure, is a characteristic of entrepreneurial wisdom. Are all entrepreneurs resilient? Yes, for the most part; only few indulge in self-pity. After bouncing back from a failure, do all learn and apply the lessons to build greater vision or stronger character? No, some recover without gaining better judgment.

Deciding to improve decision-making judgment is a matter of choice. This section explores what you can do to turn experiences, both good and bad, into wisdom and better judgment.

Accepting personal responsibility

You've no doubt read the headlines when a senior level decision-maker blames employees for some unethical action the company was accused of. To gain credibility and respect in a difficult time, however, you're better off accepting responsibility. Being able to bounce back from a setback is easier when you take the higher road and lead because you can then focus on rebuilding rather than covering up mistakes and protecting reputations.

Acceptance of personal responsibility moves you into a leadership stance where you engage in learning what you didn't pay attention to (or ignored) or important signals that you missed. After you've experienced a failure and learned from it, you'll be less likely to stick to a business strategy, for example, that doesn't keep you current with the market and/or ignores the implications on the morale or health of the workplace.

Separating good judgment from judging others

It's very easy to judge others and yourself for screw-ups. We've all done it. But blaming and judging don't improve personal or collective (company) judgment. Developing better judgment requires letting go of your own limitations and your ego's needs (I explain the role of the ego in decision-making in Chapter 4) and gaining access to a wider set of resources within yourself and your team.

Suspending blame and self-judgment

Suspending blame or self-judgment is an awareness best understood through the words of Viktor E. Frankl (psychiatrist, holocaust survivor, and author of *Man's Search for Meaning*) who said, "Between stimulus and response there is a space. In that space is our power to choose our response. In our response lies our growth and our freedom." The mind makes sense out of received data fast. It typically adds, without your consent, an emotional evaluation about whether the information is good or bad. As soon as the evaluation is added, you've missed the moment to chose a different response. Suspending blame and judgment means letting go of the idea that something is bad. Perhaps losing your job is the best thing that could happen. Perhaps the mistake you've made gives you strength and insight you didn't have before.

By taking advantage of the space between the mistake made and how you respond, you can elect to see ahead, not by ignoring your responsibilities, but by learning how to move forward in a wiser manner. You'll shake up routine thinking so that a more enlightened view can enter. You'll accept responsibility for what happens next (future-oriented) rather than flog yourself for what didn't happen. Forgiving yourself or others may be a part of the process.

By working together to uncover what happened and why and doing so in a way that sets aside judgment and blame, you improve the capacity of both individuals and groups to make better decisions. It frees the thinking in a way that turns mistakes into potential breakthroughs and opportunities to achieve higher levels of performance.

Building organizational judgment can take place only in an environment that demonstrates a commitment to organizational health; otherwise, people don't focus on growth; they focus on protecting themselves from criticism. Head to Chapter 13 to find out how to create a healthy work environment and company culture.

Communicating authentically

Admitting a mistake or failure requires two key leadership qualities: courage and honesty. Explaining in an open, honest, and transparent manner what happened, why it happened, what was learned, and what it means to those affected is essential, even if all you can say is, "I'm sorry." Communication must come from a genuine place in your being. Otherwise, the words are shallow, lack credibility, and don't honor or respect the people who've been adversely affected by the circumstances.

Blame and judgment — often the product of negative and frequently hidden emotions — cannot leak into any aspect of communication. If you haven't cleared those out of your system, take time to recognize and deal with your emotions before you step forward to acknowledge events, because your audience will be able to detect how you feel, even when you try to hide it. Mixed messages result when what you say doesn't match how you feel. By speaking openly and sincerely, you gain credibility, loyalty, and respect, even in times of failure. See Chapter 5 for insight into how you can attain the inner peace necessary to deal with emotions that can undermine successful communication.

Reinventing your self-identity

Occasionally a cascade of events pulls your world apart on every level, threatening you with the loss of your business, your family and key relationships, your money, and all you identify with. During times like these, you have an opportunity to examine who you really are, figure out what you want from life, and decide what your life stands for. This soul-searching can result in profound discoveries that may lead you to reinvent yourself.

The pursuit of success can often blind ambition to the point where what truly matters to you gets repressed or overlooked. Usually, you get a signal — a gut feeling that it's time to do things differently. But if you ignore the early warning signs, the message intensifies until your life is left in ruins. Or so it seems. The crash could be the start of a new beginning.

Humility is a leadership quality, and you earn it through the experience of having nothing left to lean on and no escape through meaningless distractions or addictions. You realize that this massive failure is an opening to reinvent and redefine yourself — who you are and who you'll become as a result of your experience. It's an entire reboot of your personal identity and how you choose to move through the world. It may feel like a trial by fire, but when you rise, like a phoenix, from the ashes, you will have gained inner freedom and self-fulfillment.

Part III
Jumping In: The How-to of Decision-Making

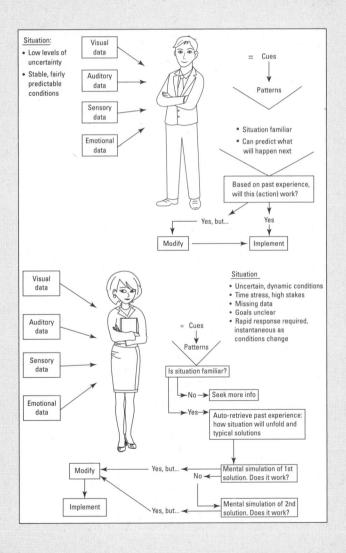

In this part . . .

- ✔ Get clear on what intuition is and isn't and how to put your intuitive strengths to work

- ✔ Look at the basic steps involved in decision-making: articulating purpose behind the decision, clarifying the goal, communicating the decision, and more

- ✔ Discover the factors that impact the timing of key decisions

- ✔ Identify your decision-making style — top-town, consensus-building, participatory, and so on — and find out which approach to use when making different kinds of business decisions

- ✔ Gain the tools necessary for making sound decisions in different kinds of business scenarios

- ✔ See why relationships are central to decision-making proficiency

Chapter 7

Understanding Intuitive Decision-Making

I doubt that any other combination of words in the English language conjures up such mixed responses as pairing *intuition* with *decision-making*. Why? Because humans tend to think that concrete, practical thinking is more reliable than intuitive decision-making. Yet most decisions — some estimates indicate more than 90 percent — are made using intuition. In other words, a lot of decisions are being made via automatic, innate processes that you and I aren't aware of.

So what creates the gap between what you see as reliable decision-making processes and what you actually rely on day-to-day? Confusion and misinformation about intuition. In this chapter, I show you a different way of viewing intuition so that you can better balance rational thinking — which you are more aware of — with intuitive thinking, which operates relatively unnoticed.

Serious and repeatedly successful entrepreneurs are dialed into their intuition and use it. Learning more about how entrepreneurs successfully use intuitive decision-making helps strengthen your awareness and mindfulness when you make decisions, and it helps you make better decisions. And here's an added bonus: When circumstances are dynamically changing and the stakes are high, intuitive decision-making takes over. (You can find the details on how your high-speed, intuitive supercomputer, your brain, makes a decision in milliseconds in Chapter 9.)

Getting the Lowdown on Intuition

In doing the research for this book, I came across many views on what intuition is or isn't. Stemming from the Latin *in-tuir,* which means "looking, regarding, or knowing from within," *intuition* is a way of knowing things without conscious thought. It isn't some kind of mystical tool. Existing science about how the brain works has cleared up a lot of the fog surrounding intuition and how it works.

In this section, I explain what intuition is, clarify some of the confusion that you, yourself, may have about intuition, and explain its benefits for business decision-making.

Defining intuition

Intuition is the process of perceiving or knowing things without conscious thought. It includes premonitions of events — often received through dreams — that have not yet happened or information that appears as a certain inner knowing, even though it may conflict with logical proof. So how you do "know" things without consciously knowing them? The answer lies in how your nervous system — which transmits information throughout your body and brain — works. Your body and brain absorb data, including feelings and thoughts, from your environment all the time. Your intuition accesses and makes that information available to you for decision-making. It helps you see what is going on at multiple levels, using all the data available, not just the kind of data your rational mind stamps as valid. (Read more about the heart's role in accessing your intuition in Chapter 5.)

Unraveling myth from fact

I admit it. I listen a lot to what people say when I mention the word *intuition*. And a lot of what I hear is inaccurate. Here I list the more common comments people have made about intuition and give you the facts regarding those perceptions:

- ✔ **"Intuition and fear are the same."** Your intuition, through your senses, picks up cues and signals from your environment. It alerts you to fear, but it isn't fear itself. Imagine staring at a sabre-tooth tiger about to attack: Your fear gets your heart racing and your body primed for action. Your intuition alerts you to the presence of the sabre tooth in advance. Instinctual reactions will save your butt.

✔ **"Intuition is the same as flying by the seat of your pants, business-wise."** Nope. Confusing intuition with flying by the seat of your pants, which refers to being disorganized, happens when you associate intuition with lack of structure or organization. Although introducing systems and processes can help you organize, excessive reliance on systems and processes exclusively can actually block intuition.

✔ **"My intuition has failed me, so I won't ever trust it again."** Most of your decisions are made without your noticing, so whether you trust your intuition or not, it still guides much of your decision-making. If you feel it's failed you, chances are you were under stress, which impacts reception and interpretation of intuitive signals. Without a proper understanding of your own intuition, you can easily mistake fear or impulsivity for intuition, yet those are very different beasts. You can read more about the feelings that many mistake for intuition in the next section.

✔ **"You can't rely just on intuition."** Absolutely true. Relying on intuition alone creates an imbalance — just as relying solely on reason creates an imbalance. To be a good decision-maker, you need to strike a balance between intuition and reasoning. I tell you how to do that in the later section "Balancing the Rational with the Intuitive."

✔ **"Intuition is a soft skill; it is hard-core rational thinking that gets you places."** Don't trust everything you think you know. An open mind is a requirement for today's decision-maker. If you take a quick look at the business case studies on what went right, you'll see that rational logic doesn't prevail in most cases. The intuitive component is often the key to a good decision.

✔ **"Intuitive decision-making can be dangerous."** A car with an unskilled or careless driver behind the wheel can also be dangerous, but most people don't abandon driving. To use intuition to improve your decision-making, you must understand how you gather information intellectually *and* intuitively. Raising your awareness on how you interpret the information you gather also improves accuracy.

✔ **"You can't trust your intuition 100 percent of the time."** True. Intuition conveys direction in a sensory manner that is unique to each individual. If you're too busy to pay attention to your intuitive signals, you reduce the accuracy of your decision-making. Additionally, intuitive messages are interpreted by your brain, which adds analysis on top of an intuitive "hit" — one reason it is often suggested that you listen to the first thought that comes to mind before your rational mind steps in to censor or add its point of view. Head to the later section "Building Up Your Intuitive Powers" for suggestions on how to develop your intuition.

✔ **"Only women have intuition. When intuition was doled out, the men missed out."** This idea is a relic from the past, based on medieval concepts of intelligence and gender, when folks believed that women were intellectual inferiors and that their brains were incapable of rational thought, leaving them to make decisions based on emotion and intuition. Yet intuition is not exclusive to one particular gender, nor is it the same for everyone. How each person accesses his or her intuition and the language it uses to speak to each person is different, as I show you in the later section "Building Up Your Intuitive Powers."

✔ **"Intuition is about emotions, and I don't trust my emotions. In fact, I am trained not to pay any attention to emotions and to stick to the facts."** Your intuition is not the same as feelings or emotions, but it does incorporate them.

Knowing how intuition differs from impulse and fear

Many people confuse intuition with fear and impulse, but the three are very different. Yes, all three can spur action, but the actions spurred by fear and impulse don't lead you in the right direction as reliably as intuition does. That's why being able to distinguish among the three is an important part of honing your intuitive abilities.

Distinguishing fear from intuition

Decisions made from fear are often knee-jerk reactions to an event or situation. Although fear is an appropriate response in situations in which you face a real threat, our environment is so immersed in fear-based messages that everything nowadays looks threatening, even when it's not. Fear-based messages are generally critical of you and your core beliefs — put-downs and other negative chatter that does nothing for your morale or confidence. In this kind of environment, it's easy to think that you are being guided by your intuition when you're really reacting to the fear you detect from the media, your working environment (which likely is focused on survival), or yourself (your own fears about your personal or financial security).

In contrast, intuition brings on a calm, peaceful feeling even when it alerts you to impending events. It often engages imagery and physical sensations to make the point. Intuition's toolbox contains some great helpers:

✔ **Gut feelings:** These are literally felt in the gut. They alert you to something you need to pay attention to.

> ✔ **Red flags:** Almost everyone has experienced these warning signals. They don't tell you that a zombie is around the corner waiting to bite you, but they do tell you that you're not traveling on the right path.

For clarity, *instinct* is associated with preset behavioral patterns that animals rely on to keep them safe; think in terms of fight or flight. *Gut feeling* is a visceral signal that something is or isn't right. You don't want to ignore either one. For the purposes of making sense of the decision-making world, consider both instinct and gut feeling as part of your intuition's tool kit.

In a culture that thrives on fear and tends to bash intuition, how do you ensure that the niggle you hear comes from your intuition rather than fear? To strengthen your defense system against fear-based decision-making, try these strategies:

> ✔ **Put your worst fears on the table where they can't hide.** Ask yourself, "What is the worst that can happen if I make this decision?" Sometimes, what you fear has already happened in your past, so you can now more objectively decide if your fear holds power as you move forward.
>
> ✔ **Identify the source of your fear.** Start to observe the source of fear, the thing that puts you on flight-or-fight notice. Ask, "What do I fear?" Doing so separates an irrational fear from a possible risk that you can address. Fear loses its power over you.
>
> ✔ **Step away from the environment to gain perspective.** Go for a walk (preferably in nature), listen to some classical music, or do anything else that relaxes you so that your brainwaves can shift to a relaxed state, the source of creative thinking.

Separating impulse from intuition

Just as a fine line exists between genius and madness, an equally fine line exists between *impulse* (acting without thinking) and intuition (understanding without thinking or conscious reasoning). Immediate decisions in extreme circumstances are guided by intuition, which just takes over. When you make an impulsive decision, however, an idea pops into your head, and you take instant action. In this case, intuition isn't guiding you; instead, you're being guided by impulsivity, a knee-jerk reaction based on fear, or a lack of self-discipline.

The difference between intuition and impulse is subtle, and discerning between the two requires close attention. As you gain the ability to perceive decisions made on impulse, you can pause in the middle of an impulsive action to consciously decide whether to take the action or not.

To become more aware of whether impulse or intuition is guiding you, observe your decision-making patterns. Notice how much you do purely on impulse. When you come up with ideas and act on them, pay attention to how well these decisions work for you. By becoming aware of how often your actions are driven by impulse, you can begin to detect patterns that will let you know whether you are getting an intuitive hit or are just being pulled in different directions on whim.

Understanding the benefits of intuitive decision-making in business

When you access your intuition for decision-making, you reap a number of benefits, such as the following:

- ✔ You can make fast, effective decisions in complex and unfamiliar situations and in high stakes, dynamically changing situations, which are often standard at the strategic and executive level.

- ✔ You gain access to deeper wisdom and intelligence.

- ✔ Your decisions are more likely to align with your core values and sense of purpose.

- ✔ You gain the energy you would otherwise lose when consciously trying to solve a problem.

- ✔ You gain greater access to creative solutions.

As a business decision-maker, you can apply your intuition to all sorts of decisions: whether to make a particular investment, buy a business, pursue a merger acquisition, engage in a joint venture, and so on.

When you rely purely on your rational mind, you unintentionally blindside yourself. Sometimes, you want something to work so badly that you listen to the facts presented only to find out later that you missed the underlying data that revealed a different reality. In such situations, try to tap into your intuition, which is there to back up your rational thinking by letting you tune into what is invisible to most.

One entrepreneur told me he'd attended an angel investor pitch event (an event where aspiring entrepreneurs pitch their ideas to potential investors). All the entrepreneur's numbers made sense, but something didn't ring true for the investor. His intuition told him not to invest. As it turned out, his intuition was right. The recruiting company gained investors but later folded.

If your decision-making is characterized by anxiety over which option to choose, or if you procrastinate because you're not sure whether you're making the right decision, the easiest thing you can do is listen to yourself.

Understanding How Intuition Works

In years past, just about any self-respecting scientist stayed well away from any sort of study of intuition because it was seen as some New Age-y pseudo-science. And for years, this neglect resulted in the perception that intuition is mystical, relied on by people who 1) make decisions using emotion instead of rational logic, and 2) seek the advice of mediums.

Years of cumulative research regarding intuition, however, paints a much more interesting picture. Gerard Hodgkinson, professor of Strategic Management and Behavioral Science at the University of Warwick, concludes that intuiting is a complex set of interrelated thinking and emotional, and biological (cellular) processes, in which there is no apparent interjection of deliberate, rational thought. The view that intuition is an innate ability that all humans possess in one form or another suggests that it's the most universal natural ability shared by all. The implication? The ability to intuit could be regarded as an inherited, unlearned gift. In this section, I explain how intuition works and how you can leverage the understanding to make more accurate decisions.

The HeartMath Institute, which has conducted two decades of research on stress management and the heart's intelligence, and others before them have shown that the heart's sensory brain detects events before it registers in your conscious awareness. In other words, the heart knows before the rational mind what is going to happen before it actually does. This *pre-cognitive knowing* is the center of your intuitive muscle, and it's directly influenced by the emotional state of your heart. You can find more about your intuitive strengths in the later section "Building Up Your Intuitive Powers."

Processing incoming data

Information comes at you all the time and at rapid rates. Consider the amount of information you take in when you're sitting in a meeting with just one other person. You receive words and facts, observe body language and facial expressions, and absorb sensory input — including tone, emotional charge, and energetic broadcasts (I talk more about energetic sensitivity in the later section "Identifying your intuitive strengths — the mechanics"). You process some of this information rationally and consciously — that is, you're aware of it and pay attention to it. The rest just happens on autopilot: You're not consciously aware of all the content in all these sensory inputs, but they are received and filed away nonetheless.

Two processors — think of them as computers — help you make sense of all this information: your conscious mind and your subconscious.

The conscious mind

The conscious mind's specialty is perceiving, organizing, and delegating, so it likes to sort the information in a logical fashion. Different kinds of thinking take the information and apply it to the task at hand. For example, you use analytical thinking to reduce information and see all the parts; critical thinking to play the devil's advocate, check assumptions or assess risk; and big picture thinking (also called *systems thinking*) to see the interrelationships and interconnections.

The subconscious mind

The subconscious mind operates like a super processor. It takes in all the incoming information from the body, the environment, and your implicit memories, and works to uncover patterns and relate whole concepts to one another, looking for similarities, differences, and relationships among them. You're only aware of a small fraction of this information.

Where you focus your attention affects what you become aware of and determines what gets processed at higher levels. In a noisy room filled with many conversations, for example, you have the ability to focus on a single conversation of interest and tune out others. Similarly, you can modulate pain from a stubbed toe or headache, desensitize yourself to sensations like tickling, and also self-direct your emotions.

The subconscious processor operates 24/7 (if your conscious mind is processing information 24/7, chances are you aren't sleeping very well!). The subconscious is the supercomputer that, while you sleep, integrates the day's experiences and processes data that saturates your decision-making environment. Your intuition takes that data and retrieves it for making decisions in milliseconds, as I explain in Chapter 9. The processing power of the subconscious is described in Chapter 5.

Forming patterns from cues

Your intuitive process draws on your accumulated databank of solutions that worked in certain conditions. The process is fairly simply. When you handle the same issues over and over again, you begin to recognize patterns. Over time, these recurring experiences become so familiar that you don't need to reference procedures; eventually, they become so ingrained that you know the solution, without having to think about it. When new information comes in that doesn't fit predictable patterns, you notice the new information and handle it differently, coming up with a different solution. When you need to make an intuitive decision, autopilot pulls from your inventory in milliseconds.

All goes well in a predictable environment. But what happens when you leave the safety of a familiar environment and enter a new one — you take a new job at a higher level or in a different sector, for example? You expand your database of cues, patterns, and solutions as you encounter different cues and underlying patterns, based on your new environment and set of circumstances.

Some people believe that intuition is only the result of accumulated experiences. This assertion suggests that you have to reach a particular age or stage in life before you can be intuitive. Clearly that isn't the case. Some young people are very intuitive, and some older people aren't.

Building Up Your Intuitive Powers

Despite assertions to the contrary, intuition isn't infallible. Nor is it something that people are either born with or not. The truth is that you can develop your intuitive capabilities and improve them. In this section, I show you how to identify your intuitive powers and give you tips for strengthening them.

Identifying your intuitive strengths — the mechanics

Research conducted by the HeartMath Institute (http://www.HeartMath.org) suggests there are three different categories or types of processes that form your intuitive strengths, or channels: implicit knowledge, energetic sensitivity, and nonlocal intuition. Your intuitive strengths aren't limited to only one of the three strengths. You can access one or more at a single time. Fortunately, you don't need to know which strength is at work, as long as it works for you. As you increase your awareness of what you are sensing, noticing, and paying attention to, you improve your accuracy.

Identifying your intuitive strengths enables you to adjust to new and different circumstances, and it increases your effectiveness in familiar situations. It also gives you a better understanding of what is going on in the social and emotional environment — data that lets you know whether a solution will work in a given situation.

Implicit knowledge

Implicit knowledge is the instant retrieval of knowledge that you've gained but can't explain logically. More specifically, it is an implicit cognitive database that holds information about situations you've encountered and the solutions that worked. It shows up as knowing without thinking. This is what most people think of when they hear the word *intuition*. It is a cognitive process based on experience and knowledge gained and catalogued over time.

With implicit knowledge, the more experience you have with decision-making, the stronger your intuition will be. Therefore, the best way to strengthen your implicit knowledge is to gain more experience in making decisions in very different decision-making environments. This is a prerequisite for anyone aiming to make senior-level, high-stakes decisions because the journey from the front line to the senior level represents a 180-degree flip in decision-making mindset. Take a look at any executive or strategic decision that has proven to be successful, and you'll find the decision-maker merged years of experience with an intuitive take on which way to go next. Rational analysis would support but not direct the conclusion. You can read more about the difference between operational and executive-level decisions in Chapter 13.

Energetic sensitivity

Energetic sensitivity refers to your nervous system's ability to detect and respond to environmental signals, such as electromagnetic fields. It is well established that, in both humans and animals, nervous system activity is affected by geomagnetic activity. Some people, for example, appear to have the capacity to feel or sense that an earthquake is about to occur before it happens. It has recently been shown that changes in the earth's magnetic field can be detected about an hour or even longer *before* a large earthquake occurs. Another example of energetic sensitivity is the sense that someone is staring at us.

Energetic sensitivity is best understood by understanding the heart's electromagnetic field, one source of intuitive perception. Your body — more specifically, your electromagnetic field — receives and absorbs data that your conscious mind doesn't perceive. An electrical current generates a magnetic field; therefore, when your heart beats, it generates an electrical field. The electrical field generated by your heart is many times stronger than the field generated by your brain. Figure 7-1 shows how far the field extends out from your body, measured by medical equipment.

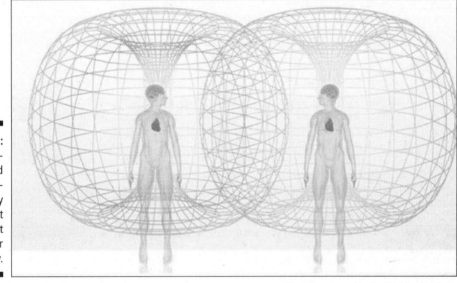

Figure 7-1:
The electrical field generated by your heart extends out from your body.

Illustration courtesy of the HeartMath Research Center

The information embedded in the electromagnetic field generated by the heart expresses the emotional state of each person, and you both emit and absorb this emotional information, whether you're aware of it or not. Standing beside someone who is happy or enthusiastic, for example, has the spin-off effect of boosting your own spirits. Conversely, an employee who arrives at work an emotional mess communicates his emotionally negative state in his interactions with customers and coworkers. Credibility and trust are conveyed or not through this invisible transfer of information.

The relevance to workplaces? Those that rely on fear or coercion impede cognitive functioning and well-being. Workplaces that boost positive emotions in the workplace, even under stress, support cognitive functioning and access to intuition.

When you are standing next to someone and your electromagnetic fields overlap, your heartbeat can be measured in the other person's brainwaves!

With energetic sensitivity, you'll have a sense for what is going on underneath the surface of a given situation, which no one is either talking about and may not even recognize. You receive that information as one or more of these signals: a hunch, an image, a physical sensation in different parts of your body, and so on. That's the good news. Now for the downside. If you're energetically sensitive, you have a tough time being in crowds and are likely to feel drained afterward, loud noises will likely be overwhelming, and working under fluorescent lights will deplete you. To read more about energetic sensitivity, check out Judith Orloff's book *Positive Energy: 10 Extraordinary Prescriptions for Transforming Fatigue, Stress and Fear into Vibrance, Strength and Love* (Three Rivers Press).

Nonlocal intuition

Have you ever known that something was taking place in a location remote from you without being told? If so, you've experienced nonlocal intuition. *Nonlocal intuition* refers to the knowledge or sense of something that cannot be explained by past (or forgotten) knowledge or environmental signals. Examples of nonlocal intuition include a parent sensing that something is happening to a child who is many miles away, or the repeated, successful sensing experienced by entrepreneurs about factors related to making effective business decisions.

Strengthening nonlocal intuition is difficult because there are no practical, step-by-step solutions on how to improve. This intuitive strength is totally intangible and unique to each person. Here's a suggestion, though: When someone you care about comes into your mind, be open to the idea that you may be picking up on an emotional signal, one that crosses time and space in an instant.

A businessman was on his way to make a critical presentation to a prospective client, with whom he had been building a relationship for months. The business man's flight was delayed by bad weather, and he knew he wasn't going to make the meeting on time. Trapped as he was on an airplane, he couldn't call the client to inform him of the delay. The businessman stilled his mind and quieted the endless mental chatter that goes with anxiety. In the resulting state of calm, he sensed that the delay wasn't going to be a problem. When he was finally able to make the call, he learned that the prospective client had delays on his end as well. In fact, the businessman's new arrival time coincided perfectly with the time the client would be available for the presentation.

Improving your intuitive intelligence

To increase your ability to access and interpret inner guidance when you need it most, you can develop your intuition muscles. Here are some suggestions:

- **Make decisions.** Don't wait to be perfect. The more experience you have making decisions, the better. Whether your decision proves to be right or wrong helps you know what works under specific circumstances.

When you're right, pat yourself on the back. When you're wrong, take time to reflect on how you made the decision and what you based your final conclusion on so that you can learn. Reflecting on decisions that proved to be flawed works with decisions you make solo, with team decisions, and with organizational decisions on a larger scale. The process for learning from failures is described in Chapter 6.

✔ **Explore your beliefs to discover whether they are limiting your perception or helping it.** Limiting beliefs reduce your capacity to perceive other information that can inform your decision-making, both consciously and unconsciously. The most entrenched belief in business, for example, is that only profit matters. If you ascribe to this limiting belief, you may overlook other key factors in your business's success, such as community goodwill or customer satisfaction.

Most beliefs are stored in your subconscious, meaning that you may not even be aware of them yourself. Therefore, try listening to what you say. Doing so can give you insight into the beliefs that may be subconsciously impacting your decision-making. For instance, if you hear yourself saying, "Self-organized teams are out of control" or "Command and control is the only way," you may discover that your core belief is that controlling people creates performance. With that awareness, you can reexamine your convictions and open up to alternatives or even experimentation.

✔ **Learn how to regulate your emotions so you can listen to yourself.** When your stress is high, your decision-making efficacy is low. Many tools are available to help you control your emotions: meditation, yoga, a walk in nature, time with pets, and deep breathing are some tried-and-true methods to help you achieve and attain daily balance. All involve helping you achieve inner peace so that your feelings and your mind can work together.

✔ **Practice predicting what will happen next.** It's a chance to sharpen your senses and strengthen accuracy on what you're detecting from your environment. Start by trying to predict which elevator will arrive first, or guess who is calling before you answer the phone. Or listen to your inner voice to help you see ahead. You may discover that you've picked up on something significant!

Improving your intuitive powers is a process, not a project, so forget about hoping you can study decision-making intuitive intelligence once and then be done. Becoming a better decision-maker takes time and attention no matter what age or stage you are at in your career or life.

Uncovering procedures that interfere with intuition

Procedures are invaluable to someone new to the job. They define specific parameters so you know exactly what to do. However, as you gain more experience, procedures become so ingrained that you don't need to refer to them anymore except under unusual conditions. Rather, you are able to spot cues and signals that tell you what is going on.

Procedures serve a purpose, but to rely on them exclusively blocks the collective intuition your company can access. The collective intuition operates faster and more accurately than a step-by-step process. Knowing this, you can do the following to hasten the transition from reliance on procedures to experience that taps into intuition:

✔ **Pair new employees with experienced mentors.** Doing so enables you to transfer the implicit knowledge more quickly and bring new staff up to speed in less time.

✔ **Reflect on whether you're relying exclusively on procedures and adjust your approach accordingly.** You want to encourage observation of the subtle cues that build rapid and accurate understanding of the situation. Remember, facts (rational approach) are seen in isolation from each other. The sensory cues (intuition) form a pattern that can reveal something.

Psychologist Gary Klein, in *The Power of Intuition: How to Use Your Gut Feelings to Make Better Decisions at Work* (Crown Business), tells of two nurses: a young nurse reading the clipboard and an experienced nurse reading the signals. The point of this story isn't whether you should trust fact or feeling. It's that both kinds of data — fact (the chart) and sensory cues (noticing what was going on with the patient) — are equally important. In this case, the latter saved a child's life.

Removing the risk of overwhelm

Have you ever felt overwhelmed? You live in the 21st century, so of course you have! That feeling occurs when you try to jam too much information through a rational mind that is simply not equipped to handle that much volume. *Overwhelm* is the signal that the conscious mind has hit overload, and you're at risk of blowing a brain fuse. Overwhelm continues when you attempt to retain control by using your rational mind. Controlling your emotions is a better way to approach overwhelm because it lets you give yourself a timeout.

Trying to think your way through information or task overwhelm is pointless. But your intuition can help — if you just free it up to do so. Step back from the situation and try to clear your rational (conscious) mind. When you stop trying to process the information mentally, you gain perspective, and your sensory skills can kick in, often enabling you to arrive at the decision you need to make. This is one of the times when relying on intuition instead of practical thinking gives you the advantage. With practice, this exercise can help you see the simplicity in any complex situation. And from that simplicity, you can unearth solutions.

Balancing the Rational with the Intuitive

If you attended business school, chances are you were taught only about rational decision-making processes. Traditional business schools emphasize the use of the rational approach, assuming that the business world is predictable. Unfortunately, it isn't.

Rational approaches have their application, but in unpredictable, fast-moving, complex, and high-stakes environments, you get faster and more accurate decisions when you use intuition. The highest performing and longest running companies in the world are both intellectually and intuitively intelligent.

Applying rational and intuitive approaches to your decisions is a lot like a dance. Which one leads? Which one follows? The answer depends on the kind of decision and the situation you're dealing with. Following are some general guidelines regarding how to balance intuition and rational decision-making in various situations. Keep in mind that these are *very* general guidelines; every situation you encounter will be unique:

✔ In fast-moving, rapidly changing, high-stakes situations, let your intuition take over. There'll be no time for any other intervention. Although the chance always exists that more information could surface, the decision can't wait. Executives or entrepreneurs making bold, high-risk decisions face this kind of situation all the time. You need to trust your instincts and stay committed to expanding your thinking to avoid narrow reasoning.

For many years, the U.S. military subscribed to an approach that required using analysis to think things through. Then in 2003, it endorsed applying intuition when it realized that over 90 percent of the decisions being made were made intuitively.

✔ In start-up companies under pressure to move ideas forward while achieving a positive cash flow, you often engage in a messy blend of intuition, analytics, and flying by the seat of the pants. In fact, you may be totally unaware of how you're making your decisions. Under these circumstances, coming to agreement on how you'll decide is a good idea. Considering that the failure rate of start-ups is ridiculously high, slowing down to be aware of how you're deciding may make your company one that makes it through.

✔ If you're an entrepreneur who makes one high-stakes decision after another, consider delegating or sharing decision-making, using a more systemized method understood by all decision-makers in the company. Doing so will relieve some pressure and bring a sense of order to what can feel like total chaos. This approach also reserves intuitive and intellectual energy for responding to the bigger questions like, for instance, whether you accept an offer to buy your company out.

✔ If your job requires adherence to specific regulatory or technical standards, you initially use the rational approach to follow formal procedural guidelines. As you gain experience, however, you can improve your add decision-making speed and accuracy by applying intuition. Refer to the earlier section "Forming patterns from cues" for ways you can foster the transition from reliance on procedures to a more intuitive approach.

✔ The higher the stakes and the more important the decisions are, the less time you have to make them. Let your intuitive supercomputer blend the facts with other information you've picked up through the social and emotional environment. Doing so gives you a strong sense of how the decision aligns with your core purpose and values.

Successful entrepreneurs and executives use their intuition as a shortcut to make sense out of vast amounts of factual and sensory information. They have an innate sense of whether they are on the right path and can readily adapt to surprises. To read more about the research that uncovered the connection between business success and intuitive intelligence, check out investment advisor Joseph Bragdon's book *Profit for Life: How Capitalism Excels* (Society for Organizational Learning [SoL]).

✔ If you make decisions under public or regulatory scrutiny — often the case in situations where accountability for public (or investor) funds is required — use a rational approach to ensure you've done your due diligence. This kind of approach makes the decision-making process transparent and ensures that you cover all the required bases. Remember, however, that the more complicated a decision is, the longer applying a rational approach takes. Use your best judgment to weigh time and complexity with speed and accuracy.

✔ If the decision is being made with remote, intact, or interdisciplinary teams or partnerships, start with an intuitive take, then explore a rational approach to make the decision, and follow up with confirming the decision using collective intuition. This strategy is best because participants in a multiparty decision-making process often represent and are accountable to their own managers, agencies, business units, or to the public. Rationally thinking the decision through together strengthens the relationship and provides a forum for the interests, needs, and diverse views of the participants to be considered; it also provides all with the information needed to communicate proceedings to those who need to know.

As I state earlier, these are broad guidelines, so use your judgment to adopt an approach that best suits each situation you encounter. And don't forget that this isn't an either/or game. The best approach is to blend the intuitive with the rational to make good decisions. Which of the two takes precedence depends on the circumstances.

The process you choose has an impact on support for the final decision. Collective support helps everyone be on the same page when communicating the decision and throughout its implementation, particularly when things don't go according to plan. It is well worth the time to ensure that everyone has achieved a comfort level with the result, that their concerns have been addressed, and that their expertise has been incorporated into the final outcome.

Why a rational approach isn't necessarily best

If you believe that rational decision-making will somehow increase certainty that your conclusion is *the* right answer, think again. Several things muddy the waters:

✔ **Human psychology:** Humans have hidden biases that operate without notice. Even when noticed, they are difficult to control. You can find information on how to deal with your own hidden biases in Chapter 4.

✔ **Temptations to commit too soon:** The need to be certain creates a serious limitation by tempting you to commit too soon to an option that may not be the best. To learn how to keep your options open, check out Olav Maassen's and Chris Matts's book *Commitment* (Hathaway te Brake Publications).

✔ **Speed and amount of incoming information:** The information environment is moving far too fast these days, and the situations are too complex to assume that a fixed approach will stabilize uncertainty.

✔ **Science:** Research in the field of psychology shows that rational decision-making isn't more accurate. In fact, the opposite appears to be the case.

Chapter 8

Laying the Groundwork for All Decisions

You make decisions for different reasons: to solve a problem, implement a new policy, take a different tact for your business, or change the way you handle day-to-day transactions, for example. No matter what the initial motivation is, gaining clarity on what you seek to achieve and what expectations you have before you get started offers all sorts of benefits. It saves time and trouble during the decision-making process, it facilitates effective communication, and it enables you to adapt to surprises during implementation.

In this chapter, I explain the things you should think through if you want to make better decisions — things like what event or situation motivates or inspires action and what the decision must accomplish after implementation. I also help you lay the groundwork to make a decision and create an action plan that actually works. So if you're ready for a no-fuss, no-muss way to make decisions, read on.

Reviewing the Essentials for Sound Decisions

Whether the decision is made intuitively or rationally (refer to Chapter 7 for details), being clear about what is to be accomplished and why provides you and your team with a clear, and preferably shared, understanding of the goal.

Such clarity is good for a couple of reasons:

- ✔ **It helps you reduce risk if things go sideways.** By having a shared picture of what is to be accomplished, avoided, and improved, you and your team can adapt and improvise as needed.

- ✔ **It establishes who you'll involve and how you'll decide.** Understanding these points ensures that the experience and diverse perspectives required to assess timing, direction, and course of action are present.

Covering these basic points alone helps you make better decisions, no matter what size business you operate.

Identifying purpose

The purpose identifies the reason(s) you're taking action. It answers the big "Why are we doing this?" and "Why do we exist?" questions. Knowing the purpose confirms priority and focus for both short-term results and longer term direction. Being clear about purpose is important for when you're making both immediate decisions ("What are we trying to achieve by taking action?") and decisions related to the company's reason for existence.

Articulating purpose at the decision-making level

At the level of decision-making, purpose points the way to the *endpoint,* the goal the decision is meant to achieve. With decisions made internally, purpose provides focus and keeps effort on track. The point is to know very clearly why you are taking action so that you can effectively communicate the purpose to your team and give a sense of priority.

A solid purpose statement provides some indication of the value — "to deliver high customer service so that the customer happily returns," for example. A clear purpose statement offers these benefits:

- ✔ **It allows your employees to adapt and adjust to emerging conditions.** When you've articulated the purpose of the decision, staff members have the freedom to react to unexpected events without needing permission. As a result, your company will be able to adjust to circumstances more quickly.

- ✔ **It clarifies how the decision serves the company, client, or customer.** A clear purpose statement connects the desired endpoint to how it is accomplished.

- ✔ **It focuses new initiatives and helps teams that aren't quite clear on what they're supposed to do.** Teams often form without knowing why or what they are to achieve. A clear purpose statement in this instance provides the needed commitment for teamwork.

The pitfalls of not clearly defining your purpose

I worked in a retail company where the stated goal was high-quality customer service, but the company did not define what "high-quality customer service" meant. To staff members, it meant that shelves were to be kept stocked. With that understanding, employees helped customers, and if the requested item was out, they explained to the customer that the item was not currently available. No options were offered. The result? Customers walked out the door without a real reason to return.

Now suppose that the company's purpose statement was like the one stated previously — to deliver high customer service so that the customer happily returns. Such a purpose statement focuses on making the customer happy. In this instance, employees would focus on customers' needs instead of shelf-stocking. As a result, they would be inclined to search for the item at one of the other stores, call the customer to let him or her know when the item comes in, or suggest an alternative.

Bottom line: Without an idea of the result (the company's definition of customer service and how far an employee can go to satisfy a customer), the concept of quality customer service had no meaning. Staff didn't know what they were trying to achieve. It was a good idea very poorly communicated.

When you are working with teams, focus on identifying the "why" for the team's work. Basically, you want to answer the question, "What can we achieve by working together?" Many team dysfunctions can be traced back to not having a good enough reason to work together.

Articulating purpose at a higher level

At a higher level, purpose articulates what a company stands for. It inspires effort. Without a sense of purpose, people are very busy, yet not all can say why or know where they are going.

At a higher level, purpose is much more than, "We exist to make money." Purpose is about how the company serves society, the community, and the environment. Defining your purpose — your "why" — helps your staff and your customers (both current and potential) know what you stand for. In addition, as author and speaker Simon Sinek says in *Start with Why: How Great Leaders Inspire Everyone to Take Action* (Portfolio Trade), the "why" is compelling and inspiring in and of itself.

A company creates meaning when its stated purpose (as well as its stated mission, vision, and intention) corresponds with its decisions and actions. Companies that post their mission statement and espoused values and then fail to connect their decisions to the words lose credibility with their employees and their customers.

> # Why, oh why, are those cupcakes so special?
>
> The inspiration behind a cupcake company was found in the aftermath of 9/11. The goal? To restore nostalgia and comfort to the world. The company's cupcakes are fancy, but they're still cupcakes. Why do customers pay twice as much for these cupcakes? Because they connect the customers to a time when life and society were less violent and more community-minded.
>
> This cupcake company isn't in the business to sell cupcakes, although that is what it does. It's in business to deliver a product that provides an emotional connection to the good old days, when life was simpler and the world felt safer.

Seeing ahead: Clarifying the endpoint

The need to make a decision starts when a problem needs to be solved, when an opportunity to improve a current practice presents itself, or when a need exists to radically change how things get done. Action is required. What you want to accomplish — your *endpoint* (essentially the goal or result) — is defined by how the change serves the company and customer. These events — the circumstance initiating the action and the endpoint of the decisions that are made in response — mark the start and finish to any decision.

Identifying what will be different

Knowing the endpoint helps you envision what a successful outcome looks like and frames the questions the outcome must address, whether you're solving a problem, changing a company policy, or articulating long-term direction.

Issues and opportunities typically motivate action. To arrive at a logical and attainable endpoint, consider what needs to be different as a result of taking action. Will an issue be resolved, an opportunity be used to advantage, or costs reduced? Articulating what will be different helps you gain clarity on what you seek to accomplish.

Articulating the endpoint

Identifying the problem in your current situation enables you recognize the issue you're addressing. If the problem you're addressing is the high cost of your company's turnover rate, you may identify endpoints such as the following:

✔ **To reduce costs of employee turnover by 20 percent by the end of the next quarter:** This endpoint uses a financial metric to signal success. When resolving problems or issues, the endpoints describe what the successful resolution of a problem or issue will be in measurable terms.

✔ **To make your company a great place to work:** Alternatively, you can step back to take a more visionary approach. For example, you may ask, "What can we do to make our company the best place to work?" This example articulates a higher goal — making the company a great place to work — that invites creative solutions and that can engage employee ideas for how to accomplish the goal.

Note the difference in focus between these two examples. In the first example, you focus on reducing employee turnover, a narrower lens that is more likely to engage a logical, rational problem-solving approach. The second example (making your company a great place to work) is far more aspirational and inspirational, and its solution is likely more open-ended. As a result, it will attract more creative solutions. Either approach can achieve the goal of reducing employee turnover by the desired 20 percent. The difference is in the process and the kind of thinking you encourage and apply to achieve the that reduction.

Clarifying the endpoint

After you articulate your endpoint, your next step is to set direction and agree on the performance results. One way is to ask team members, "What changes do you want to see or observe when the change is complete?"

If, for example, the endpoint is to make your company a great place to work (the second example from the preceding section), you can ask something like this: "When asked why our company is the best place to work, what would employees say?" Possible ideas could include, "We have a self-directed learning and development plan in place," or "We have a space set aside to kick back and casually exchange ideas."

When using this method, avoid answers that are actually steps in the process rather than the endpoint. For example, if you want to see a reduction in employee turnover, you wouldn't fill in the blank with "when we understand why people are leaving." This is akin to saying the endpoint of building a house is finishing the blueprints. Uncovering why people are leaving is only one step of many toward achieving the stated goal. A clearer endpoint in this scenario would be something like, "We will have reduced employee turnover when employees see themselves as valued members of the family and choose to stay instead of seek employment with a competitor."

When processes miss the point

ABC Company creates a new compensation plan every year for its sales reps. Ostensibly, the goal behind the new compensation is to create an incentive for salespeople to increase business from existing clients, add new clients, and develop new markets. In this particular year, the endpoint wasn't clearly defined. A sales rep, upon receiving the new compensation plan, did some calculating. She discovered that, if she did nothing all year but make check-in calls to existing and former clients, her compensation would be one penny less than the year before.

Do you think the company achieved its objective: to stimulate business development or inspire the sales force? The compensation plan obviously missed the mark.

A poorly thought-out or unclear endpoint can waste time and effort and confuse employees. Your team needs to know what your expectations are without having to second guess by finding out, as they go through the process, what you don't want. For an example of how a poorly thought-out endpoint can actually hurt employee performance and improvement goals, see the nearby sidebar "When processes miss the point."

Ineffective communication almost always results in a disjointed effort because not everybody knows or understands the endpoint or the destination you're all working toward. Therefore, when you want to effectively communicate the endpoint, communicate it to the group to avoid having it passed on from one member to the next.

Determining timing: Why now?

Timing is everything. When assessing any decision, you have to figure out whether your action plan needs to be put into effect now or whether it can wait. Some companies operate permanently in crisis mode, treating everything as urgent; others apply a more strategic approach and rely on an intuitive sense for timing entry into new markets, for instance, or initiating new product development.

Factors determining timing include the following:

- ✔ Detecting or discovering unstated emerging needs in the marketplace
- ✔ Recognizing social changes that open opportunities for innovation

✔ Knowing when to stop, change direction, or walk away

✔ Identifying innovations that meet multiple needs and for which an implicit demand exists

Your company's priorities

How important is taking action to achieving long- or short-term company goals? Priorities speak to importance. Companies that track performance by using quarterly targets risk compromising strategic direction. You must consider both the short term and the long term when you set and communicate priorities.

The long-term direction of your company

Working toward longer term or strategic goals happens in incremental steps. Keeping an eye on the long term helps you avoid missing opportunities to adapt quickly.

Consider, for example, the plight of traditional book publishers. Many failed to adapt to the emergence of online book buying. In fact, one company — Borders Books — outsourced its online division and, unwittingly, its future existence when the company failed to consider consumers' changing preferences for books and music.

Your company's short-term goals

Because they are easy to react to, short-term goals often steal focus away from longer term goals. Start-up companies and small businesses are particularly tempted to deal only with immediate needs, abandoning the steps required to ensure long-term sustainability for the excitement and thrill of taking action now. Knowing why your company exists and who would care if it disappeared helps you gain clarity on what you need to achieve in the short term that helps you stay in the game for the longer haul.

It's tempting when working in short-term time increments to attempt to do too much all at once, which can overwhelm everyone. Instead, step back to select strategic priorities. Doing so helps conserve energy while retaining focus on attaining key results.

How the decision affects other areas of your company

Consider the ramifications or implications of your decision and actions. How will the result positively or negatively affect other areas in your company? Too often, decisions are made without regard to the implications on other business units or on other decisions under consideration. Stepping back to see what else is going on, combined with communicating intent and discussing consequences, helps avert unintended consequences. Unintended consequences are more thoroughly covered in Chapter 6.

How urgent the situation is

Will deciding now prevent the escalation of even bigger problems later? When making this determination, keep in mind that some decisions are urgent and some just look that way. You can tell the difference by observing whether your company's workplace treats everything as an emergency — something I think of as deliberate crazy-making. When everything is an emergency, it's hard to separate real from reaction. To take proper action, consider the consequences of not taking action in terms of employee health and safety or company repu-tation. Use agreed-upon anchors to assess the situation. Failing that, know what you are basing your decision on so you can deliberately choose.

Every company has its own internal dynamic that impacts what issues are deemed urgent and how soon to take action. Here are some considerations:

- ✔ **Decisions deemed urgent and important to your organization:** These decisions often fall into the realm of executive decision-making and are made quickly, using intuitive decision-making.

- ✔ **Decisions that are urgent but not as important as other items on your plate:** For these decisions, identify the implications of parking the deci-sion for the time being and the triggers or signals that will bring the decision to the forefront. Also consider whether taking action in one area will address the situation.

    Every decision has a time stamp on it; if it's important, you can't delay it forever. Additionally, some decisions are related. With respect to timing, use the factors cited in the earlier section "Determining timing: Why now?" for guidance. You are using your intuitive intelligence. See Chapter 7 to discover how to tap into and strengthen access to your intuition.

    In time-crunched workplaces, it's tempting to defer important long-term decisions, but doing so creates a decision-making environment in which you and your team end up fighting fires from moment to moment. Use your judgment when deciding whether you should postpone an impor-tant decision and notice if deferring decisions becomes a habit.

- ✔ **Decisions that are important but not urgent:** If the situation is impor-tant but not urgent, the decision may be one that serves a longer term goal. For decisions that are strategically important, command time to do the necessary analysis, even though making the final decision isn't urgent. Financially based decisions, like investment or technology deci-sions, for example, need time so that you can pull together the informa-tion required to weigh and make a final decision.

- ✔ **Decisions that are neither urgent nor important:** These decisions can take up most of your day. They happen at rapid speed and may not require your conscious input. However, when small decisions start replacing bigger, more important decisions, such as those that define company direction, you need to step back and take a look at where your efforts are going. If necessary, delegate the smaller operational decisions to those who, because they have access to real-time information you have to seek out, are in a better position to make the decisions.

Everything is urgent in start-ups or in companies struggling to survive. In such environments, decisions are made on the fly in reaction to new information, and fear or panic often reigns. The underlying message? "React now, or the sky will fall!" A company in constant survival or crisis mode may be in the habit of making knee-jerk reactions instead of letting logic, reason, and good sense prevail. If you see yourself in this situation, step back to gain perspective. Sometimes, doing nothing gives you the time to reflect and take a more thoughtful approach.

Whenever health and safety are involved, take action. Period. Companies that defer costs by choosing not to make their workplaces safer run the risk that their employees will pay the price with work-related injuries and chronic illnesses.

The availability of resources

When resources — money or time — are scarce (a dilemma most organizations share), decisions get delayed. Perhaps the problem isn't availability of resources, but how creatively the resources are managed. If you're delaying a decision because you lack the resources, explore creative and unconventional methods of resource allocation. Ask whether you can achieve the particular task in a different way. Think how an outsider — someone outside your workplace — would solve the problem. A fresh look and a different perspective can reveal a different approach.

The information available

Obviously, you don't want to act until you have all the necessary information and have analyzed it sufficiently. Yet delaying a decision as you wait to assimilate all the information and complete your analysis can be a trap.

New information will always come up. You can make a decision based only on what you know now. So how do you know when you know enough? At some point, you'll feel it purely in your gut. This "gut feeling" — a product of your intuition and your accumulated experience — will enable you to make an informed judgment call. By combining analysis of the situation with your experience from similar decisions in the past, you'll be able to decide. At the same time, pressure can impair your rational and intuitive faculties, so use the tips and tools in Chapter 5 to gain a state of calm. Then decide.

Business decision-makers aren't the only ones to benefit from being intuitive about timing. Organizational judgment is improved when companies also balance analytics with good sense. Head to Chapter 7 for more on the role intuition plays in decision-making.

Assessing commitment: Your own and your colleagues

You can have the best team in the world working collaboratively, but if you or your colleagues are not committed to turning the decision into a reality, you may just as well go to your favorite coffee shop, order copious amounts of caffeine, and buzz out. Commitment can be undermined by the following:

- **Poorly thought-out plans or decisions:** Plenty of half-baked ideas end up being implemented without being thought through.

- **Task fatigue:** When a company piles one action on top of another, task fatigue results. Employees appear uncommitted when actually they're exhausted.

- **The scope or viability of the proposed task:** The overwhelming size of what must be implemented or how workable the solution or plan is perceived to be are other factors that can cause commitment to waver.

- **Lack of emotional engagement:** Lack of commitment for moving forward on a decision may indicate that team members are not emotionally engaged. Emotional engagement inspires employees to contribute to something that holds meaning. Intellectually, the task can get accomplished. But when efforts are half-hearted, initiatives that are more mechanical than meaningful won't gain support, despite the best intentions of employees.

I can practically guarantee you that, without staff commitment to the decision or change, the decision won't be implemented. Wheels will spin. Determining the commitment level for you and your team members is imperative. You must assess the commitment level early on and monitor it as the decision is implemented. You can detect the level of commitment as you consult and gather information internally from employees and colleagues, and externally from partners by paying attention to the items I outline in this section. Commitment isn't something you force. It's inspired through the merits of what you're doing and how it contributes to a higher purpose (refer to the earlier section "Identifying purpose").

Team and organizational dynamics

Team and organizational dynamics refers to the quality of working relationships between individuals and teams. It embraces how conflict is used, the degree of trust, and the level of support between coworkers. When observing dynamics, remember this key principle: Energy flows where attention goes.

A lot of attention going into turf wars and unhealthy competition works against collaboration and implementation. Conversely, when the collective attention is focused on achieving the goal, a better chance exists that all parties will work together to deliver on achieving performance goals.

To observe organizational and team dynamics, consider the following:

- **Is information openly and honestly exchanged?** If the answer is yes, then decision-makers have more trustworthy information available than they do when the answer is no. If the answer is no, information is likely used to serve personal interest. The effect is a "watch your back" ethic that undermines making and implementing decisions.

- **Are resources hoarded or shared?** In workplaces where performance appraisals reward personal effort, there is little incentive for one team to help another out unless enough goodwill exists to overcome that barrier. The degree to which employees and business units are encouraged to share resources to meet company goals reflects how highly decision-makers value team effort over controlling the way things get done at a personal performance level.

Where your coworkers can contribute

Uncover the wisdom and experience from other members of your team by finding out what they've learned, good or bad. By exploring the following, you can flag potential pitfalls early on in the decision-making process:

- **Whether coworkers have worked on similar issues before or under the same conditions:** If so, find out what worked and what didn't, and why.

- **Whether coworkers are willing to support you, either actively or as a sounding board:** Active supporters are those who actively participate in the decision-making and implementation, while sounding boards are those who, although they are not actively involved in your project, can offer useful guidance and advice.

What those higher up in the chain of command will do

Many good decisions have been waylaid by lack of support or political maneuvering on the part of those higher in the chain of command. Therefore, if your decision is affected by (or must rely on) the actions or support of people higher up in your organization, you need to gauge the degree of support you can expect. As you try to uncover this information, pay attention to the following:

- **The organization's internal politics:** If infighting, deceit, and manipulation are used to increase political status internally, you need to know upfront so that you can be better prepared for initiatives to be hijacked for personal gain or dismantled if the initiative has risk of failure.

Highly charged political environments are characterized by power brokers watching to see which horse will take them to the finish line fastest and switching positions at a moment's notice. In such environments, you can expect people to say one thing and do another. Therefore, keep your options open for longer before you commit to one course or another.

✔ **The management style:** Decision-making environments that rely heavily on a command-and-control style of management prevail even in small to medium-sized companies. A command-and-control environment, in most circumstances, relies on authority to dictate decision-making. You can expect your initiatives to be commandeered by your superiors and decisions to go through a lengthy process. Dealing with a command-and-control environment, characteristic of a more traditional approach to management, is more a matter of learning how to navigate the interpersonal relationships.

Conversely, when those higher up in the chain of command see themselves not as commanders but as peers and part of the collaboration, you can breathe easier. The values underpinning collaboration create a more trustworthy decision-making environment. You'll be able to better gauge and trust the degree of support your decision is likely to garner and know you can rely on securing the resources you need. (Head to the later section "Factoring in management style and working environment" for information on these styles of management.)

Calculating the risk and impact of doing nothing

In fast-moving, complicated, and unpredictable situations, decision-makers can hesitate because they fear making a mistake or are overwhelmed by uncertainty. Hesitation, once it becomes a habit, weakens personal and organizational confidence. But make no mistake: Doing nothing is a decision. If you choose to do nothing, make sure it is a choice instead of a default position for coping with the unknown.

Factors to consider before deciding not to take action

Like any decision, the decision to do nothing needs careful thought. Here are a few factors to consider before you decide not to take action:

✔ **Whether waiting will cost more financially or have a negative impact on key relationships:** Reflecting on the financial risks of inaction or delay helps you decide whether doing nothing is really the best option. Money doesn't have to be lost all in one big chunk to be harmful to your business's finances. Some costs occur a little at a time, but over time add up. Although you may be tempted to delay making a decision that addresses what I call the "slow-leak" issue, doing so works against the company's financial viability.

✔ **Whether the problem you are addressing is more serious and likely to scale up or expand if you do nothing:** Problems that have a tendency to expand and get worse if ignored include issues like maintenance problems (such as leaky valves), health and safety concerns (such as outdated or improperly functioning machines), interpersonal problems in the workplace (such as bullying, destructive conflict, and infighting), and unethical behavior (theft of supplies or issuing false invoices).

Whatever is tolerated is considered acceptable, and the behavior can escalate as a result. If employees are stealing from the company, bullying others (it happens more often than you think), or behaving in other unethical ways, and management is aware of these issues and takes no action, the company has a serious problem. You need to face the issue. See Chapter 19 for how to set ethical standards as part of a healthy workplace.

✔ **Whether doing nothing will cause a safety problem:** You never want to turn your back on a situation that presents a safety or health concern.

As soon as you are aware of a health or safety risk, doing nothing is irresponsible and could be catastrophic. Taking shortcuts during a construction project may save money, for example, but if it increases the risk of injury to the public, it could lead to civil — and possibly even criminal — suits.

✔ **Whether delaying will result in higher social or environmental costs:** When a company's actions negatively affect public health, the situation requires immediate action. Instead of being on the wrong side of the law, companies can remediate the problem or take full responsibility and address the issue.

Don't assume that only big companies can cause significant environmental damage. Even small companies or single individuals in any size company are capable of making big mistakes that the community or environment pays for. For example, an employee from a lawn-treatment company contracted to spray herbicide may clean his tank and dump the wastewater into the ditch that runs into the community water supply.

Recognizing when it's better not to act

Sometimes doing nothing is better than the available alternatives. Doing nothing may be a better option in these situations:

✔ **When confusion is greater than clarity:** Stress, fear, and doubt wreak havoc with the mind, denying access to the calm emotional state that enables decision-makers to stay receptive to new information. So take time to clear the chatter and calm the nervous system before you decide.

✔ **When lack of commitment suggests implementation won't succeed:** If the team isn't totally committed to the decision and direction, any action or plan may end up being flawed or stalled. In this case, wait until the commitment level is stronger or until the reasons for hesitation become clear and are resolved.

✔ **When you detect that something isn't right:** If coworkers or staff exhibit unusual behavior (like declining performance), that may mean pressures from home or addiction issues. In this case, suspend the decision until you know what you are dealing with. Monitor and observe the situation. Then before making a decision or putting your hunches to the test, verify your suspicions by asking questions and checking your facts.

As the preceding list makes clear, sometimes, the best decision is to do nothing. However, make sure that you're not sticking with the status quo just because it feels familiar and safe.

Some companies seem to believe that by pretending nothing is changing, nothing will. This approach is a risky one. Business conditions are dynamic and unpredictable. As a business leader, you are far better off developing skills that enable you to work in uncertain and unpredictable environments rather than hoping that everything will stay the same or return to the way they were before. The ultimate guide regarding when to wait and when to act is self-awareness; you can read more about that in Chapter 5.

Deciding Who Decides

Where order and structure are important to a company, employees are expected to follow established procedures. Such a "flight plan" clarifies who does what so that each team member knows his or her role and what to expect. In this section, I explain how to decide who makes the final decision and share the various factors — management style, working environment, authority structures, and so on — that influence the dynamics of decision-making.

Factoring in management style and working environment

How things get done matters. Some organizations are hierarchical; that is, decisions, instructions, information, and so on, tend to flow from top to bottom. Other organizations have structures that tend to facilitate a freer flow of information; as a result, decisions tend to be more collaborative. Observing the path decisions follow within the organization increases awareness of how power is used. You can apply this knowledge to determine how best to proceed:

✔ **Hierarchical organizations:** In hierarchical organizations, decisions typically flow downward, and decision-making authority is allocated and governed at each level. I call this the *command-and-control decision-making model.*

In companies that focus attention on the bottom line (these companies typically have lower levels of self-awareness, as I explain in Chapter 5), a silo mentality is created. In a silo, functions are isolated and often compete with the rest of the organization, even at the expense of the company's goals or customers' satisfaction. You can see this mentality at work when one department is unwilling to share information or expertise with another. Competition can be healthy, but not this kind.

✔ **Networked organizations:** In networked organizations, information flows freely and is openly shared. Decisions tend to be made by consensus. A manager's role isn't to control or direct performance but to support teamwork by clearing the barriers that can stop work from getting done in order to achieve a common goal. Such an environment increases efficiency and supports collaboration.

The buck stops where? Authority and responsibility

In this context, the term *authority* refers to the position a person holds in the company and the decision-making power that goes with that position. The authority you have in your company determines how you to carry out your responsibilities, provide direction to others, take charge of a situation, or make decisions regarding allocation of resources. Those with *approval authority* sign contracts and can commit the company to a financial or strategic direction. Approval authority is where the buck stops, so to speak.

The term *responsibility* refers to the legal and moral duty to perform a task to completion, and it points to the person who faces the music if the task fails. *Collective responsibility* relates to the performance of a group, regardless of individual contributions.

The kind of responsibility and authority that fall on your shoulders depends in large part on the structure of your organization:

✔ **Self-organizing or flat companies:** In self-managed or "bossless" organizations, the management tier is missing. Each person plays a management role. Responsibility and authority are pushed out to all employees. Everyone is accountable and holds the authority, although some companies may assign specific areas of responsibility to someone with greater aptitude or experience. The responsibility of overseeing the financial health of the company may fall to one of the partners who happens to be stronger in financial expertise, for example. Work is focused on achieving the goals of the company and getting the work done instead of managing the people.

✔ **Hierarchical organizations:** Hierarchical companies are often associated with top-down authority. Hierarchies exist without use of authority to wield power, but for the most part, executives, managers, and supervisors (management tiers) hold authority and responsibility unless decision-making is decentralized. Some organizations centralize all decision-making authority, which has the effect of making the approval process time-consuming. In others, decision-making is decentralized, so the company is more agile and able to respond to emerging conditions.

If you know how your company is organized and how authority and responsibility flow, you know how to move decisions through the organization. Companies using hierarchical, authority-based decision-making are structured around organizing working relationships. The difference in focus makes a big difference as to how powerful a company becomes.

Investigating Decision-Making Models

When it comes to how decision-making authority is used or abused, the size of a company doesn't matter. Even super-small companies can have a hierarchical, authority-based structure and use the command-and-control approach, where the boss acts like a dictator rather than as part of a team working to achieve company success. And large companies can elect not to have bosses at all, using a clearly outlined approach to decision-making and employing cooperation and collaboration within specified time frames. Some companies use a hybrid approach, which combines unit titles and "heads" who hold decision-making authority but employ a participatory and open approach that enables better information flow.

Deciding on a structure is a matter of intentionally selecting an approach to decision-making that has the best chance of achieving speed and real-time information, and is matched to your values. Many self-organized companies have almost more structure than those ruled by authority-based hierarchies, but it's aimed at defining personal responsibilities for getting work done.

In this section, I explain how decision-making power and authority are used in each of these approaches. For more general information on the impact of company structure on decision-making, head to Chapter 3.

Relaying top-down decisions: The command-and-control style

Decisions made at the top of the organization set direction and guide goal setting. These decisions tell staff and customers what is important to the business and what it means to them. As a result, the *way* decisions on direction and goals are communicated sets the tone for *how* the goal gets achieved and whether people do their part out of obligation or enthusiasm.

In a classic command-and-control management style, decisions get relayed down the organizational layers, with each layer receiving its mandate from the layer above. To the line-worker, the decision comes from the supervisor; to the middle manager, it comes from a director; and so on up the lines of authority.

Here are some typical scenarios and dynamics characterizing top-down decisions:

- ✔ **When something goes awry, people tend to blame the person at the higher level.** The blame game creates a gap between *we* and *they*. It's a critical organizational challenge for many companies, including small ones. How you engage others and make your decisions can help achieve collaboration.

  What you can do: Promote early engagement across functional expertise and among those involved in creating and communicating a decision. Doing so sends the message that you recognize the value these folks bring to the table. For suggestions on how to build consensus among teams and strengthen relationships, head to Chapters 11 and 12.

- ✔ **Because decisions can feel imposed, many employees are left with the impression that they have no control.** Management that micromanages staff tends to overlook or disregard creative ideas. In the end, employees become passive, waiting to be told what to do because it's less risky.

  What you can do: Although individual employees may not be able to influence *what* the decision is, they can directly influence *how* it is delivered. When management focuses on what needs to be accomplished, staff can add ideas and shape the outcome in those places where the decision and action steps are less defined.

- ✔ **The workplace environment becomes internally competitive, and business units may not talk to each other enough to facilitate exchange of expertise or experience.** This situation typically occurs when working relationships are excessively controlled. Business units are organized vertically — with the effect that silos, rather than cross-team interaction, form (refer to the earlier section "Factoring in management style and working environment" for more on silos).

What you can do: Open lines of communication and work to break down the walls. To facilitate sharing of key information, identify and eliminate procedures and measures that block information exchange and collaboration. Effective communication of decisions conveys expectations; then throughout implementation, it relays how things are working at an operational level, for example, or shares customer input.

Top-down decision-making is a high-risk management style in dynamically changing business environments. Top-down decisions require buy-in. *Buy-in* means that a decision is being *sold or told.* In other words, the decision is being imposed, and support must be gained through coercion or influence. The result? A lot of effort expended on convincing others that the decision is a good one. Without buy-in, you end up with lack of commitment, inaction, or, in the worst cases, sabotage. If you don't achieve buy-in, the real problem isn't whether the decision is a bad one, although it may be, but that employees weren't engaged in shaping the implementation or adapting the decision to fit day-to-day realities. People have creative talent, and they want to use it. Providing them with the opportunity to do so is just plain smart.

Using consensus

Consensus is a group decision-making process in which the final outcome requires agreement by all parties involved. To gain consensus, you invite diverse perspectives so that the groups can explore the issue from different angles. Consensus adds value by building support and commitment for implementation of a decision and action plan. It is a chance to collectively examine and predict the consequences in the short and long term. You can find more on consensus decision-making in Chapter 11; in the following sections, I share a few key points about using this kind of model.

Effectively using the consensus model requires that all participants share a common picture of the direction and vision they're working toward. It doesn't mean that everyone sings exactly the same notes in unison or that everyone is fixated on a precise, one-way-only strategy for achieving the goal.

Dealing with differences of perspective and opinion

In an effective consensus-building model, differences of perspective are given air time; they're not received as irritants or roadblocks but are viewed as offering value to the process.

Being aware of the thought processes and emotional undercurrents that occur within the group helps create a better consensus-building experience. Doing so lets the group identify and immediately address issues that may come up. Consider designating someone to keep an eye on dynamics. Consensus processes fall apart when differences of opinion fall into the camp of "I'm right," which really means "they're wrong."

Serious reservations or concerns need to be presented so that they can be addressed. In fact, probing and sometimes difficult questions can reveal insights you need. Breakthrough decisions often come by listening to the person concerned about something no one has felt comfortable saying. Keep these points in mind:

✔ Working environments or teams that value harmony above all else tend to pressure individuals to conform to what the majority feels is the best decision instead of actively pursuing the point of objection. Rather than pressuring group members to conform, explore the underlying issues and encourage team members to ask questions out of genuine curiosity. Such questions may uncover hidden issues and quite possibly valuable insights

✔ If you are dealing with cynics, then remember that the value of cynicism is to add critical thinking at points where team members may be tempted to press on, assuming nothing will go wrong. If the group doesn't include any cynics, then be sure to add a dash of cynicism as a necessary check. Doing so ensures that potential trouble is identified and addressed before moving on. But beware of too much cynicism, which can stall the forward progress of your decision-making and mire the conversation in negativity.

Making decisions that are acceptable for all

In consensus decision-making, participants should focus on making the decision in a way that is acceptable for all.

Consensus doesn't work when the right to veto is allowed. In a traditional consensus process, veto is allowed, but giving veto power to any one person can twist the experience into a power game aimed at serving self rather than common interests, negating the whole value of a consensus process.

Devoting the right amount of time to making the decision

Getting a decision right in the first place can take time, yet if the process goes on too long, people lose interest, and you lose valuable momentum. To offset that risk, structure your time frames but allow for a window of flexibility. Your intuitive sense of timing can help you get the timing right; head to the earlier section "Determining timing: Why now?" for guidance.

Workplaces that value fast action more than sound decision-making tend to have higher tolerances for doing the work twice instead of thinking through the decisions in the first place. When you're under pressure to decide, you may be tempted to take shortcuts, like bypassing the needed professional advice and or not pursing helpful input. Overlooking key data because you're under pressure to take action can lead to mistakes and less-than-optimum decisions.

Building a Team for Participatory Decision-Making

Whether your company uses a command-and-control or consensus-building style of decision-making, you may be working with a team. Making decisions as a working group or team strengthens the commitment to implementation and helps bring all the issues to the table for consideration. In deciding who you'll involve in decision-making, consider factors such as the following:

- ✔ **Who has experience or expertise that could bring value to the team?** Bring in expertise from across functions within the organization. Also consider involving customers who add value through their needs and perspectives and through relationships.

- ✔ **Who will be impacted by the decision?** Build in viewpoints from those impacted by the decision, whether the impact is anticipated to be positive or negative. This could mean adding your best customers to the team.

- ✔ **Who will be responsible for implementing the decision?** Involving in the planning process those who will be implementing the decision is just plain smart. By addressing operational considerations in the beginning (these considerations all too frequently get left out of the early decision-making discussion), you can make implementation go much more smoothly. If, on the other hand, you ignore the valuable experience and knowledge that the people implementing the decision have, you risk creating resistance and extra cost.

Engaging and designing the solutions together as an interdisciplinary team draws on the brain trust within the company and offers a better chance to foresee what may not go according to plan. In short, it helps you troubleshoot. It also helps you strengthen internal relationships. Keeping people — especially those you need to achieve success — in the dark makes no sense. You can find participatory decision-making tools in Chapters 11 and 17.

Chapter 9

The Nitty-Gritty: Walking through the Decision-Making Process

As a decision-maker, you face all kinds of situations in your business. Each situation calls for a different decision-making approach. Some approaches are rational and analytical; some are more intuitive. Despite their differences, both rational thought and intuitive thought gather and make sense of information in an attempt to arrive at the best course of action.

Whatever approach you use, you can benefit from understanding the basic steps to making sound decisions. In fact, for every decision you make, you'll touch on — accidentally or intentionally — the steps I outline in this chapter. I also show how your intuition enables you to make rapid fire decisions in quickly changing, high-risk situations.

Clarifying the Purpose of the Decision

Being clear on why you are taking action guides implementation. Establishing purpose (the *why*) is a must-do, front-end task because, when you know why you're doing something, you reduce the risk of mistakes and misunderstandings when circumstances change. Purpose provides the focus for thinking, action, and all the micro-decisions that lead to the result.

Identifying the reason for the decision

Decisions are made for several reasons. In business, the two most common reasons for making a decision and taking action are to address a problem or to seize an opportunity:

- **Solving a problem:** Operationally, when equipment isn't working, products aren't delivered on time, or customers don't receive what they ordered when you promised it, it's a problem. When problems occur, you need to take action to find out why the problem exists. In a flower shop, for example, having the fridge that supposed to store today's shipment break down and not having a backup is a problem. The question is, is this simply a mechanical glitch or is the situation far more serious?

- **Seizing an opportunity:** Opportunities take many forms: a serendipitous encounter with someone who has the potential to become your biggest buyer, for example, or a change in zoning laws in an area where you want to expand. Other opportunities come dressed as problems: Employee disengagement, for example, is an opportunity to create a better workplace. Recognizing opportunities means seeing situations like these not as problems to be solved, but as a chance to do things differently.

When the reason for making the decision is clarified, being super clear about what you are hoping to achieve (the outcome or result) provides the focus for getting there. Make sure you can articulate the following (refer to Chapter 8 for details on creating a purpose statement):

- Why you're taking action now and not later
- What will be in place when the action plan is complete
- What conditions you want the solution to meet

Providing a compelling picture of the desired outcome mobilizes the minds and hearts of employees and other affected parties.

Taking a tactical or strategic approach

Actions can be propelled by urgency (you need to do something fast) or inspired by vision and opportunity in the longer term. Articulating what you want the decision to achieve gives you a good idea about whether you need to take a tactical or strategic approach.

To understand the difference between strategic and tactical actions, consider this situation: The workload at your company has become intolerable, and your employees are stressed and requesting overtime pay. In addressing the problem, you can take a tactical approach or a strategic approach:

✔ **Tactical:** You look at options that solve the immediate problem, like outsourcing some of the work or hiring someone to alleviate the burden on your employees.

✔ **Strategic:** You step back to observe how work is being delegated and communicated, how existing resources are being used, and so on, so that you can discover and address what is creating the pressure in the first place. With this knowledge, you can institute changes that in the long run will reduce employees' stress and workload.

It's easy to make the pain go away by taking action quickly before you truly understand the situation. Doing so can result in having to revisit the problem when the solution proves to be ineffective. Companies, for example, sometimes fix undesirable employee behavior by sending them off to training rather than exploring what is creating the situation in the system (culture) itself.

Taking the Blinders Off: Eliciting All Relevant Info

Many decisions that fail do so because they were made using narrow thinking. You don't know what you don't know. Narrow thinking can torpedo your business decisions. Consider the business owner who, when her decisions were questioned, always answered, "I know what I am doing." She carried on . . . right into bankruptcy. To avoid the dangers of limited thinking, try to gather relevant information from as many different perspectives as possible, especially the ones you disagree with.

In this section, I outline sources of information and tell you how to vet the info you find. For more information about how different ways of thinking can be used to advantage, head to Chapter 7.

Doing your research

Depending on the issue you're confronting or the reason you're taking action, you may have to conduct extensive research, consult with colleagues who have already successfully faced a similar question, and consult with employees and customers. When doing so, your intention must be to learn rather than to confirm that your own ideas are right. A genuine inquiry builds trust and uncovers key factors critical to decision-making.

The primary goal at this stage of the decision-making process is to look at the situation from as many different angles as you possibly can. Sometimes this task can be difficult, especially when you don't agree with the ideas you hear, but it is well worth doing nonetheless. Doing a thorough job of gathering information gives you a wide variety of viewpoints to consider, uncovers potential pitfalls, and reveals unstated needs that must be addressed if your decision is to be effective.

Following are some ways you can gain the varied insight and information you seek:

- ✔ Monitor and participate in LinkedIn discussions that are relevant to your business.

- ✔ Subscribe to online newsfeeds like the Huffington Post or other international, national, and regional news outlets.

- ✔ Participate in professional associations where you find your clients and customers.

- ✔ Ask employees, customers, and clients for input and information by using focus groups or surveys.

- ✔ Host information sessions to find out how the constituent groups see the situation.

- ✔ Consult with your colleagues to find out their views about the project or initiative.

- ✔ Give employees an opportunity to ask questions of people in leadership and management positions in an open and honest fashion.

The information-gathering stage is typically fluid and fast rather than overly structured. To find out more about how your company's structure guides the manner in which information flows and is shared, refer to Chapters 3 and 12.

Gaining some distance to stay objective

You can see a situation more clearly when you haven't got your nose in it. For that reason, when you gather information, you want to maintain some distance. Doing so helps you objectively assess the information you receive. You'll be better able to see which questions you need to ask and to recognize who needs to be involved.

Gaining distance is easier said than done, for two reasons:

- ✔ **You are the one who has to remember to pull back and reflect.** If you don't build time to reflect into your decision-making process, it won't happen.

✔ **You have a blind side — unknown biases or, worse, prejudices — that work against your decision-making.** Chances are you are unaware of these biases in yourself but can spot them easily in others. To avoid being blindsided by what you can't see in yourself, ask someone you trust to point out when you're overlooking the obvious.

Your beliefs guide which cues you pay attention to and how you interpret them. Yet your views and perceptions are limited — limited by how much information you've had access to and the experiences you've acquired in your lifetime. Keeping an open mind is a way to maintain a check and balance on your perceptions. It opens your eyes to what others see that you can't. It also helps you be more effective. To ensure that you aren't restricting information to only what you're familiar with, follow these suggestions:

✔ **Remain curious.** Approaching each situation with an inquisitive mind expands perception. Chapter 5 discusses what influences perception.

✔ **Notice when you are being defensive or feel compelled to prove that you're right.** Take these emotional reactions as signals that you're thinking rigidly or feel threatened. They're good indicators that you're overlooking important information that can change how you lead.

Chapter 4 has more information on how beliefs and biases influence your perceptions and how to ensure that they don't derail your decision-making.

Paying attention to different perspectives

Gathering accurate information in a highly interconnected communication environment is challenging, especially because each person can see only a part of the overall picture. What people see depends on their unique perspectives, and what they understand is determined by what they know about their part of the picture. For this reason, you need to pay attention to as many different perspectives as possible. When gathering intelligence, try to do the following:

✔ **Use as many different sources as you can.** Take into account personal experience, factual data, and the social and emotional factors that will impact both the decision-making environment and the implementation situation.

✔ **Pay attention to conflicting information.** Conflicting info points to holes in the picture and is a signal that you need to keep seeking information from different people. Try asking the kinds of questions a person completely unfamiliar with the topic would ask. This strategy can shine a light on how the different views converge to form the big picture.

✔ **Incorporate diverse perspectives, especially ones you may not agree with, into your thinking.** Such perspectives highlight the things you need to consider when making the decision; they also provide insight into the factors that should be addressed when putting together the action and implementation plans.

Separating fact from speculation

Facts — like how much money was allocated for a project and how much was spent, how many employees work for the company, what the employee turn-over rate is, and so on — can be verified and proven. At some point, however, facts can get mixed up with opinions (based on perceptions) and ideas. The key is being able to discern between them, and the challenge is being able to do so in the midst of change.

When people are in the midst of change and the future is unknown or uncertain, they start guessing about what will happen in order to feel more certain about what lies ahead. Before long, speculation is running amok because people don't know what to expect, or they lose confidence in where and how they fit into the changing world.

When people start filling in the blanks themselves because they don't know how they fit into the company's bigger picture, you know that the company has failed to communicate its intent and the direction of its decisions sufficiently. When you hear speculation, you know that more open communication is necessary and that the decision must take into account the shaky confidence among the company's employees. Whatever you do, don't confuse speculation with information for decision-making.

You can address speculation in two ways:

✔ **Find out what people are saying — do they see the consequences of the initiative in a positive or negative light?** Doing so lets you discover important concerns related to the decision's outcome so that you can address them, if necessary.

✔ **Communicate.** Outline what is known and not known. Explain the direction. Doing so helps reduce worry.

Including feelings as information

The idea that humans are logical beings is nice, but it's not realistic. Although facts appeal to the rational mind, feelings guide what people do. Therefore, when you're gathering information, you want to include the emotional environment. Doing so can provide valuable data.

When one of your decisions isn't being implemented or, worse, it backfires, chances are you've failed to consider what matters to people. Unless you consider both the emotional needs and the social needs of the people affected by the decision, you risk being out of sync with customer needs or overlooking small things that can make a big difference to employee well-being and performance or to customer loyalty.

You don't find this kind of information in reports or data charts. You find it by making connections with people, being genuinely curious, and listening actively, with your mind — not your mouth — wide open.

Whether you use surveys combined with in-person relationships, engage in joint projects, or facilitate open lines of communication with employees and customers, you can follow these simple strategies to discover what matters to your employees and customers:

- ✔ **Ask questions about what works and what doesn't.** If you're testing a new product, the best way to elicit useful information is to give staff or potential customers the product and find out how it works for them both practically ("Did your clothes come out clean?") and in terms of meeting values or specific preferences ("How did you feel about using the product?") The responses offer insight into what works and what doesn't for the market you are reaching.

- ✔ **Build trust with your employees so that, even when they do tell you things you'd rather not hear, they don't have to fear reprisal or punishment.** Not every business owner is prepared to hear that he or she sounds like Attila the Hun. But you must be able to receive difficult-to-hear information without breaking down into a pool of tears or going into a fit of rage. Neither approach builds confidence or credibility.

- ✔ **Engage with the community by building partnerships with local non-profits and other local businesses.** Such partnerships provide a steady stream of information on what matters.

In the Sustainable Food Lab (`http://www.sustainablefoodlab.org`), companies partner with nonprofits to insert sustainable practices into the food supply chain. This large collaboration, in which the partners bring totally different mindsets, develops internal leadership skills while simultaneously tackling a bigger issue.

Knowing when you have enough

Gathering information isn't about feeling absolutely certain or waiting until everything is perfect before you act. It is about feeling 80 percent satisfied that you've looked at the situation from as many directions as possible and that you have enough information to make a good decision. Then you are ready to move on. When determining how much information is enough, consider the following factors:

✔ **The amount of time you have available:** Stay open to new information until the full-stop deadline for making the final choice arrives.

✔ **Whether you're satisfied you've asked enough questions and have enough information:** You'll know by answering the question, "Do we have enough information to analyze the merits of each option or scenario under consideration?" If your answer is yes, you're good to go.

Knowing when enough information is enough is never a precise calculation. Only after you reflect on the decision to gain knowledge from the process do you learn, one decision at a time, how to determine how much info you need. Intuitively, you'll most likely feel a sense of calm centered in your gut or heart.

Sifting and Sorting Data: Analysis

After you gather information, the next step is to make sense of it. In short, it's time to analyze the data. Factors that determine how you'll proceed include how much time is available and whether you need to justify your decision to investors, customers, employees, or shareholders.

Conducting your analysis

Follow these steps to sort and analyze the information you've gathered:

1. **Identify the facts, data, and raw numbers relevant to the decision and determine how you'll crunch the numbers so they can inform the decision or selection of options.**

   Big data is the term given to the proliferation and abundance of data decision-makers must consider. Computer programs available for analyzing complex data include spatial, visual, or cloud-based presentations. For an example, see http://www.spatialdatamining.org/software. You can find a list of the top free data analysis software here: http://www.predictiveanalyticstoday.com/top-10-data-analysis-software/.

2. **Sort the social and emotional information into themes.**

   The themes can be *trends* (the direction for societal preferences), *dynamics* (the interrelationships that exist), and needs or preferences (which point to the underlying values that inform decisions), for example. These things tell you about what lies ahead so that you can predict what the response will be to your decision. Use them as a lens to identify what you need to consider in choosing options, or to ensure that you meet social and emotional needs during the implementation process.

3. **Identify the considerations you see as relevant to either making the decision or implementing it.**

   To synthesize what's important to consider in your decision-making, explore the facts (the rational-logical portion) and what is going on in the situation (feelings/emotions or relationships/social). Pull out the main ideas to use in subsequent steps. You can either use a mind map, a method to visually map related ideas (see Chapter 11 for how to draw a mind map), or you can tuck related ideas under the key points so you can see the relationships between the information you've gathered.

   For example, if you're launching into a new market, as Target recently did into Canada, you'd want to ask Canadian customers what Target products they prefer. Customer preferences would be a theme; the product, price point, and customer expectations for service would form a part of the background decision-making.

4. **Map out consequences — how the decision will impact staff, customers, employees, and suppliers, for example.**

   Knowing the consequences helps you make adjustments and informs what and how you'll communicate any changes to your listeners, based on what they currently expect or are familiar with. (The mind-map tool I describe in Chapter 11 gives you an effective way to identify consequences.)

5. **If you are using a rational decision-making process, select criteria you'll use to consider options before making a final selection.**

   You need to identify the criteria you'll use to assess the options under consideration. Refer to the later section "Establishing and weighing criteria" for details.

By now, you'll know which information is most relevant, whether you're relying exclusively on analysis of the data or combining it with your intuitive know-how. If you're making your decision purely intuitively, you'll use what you perceive to be important and will rely on how the data is presented to pull out key points.

Throughout your analysis, keep communicating with your team. Doing so not only helps everyone know what is going on, but it also encourages dissenting views and alternative perspectives to come forward.

Critically evaluating your data

Mistakes get made when critical thinking isn't applied. When you think critically, you become your own devil's advocate, so to speak. You examine and reflect on your own thinking and question assumptions or conclusions.

If you find critical thinking hard to do solo, enlist a colleague's help or engage the entire team by doing some individual reflection first and then coming together to exchange observations.

To critically evaluate your data, ask these questions:

- ✔ What aren't we saying? What are we overlooking?
- ✔ Where are we making assumptions, or what assumptions are we making?
- ✔ Where are we superimposing our own values and views on top of the information we are looking at?
- ✔ What could possibly go wrong?

Critical thinking and skepticism aren't the same, although they can both bring value. Whereas critical thinking is an intellectual exercise that challenges the validity of an idea in order to test its worthiness, skepticism is a whole different kettle of fish. When skepticism rears its head, you hear comments like, "We've tried that before" and "This will never work!" The skeptic offers criticism without offering insight. If you fall into this trap, you run the risk of dismissing an idea without truly evaluating whether it has merit, and if you dismiss a skeptic simply because his or her comments aren't helpful, you're missing an opportunity to learn something valuable. If you have a skeptic on the team (or you begin to hear your own inner skeptic), find out what can be learned from the skeptic's past experience that may help the current situation.

Making assumptions intentionally . . . or not

Decisions get made all the time based on assumptions. Assumptions can be calculated guesses you make when you're missing essential information, or they can be ideas you accept as true without proof and without thought. Depending on what kind of assumption you're making — the educated-guess kind or the I-believe-it-just-because kind — assumptions can help or hinder your decision-making.

Making assumptions allows you to convert uncertainties into something you can work with, at least temporarily. Assumptions also give you a way to move forward until new information clarifies any uncertainty and presents an opportunity to think through your priorities so that, if something unexpected happens, you can quickly change direction. (For more on priorities, head to the later section "Implementing the Decision.")

Using assumptions works under these conditions:

- ✔ **You know you're making them.** When essential information is missing, you intentionally convert the unknowns into assumptions. Suppose, for example, that your office is planning to move to a larger location. You don't have data regarding your company's growth rate or the number of telecommuters it employs — information you need when determining which of the new sites has enough room to accommodate your work force. Therefore, you make the assumption that, over the next five years, the staff count will double and that telecommuters will be physically in the office one day each week. These assumptions let you fill in the blanks and move on.

- ✔ **You adjust your assumptions as new data becomes available.** As conditions change, you review your assumptions and adjust them to fit the emerging reality. If the information you needed in the first place becomes available, you can eliminate the assumption altogether.

Assumptions don't work when you're not aware that you're making them or when they are left unchecked and then prove to be inaccurate. If you aren't aware of your assumptions, or you don't test the assumptions you've knowingly made against the reality of the situation you are in, you may be operating under a dangerous illusion.

Check your assumptions before making a decision to see what unnoticed thoughts are sneaking into your deliberations. To uncover underlying beliefs, openly ask what assumptions you and your team are making. Without declaring the assumptions, you risk making a poor decision that seems sound initially but undermines your efforts later.

Establishing and weighing criteria

In a rational decision-making process, you use the information you gather to establish criteria that specify what each of the alternatives under consideration must meet to accomplish your goal. You can create the criteria on your own (for personal decisions) or collectively, as you do when you work in a team or in a collaborative venture.

Establishing a list of criteria by which to judge the options in front of you offers benefits like

- ✔ Helping you think the decision through
- ✔ Bringing the most practical alternatives to the surface

✔ Providing a clear structure that guides the evaluation process

✔ Helping the decision-making team agree on what it is looking for

✔ Making the thinking behind your final choice visible, clear, and precise — which is especially important when you make decisions that are subject to open scrutiny

Criteria specify the conditions that must be met for an option to be considered. I explain how to establish and weigh criteria in this section.

Listing and sorting your criteria

Start by making a short yet complete list of the conditions that must be met. If you are hiring, for example, list the criteria any viable candidate must have. You don't want to be the company who hired a VP only to find out he is afraid of flying!

Sort the list items into one of two categories: Must Haves and Comparatives.

✔ **Must Haves:** Think of the Must Haves category as the go/no go category. The option being considered (or the candidate in the case of a hiring decision) either meets the criteria or doesn't. If it meets the criteria, it moves on in the review process. If it doesn't meet the criteria, it's out.

Be sure to test the items on the Must Haves list to make sure list they are essential. For example, imagine that you're hiring a new sales manager, and you think a degree is essential. To test this criterion, ask, "If a candidate comes along who brings experience worth far more than a degree or who lacks a degree but has a proven track record, do we still reject that candidate because of his or her lack of degree?" If you say that you would still consider this candidate, even without the degree, then the criterion of having a degree is comparative, not essential.

✔ **Comparative:** The Comparative category holds the measures you'll apply to options that pass through the first screen (the Must Haves). You assign each criterion a rating (weight) based on how important you or your team think it is. I explain how to assign and use ratings in the next section.

Weighing your criteria

Comparative criteria are usually assigned a weighting from 1 to 10, with 1 indicating not important and 10 indicating very important. (Anything below 6 probably isn't important enough to be a criterion.) In this section, I give you two tools to help you apply criteria in your decision-making.

Scoring your options with a little math

When you're considering several comparative criteria, each with a different relative importance, follow these steps to see how the different options stack up:

1. **Create a table in which you list each comparative criterion and assign each a numeric value out of a total possible 10 points.**

   Importance, or relative value, is determined relative to the other criterion.

2. **For each option being considered, assign a score assessing how well the option meets that criteria.**

   Measure each option against the criteria, scoring each by using the relative weighting you've assigned. If the comparative criteria has a high possible score of 8, for example, and the option under consideration fully meets the criteria, give it an 8. If it doesn't meet the criteria, give it a lower score.

3. **After you score each of the options, multiply the option's score by the criterion's relative value and — voila! — you have a final tally.**

   For example, if the relative value of a criterion is 8, and the option was scored a 6, the final tally is 48. Table 9-1 illustrates how to use criterias' relative values to evaluate the options. Place the option at the top of the table and evaluate each alternative, using the scoring sheet. When you are done, you'll have a score that tells you how well the option did against the criteria you set.

Table 9-1	Scoring Option A — an Example		
Criteria	*Relative Value*	*Option #1 Score*	*Final Tally for Option #1*
User-friendly for the customer	10	8	80
Easy to repeat	8	5	40
Fits into an airplane storage space	8	6	48

4. **Add up the scores for each option to get a total for each alternative.**

   Taking this extra step lets you compare, at a glance, the total scores to see which of all your options has the highest score.

Using such a scoring sheet enables everyone to see the collective thinking. You can either have team members fill out the scores together (assuming you're all on-site), or have them fill it out online. The scores are then compiled to show how the decision-making team ranked the options.

Applying thinking tools: The Pugh Matrix

The Pugh Matrix, designed by Professor Stuart Pugh, answers the question, "Which option will most improve what is in place now?" by including a baseline in the calculations used to weigh comparative criteria. The use of the baseline indicates whether the option will positively improve or negatively subtract from what is currently in place.

To use the Pugh Matrix, follow these steps:

1. **Make a list of five or fewer of your most important criteria or conditions.**

   More than five and the list gets cumbersome. Ten is way too many.

2. **As you consider each criterion and each option, ask, "Will the result be better or worse than the current system?"**

   If the option is better than the current system, assign it a +1. If it is worse, assign it a –1. Table 9-2 shows an example of the Pugh Matrix in action.

3. **Tally the pluses and minuses to see which is the best option.**

   In this example, Option 3 dominates with three pluses and one minus, making it the logical choice.

Table 9-2	Assessing Options, Using the Pugh Matrix			
Criteria	**Baseline (What We Have Now)**	**Option 1**	**Option 2**	**Option 3**
1	0	+1	–1	+1
2	0	+1	+1	–1
3	0	–1	–1	+1
4	0	–1	–1	+1

Avoiding analysis paralysis

An organization that delays making a decision for too long is most likely stuck in the analysis stage. If you were to ask why a decision hadn't been made, you'd hear reasons like, "There isn't enough information,"; "Conditions are changing too quickly,"; or "We have too many options to choose from." The result? No decision is made or no option chosen.

Companies and people find themselves in this predicament for a few reasons:

- ✔ They overthink and overanalyze the information, the options, or the implications of the decision.
- ✔ They operate from an underlying fear of making a mistake.
- ✔ They are totally overwhelmed by uncertainty or internal chaos from too much change.
- ✔ They see either no clear option or far too many options to choose from.

Not making a decision that needs to be made increases the pressure that employees feel, which in turn leads to consequences such as stress-related illness, frustration, low morale, and poor performance. Not good. In this situation, employees have lost trust in the company's intuitive intelligence.

How do you shift out of analysis paralysis? What can you do to restore employee morale? Start by recognizing that conditions are changing constantly. To regain control and pave a path that enables you to make concrete decisions and action plans, follow these suggestions:

- ✔ **Identify decisions that are easy and ready to go, and take action.** A bit of success will build momentum, and these low-stakes, low-risk decisions are not hard to implement. So take action on them.
- ✔ **Make one decision at a time.** Limiting yourself to one decision at a time allows for the smoke of confusion and frustration to clear. Solve one problem and then move on to the next.
- ✔ **Get a fresh new perspective on the decisions under consideration.** Ask someone from outside the unit what he or she would do. Or change your environment to see the decision from a different context.

Research shows that more information doesn't necessarily mean better decisions. Hesitating to make the decision because you don't have the absolute best information is a trap. It means that you need to be perfect or right. Avoid it.

- ✔ **Trust in yourself and your colleagues.** Working from a base of trust is much easier than working from a base of fear. Sure, it may require a leap of faith, but let go of hesitation and move forward. Although a bit unsettling initially, if you take gradual steps, you can help build momentum and restore confidence, and soon things will get rolling again.

Analysis isn't bad or good. It is just one way of thinking. There are other ways of thinking, each offering a different benefit. Analysis reduces. In analytical thinking, you take the picture apart. Yet in a business environment where complexity and diversity dominate, big picture thinking is necessary. For that reason, analytical thinking may not be the best option. Flexibility is necessary.

Generating Options

In decision-making, the term *options* refers to the different alternatives or solutions under consideration. Whether you are buying a computer, upgrading office space, or hiring an accountant, for example, you must decide which alternative offers the best solution. Some decisions, like purchasing equipment, must result in the selection of only one out of several alternatives. Other decisions may benefit from working with more than one option simultaneously.

In this section, I explain how to come up with options, how to work with the risk of uncertainty, and what to do when you have too few or too many options to choose from.

Avoiding the one-option only trap

When you're making a decision, having only one option to consider isn't really an option. When you focus on only one idea to address your dilemma, you face two risks: that your (or your team's) tunnel vision has bypassed potentially better solutions and that any decision you make will keep you safely, and potentially stagnantly, in the status quo.

There are two reasons for thinking you have only one choice:

- ✔ **Narrow thinking:** In this case, you consider only what has been done before, regardless of whether it's worked. You disregard creative or unproven ideas.
- ✔ **Fearful thinking:** In this case, the decision is being triggered by fear, or the decision-making environment is characterized by fear or being afraid to take a risk.

 The rationale underlying narrow or fearful thinking when making a decision is that, if nothing changes, then nothing will change. It's a way to stay on familiar ground and stick to the status quo. And it brings on employee disengagement, the inability to retain talent, stress, and, ultimately, poor decisions.

Broadening the option pool by tapping into others' creativity

The solution to overcoming narrow or fearful thinking is to reawaken and apply creativity. Seek ideas and additional options by involving employees, customers, suppliers, and other involved parties (and don't forget to give credit where credit is due!). Tapping into additional sources' creative ideas helps you avoid missing an optimal solution no one has yet thought of.

Think of options as opportunities. You can generate options by taking creative steps to reach out and look for ideas that would otherwise escape notice.

Brainstorming has long been used to come up with ideas, but in brainstorming, strong-willed people too often end up pressuring others to conform to one view — theirs! Because creative work is best done privately — most brilliant ideas come up in the shower or when you're gardening — I recommend that you take a different approach. Follow these steps:

1. **Ask team members to identify one or more solutions on their own.**

   Independently coming up with ideas enables creative ideas to come forward that might otherwise not be heard in a group setting.

2. **Collate potential solutions so that you have access to a wider range of possibilities.**

   Bringing the ideas together allows the team, whether working remotely or in the same location, to see which alternatives fit.

3. **Discuss the merits of top ideas.**

   Bring the top ideas forward to work with. Solicit team members' perspectives on which alternative appeals and why it has merit. Include any risks associated with the option, as well as its pros and cons.

   Always consider dissenting views because they hold valued insights. Collaborating may result in creating a new solution or, at minimum, identifying the most viable alternatives.

4. **After discussion, short-list the alternatives — have participants select their top three choices, for example — and then gain consensus from the team.**

   An easy and reliable way to short-list is to use dot voting, in which you give participants dots (you can buy these little dots from stationary stores) that they then use to identify the alternative(s) they find most appealing.

   Dot voting is a great way to rank ideas or to see where the preferences lie. You don't use it to make the final decision. In addition, there are some rules, like how many dots you hand out (this number is based on how many people you're working with and how many choices are under consideration) and whether you can let participants load up their dots on one idea (it's generally a no-no!). For detailed instructions on dot voting, head to Chapter 11 or go to http://www.dotvoting.org.

At this point, you should have a short list of viable options that you keep open as you move forward.

Vetting your top options

If you are using a criteria-based decision-making process, you can now match your options against the criteria you set earlier on. Refer to the earlier section "Establishing and weighing criteria" for details. Otherwise, you can either select one or several to move forward on simultaneously. Keep reading for the details.

And the winner is! Selecting one option

Looking for one option or solution works best when you need only one solution, such as when you buy a software package, select a new location for your office, and so on. In these cases, you need to select the single, best option that meets your needs.

A super-rational decision-making process works well in predictable environments where the information isn't moving at breakneck speed and you can take the time to deliberate. The process I outline in the earlier section "Establishing and weighting criteria" — especially in regards to using a scoring sheet or the Pugh Matrix to discover the best option in front of you — can help you do that.

Using scenario forecasting

In the case of project implementation or, at a higher level, determining strategic direction, new information pops up all the time. The situation is unpredictable and quite fluid. Selecting a single option to adhere to is like trying to put a foot down while the train is still moving. Instead, view your options as scenarios. Doing so helps in situations where there are multiple possibilities in fast-changing circumstances.

In uncertain decision-making environments or when you're forecasting into the future, keeping your options open is a better approach because fixing on one solution too early can create stress (you're forcing a solution that doesn't quite work) or result in a missed opportunity (you overlooked a solution that would work better). When the decision-making environment is complex and rapidly changing, you can't afford to be inflexible in your approach.

Scenario forecasting, an approach to risk management explained in Olav Maassen's and Chris Matts's book *Commitment* (Hathaway te Brake Publications), is a way to keep options open by exploring scenarios and changing how you allocate resources. In scenario forecasting, you prepare for a world with multiple possible futures by creating a concrete plan for dealing with an abstract but probable future event.

When you use scenarios to prepare for future events, you're truly thinking big and mitigating risk exposure. Fortune favors the prepared. Consider FedEx, for example, which relies on petroleum as its energy source. If the global forecast predicts a world shortage of petroleum, rising gas prices will increase FedEx's risk of relying solely on one fuel source. By working through this kind of scenario — imagining a world in which petroleum is in short supply or imagining options that address the problems caused by a shortage of petroleum — FedEx can identify various ways to mitigate its risk. It may look at strategies that reduce energy use, identify reliable sources of alternative energy such as biofuels, or investigate other options that alleviate reliance on petroleum.

Assessing Immediate and Future Risk

Working with risk is risky. Although your mind can assess risk logically, psychologically, you handle risk in a totally different way. In this section, I explain how to calculate risk in your mind, look at how human psychology works when facing risk, and, finally, show you how to avoid underestimating risk.

Identifying risks

Calculating risk rationally engages your mind in a way that identifies the risk and assigns a value to how serious that risk is. Follow these steps:

1. **Start by asking the question, "What can possibly go wrong?"**

   The answer identifies potential risks arising from different sources. These are unique to the situation. For instance, in bridge building, one way you'd use this lens is to uncover potential engineering flaws. In marketing, you'd use it to identify assumptions being made about the market.

2. **Ask yourself, "What is the probability of this event happening?"**

   Assign the probability a high, medium, or low rating. This step separates the big risks from the tiny ones and helps you identify the likelihood that you'll face the risk in reality.

   If you detect a risk that is lying on the periphery of what everyone is paying attention to, name it.

3. **Identify the seriousness of the event's impact on your business, using the high, medium, or low rating.**

   This step isolates the risks that may have a low probability of happening but very serious consequences if they do — a reactor failure in a nuclear power plant, for example. On the other hand, a number of risks may surface that have both high probability and high seriousness.

   By looking at probability and seriousness together, you identify risks that you need to address in the decision-making process, either by making a contingency plan or by addressing the risk early on in the process to prevent it entirely or mitigate its effects.

4. **Develop and incorporate ways to prevent, mitigate, or eliminate the risk into your decision-making process.**

   If you can't prevent it, plan to have a backup plan. For instance, in the case of electrical outage, most buildings have a backup generator. How far you take efforts to mitigate risk depends on the seriousness of the consequences.

Considering people's response to risk

When a risk is real, specific, concrete, or immediate, it is much easier to relate to. For instance, when you jaywalk across the street in a high traffic zone, the risk of being hit by a car is pretty real. Conversely, a risk that is possible but not tangible — such as the chance of needing trip interruption insurance — is treated differently. Why? Because of human psychology. Consider the following points:

✔ **People naturally tend to focus on the tangible and discount the theoretical.** In other words, you're more likely to pay attention to a specific risk you're facing in the moment than to anticipate a risk that may happen in the future. This tendency explains why attention goes to what actresses wear to the Oscars rather than rising sea levels, or why a contractor substitutes inferior, low-cost materials to meet budget rather than focus on probable future risk (the stability of the building and the possibility that the inferior product may fail).

✔ **Especially when making complex decisions, few people see *unintended consequences,* the unanticipated, wider effects that result from an action.** Think of a spider web. If you jiggle one strand, the whole system is affected. The decisions you make can have similar effects. If you limit your attention to only one strand — that is, you make a decision looking only at one part of the whole picture — you won't see how the strands are interconnected. Such tunnel vision causes decision-making errors.

When you see the big picture, you can more accurately identify the direct consequences of a decision and action plans, and you can predict the indirect effects. Doing so reduces the chance that you'll be blind-sided or make a decision that takes a nose dive. Use a mind-mapping process, which I explain in Chapter 11, to see how a decision may play out and to see who will be affected directly and indirectly.

✔ **People perceive the future as distant, unknown, and not concrete.** Traditionally, the majority of companies have operated on the assumption that climate change wasn't relevant to business sustainability over the longer term. The probability of climate change, given the way risk is assessed psychologically, has not traditionally been factored into decisions about how resources are used or the carbon footprint of business activity. Consequently, actions that could have reduced carbon outputs were not taken. Now, according to the Carbon Disclosure Project's survey, S&P 500 companies estimate that 45 percent of the risk will surface in the next one to five years, with some costs of production already being felt. The effect of the psychological tendency to see potential futures as a slide show is that action is delayed resulting in a higher cost later on.

In the traditional sequence of think-plan-do, risk isn't real until you reach the doing stage. As long as you are thinking or planning, things that go bump in the night — the consequences of your actions — aren't real. But when you take action, people react, and consequences show up. To assess risk, you must be able to conceive the reality of things going wrong. You can reduce the risk of making errors in risk planning by imagining the possible scenarios and describing in real terms what would happen as a result of the options you're considering. This exercise gives you a better sense of whether a particular path improves the situation, makes it worse, or has no effect. Looking at each option through this lens better prepares you for implementation.

A fresh mind sees things a tired mind can't. If you are confused, hold off your decision until you have regained clarity, which may take only minutes or a day or two. Sometimes the best way to gain clarity is to relax and not think about the decision or situation at all. Take a break and remove yourself from the environment: Take a walk in the woods, go to a show, go to the gym, spend time with family. I explain the value of a relaxed emotional state in the later section "Making the Decision."

In situations where uncertainty reigns, the human tendency is to decide now — even if it means being wrong — just to restore certainty. Those who are uncomfortable with the unfamiliar or who feel unsure may commit to an option far too soon. To understand how to assess risk in the context of uncertainty or unfamiliarity, head to Chapter 3, and to find out about your personal relationship with risk, go to Chapter 5. Both discussions can help you know when to wait, when to move forward slowly, and when to make a radical move.

Mapping the Consequences: Knowing Who Is Affected and How

Most decisions that backfire do so for two reasons:

✔ The people who must implement them aren't involved in the decision-making.

✔ The decision fails to take into account the emotional needs and values of the customer (or anyone else impacted by the implementation). These needs and values aren't limited solely to the impact that the decision has on people. The impact of the decision on the environment and on the community the business resides in is also an important consideration.

A popular tool for mapping out who or what the decision impacts is a mind map (the brainchild of Tony Buzan, expert on the brain, memory, creativity, and innovation). Mind maps, which you can read more about in Chapter 11, are incredibly useful because they help participants tap into both creative thinking and linear-logical thinking. Mind maps graphically represent the various aspects of a topic. In the case of decision-making, they can bring the pieces of the puzzle or process into one visible picture.

To create a mind map of internal relationships, start by mapping out which staff or internal business units are involved (ask questions like "Which departments are required for implementation?" and "Who needs to handle sensitive issues?"). Then add maps to include the implications on those directly or indirectly affected by the decision. Be sure to include social, emotional, and environmental impacts such as employment opportunities, a decrease in property values, the destruction of wildlife habitat, and so on. Such a map helps you see the relationships between different parts of the situation so that you can better prepare and build in ways to either reduce the risk of negative impact or devise a strategy for addressing it.

Making the Decision

An effective decision has these characteristics:

✔ **Reflects a positive attitude:** Negativity is like glue. It slows everything down, saps energy, and undermines momentum. If your attitude is negative during the decision-making process, or if the decision-making environment is highly stressful, you'll make a poor choice. Period. Chapter 21 describes how to find your inner calm so you're in peak shape for decision-making.

Negative attitudes and critical thinking are not the same thing. Critical thinking improves a decision. Head to the earlier section "Critically evaluating your data" for an explanation of the difference.

✔ **Aligns what you think and how you feel about the final choice:** Pushing forward because you feel obligated is draining. When your heart just isn't in it, even if you think the idea is a good one, nothing happens, or if it does, it takes a lot of effort and can feel quite depleting.

✔ **Balances your intuition with your rational, analytical work:** Ideally, you want your gut and your mind working together, each providing a check and balance to the other. One entrepreneur told me, for example, he'd been to a investor's meeting where the pitch sounded good and the numbers looked sound, but because he had a bad feeling about the deal, he didn't opt in. Chapter 7 describes how intuition works and how to use your intuition to inform your rational-analytical sense, and vice versa.

✔ **Includes time to contemplate and reflect:** Time can be your ally when you're deciding on a course of action. Often the best ideas occur when you're relaxed and doing something other than concentrating on the decision. In Chapter 21, I tell you how to achieve a peaceful emotional state that lets effective decisions come forth.

Bias, prejudice, and doubt influence decisions whether you realize it or not. Here are some suggestions to help you overcome the three:

✔ **Doubt:** Doubt simply signals that a hidden fear is getting in your way. Ask yourself, "What's the worry?" When you put the fear out in the open, you often find that the doubts and worry lose their power over you.

✔ **Bias and prejudice:** Prejudice and bias create a blind side, and you need help from others who can point out what you can't see. To minimize the chances that unseen bias and prejudice are influencing your choices, notice when you are leaning toward one solution or perspective over another. I talk about bias and prejudice in Chapter 4.

Communicating the Decision Effectively

Transparency of information creates trust, which is important in business environments and vital when change is being made. Decisions made behind closed doors are always suspect. Therefore, after the decision is made, you need to communicate it. *How* you communicate the decision is everything.

Basically, you want your message to summarize the decision you've made, why you've made it, and what it means for the audience you're addressing. When you communicate your decision, include the following:

- ✔ **The reason the decision was necessary:** Include a brief summary of the opportunity or issue the decision and action plan address. Explain the "why."

- ✔ **The final decision:** Pretty straightforward.

- ✔ **The implications:** What the decision means to both your internal network and your customers or clientele. Address how the solutions will help and speak directly to the changes that these groups would be likely to see as losses.

Few things are worse than hearing that tired old phrase "Out with the old, in with the new." People fear loss and change more than they value gain. Meeting emotional needs when you are both making and communicating a decision is frequently overlooked but of vital importance. People are less interested in the decision itself and more interested in what that decision means to them.

- ✔ **What will happen next and what you need them to do to support the decision:** Feedback and feed-forward information allows for adjusting to change.

To avoid a backlash, make sure you address the key concerns that were raised during the information-gathering process; refer to the earlier section "Paying attention to different perspectives."

Credibility comes from speaking from the heart, genuinely and honestly. Tell your team and all parties involved what you know and what you don't know. Don't feel you have to cover the nitty-gritty details. What they need to know is just what is expected and what the resulting decision means to them personally and professionally.

Implementing the Decision

Finally — it's time for action (as if you've been sitting around all this time)! Getting things done is where rational and logical thinking really delivers. So what do you do? You create an action plan. This section has the details.

Putting together your action plan

An action plan guides the implementation of the decision and helps monitor progress. The more complex the task, the more people involved and the more key activities and subactivities are needed. In an action plan, you list the tasks that need to get done, identify the parties responsible for each task, set timelines for completion, and indicate what successful completion of a task looks like.

To put together your action plan, follow these steps:

1. **Individually or collectively list all the steps that need to be accomplished to get the job done.**

   Involve the team and any other units that will be involved in the implementation of the decision. Doing so ensures that no task gets inadvertently left out.

   If you're doing this task in person, put one action step on a sticky note or 3-x-5-inch index card. Then you can rearrange them easily to get the timing and order worked out.

2. **Set priorities.**

   Some actions are immediate and some can wait. To establish which decisions or parts of an action plan are more critical, set priorities. For additional information on priorities, refer to the next section.

3. **Pull out higher-level action items and then rearrange the sub-activities so that each appears beneath the higher-level action it is associated with.**

   The higher-level actions are like parents to the rest; taking care of them resolves other issues down the line. (The term *parent-child* refers to actions that are related to one another. By taking action on the parent, you look after the child. Noticing such relationships allows you to leverage your efforts.)

   For instance, if you're starting a company, the higher-level action may be to get the company legally registered. Sub-activities could include deciding what legal registration fits, generating and submitting names for the company so that your company's name isn't already taken, and so on.

   This step lets you see how each sub-activity contributes toward your overall goal; it also helps you identify the tasks associated with each action step.

4. **For each task, indicate who is responsible for the task.**

5. **Set time frames for completion or, at minimum, checkpoints for review.**

   Avoid the label "Ongoing." "Ongoing" may lead people to assume that things are moving along on this action item when, in fact, it may be stalled or overlooked.

6. **Define what the task will accomplish so that the endpoint is clear.**

   Agree on what successful completion will fulfill. Everyone involved in implementation needs to be on the same page, holding the same picture of what the result must accomplish so that they can adapt during implementation as conditions change. As pointed out in Chapter 8, doing so enables flexibility as new opportunities or information surfaces.

Action plans change all the time as new information alters the course. Be prepared to adjust. Use this kind of framework to jump-start the launch. After that, communication with your team will keep track of what is happening.

For large, multiparty projects, sophisticated project management software is necessary. Here are some helpful links:

✔ For a list of top ten free (open source) project management software programs: `http://www.cyberciti.biz/tips/open-source-project-management-software.html`

✔ For programs for remote teams: `http://www.hongkiat.com/blog/project-management-software/`

✔ For general project management programs: `http://www.softwareadvice.com/project-management/`

In addition, social collaboration tools help facilitate information exchange. A range of solutions are available, and new software products pop up all the time. Companies like `http://www.Nooq.co.uk` facilitate rapid information exchange in small to medium-sized companies. IBM social platforms or Microsoft's products, like Sharepoint, offer large-scale content management solutions. Go to `http://mashable.com/2012/09/07/social-collaboration-tools/` for details.

Deciding what is important: Metrics

You've probably heard the business maxim, "What gets measured, gets managed." In short, metrics matter. Establishing the measures you'll use to track performance ensures you pay attention to what matters and to whom — the customer or internal operations? Pick the right metrics, and you get information that helps you make good decisions; pick the wrong metrics, and you may inadvertently create issues that you then have to deal with. In this section, I offer two examples of how your choice of metric can support or undermine your business goals.

Example 1: Customer service

Getting the metric right can take awhile, but knowing what you want to achieve is the place to start. Suppose, for example, that you work for a telecommunications company, and your company wants to improve customer retention. To achieve that goal, it targets the customer service function and decides to use length of call time as its metric, assuming that shortened call time will result in greater customer satisfaction and retention. Sounds reasonable, right? After all, no one likes being on a customer service line for what seems like an eternity.

Now put yourself in the customers' shoes. Imagine being on a call with your mobile provider where your problem *never got solved* but they had you off the line in less than five minutes. Do you, as the customer, consider the call a success? Not a chance. If customer service performance is measured by the length of call time rather than whether the customer's problem was successfully resolved, you have not actually improved customer satisfaction or retention, although you may have improved call time. The customer will be a long way from feeling delighted. In fact, you may have annoyed the customer so much that he looks for another provider.

Now suppose that the metric you use is whether the customer's problem was solved to his or her satisfaction. Chances are your company would have happier customers who are more likely to continue to use your service.

Example 2: Employee retention

Suppose that you want to reduce turnover rate because you know that replacing people is costly. The metrics you use to measure the actual costs of losing an employee direct the focus of your efforts to retain people:

- ✔ **Viewing the situation from a mathematical perspective:** When an employee resigns, you can calculate the costs in a relatively simple mathematical equation:

    cost of one lost employee = that employee's salary + replacement cost + training time

  With this calculation, you may discover, for example, that having to replace an employee costs you 2.5 times the lost employee's salary.

✔ **Taking a holistic view of the costs:** Note that the preceding equation misses the hidden costs. How much, for example, does it cost to replace the knowledge and experience that walked out the door? The lost clients? The customer loyalty to staff? The damage to your company's reputation? These factors can't be measured and yet are important for weighing how well things are working.

Setting priorities

To ensure that you do the tasks in the correct order and to allocate resources, which tend to be in chronically short supply in most businesses, you must set priorities. By setting priorities, you know what to pay attention to first and where to direction your attention so that you don't try to do everything at once.

In establishing priorities, think in terms of these three categories:

✔ **Essential (1):** These are action items that must be started immediately after the decision and action plan are finalized. Indicate essential action items by using the number 1.

✔ **Important (2):** These action items are not essential but still important to the overall success of the plan. Indicate these by using the number 2.

✔ **Nice (3):** Think of these action items as frosting on the cake. They're not essential but would be nice to implement. Assign them a 3.

Learning from the implementation process

As the implementation of the decision unfolds, you'll find yourself making adjustments to your plan due to practical and emerging realities as unintended consequences and changing conditions unfold.

Adapting to changing realities

As you implement your changes, monitor the consequences of the decision and adjust the implementation plan to reflect what is happening. Here are some suggestions:

✔ **Pay attention to whether too many negative results show up and you find your red flags working overtime.** So that you can adapt quickly to the emerging realities, try these tactics:

- **Agree with the team ahead of time that any team member can call a review meeting in the event that a concern or opportunity to improve the action plan arises.** During this meeting, the team can collectively decide how to respond to the changing conditions.

- **Have a contingency plan ready.** This is one way you can use the scenarios developed during your planning phase. You can also develop contingency plans out of your risk assessment. See the earlier section "Using scenario forecasting" for details.

✔ **Treat unexpected occurrences as a potential opportunity to creatively improve the work you're doing.** Some unexpected events might be negative consequences, but a creative approach can convert a potential problem into a creative opportunity.

Reflecting on what happened

Unless you and your company are devoted to learning, you'll fall into a pattern of recycling the same decisions over and over again. You can use self- and organizational awareness to avoid this fate. Companies that develop this awareness have a clear edge. One way to increase self- and organizational awareness is to take time for reflection. Following are two approaches:

✔ **For bigger decisions that went badly sideways, collectively reflect on each part of the decision-making process.** Ask probing questions, like

- What kind of thinking was applied (analytical, big picture, causal, and so on)?

- What assumptions were made?

- What questions weren't asked?

- What flags were ignored?

Applying a critical and constructive review allows the organization to learn from the decision-making process.

✔ **Schedule a time weekly or monthly to engage in reflection within the business unit.** As a group, ask questions like, "What do we need to stop (or start) doing?" and "What do we need to improve?" Then incorporate results back into your day-to-day work. This systematic method lets you stay on top of what's going on and gives you an opportunity to identify actions that are habitual but useless as conditions change.

When a decision turns out to be a failure or doesn't play out according to plan, reflection gives you the tools to recognize what went wrong, learn how to avoid repeating the errors, and improve your future decision-making endeavors. The process of using mistakes to strengthen decision-making is found in Chapter 6.

Decision-Making on Auto-Pilot: Intuition in Action

Most decisions happen instantly (the whole decision-making process may be over in milliseconds) and are made entirely without your conscious knowledge. When you don't have time to consciously work through the decision-making process, what do you do — take a wild guess? No, you use your intuition.

Intuition is the ability to know or identify a solution without conscious thought. And where does this ability come from? One source is from experience you gain by making decisions, something called *implicit knowledge,* which I describe in Chapter 7. With implicit knowledge, the most recognized form of intuition, the more experience you have making decisions in diverse, complex, unstructured situations, the faster and more accurate your decisions are. In this section, I provide more details into how intuition works in both stable and highly volatile situations.

Grasping intuitive decision-making

When you're under pressure, you may not have time to mentally generate different options, evaluate their practicality, and then choose one. You need to act quickly! Intuition equips you to make fast, accurate, and workable decisions in complex, dynamically changing, and unfamiliar conditions. Higher level strategic decisions rely heavily on intuitive intelligence, for instance. Here is how your supercomputer, your intuition, operates:

1. **Processes incoming information at high speeds.**

2. **Selects pertinent factual and situational information from a ton of data.**

3. **Scans for cues and patterns you've come across before.**

4. **Decides whether this situation is typical or unfamiliar.**

5. **Runs scenarios from your inventory of what has worked before to see how the solution will play out in the current situation and then adjusts the solution to fit the situation.**

6. **Picks one and — shazaam! — the decision is made.**

And it does all this in milliseconds!

Taking a closer look at intuition in different situations

As the preceding steps indicate, part of the intuitive decision-making process is an assessment of whether the situation is typical or atypical. If the situation is typical, your supercomputer retrieves options that have worked before, rapidly tests them, scans them for weaknesses, and modifies them if necessary before selecting one. This process, described by Gary Klein in several of his books, most notably *Streetlights and Shadows: Searching for the Keys to Adaptive Decision Making* (Bradford), is illustrated in Figure 9-1.

If the situation isn't typical, your supercomputer goes into overdrive. This is where experience matters. Your internal supercomputer looks for more information until it senses that enough has been gathered, and then it runs through some scenarios to see which one will work, makes any necessary adjustments, and — BAM! — decision made! Figure 9-2 shows this process.

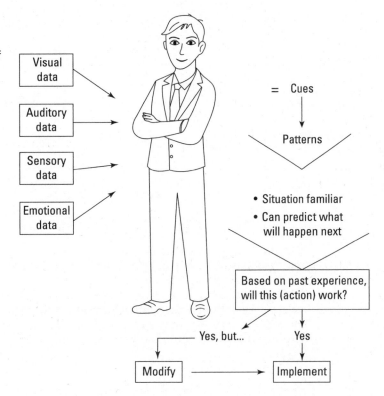

Figure 9-1:
Intuitive decision-making in stable, fairly predictable conditions.

Time elapsed: Milliseconds

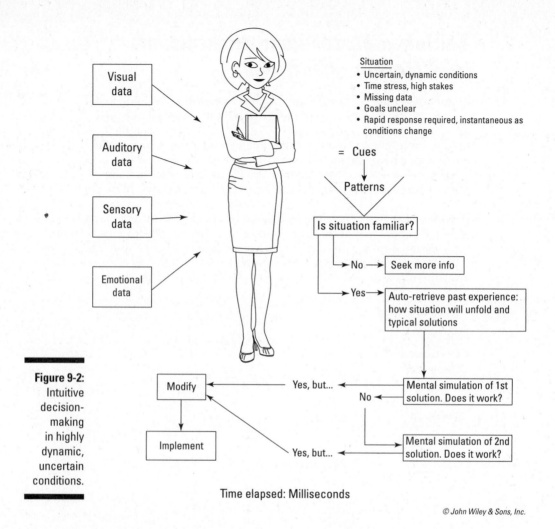

Figure 9-2:
Intuitive
decision-
making
in highly
dynamic,
uncertain
conditions.

Time elapsed: Milliseconds

© John Wiley & Sons, Inc.

Quite frankly, neuroscientists still aren't sure how the brain selects the right information from so many signals. One thing is for sure: Intuition is efficient, and it works, especially when there isn't any structure to lean on, when you aren't really sure what will happen next, when conditions are volatile or ambiguous, and when there is an immediate reaction to events. Chapter 7 takes a look under the hood to see the mechanics of intuition so that you can identify your natural intuitive strengths and improve your interpretation of the signals you receive.

Chapter 10

Tackling Various Types of Business Decisions

*U*nless you know how to think through a decision, you can easily find yourself talking about 12 things at once and wind up feeling scattered or confused. The key is to become familiar with the steps involved in decision-making. The more familiar you are with these steps, the more easily you'll be able to apply them to different kinds of decisions, making your approach more automatic. Knowing how to think things through helps you figure out what is happening now and what needs to happen next, whether you're in meetings, having casual conversations, or working on a project. These steps also help you change direction when necessary.

In this chapter, I take you through different kinds of decisions you're likely to face in your business, explain the thinking in each scenario, and highlight some key issues to keep in mind.

Visionary Decisions: Getting a Grip on Direction and Focus

Vision is a long-term view that articulates the company's contribution to the world. Consider it a visual and visceral description of what inspires the company's decisions and guides direction. It hooks your imagination.

For vision to inspire action, it must emotionally hook customers, employees, and supplier networks that contribute to company performance. Here are a couple of examples:

- ✔ **HootSuite:** HootSuite is a pioneer in social media management. According to CEO Ryan Holmes, HootSuite's goal is "to empower people and brands to reach global markets, using social media — to help them connect, inform, and succeed like never before."

- ✔ **Patagonia:** Patagonia is an outdoor apparel company. Its whole reason for being reflects the intrinsic values of the company's founders and employees: a minimalist lifestyle that goes with surfing, climbing, and other sports that leave motors behind. Patagonia's vision: "Build the best product, cause no unnecessary harm, use business to inspire, and implement solutions to the environmental crisis."

In business, having a shared vision lets you establish long-term goals that align with your reason to exist. At a high level, vision helps people understand the company's purpose; at a lower level, it helps them aim for the right project outcomes. People know where they fit, how they can contribute, and where the company ship is going. A well-articulated vision inspires the best from different business units, your professional networks, your suppliers, and your customers. Holding a clear vision for where you are going and what you seek to achieve generates outstanding performance. And, when the darker moments arrive, it can keep you focused and help you stay the course.

To apply your vision statement to decision-making, ask questions like, "How does this decision align with our vision (and values)?" You'll get a clear sense of whether the direction under consideration is taking you where you want to go.

Developing a vision statement engages employee creativity, so be fun, visual, and playful. A vision statement is flat when viewed as an intellectual exercise. Vision evokes an emotional connection to the company's values, as long as what the company does is consistent with its vision. When you use your vision statement as a barometer of how on-target your decisions are, you instill integrity into the decisions-making process.

Strategic Decisions: Moving from Here to There

Strategic decisions are typically made at a higher level, have higher risk, and focus on a company's longer term interests. Strategic decisions set direction and point toward the long-term vision.

A failure in vision: Eastman Kodak

Once *the* company to go to for film and film processing, Eastman Kodak, known globally simply as Kodak, failed to recognize that digital technology would change the face of photography. Consequently, the company missed the chance to adapt from selling film and film processing to digital photography, even though it knew change was on the horizon a good ten years before it happened. It filed for bankruptcy in 2012.

Although Eastman Kodak has since emerged as a smaller digital-imaging company, by failing to use foresight — either by not recognizing the profound impact the switch to digital photography would have or by refusing to adapt its business model as necessary — Kodak missed the opportunity to do things differently when the timing was best.

Here's an analogy. Think of a road trip. You first pick a destination (at a high level, this is the equivalent of your company's vision; at the project level, it's the equivalent of a goal), and then you decide which roads you'll take to get there. Strategic decisions make up the route to your destination. In short, the vision is your destination, and your strategy is the way there.

Strategy fails when the sense of the future is fuzzy, short term, or non-existent, and when a high level of attachment to the current strategy exists. In these instances, the results can be dire. Failures in strategy can doom a company, as the fortunes of Eastman Kodak demonstrate (head to the nearby sidebar "A failure in vision: Eastman Kodak" for the details).

Making high-level strategic decisions

You have your vision, you know what you offer to customers, and you know why you exist as a company. You also know what sets you apart from the competition. Next up? Strategy. Strategic-level decisions, which are often complex and high-stakes, describe what direction you'll take to fulfill your vision. Consider these examples:

✔ A marketing strategy outlines your customer's current and anticipated needs and how you'll deliver your promise to meet those needs through a satisfactory buying relationship. It outlines delivery channels and customer feedback mechanisms, and can engage the customer in helping you define or refine your product or service offerings. Your marketing strategy will be guided by longer term goals but must be able to adapt to social change. How you approach marketing will change as you move from starting a business to having an established brand. It will also change as market conditions change.

✔ An information technology strategy outlines how you'll use technology internally (to support productivity and internal communications) and externally (to deliver product or service to customers and stakeholders, and to facilitate communication and build brand recognition). Technology moves quickly, so internal systems are big investments. Your strategy will outline how you'll stay up to date so that you can provide employees with the support they need to optimally deliver customer satisfaction.

The challenge with making high-level strategic decisions is that you generally must do so when the relevant facts are still uncertain — a typical scenario in fast-moving situations. These kinds of decisions are also complex (you must explore many layers that cross all functions within and beyond your company's borders) and high risk (a mistake could result in failure, high cost, or serious loss.)

Making strategic-level decisions employs all your skills and intuitive instincts. It forces you to expand your knowledge base to understand all the company's functions and to develop your partnership skills so that you can to build trustworthy relationships. Although you'll be responsible for making the final decision, you can't work in isolation; otherwise, you risk overlooking key information or considerations. To read more about making strategic-level decisions, head to Chapter 13.

Strategic decisions provide direction at a higher level, regardless of how big your company is. Small companies can while thinking globally. To use strategy as a smaller company, practice seeing yourself as a global player so that you don't fall into the trap of hoping nothing will change or affect you. Bookstores that didn't pay attention to the changes that social media and digital publishing brought about no longer exist. Expanding your thinking to see ahead helps you prepare for change.

Applying strategic thinking to lower-level goals

You can also apply strategic thinking to achieve lower-level goals. If your assignment is to create a strategic plan to reduce employee retention, for example, you would follow these steps:

1. **Gain clarity about the present situation by asking, "Where are we now?"**

   To reduce employee retention, you would analyze things like employee turnover, how your company's turnover compares with the industry average, and why employees are leaving your company. You may describe your present situation as follows:

   > We're losing 14 percent in turnover of high-value employees annually at a hard-dollar cost of $200,000.

   Note: There are other costs that aren't measurable. I talk about these in Chapter 9 in the section on metrics.

2. **State your desired result (where you want to go) by asking, "What do we want to achieve?"**

   The answer to this question should describe the endpoint as specifically as possible, covering both the relevant facts ("We saved $__ by reducing loss due to employee turnover") and the relationship side ("We improved our workplace environment so that high-value employees know they are valued and choose to stay"). In the example you may state your desired result as follows:

   > Retain 95 percent of our talented employees annually.

3. **Identify the tasks or actions you must take to move from your present state (Step 1) to the future state you identified in Step 2, by asking, "What needs to be done to achieve the desired result?"**

   In the example, you would ask, "What needs to be done to achieve 95 percent retention of talented employees that are currently being lost to other firms?" This last question should give you a long list of actions, but only a few qualify as strategic.

4. **Organize your list into strategic and tactical (nonstrategic) action items.**

   The strategic action items capture the Big Idea and serve as an umbrella for the rest. Pull those out, and you should have a super-short list of top-notch actions that lead the way. All the other action steps fit underneath to become steps on the road ahead. For instance, you may decide to use social media as your marketing strategy. Tactically, you'd need to select which social media platforms to use, followed by launching a Facebook page and building your profile on Facebook. (Remember, tactical action items refer to the more specific, how-to-get-the-job-done actions.)

Strategic directions come from filling in the gap between the present situation and the end result. They describe why the direction was selected over other alternatives and how you'll move from your current state (identified in Step 1) to where you want to go (revealed in Step 2). The tasks or action plans you put in place help you successfully accomplish your goal.

Adjusting your strategy as necessary

Today's business environment is just moving too fast. Strategy must remain fresh, vibrant, and in tune with emerging reality. To keep pace with changing realities, you must keep your strategy in the foreground. Ask yourself these questions weekly:

- ✔ **"Why are we doing what we're doing?"** and **"What are we seeking to accomplish in terms of mission or vision?"** You'll check and validate your focus or direction.

- ✔ **"Who are our customers?"** and **"What do they value and care about?"** You'll identify and alter any assumptions being made about who the customer is, what your customers care about, and how they make their decisions. In a changing social environment, these questions helps verify that you aren't relying on an old strategy in new circumstances.

- ✔ **"What results are we getting?"** You know what you want, but how things are playing out may be quite different. Unless you recognize the effect of the strategy on employee or customer retention, for example, you may stick to an obsolete strategy.

Operational Decisions: Seeking Out Efficiencies

Operational decisions target how things get done both efficiently (speed and best use of resources) and effectively (how well did it work?). Operational decisions occur on a daily basis and can be implemented quickly. The direction you set guides *what* gets done. The values of the company, conveyed through leadership and the workplace culture, guide *how* work gets done.

Going to frontline employees for ideas

When seeking out efficiencies, no one knows better where to find improvements than the people immersed in the operation — frontline employees who face the customer daily and maintenance workers or equipment operators who know what is working and where barriers exist that they have to work around. These employees work at the intersection where what gets done collides with how it is accomplished. How you tap into their expertise depends on your company's structure and culture:

✔ **In companies dedicated to learning:** Improvements to efficiency flow through both informal and formal information feedback mechanisms put in place to keep the company responsive. In these companies, employees tasked with making operational decisions have the same power to make change as those at the top of the organization.

✔ **In medium-sized to large companies organized by hierarchy, where decision-making is centralized in positions of authority:** Those higher in the organization may forget to listen to frontline or operational decision-makers. As a result, a gap can develop between what upper management says it wants to see happen on an operational level and what is practical and fits operational and customer realities. If you're seeking ideas for improving efficiency and effectiveness, ask staff implementing the day-to-day processes and listen carefully to the answers. Suspend any preconceived ideas you have about how things should get done. Your frontline troops know, and, provided that you've instilled a sense of trust in the workplace, they'll tell you what you need to hear.

Toyota's efficiency expertise transforms New York food bank

In some cases, knowledge that is gained in one business can bring a valuable perspective to a totally different type of business. To see how looking beyond your company — or even your industry — for solutions can yield the answers you seek, consider the impact Toyota's expertise had on a New York City food bank.

The Community Kitchen & Food Bank of West Harlem is a charitable organization that provides upwards of 50,000 free meals a month. It faced three problems: long lines outside, a long wait (upwards of an hour-and-a-half for meals), and a dining room that, on average, used only about three-quarters of its capacity.

Toyota, a corporate sponsor of the charity, decided to offer its business efficiency expertise, rather than money, to help the Community

Kitchen overcome these challenges. Specifically, it wanted to apply the concept of *kaisen*, or continuous improvement, to the Kitchen's operation. In so doing, the Toyota team reduced the wait time for meals from 90 minutes to 18 minutes, thereby eliminating the long lines, and filled the dining room to 100 percent capacity. Toyota has since shared its efficiency expertise with other food pantries, helping them provide services more efficiently and quickly.

The initial reaction to Toyota's involvement in the operational processes of food pantries was skepticism. After all, what could a car manufacturer possibly know about feeding the poor? But the company's success illustrates that the best ideas can come from anywhere.

Company culture makes a difference in the search for greater efficiency. In companies where you get ahead by stepping on others, employees are less likely to respond enthusiastically to a request for great ideas because they've probably watched a superior seize their ideas and present them as if they were his. This kind of environment creates passive employees who wait to be told instead of taking initiative.

In a company where employees own their ideas and receive recognition for their contribution, however, creative adjustments are made all the time, enabling the company to keep pace with changing social and economic conditions. Respect is at the heart of good working relationships. See more on what makes working relationships and workplace culture a positive force in decision-making in Chapter 2, and head to Chapter 3 for details on how workplace structure affects how things get done.

Making operational decisions: Things to think about

You'll be making operational decisions if you work in retail; manufacturing; maintenance of roads, aircraft, or cars; or other areas where technical specifications or regulations provide a structured framework. Operational decisions are specific, concrete, and, more often than not, made in predictable circumstances with everyone being very clear about what role they perform. Making operational decisions typically relies on procedures (following technical specifications in the case of equipment maintenance, for instance). As you gain experience, you apply that know-how to quickly trouble-shoot, diagnose, and take action.

If it's your first day making operational decisions, your first task is to become very fluent with the regulations or technical parameters of the work, particularly the safety issues. Also ask questions when you're in doubt or unsure of what to pay attention to, particularly in terms of safety issues. (Remember, when you're navigating a different operational environment, there is no such thing as a dumb question!) Finally, try to team up with someone who's got a ton of experience and is willing to share his or her expertise. A mentor can guide you through the decision-making process from start to completion, and you'll gain a lot of insight a lot faster than you would working alone or reading a manual. You can read more about making decisions that impact the safety of others in Chapter 19.

Financial Decisions: Raising and Protecting Your Cash Cow

Whole books have been written on the myriad topics related to company finances. In this section, I point out a few things to consider so that you are prepared when the time comes to make strategic and operational financial decisions.

Securing financing

Financing is a top issue for all companies, but the good news is that the methods for finding funding expanded after banks became more risk averse, and innovative lending and funding approaches emerged to meet the needs that the banks weren't prepared to address.

Making financial decisions to secure funding is usually triggered by three events:

✔ **Starting up the company:** You need to decide how much money you need and what is the best source. In addition to conventional sources of funding, such as bank loans, family, and friends, you have access to other sources such as crowdfunding, microfinancing, and peer loans.

Finding sources for start-up funds is a big topic; you can get quick definitions of the key options at http://www.dummies.com/how-to/content/business-financing-terminology.html.

✔ **Operating the company:** You may need to seek funds to help you manage your cash in tough economic conditions or slow seasons, or to acquire new assets. Funds for acquiring assets can come from your current cash flow or from a loan or investor.

✔ **Growing and expanding into new markets:** You may seek financing to support your company's growth (size) as well as its expansion into new markets. Funds for this purpose come from internal cash flow or external investors such as private equity or venture capital firms.

Several books are available to help you understand funding options and secure funding. Check out *Small Business Finance All-in-One For Dummies,* by Faith Glasgow (Editor); *Small Business Financial Management Kit For Dummies,* by Tage C. Tracy and John A. Tracy; and *Venture Capital For Dummies,* by Nicole Gravagna and Peter Adams, all published by John Wiley & Sons, Inc.

Sustaining cash flow

One of the most valuable tools for making financial decisions is a cash flow statement. Why? Because making better decisions is just easier when you can see how much money is coming in, how much is going out, and how much you have left at the end of each month over a 12-month operational period.

Cash flow statements are used to manage growth and make big purchases. For that reason, knowing how your cash requirements match up against monthly revenues and business revenue cycles over the year enables you to better finance your company's growth and make decisions about acquiring new assets. Templates for preparing a cash flow statement are available online (`http://office.microsoft.com/en-ca/templates/12-month-cash-flow-statement-TC001017512.aspx`).

Avoiding the five most common financial errors

The fortunes of a company are based on two major factors. The first is the relevance of a company's purpose to what's important to customers, and this leads to the second: the company's profitability. If you clear those hurdles successfully, the next step is to ensure that the money is managed wisely. Here are the five ways financial decisions fall down and ways you can avoid these traps:

- **Overestimating projected revenues:** Err on the conservative side so that, if your customers aren't as enthusiastic as you think they'll be, you're prepared.

- **Underestimating or not addressing your immediate budgetary requirements:** There is a temptation to ask for less than you need, but doing so works against your success. If you need $50,000 to launch, ask for at least that much.

- **Thinking that, if you have revenue, you also have cash flow:** Revenue means cash is coming in. Cash flow tells you how much is staying behind to cover surprises and unexpected expenses. Rely on your cash flow to see how incoming and outgoing funds balance out.

✔ **Forgetting about taxes and other regulatory costs:** It's especially easy as a sole proprietor to forget to set aside money for the taxman. Set up a separate account for your tax money so you don't think you have access to cash that will be claimed by the government later.

✔ **Underestimating business development cycles:** Every business is different in terms of how long it takes from the time you promote your services and products to the time you gain new customers, much less keep them. Research the average development time characteristic of your business and then use a conservative estimate when calculating growth or revenue projections. Gaining experience in the marketplace helps. Over time, you'll get better at deciding what lies ahead while managing what is in the bank account.

Problem-Solving Decisions: Getting to the Root of Issues

When faced with a business problem — something is not going or performing the way you expect — you go into problem-solving mode, in which you try to uncover the cause of the problem and then remedy it. You can take one of two approaches when working with problems:

✔ You can seek out the root of the problem — the thing that is impeding the desired outcome — and fix it.

✔ You can treat the problem as a springboard for creatively (and intuitively) finding a way to work around the issue until it goes away.

Notice the key difference between these two approaches? The first looks back and employs more analysis; the second looks forward and engages creativity and intuition. Which strategy you use depends on the complexity of the problem.

Uncovering and addressing the root cause

In simple, uncomplicated circumstances involving an issue that must be resolved, you look for the root cause of the problem so that you can fix it and thereby solve the problem. Begin with the question, "What went wrong and how do we fix it?" This question starts a process of following the trail back to the point where something happened that caused one or more problems (a glitch on the assembly line that resulted in the unusual number of errors in the final product, for example). This strategy can be effective, provided that you keep these points in mind:

- ✔ **You use it to address the problem, not affix blame.** Sometimes, when you look back, you discover that someone — rather than something — is the root of the problem. In these cases, you need to use this as a learning opportunity. If a person made an error, did that person have sufficient training? Understanding why an event took place helps improve practices.

  Too, often, however, this strategy is used to place blame, a practice that is very distracting and works against productivity and developing trustworthy working relationships.

- ✔ **The problem is a simple one.** You can trace back to find the cause when you're dealing with a simple situation: a valve isn't working, for example, or the engine isn't running. But using a problem-solving analysis with complex problems almost guarantees that the problem will come back. In those situations, a more creative, intuitive approach is typically the better option, as I explain in the next section.

The effect of perspective

When you investigate a problem to find its root cause, you'll encounter different perspectives, making it pointless to insist that one view of the problem is the only "correct" view. Things are rarely as they seem, and everyone has a different perspective. Take a car recall. To the consumer, it is a safety issue and huge inconvenience. To the company, it is a quality-control issue. To the executive, it is a decision-making focus error. The project manager may view it as a personal failure, and the engineers may see it as a process issue.

Determining the root cause will take multiple approaches, depending on whose point of view is driving the inquiry. The Toyota recall example in Chapter 13 describes how the CEO of Toyota addressed the issue internally while simultaneously appealing to customers' interests. The important thing to know about problem-solving is that reaching agreement on what the problem is requires that you take into account the different perspectives, with each contributing to the company's overall learning and development.

Tackling problems creatively

Issues involving technology, organizational change, or other situations where interpersonal relationships or interconnectivity between parts of the system (technology software, for instance) are deep and multifaceted make finding the root cause either impossible or ineffective. In these situations, a creative approach is the better problem-solving strategy. You use a creative approach whenever you're dealing with human dynamics and complex situations because what appears on the surface is just the tip of the iceberg.

Look for patterns. Does the issue keep coming back no matter what you change? It may take different forms, but is it still the same issue? When issues recycle, it tells you that the root cause is hidden somewhere in the company's performance system or is the result of an outdated, underlying cultural belief. In other words, systems and procedures are rewarding behavior you don't want instead of behavior you do want. You'll find more on how workplace culture drives decisions in Chapter 3.

Systemic problems in complex systems, most often technological in nature, are great opportunities to use a creative problem-solving approach. Why? When software settings seem to have a mind of their own — your password randomly stops working, for example, or your email settings reset themselves for no explicable reason — finding out why isn't effective. It is worse than looking for a needle in a haystack, given the variables and random nature of complex systems like software. Instead of looking backward for the root cause, find creative solutions by looking ahead. Here are some suggestions:

- ✔ **Experiment to find what will work to solve the problem, using a forward focus.** Reset your password rather than trying to find out why it stopped working. This is why most technology products have tech support, not just to help you navigate the how-to manual but to also address the issues that the manual couldn't predict.

- ✔ **Invent creative solutions to adjust how work gets done so that the focus is on achieving goals rather than modifying behavior.** Interpersonal issues are often tackled by trying to fix the people. Instead, collaboratively develop a totally different approach to how work gets done so that the focus is on achieving goals rather than changing behavior.

- ✔ **Use creative processes and joint ventures to come up with innovations that mere mortals view as impossible.** Taking a "fix this problem" approach implies that something is always wrong. In complex situations like organizational interactions, using what isn't working to invent a better approach creates better results.

Making Partnership and Joint Venture Decisions

When you are limited by time, money, resources, or expertise, partnerships and joint ventures can be of tremendous value:

- ✔ In a *joint venture,* two companies agree to combine their resources to accomplish a specific task, and the venture exists for a specific time period. Joint ventures provide companies large and small with expanded capacity to reach new markets or to market products and services.

- ✔ *Partnerships* are formed when two or more people combine expertise to run an enterprise. In a partnership, an ongoing working relationship is established. Ben & Jerry's Ice Cream is a good example of a well-known U.S. partnership.

Trust, mutual fairness, and enough differentiation to create value are the ingredients that make either of these arrangements work.

Determining whether to pursue a joint venture or partnership

Success in a joint venture or partnership is based on what you want to get out of the relationship and then whether the values between the involved parties are compatible. To assess the value of entering into a partnership or a joint venture, ask these questions:

- ✔ **How can the other company help us?** What does it bring that we value? What strengths does it have that complement ours? The answer identifies the value, strength, or benefits you expect to gain.

- ✔ **How can we help the other company?** What do we bring that the other company values? From its perspective, what does the arrangement offer in terms of added value, strength, and benefits?

Each party answers these questions on its own; then the two parties meet to see how their answers match up. By combining the two lists, you can see how closely matched the perceptions are. Focus on whether your companies can support each other in your endeavors. Through reciprocity, you both gain.

After you work through the points to determine whether yours is a match made in heaven but before you ink in the agreement, give yourself a night's sleep. Doing so gives the team time to pull any uncertain points forward for discussion. If things look and feel as good as they did the day before, then you likely have a relationship that will work.

Without a good working relationship between the two companies, the partnership or venture simply won't fly. Trust and commitment are two central ingredients to making cooperative working relationships work. One way to determine how strong these qualities are in your partnership is to consider how your two companies will handle situations in which things go wrong. If the answer is to blame the other guy, your partnership or venture is in trouble. If, however, the two of you can have a conversation, lay the issues on the table, find a solution, and then move on, you're closer to a relationship that will work when things go sideways.

The bridge that went down

What makes partnerships and joint ventures work is willingness to take responsibility, be truthful, and collectively focus on finding solutions no matter what. To illustrate this point, consider the story of a bridge demolition contract, in which the contractor told his foreman to take down the next bridge. So the foreman demolished the next bridge in view. The problem? The demolished bridge wasn't on the list of bridges to be destroyed. The mistake? The contractor meant the next bridge *on the list of bridges to be demolished;* the foreman assumed the next bridge was the next bridge in view. It was a simple but costly communication error.

Rush hour traffic was due to cross that bridge later that afternoon. Yet rather than spend time assigning blame, everyone who needed to be involved in resolving the situation got together, made a plan, and delivered. By the time afternoon rush traffic began, traffic was successfully redirected. After the urgency had been addressed, a conversation began to determine what had gone wrong, how to avert a similar miscommunication in the future, and how to handle what came next, not the least of which was replacing the bridge that had been accidentally taken down. During this period, the team's focus was on moving forward, learning from what happened, and not on pointing fingers.

Chapter 11

Exploring the Decision-Making Tool Kit

In This Chapter

▶ Exploring ways to engage your team when the decision comes from the top

▶ Investigating negotiation and consensus-seeking as decision-making strategies

▶ Getting teams involved through participatory decision-making

*E*very company approaches decision-making in its own unique way. Many rely on the formula taught in business schools, *think-plan-do*. This approach is very logical and predictable — even comforting — unless it winds up looking more like do-think-redo, a real possibility for companies that are in a hurry 24/7. Other companies approach decision-making more randomly. They make one decision after another, hoping that, by throwing enough ideas against the wall, one will eventually stick.

Whichever approach you use, you must choose the tools that best fit the working environment and produce the desired results. Your effectiveness as a decision-maker is also dependent on how you use your authority to communicate with and engage your team.

In this chapter, I explain how your communication style can impact team engagement in the decisions, show you different approaches to decision-making, and provide a few tools to use for participatory decision-making.

Adopting an Approach That Gets Engagement and Results

Many companies are organized around layers of authority, both in terms of reporting structure (you report to a boss who reports to a boss who reports to . . . well you get the picture) and decision-making, in which decisions are made at upper levels and relayed down for execution. In this section, I identify the two main kinds of top-down structure and explain how people in authority can use it to engage, rather than alienate, their employees during the implementation process.

Note: In this chapter, I used the term *top-down decision-making* to refer to situations in which the boss makes the decisions, sets the direction, and then looks to staff to implement those decisions.

Differentiating between authority and power

Power and authority have come to mean the same thing, but in reality they are quite different. *Authority* speaks to the legally designated power that goes with holding a position. *Power* emerges comes from the integration of a full spectrum of intelligences and awareness. The difference is evident in how companies organize themselves:

- **Companies that organize work around *how* work gets done focus on managing the people:** Authority and power are viewed as synonymous. While company size can make a difference, what makes the bigger difference is your relationship with how you use authority as a replacement for true empowerment. Generally, the top levels of power and decision-making authority in hierarchical companies make the decisions and relay them down for implementation. Even in small companies (those with 2 to 150 employees), the boss often makes decisions with little or no input from his team.

- **Companies that organize around getting the work done hand the power to their employees:** Authority may still be designated with leads, but the power to get the work done is distributed using very explicit peer-accountability agreements. Rather than authority compelling engagement, peers and a sense of shared accountability foster engagement. Ways of organizing work that replace traditional top-down, authority-based decision-making are gaining attention.

If the strategy is to use authority to compel performance, something is in the way of engaging employees to naturally focus on getting the work done. Yet when the focus is on achieving the business goals and the company is organized around getting work done, then engagement is quite natural, assuming that the purpose is shared and inspiring.

Powering up a more engaged workforce

Whether a decision feels imposed or is received favorably depends on the health of the workplace, and *that* depends on how you, as a person of authority, use your personal power.

When power is used to work *with* employees, as peers working together, employees have the freedom to determine how to achieve the goal. In this environment, employees feel a strong sense of control because they know that they can take initiative without jeopardizing their careers. When the workplace is healthier and positive, chances are employees will perceive decisions as clear direction, knowing they can shape how the decision is implemented. During the implementation process, they have the freedom to contribute their creativity and ideas.

When power is used to gain control *over* employees, managers tend to micromanage employees and their work. This kind of environment represses employees' creative contribution and individual growth, ultimately creating passive employees. The cost of stress-related illness is an explicit indicator that a company is using authority to hold power over employees rather than choosing to engage them emotionally and intellectually in achieving business goals. In these conditions, you may notice the following:

- ✔ **The decision may be implemented right away, but workplace morale falls to extremely low levels.** Don't be too surprised if you see higher costs in stress-related illness, depression, and absenteeism.

- ✔ **Decisions get implemented . . . eventually.** The more cooperation needed between units, the longer implementing the decision takes. When power is used over others, an unhealthy competitive environment surfaces. In large companies, the term commonly used to refer to this phenomenon is *silos,* but similar dynamics can show up even in small to medium-sized companies.

- ✔ **Subtle but effective resistance occurs.** In this case, the decision either never gets implemented, or the implementation happens slowly. Resistance also arises when staff are given one choice, the one that comes from the top. In this scenario, staff feel like they have no control and are being treated like children, which can be pretty annoying. When employees believe that they have no control, they will get the job done but with a higher level of stress because their creativity is being stifled.

Employees bring the fuel for achievement. The workplace environment can boost or drain enthusiastic engagement. The failure to implement is the first sign that authority is being used without sufficient understanding of what makes the workplace work for people.

Engaging in Formal Decision-Making Methods

A few time-tested tools can help you arrive at many of the decisions your company must make on a day-to-day basis. In this section, I show you some of these methods for arriving at decisions. If you've been in business awhile, these will look familiar to you.

Using negotiation to make mutually acceptable decisions

In decision-making, you often face a situation in which you think one course of action is best but another party is at odds with your recommendation. In this situation, you two can negotiate to arrive at a decision that meets your needs and the other person's needs.

In decision-making, negotiation is good for handling simpler tasks, like deciding where to lease space or coming to agreement on salary level. Negotiation is also used in more complex discussions, such as determining a company's value so that the owners of both the company being sold and the company doing the acquiring feel that the price is fair. Although you would not use negotiation to start a joint venture (you'd get to know one another instead), you do engage in negotiation throughout the joint venture relationship to work out how you'll work together.

Following are the general steps you follow in a negotiation:

1. **Prepare to negotiate by gathering all necessary information, discussing with your team what you need to achieve as an outcome of the negotiation, and clarifying your goals.**

   This steps lets you know what you need to gain and what you can let go of. It also lets you recognize when the agreement meets what you've defined as success.

   Focusing on personal motives can negatively influence negotiation. So be sure that you're clear about what the company needs to achieve as success and to identify where your own career motivations overlap.

2. **Negotiate toward a win-win decision, in which all parties gain.**

   Try to avoid win-lose outcomes, in which one party wins and the other party loses. In this type of scenario, compromise has traditionally been the name of the game, but in reality, compromising means losing something important.

3. **Arrive at and implement an agreement on the decision and course of action or next steps.**

    After finalizing the agreement and creating a definitive course of action both parties are committed to, you're ready to go!

To be an effective negotiator, you need to be able to stand up for what you want and know when to yield to achieve your goal. Yet not everyone is a master of negotiation. Fortunately, it's a skill you can learn. Two excellent resources on how to negotiate are *Negotiating For Dummies,* 2nd Edition, by Michael Donaldson and David Frohnmayer (Wiley), and *Getting to Yes: Negotiating Agreement Without Giving In,* by Roger Fisher and William Ury (Penguin Books).

Seeking consensus

The word *consensus* comes from the Latin verb *consentire,* which means "to feel together." In consensus, diverse parties come together to lay out what they see as the issues and what their interests are, and then collectively explore solutions and agree on a solution.

Consensus requires a higher level of self-awareness and personal mastery because team members may disagree on important points or bring hardened positions to the discussion that they aren't willing to soften. By dealing with these kinds of conflicts in a way that helps the group see the merits in each point, you create an environment where everyone is better able to work collaboratively and achieve a better outcome. In this section, I explain what it takes to build consensus and what common consensus-building traps to avoid.

Looking at the pros and cons of the consensus model

In business decision-making, consensus lets you check how ready participants are to reach closure and agree on a final decision. It can also check the degree of solidarity. Furthermore, trust and open sharing of information make consensus effective because, after a decision is made, it has the support of those who participated. Table 11-1 lists the pros and cons of using the consensus model.

Veto has traditionally been part of the consensus process, but it has caused nothing but trouble. If the veto is allowed in the final decision-making, it provides an opening for special interest groups — or one individual — to revert to the status quo. Rather than use veto, use a tool like the Gradients of Agreement tool so that the ability to kill a decision doesn't lie in the hands of one individual.

Table 11-1	Pros and Cons of Consensus Decision-Making	
Pros	**Cons**
Team members are involved and feel valued as long as their inputs are respected and incorporated into the final outcome.	Building the trust and commitment necessary to move forward can take time.
It builds commitment, empathy for differing views, understanding of the implications, and support for a decision.	When voting is used to make the final decision in a consensus process, the majority rules, which negates the whole point of working toward consensus, especially in low-trust environments.
It provides a forum that enables participants to contribute viewpoints and gain understanding.	Conflicting views can be used to discredit the process.
Although it takes time in the front end, it delivers commitment to implementation on the back end.	Those with hidden agendas can try to manipulate the result to serve their interests at the expense of others.
It builds relationships, engages the good will of all involved, and can build trust.	

Avoiding the "perfect harmony" trap

A common assumption with the consensus model is that everyone must be in near-perfect agreement. This mindset creates obstacles to gaining consensus because differences are perceived as undesirable. If you have disagreements, the thinking goes, you haven't reached consensus, but that isn't actually the case. Conflicts are actually beneficial in consensus decision-making. Here's why:

✔ **Conflict helps you avoid tunnel vision.** Working with the consensus model is a great way to air out disparate views, ensure that enough information is available to make the decision, and ensure that the implications are seen through different values and worldviews (especially important in cross-cultural situations).

✔ **Conflicts can strengthen relationships and foster understanding.** Conflict isn't about one party fighting with another. It is about different views or values colliding. The collision opens the door to curiosity and understanding. Asking questions that explore underlying values and beliefs results in better decisions and solutions. Relationships are strengthened. The more understanding and acceptance (not necessarily agreement) there is of everyone's perspective, the better.

Empathy as the vehicle to higher consciousness

More than all the other processes available in your tool kit, consensus and participatory decision-making build empathy. *Empathy* is the deepest expression of the profound connection between one person and another. An empathetic person experiences others' emotions and experiences as if they were his or her own. Empathy is an important quality for emerging leaders because without it, high performance and agile workplaces can't be developed, nor can the relationship between humanity and all that sustains life on this planet thrive. Building empathy in company cultures is the key to staying relevant to society.

In his book *The Empathic Civilization: The Race to Global Consciousness in a World in Crisis,* social thinker Jeremy Rifkin suggests that the way to avert the further ecological breakdown of our planet and its economic collapse is to develop global empathy and, with that, human awareness. Global empathy transcends fear created out of self-interest or cultural differences so that the human experience and decisions are reconnected to the bond that connects humans to all life. By embracing empathy to expand what is taken into account in business decision-making, business can become an invaluable force for positive change.

With strengthened empathy, we can engage our collective ability to care for the air, water, and food sources, and we will have the capacity to collaborate to overcome the challenges — such as the effects of climate change — that affect us all. In short, we can make decisions that forge the future of civilization.

When consensus-building entered the decision-making scene in the 1960s and 1970s, it arrived at a time when handing out mandates seemed more efficient than working with people. The perceived cost of getting everyone in agreement was speed and effort. Yet what businesses have since learned is that, although driving a decision through without agreement may look more efficient, it isn't more effective. Many companies are now grappling with the reality that decision-making is less effective without the engagement of the people it affects.

Using Participatory Decision-Making Tools

Participatory decision-making engages a team to make decisions that are owned by all participants. By owning the decision, participants accept responsibility and accountability for the resulting outcome. The size of the team, the kind of decision, and the amount of time allotted for participants to contribute to the discussion determine which tool is most appropriate.

When you actively engage staff or teams in decision-making, you can use a variety of tools to augment and streamline the decision-making process. These tools include the Gradients of Agreement tool, dot voting, and mind mapping, all of which I explain in this section.

An excellent resource for participatory decision-making is *Facilitator's Guide to Participatory Decision-Making,* by Sam Kaner (Jossey-Bass).

The Gradients of Agreement tool

The Gradients of Agreement tool is a visual way to check where a large team or small company stands with respect to the decision under consideration. It can also be used for finalizing a decision when the group feels it has enough information and is ready to decide.

You use Gradients of Agreement in the following situations:

- ✔ When testing the commitment to a decision can help unify communication and implementation
- ✔ When participants need to know how much support a decision has, as well as what is guiding the decision
- ✔ When you're working with a larger group of people (more than six, for example) and you want their participation
- ✔ When you need to determine where strong, differing opinions exist so that you can explore them more deeply

With this tool, participants stand beneath the placard that best characterizes their feelings about the decision at hand. It may seem odd to be standing up rather than doing everything at a boardroom table, but getting people moving helps foster energy and engagement. Keep reading for instructions and guidance on using this tool effectively.

Where differences in viewpoint emerge, these differences serve to spark further discussion. When participants are undecided, more often than not, the information is either insufficient or the implications need to be further explored. This tool gives you a way to ensure that needed conversation takes place so that gaps in information or understanding are filled in and people can hear perspectives in an informal, preferably fun way.

Using the Gradients of Agreement approach

To use the Gradients of Agreement tool when everyone is in the room (and not spread around the world), follow these steps:

1. **Write the following headings on 8.5-x-11-inch sheets of paper: "Strongly support," "Support," "Undecided," "Mixed Feelings," and "Can't Live With It."**

   The labels mean the following:

Label	Translation
Strongly support	I really like it.
Support	I can live with it.
Undecided	I need more information.
Mixed feelings	I don't like it in its present state but I do not want to hold things up.
Cannot live with it	I do not want to be associated with the decision or involved in implementing it.

2. **Pin these headings across a long wall in the meeting room.**

   To make sure everyone in the room can see the categories, place the headings above head height. Also space them so that you have enough room under each for people to congregate.

   Basically, you're setting up a human wall chart (assuming you have 15 or more people). The set up must allow participants to stand beneath the headings that fit their views and to see where others stand.

3. **In the presence of the group, confirm that the group is at the point where all participants want to see where group members stand with respect to the decision.**

4. **Assign one or two people to the role of observer.**

   Observers share what they see after participants have taken a stand (Steps 7 and 8). In doing so, they help the group see how strongly the group is in agreement.

5. **Introduce the decision.**

   For example, if the decision is to change workplace practice to openly communicate issues as they arise, ask "How do you feel about the idea to openly communicate issues as they arise?"

   You can test the understanding of people who are new to the Gradients of Agreement system by asking a fun question such as, "Driving and texting don't mix. Where do you stand?" Then ask them to stand in front of the label that best represents their feelings. Practicing lets you ensure that group members know what to do.

6. **Ask participants to select the label that best matches their feelings about the decision and line up underneath it.**

   Having the group line up underneath the wall-mounted headers enables everyone to see how each person feels about the decision at hand.

7. **Ask people standing under each label to discuss among themselves why they chose that label; after about five to ten minutes (depending on the size of the cluster under the label), ask them to share what they learned from each other with the whole group.**

   Sharing this information allows everyone to hear others' thoughts and assumptions.

8. **Tell people that they can move to stand under another label if they've changed their minds, based on the discussion in Step 7.**

   Don't be surprised if people move to a different column.

9. **Ask the observers (see Step 4) to share what they observe.**

   Comments may raise reasons why the decision makes sense, why feelings are mixed, what is needed to clarify confusion, or what information is missing. This gives the group, who can't see the whole picture, a chance to hear from someone watching.

10. **Ask if anyone has questions, particularly if the groupings indicate a difference of opinion — you have groups distributed at opposite ends of the spectrum, for example.**

    You and they need to know where differences lie and what is needed to understand divergent views. This isn't a time to draw conclusions, just explore perspectives and perceptions.

11. **Ask the observers whether they feel the decision is clear or whether more work or conversation is needed; then ask whether they can comfortably support the decision.**

Interpreting the clusters

The way people cluster under the labels indicates the level of agreement. If the majority are under the Strongly support and Support labels, you have commitment. If most fall under the other labels, you don't. When you have a mix, something more is needed: more time, more information, or more conversation. Explore and document dissenting views, which offer insight, and then revisit the decision later.

An easy way to see the breakdown is to create a scale from most to least supportive of the decision. You would arrange your columns as shown in Table 11-2 and then under each label jot down how many people are in that group. Using a scale like this makes opinions visible to all.

Table 11-2	A Gradients of Agreement Scale in Action			
Strongly Support	*Support*	*Undecided*	*Mixed Feelings*	*Can't Live with It*
1	2	5	4	2

If you saw a scale like the one in Table 11-2, you would see that the group is pretty ambivalent about the decision. Only three participants support the decision; two are completely against it, and the majority are either undecided or have mixed feelings. Obviously, more info and discussion is necessary!

You want to find out why people feel and think the way they do about the decision. The questions you might ask include the following:

- ✔ **What information do the folks who feel undecided need?** You'll learn what information is either missing or misunderstood.

- ✔ **Why can't the decision under consideration be lived with?** You'll learn what risks aren't being taken into account and what needs to be considered for the decision to become acceptable.

- ✔ **Why are feelings mixed?** You'll learn what doubts or concerns are creating indecision or lack of confidence in the solutions under consideration.

- ✔ **What is appealing to those who support or strongly support the decision?** You'll learn how the decision meets some interests. Sharing perspectives will bring forward a clearer picture of what needs to happen before a decision deserves support.

Pushing through dissent to avoid conflict isn't a good idea. Chances are others share the same view but aren't willing to say so, and ignoring the concern may alienate more people than you realize. Instead, use dissenting views to gain greater understanding. Stay curious and, when you ask questions, try to avoid bias about what is a "good" or "bad" answer. By suspending judgment, you gain insight.

Dot voting to gauge opinion and progress

Dot voting helps you arrive at a decision, using the little sticky dots you buy in stationery stores. These dots come in different sizes, colors, and shapes, giving you plenty of options for how to use them.

Dot voting is a quick and easy way to discover the opinion of a group, either in person or online, letting you skip past the heavy duty debate and deliberations. It also helps engage everyone in the decision because, by its nature, it doesn't allow any one person or group to dominate, and it ensures that everyone participates.

Dot voting has numerous applications. In this section, I outline the basic rules and instructions for dot voting. For more information and an online voting platform, go to http://www.dotvoting.org. And if you're interested in seeing how dot voting can be used for governance and community participation, head to http://www.dotmocracy.org.

Getting your dots in a row: The rules

Dot voting is really pretty simple: Each participant gets a certain number of dots and can use them to indicate which of the presented options he or she prefers. By the time a dot voting session is complete, the entire group can easily see which options have the most or least support. And if the distribution of dots doesn't reveal a clear preference, the group knows that more discussion is needed.

Here are the basic rules (keep in mind that you can modify these as needed for your particular scenario):

✔ **How many dots do you give each person?** You have two choices:

- **Do the math.** Take the number of people you have, look at the number of options and number of ideas they have to pick from, then roughly divide the number of participants by the number of ideas and give each team member that many dots. If you have 20 participants and 5 ideas, each participant gets 4 dots. If you're setting priorities, lean toward 3 to 5 dots, regardless of group size. No more.

- **Go with your gut.** This method depends on what type of decision you're trying to arrive at and the number of possible options or answers. For instance, if you're seeking to identify top level priorities, 5 dots is tops. If you're looking to take a whole lot of ideas and pull out the key themes for discussion over a set period of time, you might allocate 5 to 8 dots. This is a place to apply your judgment. With experience, you'll learn what works best to pull out clear results. You can always ask your team for guidance.

✔ **What kinds of decisions lend themselves to dot voting?** Dot voting is great for the following:

- Making smaller, low stakes decisions like determining what topics to cover in the next 30 minutes

- Quickly gauging agreement and moving forward on a decision

- Making decisions when a formal decision-making process hasn't been worked out yet (as is often the case in start-up or small companies)

- Clustering ideas together into themes or categories

- Identifying priority areas

- Identifying divergent ideas that you don't want to miss or checking to see whether any issues have been left unaddressed

In general, there is resistance to using dot voting to make a final decision in low-trust environments where creative thinkers get overruled or ignored or where the resulting decision is used to force compliance. In high-trust workplace environments, where divergent views are respected and heard, using dot voting to decide typically isn't an issue.

When purchasing dots at your local office supply store, you can buy a different color for each category if you need to sort the ideas, as you would do when you're setting priority or distinguishing between current and future scenarios, for example. Also, if you don't have access to sticky dots, different colored felt pens work fine, too.

Connecting the dots, step by step

When all your dots are in a row, you're ready to do some dot voting. Follow these simple steps for your next dot voting session:

1. **List the ideas or actions you're working with.**

   Put the ideas on sticky notes; list them on 8.5-x-11-inch sheets of paper, one idea per page; or make a list on a flip chart, being sure to allow enough space between items for participants to place their dots. Whatever medium you choose, it must be large enough for the group to read and have enough space for the dots that will be positioned there.

2. **Distribute a specified number of dots to each person and ask participants to place the dots beside their preferred choice(s).**

   If you use colors to sort ideas out, then explain what each color represents.

3. **Apply the dots and then step back to discuss the results.**

   The focus for the discussion is guided by the purpose for using the dots. If you're identifying priorities, you'll pull out the ones that received clear support and then talk about ones that received underwhelming support. Find out why the idea was viewed as important, even if only by one person, and then work out how to handle it so the idea is respected rather than dismissed.

4. **Check each person for wayward dots before adjourning the meeting.**

   Sticky dots have a way of sticking to your face, hands, and random other places!

Voting as a blunt decision-making tool

Although voting can be used to indicate the pulse of the group, you don't want to use it to decide whether actual consensus has been achieved. Why? Simply put, when the majority rules, you don't consider divergent views, and the focus is on conforming to a majority conclusion. This is risky when divergent views offer a great deal of insight and potential opportunities. If you use voting in your decision-making sessions, keep these points in mind:

✔ **Limit its application.** In business, voting is most often used as a simple way to indicate whether team members are "in or out" — that is, in agreement or not.

✔ **Be careful that it isn't being used to replace needed discussion.** Simply taking a vote (or a series of votes) isn't enough to ensure that key issues are aired and resolved. Failing to engage in needed discussion will bite you later when you need commitment for implementation.

✔ **Ensure that everyone is working with the same base of information.** To do so, you must engage in discussion and an exchange of perspectives. Remember, more minds are better than one!

Visualizing consequences, relationships, and ideas: Mind mapping

Mind maps are spatial representations of related ideas. They draw on the brain's ability to make associations between multiple ideas to form a unified image — the big picture, so to speak, Therefore, when you need to see relationships — who is impacted by the decision under consideration, for example, or what steps you need to take to implement a decision — draw a mind map. Mind maps are great for visual learners, but they also draw on whole-brain thinking, which is handy in complicated situations.

Creating a mind map

In a mind map, the central idea appears in the middle and branches extend from it. Each branch represents a key idea, which itself may have branches extending from it, and these sub-branches may have branches, and so on, creating a web of connections between ideas. Figure 11-1 shows an example of a mind map showing basic company relationships.

To create a mind map of an idea, follow these steps:

1. **Gather together a large sheet of blank paper, colored pens, and, if you like, images.**

   Color can be used to highlight each branch or to separate categories from one another. You can either write the ideas down or use pictures (cut them from magazines or draw them yourself) that graphically capture the idea.

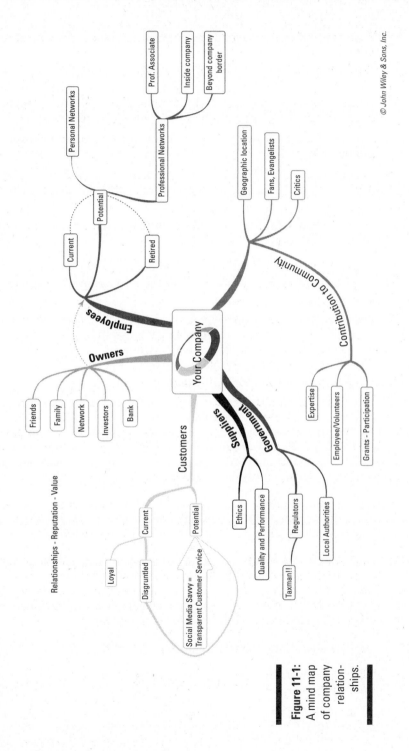

© John Wiley & Sons, Inc.

Figure 11-1:
A mind map of company relationships.

2. **In the middle of the page, draw an oval and place the central idea within the oval.**

   The central idea could be "New product launch," "Marketing plan," or whatever forms the central task, decision, or action needed to move the work forward. In Figure 11-1, the mind map seeks to highlight basic company relationships, and the central idea is "Your Company."

3. **For each main category related to the central idea, add a large branch and label it.**

   You can also use different colors to mark different categories. For Figure 11-1, the branches include "Owners," "Employees," "Customers," and so on.

4. **Add sub-branches as needed to the big branches to represent the ideas related to them.**

   Write the second- and third-level topics near the big branch they relate to.

5. **Continue adding sub-branches until the mind map shows all the ideas you have in your brain.**

   Concepts and ideas evolve. If you use a large sheet of drawing paper, leave lots of room around each main category so that you can add second- and third-level ideas as they arise.

Using the mind map in decision-making

The mind map is useful in decision-making because it lets you see how all the components interact. Such a view allows you to predict consequences and ensures that you've identified the implications of your decision on people who are either affected by the decision or who care about your company's actions. It's a way to bring individual pieces of the decision into one place where you can visually recognize the interrelationships.

Used well, a mind map can help you identify whose interests you haven't considered, predict consequences you may not have foreseen, and identify risks you may have missed by assuming nothing could go wrong.

The mind-mapping process is powerful. Although it may seem time consuming, it's worth the investment to visualize the larger set of factors or relationships touched by your decision or your company's activities. Besides, drawing these webs is way more fun than making long lists. Software is available to help you create mind maps. Here are two I recommend:

✔ **For purchase:** Tony Buzan's iMindmap, at `http://www.imindmap.com`

✔ **For free:** FreeMind, at `http://sourceforge.net/projects/freemind/`

Chapter 12

Strengthening Relationships with Employees and Customers

In This Chapter

▶ Strengthening workplace well-being to achieve customer loyalty

▶ Building goodwill and trust with customers and community

▶ Using social media to build genuine relationships

▶ Consulting with employees and customers

▶ Integrating open flow of information for better decisions

*M*eaning matters. The desire to pursue work that has meaning is powering a revolution in business thinking. No longer is profit considered the only purpose of a company; today innovative start-ups dare to do things differently by setting business up to create a positive change in the world while making money.

The focus has shifted from making money at any cost to making money so that you can give back, solve a societal or environmental problem, or take up a cause. The growth of this movement is bringing about some important changes: It has produced new kinds of companies that don't fit traditional funding models, and it emphasizes the value of stronger relationships with employees and customers. What lies in front of companies that accept or embrace this new kind of business environment is an exciting chance to do things differently, which begins by restoring trust in relationships with employees and customers.

In this chapter, I show you how building relationships with employees has a ripple effect on customer loyalty, share a tool you can use to better understand customer/client values, give you ideas for formally consulting with customers and employees, and explain ways you can put informal feedback mechanisms in place.

Improving Well-Being at Work

To many, the idea of improving well-being at work sounds like a soft business issue. After all, what does waking up in the morning and feeling excited about going to work have to do with increased customer loyalty? As it turns out, everything.

Don't believe it? Do a survey of one: Ask yourself: Does working with a great team of people and doing work you love make a difference in your personal and professional relationships? Do you feel inspired to meet a sales quota or to ensure that your customers leave happy and with what they wanted or needed? How you *feel* about your work impacts how you *do* your work.

Engagement statistics indicate that 70 percent of employees in the United States are emotionally disengaged from their work and that 75 percent who voluntarily leave their jobs quit their bosses, not their jobs. On the flip side, companies who engage their employees by finding ways to connect the work to their employees' values and desires to make meaningful contributions enjoy two-and-a-half times more net income than competitors who don't. If numbers appeal to your rational mind, then these numbers point to the value of a healthy workplace.

From happy employees to loyal customers: Creating a ripple effect

The most logical way to cut costs, improve revenues, and create happy customers is to rebuild trust with employees because, when employees feel enthusiastic, that enthusiasm spreads to customers. This strategy has worked for big companies like Southwest Airlines, as well as for small and medium-sized companies, who are changing the workplace environments to produce a ripple effect from inside out.

Here are the things to keep in mind as you seek to improve well-being at work:

✔ **Start at the top.** Establishing healthy working relationships starts with you. Accepting personal responsibility for your emotional health and your capacity to connect and build meaningful relationships with people, regardless of your role in the company, is at the heart of healthy personal or professional relationships. Although it's easy to get absorbed with your to-do list, switch your focus to acknowledge your team when you arrive at work. Greet each one personally and take a genuine interest in his or her well-being. Being present with the people you're with and observant of your emotional state builds connection, which builds community.

✔ **Address the personal and work-related issues that affect employee relationships.** Times occur when you need to be more than an employer paying a salary. Employees under stress from home or other pressures act out. Rather than punish the symptoms, direct your attention to finding out what is going on and then help the employee develop better emotional and social skills. Doing so benefits customer relations, employee retention, and the overall atmosphere in the workplace. Instead of giving attention to the latest drama, focus on supporting better responses to pressures.

✔ **Put in place systems that enable you to foster healthy relationships, both with employees and with your customers.** Some companies operate with unwritten rules, such as "Don't tell the boss anything he doesn't want to hear." Yet this works against effective performance. Instead, set up regular forums where employees can have open access to you. If teams are remote, find ways to let employees see your face and ask questions (try Google Hangouts on Air, for example). If you're on-site, go to where your employees are. Host annual vacations for the entire company, families included. Finding opportunities to celebrate the good news and talk through the more difficult issues keeps relationships healthy.

R.J. Allen Construction, an example

R.J. Allen Construction, Inc., a company with fewer than 100 employees, specializes in demolition and concrete cutting. Andy Allen, CEO of R.J. Allen Construction, has created a workplace that shows how a leader's decisions can begin the ripple effect that leads to a workplace that fosters respect and, ultimately, customer loyalty.

Beginning at the top

Andy faced several challenges simultaneously; his divorce, which was difficult, occurred during the same time that the company was in the process of moving from flying by the seat of its pants to putting systems in place. To navigate these challenges, Andy hired a psychologist to work with him and his staff on team building, self-knowledge, and communication skills. He also enrolled everyone in a management action program course and hired a personal coach. When the emotional pressure of his divorce left him barely able to cope, Andy knew his decisions would suffer, so he turned to his team and told them, "Look. I am barely functioning. I need you to look after things while I look after myself." And then he took himself to a therapist.

Andy's decision highlights the importance of accepting personal responsibility as the linchpin for developing well-being and customer loyalty: Faced with two options — deep-six his company so his ex-wife wouldn't get a thing or rise above the drama by digging deeply into his inner resources — Andy invested in himself and dug deep. The result? He has become a leader and role model for his staff. For R.J. Allen, that's how the ripple effect began.

Addressing issues that affect employees' personal and on-the-job relationships

A top-notch foreman on Andy's team had a habit of indulging in inappropriate behavior both at work and at home. He'd vent his anger, unchecked. Andy called him on his behavior and issued a warning: The next time the foreman lost his temper, Andy would terminate the foreman's employment. When the foreman told Andy that he wanted to learn how to handle his anger in a more constructive way, Andy offered the foreman help, as long as the foreman was committed to doing the personal work required. Since then, more employees have stepped forward for help with the deeper issues that affect their personal and on-the-job relationships. In addition, upon learning that a few employees struggled to pay their mortgages and recognizing that many had never been taught ways to manage money, Andy offered to help employees set up a savings plan and set aside $20 a month from each paycheck into this account. In addition to helping the employees, Andy's policies also helped the business: Employee turnover decreased.

Putting in place systems that promote good relationships and decisions

Before the introduction of systems, R.J. Allen took any job it could get. Turning nothing down, the company was in the game to survive and was far too busy to deal with the recurring issues that hijacked productivity to uncover why the same problems repeated. The company was too busy to find out which projects made money and which ones didn't. When the financial systems were in place, however, the company was able to identify profitable from unprofitable projects. It also discovered that the clients it was spending the most time on — the crankiest clients — were tied to the least profitable projects. This realization changed R.J. Allen's decision-making process. Rather than take any project, it carefully considered the working relationship as well as the value or opportunities the potential projects offered. The result? The company switched its focus to taking high-value projects whose clients valued trusting working relationships.

When the CEO leads from a deep and authentic place, the overall effect is profound and touches everyone. R.J. Allen, for example, has become flexible, adaptive to very different customers, and more efficient, investing a lot in interpersonal communications. The result of these changes? Most of R.J. Allen's clients are loyal, repeat customers, and many now consider it the go-to company for demolition work.

Recognizing the Consumer as a Change Agent

When I look across the landscape of business sectors — manufacturing, information technology, finance, or retail, for example — I notice that some companies are more progressive than others. That is, they are more adept at recognizing when the time has come to radically change what they're doing and switch to a different approach.

In Chapter 1, I talk about big-picture trends that influence the business landscape and put pressure on companies to adapt. What I want to focus on in this section is how the consumer is changing and how you can position your company to meet your customers' immediate needs and keep pace with their emerging desires. In short, the consumer is becoming a change agent for your company. So what can you do? Keep reading to find out.

Keeping an eye out for trends

Regularly keeping pace with bigger picture trends helps you see ahead and adjust now. Business is moving toward a *collaborative economy,* meaning customers and the community want to participate in your product development and will help you promote your product, based on its merits and value to their lives and to the environment. To keep appraised of broader trends, do the following:

- ✔ Refer to the annual compendium of trends put together by companies such as Deloitte (`http://dupress.com/periodical/trends/business-trends-2014/`) or PWC (`http://www.pwc.com/gx/en/ceo-survey/`) for their annual CEO surveys.

- ✔ For small and medium-sized companies, monitor what is going on with start-ups, social innovation initiatives, and thought leadership websites like `http://www.managementexchange.com` or `http://www.Management-Issues.com`.

- ✔ Attend conferences such as `http://www.Business4Better.com` or `www.ConsciousCapitalism.com` or conferences that present trends in your sector.

- ✔ Follow radio programs or podcasts presenting information on trends or ideas that don't fit into current mainstream thinking. For example, `http://todmaffin.com/category/cbctech` provides information on technology trends.

To find out more about the collaborative economy, see Rachel Botsman's TED talk, "The Currency of the New Economy Is Trust" at `https://www.ted.com/talks/rachel_botsman_the_currency_of_the_new_economy_is_trust`.

Chatting up consumers

A great way to stay apprised of what your customers need is to simply spend time informally chatting with them. Ask things like why do they use your services and why would they (or would they not) recommend your services or product to a friend. Getting input from customers gives you insight into ways you can build relationships that support your community and your customers. By acting on the information your customers give you, you make yourself too valued to your community of customers to fail.

Learning starts when you admit that you may not know everything there is to know. When you talk to your customers, ask your questions from a place of genuine curiosity; set aside any preconceived notions you may have about what you think you'll hear. By keeping your mind open, you give intuitive insights the opportunity to emerge.

Reconnecting Business to Customer Service

By 2017, the Millennial generation, born roughly between 1977 and 2000, will have the biggest buying power of any generation in history. That says a lot, given that their current buying power is $215 billion. These consumers buy differently than other generations: They rely heavily on social media and either question the rules or rewrite them. Boomers, born between 1946 and 1964, also hold big purchasing power. Both generations value authenticity and trustworthiness, and this set of shared values changes how companies need to relate to them to get and keep their business.

Here are some big changes in buyer behavior to keep in mind if you want your company to remain relevant to consumers:

- ✔ Consumers of all ages use the Internet and social media to research products and companies. Then they either buy online or head to a brick-and-mortar store for their purchases.

- ✔ More and more customers are giving their business to support companies whose values match their own. Apps are becoming increasingly available to support consumer decisions. The app Buycott (`http://www.buycott.com/`), for example, helps consumers align their spending decisions with their personal principles and values. (To see a list of eight such apps, check out `http://www.maclife.com/article/gallery/8_apps_fair_trade_and_ethical_shopping`.)

- ✔ Customers turn to social media to determine a company's motive: Does it just want to look good, or does it interact from a genuine sense of care?

In this section, I explain the gap that lies between what companies are doing now and what they need to do to keep and strengthen customer loyalty. I also show you a tool for understanding your customers and discuss how social media can both widen and close the gap between what your company offers and what clients and consumers are looking for.

Bridging the gap to connect to your customers

It's easy to say that your company is connected to its customers. After all, don't customers buy your products, and don't you have a customer service line? But the connection between your company and your consumers isn't limited to the challenge of communicating your message or to your customers feeling good about their purchases. You also must ensure that your customers know that you value them for more than their contribution to your bottom line. How you interact with your customers, respond to their concerns, and engage them in designing products and services sets you apart and creates shared value.

One survey suggests that only 23 percent of customers think that companies value their business and will go the extra mile for them. Worse, the two biggest buying generations — the Millennials and Boomers — believe that customers care more than companies do. Until trusting relationships with customers and employees are rejuvenated, consumers will trust the opinion of other consumers over company information.

For your company to separate itself from the pack, you have to be different and creative. Even the neighborhood meat market can't afford to be complacent as ecological consciousness rises and people alter their diets to reduce meat consumption. Here are some steps you can take to close the gap between your company and your customers:

✔ **Go to where your customers are.** If your customers are between 16 and 50 years old, pay attention to the social media such as Facebook, Pinterest, or Twitter. For information on how to use social media to learn about your customers, head to the later section "Using social media to obtain feedback."

Social media trends are important to monitor as the terrain changes. Facebook, for example, changes its algorithm without notice, so advantages that used to be there for business require adaptation. To track social media trends, some sites make it easy; check out `http://www.socialmediaexaminer.com/social-media-marketing-industry-report-2013/`, for example.

> ## Air France, lost luggage, and Twitter
>
> Twitter is one place where real-time service can resolve issues quickly. Take the customer who flew Air France over Christmas, arriving without her luggage. A month later, traditional customer service channels had produced nothing. After the traveler posted a "They don't care" message on Twitter, Air France caught the tweet and responded. Within 48 hours, the woman was reunited with her luggage. What mattered most to this customer? Empathy. Established customer service procedures couldn't do what a 140-character tweet could. Had Air France not been on Twitter, it would have missed the tweet and the opportunity to turn an unhappy customer into a satisfied one. (Companies using social media must also monitor the feeds so that an irresponsible post can be addressed before it turns into a viral rant.)

✔ **Eliminate machine-like attempts to deliver customer service.** Working your way through a never-ending phone tree doesn't have the same touch as a personal exchange. Engaging in direct communication is key. New technology-based mobile tools are emerging which, when used properly, can open up dialogue.

Check out echo**bravo** (`http://www.echo-bravo.com/`), a tablet-based app that generates a report card and collects improvement suggestions. Companies with repeating, ongoing customer interactions, like restaurants, hairdressers, and hospitals, can get immediate feedback and start a conversation with customers before those customers even walk out the door.

✔ **Take a closer look at what you're measuring.** The metrics you use to evaluate or reward performance indicate what matters and impact what your employees pay attention to. Head to Chapter 9 to discover how to ensure that the metrics you use support rather than undermine your customer service goals.

Getting inside the customer's head: Empathy mapping

When you want to understand your customers, an empathy map, like the one created by the design consultancy firm XPLANE (`http://www.xplane.com`) (see Figure 12-1), can be quite useful. An empathy map helps you draw a picture of your customers and understand their needs. Since its initial implementation, the empathy map has been adapted and adopted for marketing, customer relations, and other purposes.

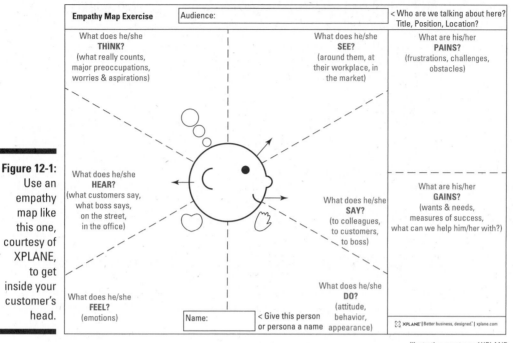

Figure 12-1:
Use an
empathy
map like
this one,
courtesy of
XPLANE,
to get
inside your
customer's
head.

Illustration courtesy of XPLANE

The best way to understand your target customer is to get inside his or her head, and an empathy map helps you see the world through the customer's viewpoint. Whether you're seeking to understand customers, users, or employees, you can use an empathy map to define what they think about and what forces are at work in their lives. Knowing this information, you can begin to understand how best to solve their problems.

To create an empathy map for your customers, follow these steps:

1. **Draw a graphical representation of your target customer on a piece of paper; give the customer a name.**

   Draw it to whatever degree of depth and insight you can — a circle large enough so you can put a description of who your customer is: Sara, 29, Digital Marketing Manager, for example. Or use a photograph to illustrate.

2. **Create categories for the information you need to see through their eyes.**

   For example, under the category "Seeing," you describe how your customer sees the world; in the category "Thinking," you describe what your customer thinks about the world. On a given day, what is this person experiencing? What is he thinking and seeing? What is he doing and feeling?

3. **Under each label, write in the customer's thoughts, feelings, and experiences.**

   You gather this information by doing the research to understand your customer's perspective on the world and then sensing what's important, based on this data.

Being able to see things from your customers' point of view *as if you were them* is key to creating empathy. The best way to get inside your customers' minds is to conduct interviews to learn firsthand what is important to them and to fill out each component of the empathy map. When interviewing customers is impossible, put yourself in their shoes. Keep in mind, however, that guessing how your customers feel and think is risky. You can also ask people on your team or frontline sales to help fill in the blanks. Offer clear guidelines to staff so they know how to deliver the information in a way that's useful.

Using social media to obtain feedback

Today, many potential customers rely heavily on user-generated content — in other words, other people's experiences — that they find posted on social media. They use Yelp, Trip Advisor, and Facebook, for example, to learn what other customers have to say about their experiences with your company or its service. Therefore, if your company isn't plugged into social media, you will find yourself in an awkward position: Your prospective customers will know more than you do about how your current customers feel about your company.

Companies relying solely on standard surveys with check boxes that let customers tick off a series of set responses limit information. The preset responses don't give customers the freedom to offer the kinds of details that can help you improve their experience. That's not to say your company shouldn't conduct surveys; just don't limit yourself to a survey as the only method for obtaining feedback. Broaden your feedback mechanisms to include social media interaction, which lets you do what a printed form can't.

To use social media for customer feedback, consider these points:

- **Make it easy for customers to find you online.** Go where your customers are: Pinterest, Facebook, LinkedIn (for professional services), Yelp, Trip Advisor (travel services), and so on.

- **Monitor comments constantly.** Your online reputation is fragile. When an issue resonates with people, it spreads like wildfire, for better or worse. Addressing issues earlier is better for everyone.

- **Develop a working relationship with top bloggers covering your sector.** Test ideas under consideration.

The upside of using social media is that you get honest feedback in the moment and a chance to fix errors or see what the customer buzz is. The downside is that, if you do not continuously improve or if you fail to respond to issues quickly, you'll miss — or worse sabotage — opportunities to attract customers.

Some companies hire people to give false feedback to help them look good. If you take such an unprincipled approach and post false or misleading social media information, you'll destroy your credibility. Make sure your company promotes honest feedback and is genuine in its communication and interaction with customers. Social media is a great way to engage directly with current and potential clients, even if you do so only through 140-character tweets — but if it's used unscrupulously, it'll backfire.

Focusing on what's important to the customer

What do you focus on as a decision-maker — delighting the customer or delighting the bean counter? It's easy for businesses to become preoccupied with internal issues and to put what is convenient or measureable at the center of decisions. It's also dangerous. When the focus of your decisions is to keep the accountant happy, you're not focusing on customer service, delivering a quality product, or ensuring that your decisions are compatible with customer values. Ironically, focusing solely on keeping costs down can actually reduce profitability.

You can do the following to ensure that your decisions don't protect the bottom line at the expense of customer needs:

- **Take time to step back before finalizing your decision.** You'll gain a wider perspective on what you're paying attention to, a perspective that helps you make better decisions — ones that don't cost you revenue by compromising customer rapport and satisfaction.

- **Consider what your employees and customers find rewarding.** Is it the satisfaction of making a quota for the month or the gratification of providing memorable service?

When you focus on the right priority — satisfying customer needs — you'll discover you are creating an experience, not just completing a transaction. These memorable and satisfying experiences are the things that encourage customers to come back again and again.

When watching costs is costly

The tale of the Ford Taurus is a classic case study of how focusing on keeping costs down can actually reduce profitability. The original project manager in charge of the Ford Taurus kept customer feedback in mind throughout the design process. The result was a car that was both a huge commercial success and over-budget. Ford replaced that project manager with one who made being under budget the priority. The resulting product came in within the budget, but it wasn't a commercial success. The second project manager's focus on budget limited the company's ability to realize the bigger goal: selling a quality product that met customers' needs. Ford forgot that, although keeping costs down is a reasonable goal, it shouldn't come at the expense of producing a product that customers want to buy.

Promoting Communication with Customers and Employees

Fundamental to building relationships and arriving at better decisions is knowing how employees and customers feel about the workplace or see your product. To create an environment that fosters the open sharing of information or differing perspectives, you must be honest about your motivation and clear about the value that this kind of sharing has for you, for your customers, and for employees. In this section, I show you how to gain clarity on your intention and give you ideas on how to set up information flow and feedback mechanisms. For more formal consultation methods, head to the later section "Tools and techniques for formal consultation."

Establishing intention and value

When you decide to consult with employees or customers, the simple question you are asking yourself is, "What do I want to achieve?" The answer depends on your purpose: Do you want to gather continuous or regular feedback; to share information openly throughout the organization; or to foster an active exchange of ideas and information? The following list helps you articulate your intention in each of these three scenarios:

✔ **You want to gather regular feedback from employees and customers.** You need to clarify how you will use the information.

How you use the information defines the health of the workplace environment. If you respond to feedback and act on it, you strengthen relationships. If you're only going through the motions to give the impression that you care, you break trust. If you gather feedback and then don't use it, you've wasted everyone's time and energy.

✔ **You want to share information openly.** If this is your intention, you must engage your team in removing barriers that can get in the way of being effective. These barriers can range from pointless procedures to interpersonal issues and egos. Placing higher value on collaboration rather than self-interest promotes openness and lets you gather ideas from your employees and/or customers to find out how they'd like to relate, communicate, and exchange ideas.

✔ **You want to actively engage employees and/or customers as a key part of decision-making.** In this scenario, make sure to clearly define your purpose. Also keep in mind that two-way communication is at the core of consultation. (If communication is one-way, you're dispensing information, not consulting.)

The business environment is shifting from companies having free license to do whatever they want regardless of the impact on communities to companies realizing that they gain relationship equity by working with communities. Although plenty of companies still feel they have the right, using economic contribution and job creation as their bargaining chips, to do whatever it takes to get what they want, this approach has left communities with high tax bills and an unwillingness to extend cart blanche to companies. The new generation of companies is setting a higher standard by placing greater value on relationships with employees, customers, suppliers, and the communities in which they live. Such companies are much better equipped to remain sustainable. You can adapt more readily, and, if trust is established and continues to be earned, you can concentrate on keeping it — a much easier task than rebuilding trust after it's been incinerated.

Be mindful that business consulting with communities and employees has a none too illustrious history, and this is especially the case when the consultation was motivated to meet regulatory requirements. If you're consulting with a community only because you must do so to meet regulatory requirements, you need to work harder and smarter to restore trust. Too many businesses have proclaimed that they want to authentically listen to a community's input, even though they've made up their minds and aren't interested in new facts or community views. The result is damaged trust, credibility, and reputation.

> ## UGG Australia: Supplier-client relations
>
> UGG Australia founder Brian Smith built strong relationships with the buyers for the large retail chains he supplied product to. These relationships were based on open, honest communication, ethical behavior, and a sense of loyalty — and they were put to the test when the going got tough. When Smith's manufacturer sold product produced for UGG to an upstart competitor, the buyers discovered what had happened, and they refused to buy from the new company. The relationships Smith had built with the retail chains were personal and dependable. Some things you just can't put a price on.

Calculating the benefits of communication

For many business owners, asking customers what matters to them and how they're doing is intimidating and out of their comfort zone. Yet businesses actively consulting with their employees and customers report these benefits:

- **Being able to monitor emerging trends:** Recognizing trends early lets you react quickly to negative patterns and use positive feedback to strengthen your company's standing in the market place.

- **Finding common ground for more workable solutions:** If you do notice negative feedback or disturbing trends, you and your team can create a solution that benefits both your customer base and your company.

- **Building trust and a broader understanding of issues:** Keeping your finger on the pulse of the marketplace, continually seeking feedback from customers, and monitoring current trends gives you a one-up on competitors who don't interact with customers or monitor trends.

- **Improving the likelihood that your solutions will succeed:** When you have access to current information, you can base your decisions on solid knowledge and data, thus giving them a much greater chance of success.

- **Making better decisions:** When you consult with fellow employees and customers, you gain the knowledge you need to make better decisions that will benefit your customers and help your company grow.

Not stepping out of your comfort zone can leave you blind to the kinds of big-picture changes — like the shifts in the values and drivers that underlie customers' decision-making — that have an indirect effect on your company's survival. For more on these big-picture trends, head to Chapter 1.

Setting goals for your interactions

So how can you realize benefits outlined in the preceding section at a more concrete level? By creating goals that will guide your interactions with employees and your customer base.

Considering a few common goals

To realize the benefits from consulting with employees and clients, you must first establish what you hope to realize through your interactions with employees and your customer base. Establishing goals helps you gain clarity on what you want out of the exchange. A few goals that immediately come to mind include the following:

- ✔ **To build relationships:** When you actively engage with employees and your customer base, you build trust and stronger relationships. Employees and customers realize your company cares.

- ✔ **To gain expertise or insight into what is important:** When you actively seek feedback from customers and employees, you know what they think is important and can consider these points when you make a decision or consider a change.

- ✔ **To identify concerns and issues that must be resolved:** Interaction with employees and customers lets you discover concerns and issues that you can then quickly resolve.

Outlining how the exchange serves all parties

When seeking interaction with employees and customers, you also need to know why the exchange is needed and whether it will benefit both parties. Will the exchange create a larger information pool than is currently available? Will it bring your company in contact with a community of like-minded people who share similar interests?

Create a list that describes what your company and the other parties gain through the relationship. When you understand how the exchange serves all parties, you'll know what everyone needs, and you'll learn where the synergies lie. If mutual gains don't exist for both parties, the exchange won't last or grow.

Clarifying what you and your team want to accomplish

To establish the overall goals for the consultation process, you must start with confirming your company's vision and values. This awareness lets you see the big picture and avoid knee-jerk reactions and the unintended consequences those actions may have.

With your vision and value in mind, you're ready to clarify what you and your team want to accomplish. Perhaps you want to share information with employees and clients, ask for perspective or opinions on a specific initiative, engage participants to help you address a specific issue, or obtain feedback on a product or service your company is launching or that is under review.

As you establish goals for the consultation process, be sure to identify who's in your client base and what their preferences or conditions are for participating. This information, in addition to your goals, will give you an idea about how to elicit the information you need — whether to use Internet surveys (high tech) or personal outreach and community participation. In the next section, I go through a variety of methods you can use for your employee or customer consultation.

Delving into Information-Gathering Methods

You can use both formal and informal methods to find out what is going on in the hearts and minds of your customers and stakeholders. Think about formal methods as those that are more impersonal and aimed at gathering data; informal methods are more personal and aimed at understanding the emotional and social values that impact what you're about to do or decide. In the collaborative economy, where the customer has more power and voice than ever before, relationship building is pivotal to sustaining relevancy and success.

Formal research is more controlled and systematic while informal research follows a more intuitive line of questioning that can reveal insights that data alone can't offer. By knowing what you hope to gain through your consultation with clients and employees, you can choose the consultation method that can more effectively help you achieve your desired results.

Regardless of the method you choose, make sure you respect the participants' time. One strategy research houses commonly use to attract public participants is to offer a reward for participation (although incentives are unethical when working with government or corporate clientele). A supplier I use recently asked me to fill out a feedback survey in exchange for a $50 Amazon gift certificate, for example. If you choose not to offer anything, keep the amount of time you ask participants to invest reasonable. I once agreed to participate in a phone survey that took over an hour! The unspoken message was clear: Your time is our time.

Tools and techniques for formal consultation

Formal consultation methods and practices include the more conventional approaches to ascertaining customer response to a new product, service, or design concept. Formal methods fall into two categories:

✔ **Qualitative methods:** These methods seek to discover the nuances of a problem or issue. Qualitative research gathers opinions, beliefs, and perspectives about the concept, product, or service.

✔ **Quantitative methods:** These methods quantify demographics, likes, dislikes, and answers to yes-no questions. Quantitative research gathers data through surveys, for example.

If your goal is to gather information, surveys or using a third party, such as a focus group, can serve you well. But if you want to build relationships, high touch personal consultation is more effective: Opt for the methods that involve interviews and conversations. The personal approaches reflect a sincere interest in meeting customers and/or employees where they are most comfortable. Keep in mind, however, that when you deal with interested parties on a personal level, you must know their preferred source of communication: online, in person, Internet news streams, mainstream news, and so on.

In this section, I identify a few common ways to gather information from employees and customers and explain the scenarios they are commonly used for.

Focus groups

A focus group is a kind of interactive research exercise run by a professional moderator in which a small group of people are asked questions and give their impressions and opinions about the product or service being evaluated. The questions are structured and consistently asked so the results can be compared across demographics. This method is used for policy development, market testing, public opinion research, and so on.

The professional research companies that specialize in this type of interactive session are skilled in asking questions, organizing the findings, and minimizing bias by keeping the name of the client (your company) confidential. Focus groups are good for gathering information, but not for exchanging it.

Surveys

Surveys include public opinion polls that track consumer trends, for instance, or questionnaires like the ones you can send to your database through services such as SurveyMonkey (http://www.surveymonkey.com). Public opinion polls are conducted by research houses with expertise in asking questions, collating and analyzing data, and then reporting on it. Surveys cover market research, product, and stakeholder or consumer surveys. With questionnaires, suitable for smaller companies, you craft your own questions and send them out to your database or post them online, for example.

You use surveys, either online or by telephone, to gauge the level of employee engagement or to assess public opinion on specific issues, products, and company brand recognition. You can also use surveys to determine whose interests need to be considered in large projects impacting a wide geographic area, like pipeline development. Surveys are impersonal, so they provide data more than insight.

Personal interviews or conversations

Personal one-on-one interviews, in which you interview a specified group, such as CEOs or team members, employ a set list of questions so that the approach is applied consistently across all interviews. One-on-one interviews serve to gather information that will support building relationships between team members or inform broader management decisions.

Interviews can be used before a project starts, to gather information; during a project, to monitor progress; or after completion, to gain individual feedback or plan a follow-up course of action. To conduct an interview, you decide what information you need and then craft a series of set questions to ask each person. A great guide to the art and science of asking questions is *Making Questions Work: A Guide to How and What to Ask for Facilitators, Consultants, Managers, Coaches, and Educators,* by Dorothy Strachan (Jossey-Bass).

In-person conversations can also be used to gain closer insight into what individuals think but don't reveal when they are in a group or team setting. You use personal interviews when diagnosing a situation or gathering perspectives on a given issue to gain insight on what isn't being said in a group context.

Facilitated consultations

In facilitated consultations, you ask an internal or external facilitator to guide you through a series of steps designed to gather a group's perspectives on a single issue or an opportunity. The facilitator works with you in advance to agree on what needs to be achieved, both in terms of accomplishing the task and doing so in a way that works for participants.

The advantage of facilitated consultations is that you can work with teams or multiple stakeholders to gather a lot of information in a short period of time. Combining personal interviews with group input illuminates organizational dynamics in companies. What people will say to you personally and what they'll say openly in a group discussion is often different. Facilitated consultations are good when you need to test the pulse of public interest in a proposal you're making.

Public meetings

In a public meeting, you invite the public to attend a meeting at a set place and time. These meetings are good for gaining information and offering feedback. The format you choose is important. Some public meetings engage a panel of speakers who participate in a question-and-answer period afterward. Another format is to set up stations around the room, with each station responsible for discussing a different topic. People go to each station and ask the host representative questions, or the host can ask participants questions.

For a successful public meeting, you must carefully balance the giving of information and the receiving of feedback; think this issue through ahead of time so people know what to expect.

Establishing informal information-gathering channels

Many companies design informal employee feedback channels and foster open, on-going communication as a way to keep everyone in the company aware of what's going on. Informal methods embrace more casual interactions, such as face-to-face conversations, or use technology to move feedback rapidly across the organization for real-time decision-making.

In this kind of feedback environment, leaders exist at every level and information openly travels in every direction. Even a company with a hierarchical structure can keep communication traveling openly; in this case, the top-down structure of the team isn't used to restrict flow of information. In addition, any size company can set up and sustain open lines of communication and the free flow of information. Here are some ideas on how you can exchange information with employees, clients, or the local community:

✔ **Participate in community associations, networks, or local initiatives.** Volunteering and sitting on local nonprofit boards are also effective ways to credibly build relationships and gain information you can feed forward into decisions.

The greatest insights come from relaxed casual conversations. Building your network of valued relationships gives you a constant source of information and insight invaluable for decision-making.

✔ **Provide opportunities for informal constructive feedback to keep in touch with employee happiness and satisfaction.** Use of apps like the Hppy app help companies track the mood of their employees. See `http://www.gethppy.com`.

✔ **Use mobile tools to transfer key decision-making information across the organization quickly.** Companies like SnapComms (`http://www.snapcomms.com`) have developed internal mobile communication tools.

Let employees know their feedback is important. You can respond to their feedback with a simple, "Thank you." When you personally recognize employee contributions, you'll gain more participation.

✔ **Rethink the suggestion box.** Most people are familiar with a suggestion box, but too many companies ignore the contents or use the box to give the appearance they care but never use the suggestions as a real feedback tool. Fortunately, one company — marketing agency Quirk — came up with a better approach. The CEO of Woohoo, Chief Happiness Officer Alex Kjerulf breaks the Quirk process down into easy-to-implement steps. Check it out at `http://positivesharing.com/2014/02/kill-suggestion-box-heres-much-better-way/`.

If you're going to use a traditional suggestion box, then keep it real. Put it out in the open — not under the counter — and be clear about what kinds of ideas you're looking for and willing to act on. If, for example, you want your company to go green, ask employees for ideas on how to improve energy efficiency.

Create a weekly question-and-answer period with high-level company decision-makers. Doing so puts everyone on the same page.

HootSuite, a social media management company, hosts Ask Me sessions, putting lead decision-makers in the metaphorical hot seat to answer questions that attending employees send via Twitter and other social media channels. Answers are shared with employees, and no questions are considered dumb or out of bounds.

The creative ways you can open information flow is only limited by your and your team's imagination. Whatever method you choose, make sure your recipe includes the following: having fun, being consistent, providing access through various channels, and ensuring two-way communication.

Method's mission, goal, approach, and benefits

Method is a cleaning company that makes products "that work for you and the environment." The company's mission: "In the same way we take the dirt out of cleaning, we strive to eliminate some of business's dirty practices." Its goal is to reduce the carbon footprint at the front end of the business rather than try to offset it at the back end.

To do this, Method's approach involves improving the environmental profile of supplier and manufacturing operations. Both Method and its suppliers benefit: Method makes progress toward its goal, enabling manufacturers and suppliers to cut cost and increase efficiency.

To stay on top of what is important to employees, Method has what it calls a "Laundry Room," where employees leave ideas, feedback, and whatever is on their minds on floor-to-ceiling whiteboards. This strategy provides a constant feedback loop, enabling decision-makers to check the pulse of the working environment.

Part IV
Making Decisions in Various Roles

Five Ways Decision-Making Changes with Changing Roles

- As responsibility and accountability increase, a decision-making style that directs and controls performance should change to a more collaborative approach. It's a difference between "Make it so" and "How can we make it so?"

- As your management style transforms from controlling others through power, fear, or intimidation to giving away control, you can work with and engage staff, employees, and customers.

- Moving into unfamiliar decision-making territory builds your inventory of what works and what doesn't so that you have more solutions available on call.

- Moving from an operational to a strategic role requires a complete shift in thinking as you move from decisions based on predictable circumstances to decisions that are ambiguous, uncertain, and high risk.

- To move from a fixed mindset to a growth mindset, you must jettison fixed notions about what makes business success. Doing so gives you resiliency and the ability to openly explore ideas.

To find out how to managers can be leaders in business, go to www.dummies.com/extras/decisionmaking.

In this part . . .

✔ Discover how, to become a better leader and decision-maker, you must change your mindset as you increase responsibility and risk

✔ Explore the role of the manager as it changes from controlling to serving employees

✔ Realize what fuels entrepreneurial ambition and resilience and discover how to tap into those forces to get the best out of your staff

✔ Put systems in place that facilitate, rather than stifle, decision-making engagement

Chapter 13

Becoming a More Effective Decision-Maker

*B*ig advances in your skills and leadership don't happen when things are going swimmingly. Your character and your strengths grow when you face tough judgment calls, deal with inner or interpersonal conflicts, or face unfamiliar territory, like a new career. Making tough decisions is only one half of being a successful businessperson. The other half is unearthing who you become as a result of the decisions you make. Such character-defining decisions — ones that determine the quality of your key personal and professional relationships from that point on — impact what happens next in your business and in your life.

In this chapter, I show you how to use challenging moments to develop your influence as a decision-maker and how to adapt your thinking by taking increased responsibility for your company's direction. I also explain how to handle yourself when things go wrong or when you find yourself confronting bad behavior. No matter what the crucible, you can grow leadership capacity and build character and your relationships in the process. Head to Chapters 4, 5, and 6 for more on growing yourself as a decision-maker.

Upping Your Game: Transitioning from Area-Specific to Strategic Decisions

When small companies grow big fast, CEOs who want to stay CEOs pretty much have to grow to keep pace with the expansion. And, according to one Harvard study, 79 percent of top-performing CEOs are hired from within. This means that if you're aiming for an executive position, your thinking and approach to decision-making have to evolve to meet your career aspirations. Accepting higher levels of responsibility changes your decision-making game.

As your responsibilities grow, no matter how that growth unfolds or how large your business, you'll be challenged in two ways:

- ✔ You'll move from making straightforward decisions to strategic and more ambiguous decisions. Ambiguous decisions don't lend themselves to a "right" answer or a step-by-step approach.

- ✔ Whereas in the past, you could specialize in — and remain comfortable with — one area of expertise, you now must embrace and understand the bigger picture.

The business environment is both complex and interconnected. For that reason, relying on only one area of expertise limits your view as a decision-maker, and you'll make mistakes as a result. To combat this tendency, try tackling decisions where more is at stake. Doing so gives you the chance to push the boundaries of your comfort zone. The idea is to give yourself a chance to stretch, not to the snapping point, but to the point where you can discover that you are capable of more than you think. The rewards? By accepting higher levels of personal responsibility, you gain freedom to make decisions for yourself instead of following directives without question. This freedom sets the foundation for ethical behavior, which you can find out more about in Chapter 19.

Any company, regardless of size, can benefit from working with a longer term view. In fact, if you want to do more than survive as a company, you need to blend strategy (the thinking part) with creativity (the innovation element) so that you can continue to adapt.

Highlighting strategic decisions

Whether you make strategic decisions or not, your decisions benefit from strategic thinking. When you think strategically, you look ahead to the direction you're heading, and you weigh risk, consequence, and other aspects of the decision-making process. In short, strategic thinking allows you to work with the uncertainty of the future and use the details you pay attention to day by day to set a direction for your company. When you think strategically, you take the big-picture view as you move from your current position to the desired possibilities.

In this section, I focus on strategic thinking because, without it, the chances that your company will fail increase. (Head to Chapter 10 to discover the basic parameters for a strategic planning process.)

Balancing short-term actions with long-term direction

Many companies fail to think past the end of next month or next quarter, and most equate being constantly busy with making progress. The problem with this mindset is that, if you don't know where you're going, you could end up going in circles and never make progress, or you can wind up someplace you'd rather not be. Strategic thinking puts the compass in your hands, enabling you to balance short-term, immediate actions (which everyone loves) with the longer term direction that makes a company resilient and valued.

Taking a bird's-eye view

Strategic thinking entails thinking conceptually to see patterns and relationships among seemingly unrelated pieces of information and then adding a dose of imagination (without getting too carried away) to find opportunity. The best way to see new opportunities is to view circumstances from a higher vantage point. When you think conceptually, you can separate what's important from what's not important, or you can take a solution that works in one place and apply it successfully to a totally different situation somewhere else.

British explorer Mark Wood approached Skype, a computer-based video and audio chat software company, to install a cybercafé in Nepal, where tourists would pay a nominal fee to use Skype to call home. The fee gave the local Nepalese children connection to the rest of the world.

If you're like many, you may prefer to avoid thinking conceptually because concepts don't tell you what to do differently on Monday morning when you show up at work. After all, the security of routinely knowing exactly what to do Monday morning is comforting . . . and a trap:

- ✔ If you don't visualize or articulate where you want to go, you're left without direction or purpose.

- ✔ Routines can blind you to what can be achieved if you were to look beyond the end of the month, the end of the project, and so on.

- ✔ Feeling certain can lull you into thinking that nothing is changing, but it is — and at rapid rates.

Putting strategic thinking to good use: Medicare-Glaser

When Harlan Steinbaum was chairman and CEO of Medicare-Glaser, his privately held, rapidly growing company needed an infusion of cash. A large conglomerate with sufficiently deep pockets arrived on the scene and agreed to buy it. Harlan stayed in the company, his new role being to oversee 6 of the 17 divisions. From this vantage point, Harlan was able to observe how the conglomerate made decisions, and he noticed that the company was risk averse; its culture focused on managing problems instead of solving them.

Recognizing that this culture wasn't one that would support expansion — the reason Medicare-Glaser needed cash in the first

place — Harlan and his partners negotiated a leveraged buy back to reclaim control. Risky? Yes. High stakes? Yes. Ultimately, however, buying the company back enabled the company to grow, which had been the original goal. The keys to this decision were the things that Harlan brought into his new role: the ability to look at the situation from a higher vantage point and the capacity to think conceptually. Doing so allowed him to recognize that Medicare-Glaser, as a subdivision of the larger company, was not well positioned to realize its original goal and to devise a strategy that would put his company on the right path to future success.

As a decision-maker, you'll make fewer strategic decisions than tactical ones (head to the next section to find out the difference), but these decisions can make or break your company's fortunes and future.

Developing your strategic thinking capabilities

As a small business owner or someone who works at the operational or managerial level, you make a lot of decisions. The practice you gain in those positions gives you the experience you need to steer through fairly predictable situations, operationally and tactically. However, with increased responsibility, your decisions change from tactical ones, which take care of current needs and projects, to strategic ones, which attempt to answer the question, "What do we want to accomplish?" The mindset shifts from managing or controlling the process (tactical) to looking for the results (strategic).

You can develop your strategic thinking by doing the following:

✔ **Step back and shift perspective.** Try to observe your business and its position in the community or market from as many angles as possible. Doing so is crucial because it gives you time to reflect so that you can see the big picture.

Don't hesitate to explore how a totally different kind of company is tackling the same kinds of issues you are. The idea isn't to transplant their ideas into your company but to gain inspiration from their thinking and come up with something that fits your situation.

✔ **Dedicate time each month to reflect on your position in the market, in the community, and in the world.** Reflect alone first and then reflect with your team. This enables you and your team to refresh your thinking with enough perspective to make creative decisions and plan for the future.

✔ **Use the insights you gain from your observations and reflection to modify or affirm your direction.** Beware the trap of thinking that once you develop a strategy you're done and have only to periodically update it. Defining and setting out your strategy doesn't mean you suddenly have the ability to control the future, and in the rapidly changing conditions of the modern business environment, things are going to change. Monitoring changes in the market conditions and then incorporating new information into your thinking allows you to stay on top of change or even totally change direction. Chapter 12 describes ways you can stay on top of outside changes.

Avoiding the perils of micromanaging

Anywhere along the path to increased responsibility, you may be tempted to hang on to control, thinking that it's part of being "in charge." Actually, letting go of control is the basic skill needed. If you don't learn to let go, you run the risk of micromanaging. As a micromanager, you direct every action and must verify the accuracy of every decision because you don't trust that your employees are competent.

Micromanaging is a really good way to demoralize staff. It shows that you don't trust your staff or that your need for perfection compels you to retain control over everything. Can you say, "Control freak"? To solve the problem, you have to first recognize that you're micromanaging and then shift your approach to a more strategic style. You do so either by identifying the tendency on your own or by asking staff.

Overcoming your micromanaging tendencies offers many benefits:

✔ You reduce your stress levels and gain engagement with your staff.

✔ Delegating lets you see the big picture, which gives you the perspective you need to think strategically.

✔ You can accomplish more when you work together with your team than you can by doing everything by yourself.

✔ Realizing that you're human and need the support of staff to get the job done makes you a more compassionate and better leader.

Are you a micromanager?

Although you likely won't admit to being a micromanager, it is a guarantee that your staff knows. Here is a set of characteristics that indicate you're probably a micromanager:

✔ **You frequently feel overwhelmed by work while others wait for you to tell them what to do.** This indicates that you're bearing the brunt of the workload and not delegating.

✔ **You dictate the end result rather than work with staff to clarify expectations.** Dictating the end results indicates that you need to be in complete control and you're not using the assets and brain trust at your disposal.

✔ **You may delegate a task, but if it isn't being done the way you want it done, you retract the assignment and put it back on your desk.** This behavior indicates that you believe you're the only person who can do the job right.

✔ **You hear these words running through your mind or coming out of your mouth:**

• **"If you want something done right, do it yourself."** If you think along these lines, you believe that you're the only one who can do the job right.

• **"Nothing can move forward until it is approved by me."** This is another way of saying that you need to be happy with the details. It also suggests that you have expectations you either haven't told staff about or haven't articulated clearly enough; otherwise, your staff would know how to accurately interpret your meaning and produce what you want on their own.

See yourself? If so, you need to overcome this tendency. Micromanaging sends the message that you don't trust that your staff will perform. Lack of trust causes confidence to deteriorate. It's also baggage that you have to shed if you want to progress to higher levels of decision-making. No single person is perfect, and one person alone, even one with a superhero cape, simply can't be a company all by him- or herself.

Letting go of micromanaging

If you've confessed that you're a micromanager, how do you let go? Follow these steps:

1. **Name, boldly and honestly, what you're attached to and why.**

   For example, perhaps you have a hard time letting go because of a fear of failure or a fear you won't get the result you want.

   Control stems from fear, so knowing what you're afraid of losing and why helps you decide whether it's a real concern and opens up the space to trust in what comes to you rather than force results.

2. **Decide whether you're ready to let go of control.**

   Keep in mind that there will never be a perfect time. Knowing that the timing is right is an intuitive instinct that fear blocks access to. Ask yourself whether letting go of intervening in team decisions, for example, would give you more freedom. If the answer is yes, then it's time. Remember, the goal is to recognize that, by opening up to new results, you'll be able to handle what happens next.

3. **Accept what happens next and trust all will be well, without your intervention.**

   There is always an empty space between what you've always done and what's next. To avoid reverting back to control, simply be patient with yourself, visualize the better approach, and trust that you'll be all right. To navigate personally, consider working with a mindfulness coach who can help you stay calm. At work, letting go of micromanaging might mean you give up making decisions team members are better equipped to make. They'll be expecting you to step in when they hesitate. Don't bite on that invite! Keep asking them what they'd do and then wait.

Often, when people hear they need to let go, panic results because they think it means letting go of responsibility or quality. But in actuality, you're simply replacing the need to be in control with trust in yourself, your management capabilities, and others on your staff. At the end of the day, the only one you can control is yourself.

If you don't want to let go, not because you need to be in control but because your staff isn't ready to independently assume the necessary responsibilities, then release slowly. Make sure you give inexperienced staff the mentoring and support to bring them up to speed. Also, encourage them to ask questions when they aren't sure. Doing so helps them grow in their careers.

Taking even more steps to improve your leadership style

As you recover from your experimental stint as a micromanager, you can continue to expand your leadership skills, and the easiest way to do so is to take time to listen to what each person on your team brings — or wants to bring — to the table. By listening deeply to your staff, you'll be able to discover breakthroughs and unique solutions. Leadership, as I explain in more detail later in this chapter, isn't about having all the right answers; it's about asking the right questions.

To strengthen your leadership style, ask these questions:

✔ **Do you expect staff to get the job done the way you would do it, or do you simply want it successfully accomplished?** The difference is a focus on the process (how it's accomplished) or the end point (success!) Micromanagers focus on every single aspect of how things get done by others. You want to focus on achieving results, using a process that respects and engages your team.

✔ **What do your staff members see as each other's strengths and what responsibilities does each want to grow into?** The information you glean from this question guides you as you decide how to allocate staff members' current skills while helping them develop new skills. It also helps staff see where their growth aspirations lie.

Based on the responses to these questions, return decision-making power to the appropriate level and people. When you give decision-making power back, the result is that decision-making has sustainability; that is, the team can perform well past the assumed targets. U.S. naval commanders who develop ship personnel as decision-makers find that they can leave and performance doesn't plummet, even if the next commander brings a less enlightened approach. In short, the crew can lead itself.

Support the team as team members come up with ways to have fun, work together, and support one another. Doing so shows that you trust your team members to solve problems on their own.

Moving from specializing in one area to working across functions

Several forces are pushing decision-makers to hold an expanded view not only of their businesses, but of their roles as well. You can read more about these and other trends in Chapter 1, but here are the highlights:

✔ **The shift away from the old notion that you're either a specialist or a generalist:** You may specialize in a function, but you'll always need to know where you fit in terms of the company's success and how the company dovetails into the rest of the world. Understanding what the higher purpose of a company is helps employees stay engaged while achieving that purpose.

✔ **The trend toward combining complementary functions into one role so that all can function more cooperatively:** Internal functions, like sales versus marketing, for example, used to compete with each other. But businesses can no longer afford to waste productive energy on unproductive competition among staff members or company divisions. The idea behind combining complementary functions is to serve the employee community and the customer, not feed competitive conflict.

✔ **The shift away from centralized decision-making, in which decisions are made by a few, to decentralized decision-making.** This structure fosters collaboration and timelier responses to change, and everyone contributes to the company's success.

As a decision-maker, how can you prepare for these changes? By taking the actions I outline here:

✔ **Seek out opportunities to work in different areas of expertise.** Working with others whose expertise differs from yours makes you a well-rounded individual and gives you insight into other areas of the company. This exposure to multiple areas gives you a new, broader perspective that can inform your decisions and help you predict what impact your decisions will have.

✔ **Participate in decision-making related to the best projects to move forward on.** Quality, not quantity, of projects aids success. You'll gain experience in seeing how projects bring together expertise from within and beyond your company's boundaries. Even if you're working on a joint venture, you'll gain insight into how very different values, criteria, and beliefs guide decision-making.

✔ **Practice empathy.** Use every conflict or misunderstanding to see through someone else's eyes. Doing so lets you use your team's diverse outlooks to your advantage. Plus, this capability is an essential quality for anyone paying attention to the workplace culture and customer relationships. The empathy map tool in Chapter 12 can help, but your greatest ally is your ability to listen.

✔ **Embrace the idea that you don't know everything there is to know.** Don't believe everything you think. There is more knowledge, excitement, and opportunity waiting, and the only thing required to tap into it is curiosity! Through social media and other resources, information can flow instantly around the world. This new reality expands what is available, and it opens new relationships from many different sources.

Displaying Character through Decision-Making

Character — essentially your moral fiber, ethics, and integrity all rolled into one — counts at every level. How you use power, whether it's personal power, which you earn by overcoming adversity, or delegated power, which you possess as you attain positions of authority, reveals your character. Character separates those who lead their lives with integrity from those who abuse authority or use force.

Mirror, mirror, on the wall: Taking a close look at yourself

How can you tell where you stand, character-wise? Use the Waiter Rule. Basically, this rule says that how you treat a waiter reveals who you are as a person. According to Bill Swanson, a CEO of Raytheon, "If someone is friendly to you (someone higher in authority) but rude to the waiter, he or she isn't a nice person." In addition, saying things like, "I know the owner and can get you fired" speaks volumes about how a person uses his or her personal power. Someone who throws the power of his position around doesn't respect his position or the power it holds and doesn't embody the traits of a good leader.

To discover how you view power, ask yourself these questions:

- **Do I think I have all the answers, or can others offer a view that I can learn from?** Reflecting on this question reveals your approach to learning. If you think you have all the answers and need to be the resident expert, incorporating the wisdom of the team will be tough. Take this mindset to the extreme, and you could qualify for dictator!

- **Do I treat those who report to me with the same respect I treat those in higher positions?** If you treat everyone with the same respect, regardless of their position, you'll know you're comfortable with authority. If not, you'll know that you attach authority to power and so might not respect its use.

- **Does my confidence shrink when I am confronted by an authority figure? Do I feel I need to manipulate to get what I want?** If your default, go-to strategy is to exert control over others or use manipulation to get your way, there's a good chance your self-esteem needs a boost. Low self-esteem leads to lousy decisions. Building confidence in yourself can help you increase trust.

✔ **Do I feel more powerful when I am delivering orders or when I am collaborating to achieve a team goal?** In other words, what floats your boat: being in charge or working collaboratively toward a common goal? Perhaps you're comfortable doing both. If you need to be in charge, can you step back and let others take the helm without feeling you've lost control?

Out of all the questions listed, the last one points to the ego. In this context, *ego* refers to your concept of self and your relationship with yourself. Most business folks still hang onto the old and generally inaccurate belief that an overblown ego is a prerequisite to achieving success. The younger generation, on the other hand, doesn't subscribe to this idea, and these "kids" are leading companies that are growing like crazy. Many people who have poor relationships with their egos protect the ego by trying to make themselves feel better by putting down or comparing themselves to others, but this is a career limiting mindset, especially in environments where collaboration is critical. When your concept of self is low, your decisions suffer because making yourself feel better becomes more important than making a better decision. You can read more about ego, self-esteem, and decision-making in Chapter 4.

Using defining moments to build character

In the same way that career-defining moments of a company's leader shape the company's future, personal defining moments build character. In these defining moments, you're typically presented with two equally held, highly important values that you must choose between.

Suppose, for example, that you discover you're booked to meet a potential new client at the same time you promised your daughter you'd attend her school play. What do you do in this situation? There is no going back and no right answer, and your response may uncover something you didn't know about yourself or another person involved. Do you do what you believe is more important or what you feel obligated to do? Cumulatively, tough decisions build character. They also change relationships.

How can you use character-revealing conflicts to transform character? There are two ways:

✔ **Find out what is important to you and then identify the underlying values.** Look at a conflicting feeling not as gut wrenching, even though it may feel that way, but as tension between two equally acceptable values. To identify the conflict, ask yourself what is important to you about each demand. Then chose the higher, more difficult path that is aligned with what matters more to you.

✔ **Take your mind off what is immediate and in your face to allow your creative side to go to work.** Step out of the workplace "noise" and do something you love to do: ski, hike, bike, knit, garden . . . whatever, but before you do so, ask yourself for insight. Then, when you're out doing the thing you enjoy, insights will pop up when you least expect. Notice when the light bulb goes on to reveal deeper values.

The idea is to free your mind, not numb it. So step away from the TV, remote control, and mini-bar.

Handling yourself when things go wrong

You may have heard the saying, "Conflict builds character, but crisis defines it." Sooner or later, something you're working on will not go as planned — perhaps with disastrous results — and you'll have to deal with it. How you handle yourself in such situations is a defining moment in the development of your leadership ability.

As a leader and decision-maker, you must be prepared to handle unexpected crises with honesty and integrity. Following are some actions you can take to prepare for, deal with, and learn from when the going gets rough:

✔ **Plan ahead.** If you don't have a team plan for a crisis, put one together and make sure that all members are on the same page regarding the following:

- An explanation of what constitutes a crisis for your business
- How to address all legal issues
- How to address public perception of what happened and what it means
- The person(s) responsible for putting the plan into action to ensure that, when bad things happen, the plan is brought forward to guide immediate action

✔ **At the time of the crisis, take action.** Move immediately to address risks to public or employee safety and offer clear information about what is going on.

Crisis experts traditionally give less than 48 hours to provide information to the public or to staff, but with the advent of social media and its capacity for instant communication, you have much less time than that. Without information, expect people to speculate.

A study in character: Akio Toyoda

At the end of 2009 and into early 2010, Toyota recalled over 7.5 million cars due to unintentional acceleration (and subsequent deaths) traced back to the gas pedal made by one supplier. After recalling over 7 million vehicles, Toyota President Akio Toyoda accepted full responsibility, saying, "In the past few months, our customers have started to feel uncertain about the safety of Toyota's vehicles, and I take full responsibility for that." His next step was to learn what happened and to address it. He did not shy away from what he discovered:

> I would like to point out that Toyota's priority has traditionally been the following: First, safety; second, quality; third, volume. These priorities became confused, and we were not able to stop, think, and make improvements as much as we were able to before, and our basic stance to listen to customers' voices to make better products has weakened somewhat. We pursued growth over the speed at which we were able to develop our people and our organization, and we should be sincerely mindful of that."

Toyota has a learning culture, and, true to form, company leaders focused on learning why the errors leading to the recall occurred. The company's president accepted full responsibility and didn't pin the blame on a scapegoat further down in the ranks. When I spoke to Toyota owners at the time (2010), they told me they were buying more shares in the company. Loyalty is inspired by care and honesty.

✔ **Show true compassion for the people affected.** Due to the violence people are exposed to everyday — violent TV shows and video games, ongoing military operations, and so on — the public psyche is often numbed to general tragedy. However, when loss is experienced at a personal level, it's very real. Therefore, when you take action during a crisis in which your business or product harms the public — whether that harm is physical or to the public trust — you must speak from your heart and put yourself in their shoes. Otherwise, your response comes across as insincere.

✔ **After the dust has settled, find out what happened and then share that knowledge.** Your goal after the crisis is not to seek someone or something to blame, but to learn from the situation. Put together a team of employees from throughout the organization and give them the job of collectively reflecting, documenting, and then sharing what is learned. Remember, sound organizational judgment comes from learning and then sharing.

A crisis can be the catalyst for doing things differently for greater benefit. It breaks up patterns and gives you an opportunity to replace useless or ineffective habits. But you don't have to wait for a crisis before you decide to think creatively about your processes.

Improving Your Decision-Making by Becoming a Better Leader

Who do people turn to in times of uncertainty, when they need to take action but don't know what action to take, or when they have a problem they can't solve on their own? Leaders. In short, leaders are the people others look to when a decision must be made. But you already knew that. What you may not know is what a leader isn't: He's not the one with all the answers, and she's not necessarily the one with the authority. In this section, I tell you how you can become a better leader, which will, in turn, transform you into a better decision-maker.

Differentiating between leadership and authority

Despite their similarities, being a leader is not the same as having authority. Knowing the difference between being a leader and being in a position of authority is necessary for operating in a world where collaboration is essential. Here are some basic definitions:

- *Authority* refers to officially possessing, often through a position, decision-making power.

- *Leadership* refers to the quality that inspires others to move toward a common goal, to overcome hardship or difficulties, and to work together to achieve the objectives placed before them. Leadership combines vision with inspiration and telling the truth.

You can see the confusion anytime someone asks, "Who is the leader?" and everyone points to the person in charge. That isn't leadership. It's where authority resides. Now that same person may also be a leader, but it isn't a forgone conclusion.

Although authority specifies which decisions you have the power to make, authority does not necessarily make you a leader. Plenty of people in authority have been ineffective leaders, and plenty of important leaders have come from the ranks of those without official authority.

Using your power for good

Leaders inspire. They turn the mundane into the meaningful and motivate others to pursue this higher purpose. They don't have all the answers, but they ask the right questions. Leaders are decisive and visionary.

Anyone can be a leader. The notion that people fall into one of two groups — either leaders or followers — just isn't accurate and has been debunked in the last place you'd expect: marine naval vessels. Even in strong command-and-control structures like the military, each person can demonstrate leadership because it doesn't have anything to do with authority. It has to do with responsibility. People are encouraged to take the initiative, come up with solutions, and act on them. This kind of trust in the capabilities of people up and down the chain of command is vital for success, not only in the military but in the civilian world, too. In fact, sustained high performance depends on it.

In environments where people are expected to take the initiative and act on the solutions they devise, the person in authority — you, as a business owner or manager — plays a completely different role: Your role is to facilitate the emergence of leadership. To foster leadership in your team, ask your employees what solutions they have to the issue at hand, and keep asking them for their ideas, even when they turn to you for direction. Then help them think through the solution (a mentoring role) and support implementation.

Some people in positions of authority wield power inappropriately just to boost their self-esteem, ego, and confidence. Doing so undermines staff morale and contribution. How you handle power and personnel when in a position of authority says everything about you.

Being a leader good enough to ask the tough questions

Groupthink — when people feel they need to conform to one view without question — is toxic for effective teamwork. It leads to important issues not being addressed and creative ideas not being offered. It preserves the status quo and leaves you and your company vulnerable.

If you move forward without clearing out the hidden issues, your leadership and your company's growth get stuck in a holding pattern, and moving forward will feel like running waist-deep in glue. You'll miss breakthrough moments in personal, team, and organizational performance.

Fortunately, effective leadership can overcome groupthink. Leaders must have the courage to ask the tough questions of themselves and their teams. Doing so puts the "unmentionables" on the table. By asking tough questions, you ensure that routine thinking doesn't block achievement of your goal. The best time to ask a powerful question or two is when things are at a standstill or when agreement has come too easily. What is a powerful question? Here's one example: "Is there something we're missing here?"

To profit from powerful questions, do the following before finalizing the decision; this exercise is especially important when you're making big, strategic decisions, like whether to accept an offer to sell your business:

1. **Take a time-out between discussions.**

   The purpose of this time-out is to give everyone a chance to ruminate on the issue at hand. Team members can take a walk together or alone. Don't give specific instructions (you don't want to lead them to a conclusion), but you can say, "Let's take some time to think about this."

2. **When you reconvene, ask for questions or offer one yourself.**

   Breakthroughs can often result when you open up the conversation to explore alternatives not usually on the table. If allowing space for reflection hasn't produced any questions, you can move to conclude the decision.

Creating Safe and Stable Workplaces

Trauma occurs when an individual is psychologically overwhelmed and unable to cope intellectually or emotionally. When the source of the trauma is a single, catastrophic event, such as a hurricane or office shooting, or ongoing and pervasive danger (such as exists in war zones), it's easy to identify. But people can also experience trauma as a result of an accumulation of factors, like unclear expectations, excessive workloads, repeated negative judgments, prejudicial behaviors and opinions, pathologically difficult people, or abusive treatment by superiors. Sound familiar? Unfortunately, one or more of these factors affects too many workplaces.

Trauma caused by the work environment has a negative effect on creativity, mental processing of information, productivity, and the ability to adjust to change. In other words, poor workplace environments cultivate poor performance and bad decisions. Conversely, when workplaces are safe, people contribute beyond what is expected, without fear of reprimand. They also make better decisions because they aren't stressed out.

The trouble with bosses

Research conducted by the Hay Group, a global management consulting firm, found that globally the majority of leaders, most likely in management roles, are blocking performance and instilling workplaces with unmotivated employees, which results in poor decision-making. These leaders give instructions and then focus on what was wrong over what was right. The subjects of the Hay Group study aren't alone. Many in leadership roles default to a command-and-control management style as a way to feel in power, particularly when things seem uncertain. As I explain in Chapter 8, the command-and-control style has its place, but for day-to-day performance, it's demoralizing. In an environment like this, decision-making can come to a standstill because people are afraid of making mistakes.

A safe workplace is one in which employees feel emotionally safe, financially secure, recognized, and acknowledged. In this section, I explain how you can create a workplace that fosters well-being, creativity, and improved problem-solving and decision-making.

Adapting your management style

Management by fear works against sound decision-making and performance. It creates an emotionally charged workplace that is not conducive to rational or intuitive decision-making. Although productivity is possible in such a workplace, this type of environment is bad for a few key reasons:

- ✔ **It makes creatively adapting to changing conditions impossible.** People will follow the rules before achieving goals or taking risks.

- ✔ **It compromises innovation.** Innovation requires creativity and risk-taking. In fear-based decision-making environments, people watch their backs and avoid taking risks.

- ✔ **It impedes seeing ahead.** Vision for the future requires intuition and empathy, two things that are in very short supply in fear-based environments.

Relying on coercion isn't logical or rational, yet it's the prevailing leadership style around the world. If you work in a complex decision-making environment, you (and your managers) need to access leadership styles that are more appropriate to creating better decisions. Management styles that free up employee creativity and open communication to difficult conversations share these characteristics (you can read more about what makes an effective manager in today's modern workplace in Chapter 14):

- ✔ They engage employees to creatively find solutions to issues.
- ✔ Decisions focus on achieving business goals rather than personal career aspirations.
- ✔ They engage in difficult conversations aimed at understanding the situation instead of seeking fault.
- ✔ They care about employee well-being, do not judge, and approach issues with open minds and hearts, enabling open and honest communication that springs from a genuine place.
- ✔ They inspire trust in the working relationships.

Workplaces that don't work for the employees don't work for the company's sustainability. A healthy, trusting work environment lets you go beyond your current productivity goals and quotas to achieve much higher performance. It really is that simple.

Taking steps to improve the quality of the working environment

One way to address negative aspects in the workplace and ensure that employees can work well together as a team is to pay attention to working relationships. The world may be unpredictable, but the quality of working relationships provides stability. In workplaces where trust, a sense of belonging, and genuine care for each other are cultivated, employees can focus on giving the company or the project their absolute best.

When the environment doesn't support high-quality working relationships, your employees spend more time dealing with office politics or covering their backs to reduce personal risk. If your goal is to create high-quality working relationships among employees, supervisors, and upper management, give the items I discuss in this section prime consideration.

Improving emotional safety

To improve emotional safety, identify barriers to trustworthy interpersonal relationships (punishing disclosure of safety risk, for example) and then work with managers and supervisors to establish accountability for better practices. Here are some suggestions:

✔ **Sustain caring, respectful working relationships.** Rather than confirm the negative, relationships must support the positive. Solid emotional support helps people recover from stressful situations, whereas relationships that confirm negativity in the workplace affirm the trauma.

✔ **Provide opportunities to talk about traumas and release emotion.** Trauma results from a painful, stressful, or shocking event that can be sudden or prolonged over time. Traumatic experiences include losing a coworker, an insensitively handled layoff, violence in the workplace, or a bullying boss. Be sure to acknowledge and look after your own feelings, as well.

✔ **Plan casual events that support social interaction, in a comforting environment.** Doing so allows the workplace community to collectively process their experience.

Often management sends the message that employees just need to get over it or that their feelings about the situation indicate weakness. This attitude only makes the trauma worse. Conversely, excessive focus can strengthen the trauma by reinforcing the sense of powerlessness. The difference lies between allowing the emotions to be processed versus repeatedly reliving the experience.

Anne Murray Allen, in her former role as Senior Director for Knowledge and Intranet Management for Hewlett Packard, suggests saying something like this to get the conversation going: "We are missing a process here. If we had it, it would make everyone's life easier. How about we all get together to create this process so it works?"

Ensuring physical safety

To ensure physical safety, set standards and live by them. In industries like construction and manufacturing, workplace safety requires watchfulness. Give experienced employees the assignment of identifying potential hazards or practices.

In companies where speed of production can undermine personal safety, employees will "take one for the team" if meeting quotas has a higher priority than workplace safety. In some workplace environments, such a priority can mean a limb lost — not something you want credit for.

Ensuring high-quality interactions

To ensure high-quality interactions between employees, supervisors, and upper management, create an atmosphere that affirms employee confidence by genuinely acknowledging effort. This suggestion doesn't mean you have to be Mr. or Ms. Nice 24/7. It means that recognition is a natural part of the interaction between you and all the employees you come in contact with.

Spontaneously praise employees for jobs well done. Include fun as part of the working day. When you have fun, don't do so at anyone's expense, but out of the pure pleasure of working with a great group of people. Your genuine enthusiasm and sincere appreciation for their efforts can make a big different, even when your employees aren't feeling so great about themselves or their work.

Being the leader you expect to see in others

When morale is low or the thinking small, small issues end up looking pretty big and people act out their frustration and lack of control. One cause of low morale is often unaddressed bad behavior — bullying, threats, and intimidation, for example — in the workplace. If you truly want your company or department to succeed, you need to address these issues.

Staff look to your actions to find out what the unwritten rules are. The *unwritten rules,* which I write more about in Chapter 12, are the de facto rules that govern behavior and expectations in the workplace, regardless of what the stated policy is. Often, the term refers to the difference between what is said — "We value respect in the workplace," for example — and what is done — managers overlook bullying behavior. Although no one may be running around the workplace waving a sign that declares, "Bad behavior is permissible!" not doing anything about bad behavior pretty much amounts to saying that it's acceptable.

Being a leader means you must firmly, yet professionally, confront tough interpersonal issues, including bad behavior in the workplace. Here's how:

- ✔ **Challenge bad behavior, including bullying and overtly expressed prejudice.** Bullies tend to be people who feel that they lack power and use anger and aggressive behavior to reclaim it. Have no tolerance for inappropriate behavior or judgment of others, but offer professional coaching or personal development opportunities so the individual can gain better interpersonal skills. In the workplace, holding people accountable for their behavior reinforces your commitment to higher standards.

  Deal with prejudice differently because it is a hard-wired belief. To deal with prejudice, pair people up so that the successes resulting from the working relationship transforms the belief.

- ✔ **Draw clear boundaries around what is acceptable and respectful and what is not.** When dealing with an interpersonal issue, take the individual aside, and, if the employee is receptive, provide a coach.

You can also try a game that builds empathy. One such game is Know Me, developed in the thick of apartheid reconciliation, as a means to respectfully disagree, learn, and forge better solutions. For details about this game and others, go to `http://knowmegame.com/johari_window.html`.

✔ **Reject pervasive negativity.** In some workplaces, grumbling could qualify as an Olympic sport. Pessimism and crankiness can be momentarily useful, but if they become persistent habits, they bring everyone down.

Negativity is not the same as critical thinking. Critical thinking is required as a check and balance; it doesn't have to be negative or punitive. For more on using critical thinking as a way to uncover better solutions and make smarter decisions, head to Chapter 9.

✔ **Tackle difficult issues.** Many issues negatively impacting the workplace are left unresolved for fear that careers will be in jeopardy if the problem is reported. When you encounter a difficult issue, openly gather the facts, skip blame or judgment, and involve all parties to develop options and solutions. Be hard on the problem and soft on the people. When you face a difficult issue head on and with integrity, you open up confidence and reinforce that all people matter, not just the ones considered to be of higher value.

It takes courage and strength to deal with adversarial or difficult situations in the workplace, but when you do, you display — and inspire — integrity and are more likely to make ethical decisions (more on that in Chapters 2 and 19) and engage in the kind of risk-taking that saves companies.

✔ **Establish clear expectations about what are and aren't acceptable behaviors for everyone in the workplace, including contract employees.** When the expectations you set aren't being followed, you must follow up and put your foot down. Trust is breached otherwise.

Management guru Edwards Deming says, "Managers talk about getting rid of deadwood, but there are only two possible explanations of why the deadwood exists: You hired deadwood in the first place or, you hired live wood, and then you killed it." Nonperforming employees are often created when you don't pay attention to how workplace conditions affect performance. You can change the workplace conditions to make them better. Head to Chapter 3 for even more on how the workplace affects performance.

Chapter 14

Making Decisions as a Manager

....

....

*W*hen companies reach a point (number of staff) where they feel the need to organize how work gets done, many automatically adopt hierarchies without considering other options. The go-to hierarchy — and the way it has always been done in business, based on the belief that people need to be directed, not trusted — is one that relies on managers to control and direct performance . . . that is, to tell people what to do and to make sure they do what is expected of them.

This model — and the manager's role — is changing. So, too, is the way in which decisions get made. Now the focus is on engaging employees and working collaboratively to make sound decisions quickly. In this chapter, I explore the overall trends affecting the managerial role, provide some tools you can use to thrive, and share strategies to help both older and younger workers achieve greater fulfillment in their work.

Recognizing the Changing Role of Manager

Traditionally run businesses are structured around authority (legal or delegated decision-making power) with the most authority/power residing at the top (the CEO and the board, in bigger companies) and each subsequent level holding progressively less authority. Think of a pyramid — a graphic that pretty accurately conveys the power structure in these businesses — the decision-making occurs at the upper levels of the pyramid, and the work happens at the bottom.

In such hierarchical, authority-based structures, especially in those with many layers, attaining approval for decisions takes a lot of time. In today's interconnected world of high-speed communication, this decision-making structure is way too slow. Recognizing that decisions need to be faster and more accurate, companies are employing options such as the following:

- ✔ **Decentralizing decision-making power.** Decision-making power that works with employees and is decentralized allows companies to respond quickly to changing conditions. Although titles like "director" may be used, these positions don't include the power to control others. The implication is that the role of managers is changing from controlling to supporting performance.

- ✔ **Distributing management to all employees as companies approach accountability and responsibility, using alternative organizational structures with no bosses.** These structures are called *self-managing* or *flat structures* or, as Cocoon Projects in Italy calls it, a *liquid self-organizing company*. Liquid organizations are adaptive, dynamic, and value-driven. Structure exists, but it isn't centered on telling people what to do. Creating value is the focus. The implication is that managerial responsibilities move to the individual, relying on peer accountability and shared responsibility to create value for the customer, colleagues, and society.

The idea of self-managed companies isn't new. Morning Star, considered to be the world's largest tomato processor, has 400 leaders and no bosses. The company is committed to operating as a community of self-managing professionals, and it's been around for over 20 years.

These novel approaches to getting work done are adaptive and focused on speed, collaboration, and employee autonomy. In this section, I tell you what you need to know to become the empowering manager you were meant to be — a new role you can leverage to help your company culture adapt.

Embracing your role as change agent

As a result of the trend toward more decentralized decision-making and flatter organizational structures, even managers in hierarchical structures are changing how they perform their roles to add value and increase engagement. They're letting go of the idea that "being in charge" defines what it means to be a manager.

This shift doesn't come without challenges, however. For managers immersed in the traditional role, letting go of being in charge can feel threatening, but it doesn't have to be. In fact, if you embrace the idea that managers are agents of change and their role is to engender respect and empowerment in the workplace, rather than to control and micromanage, you'll find that this new kind of management role is actually much more powerful and significant.

In the end, no matter what management structure you prefer, your role is to restore autonomy to employees so that they are free to achieve goals and be fully responsible for their achievements. Self-management is combined with mutual effort; each person contributes to and supports every other person's success, and the role of the manager is to bring out the best in people and to foster their natural desire to work together.

The role of the manager is changing from controlling performance to supporting it. As a result, your management mission is fairly simple: Find what your team needs to achieve the goal and then identify and remove barriers that get in the way of accomplishing it. Being a change agent means that you engage employees with what matters collectively. With employee engagement comes collaboration, creativity (where it makes sense), and completion (execution).

Recognizing the limits of hierarchical authority-based structures

The very nature of a hierarchical authority-based organizational structures implies that direction comes down from the top and performance moves up from the bottom. Although this is an orderly image, it is also an illusion. The organization chart shows how reporting takes place and how resources are allocated, but it doesn't determine how work gets done.

Direction may come from the top, but performance actually takes place in networks that cut across the company. Even in command-and-control organizations, goal-oriented performance runs on networks. This idea is based on research conducted by social biologist Dennis Sandow, who uncovered the natural and recurring pattern in organizations of all sizes including, most notably, Hewlett Packard.

Because people's networks extend beyond the boundaries of their official departments, managers who try to control performance are more likely to suffer nervous breakdowns than to succeed because much of what impacts performance is beyond their purview. Why hang on to that much stress?

Adapting your management style

If you can see the value of managing differently, the next logical question is, when do you tell your team how to get the work done and when do you get out of their way? Managers know that providing the team with what it needs goes with the turf. So the bigger challenge is moving from telling and directing the team to supporting and serving it. The changing role requires a higher order of leadership, one that brings more of your natural talents to bear. In this section, I tell you how to make this transition.

Understanding what gives you personal satisfaction

Making the transition from a manager who tells and directs to one who supports and serves starts with self-awareness. Understanding what gives you personal satisfaction is a key first step in understanding what you think a manager's role is. Ask yourself these questions to examine your preferences and discover how you view your role as a manager:

- **Do I feel most powerful and satisfied when I tell others what to do or when I help them succeed?** Your answer to this question tells you whether your self-worth comes from within or from having control over others. If you need to have control over others, then see how to stop being a micromanager in Chapter 13. Be aware that while you may prefer to be in charge, your employees may prefer a more team-based approach.

- **Do my employees know more than I do, and if so, how do I feel about that?** This question helps you identify whether you value your expertise as much or more than your ability to develop strong and respectful working relationships. If you need to be right and have all the right answers, you'll find that letting go of the need to control will be difficult for you. Keep in mind, though, that trusting that you bring more than just your expertise to the table gives you the advantage.

Building trust in yourself and your team

As I mention earlier, managers around the world, when faced with uncertain situations, tend to revert to directing, controlling, and — in the worst instances — intimidating their employees, even though those strategies don't help them achieve their goals as much as they help them feel in control. So how do you avoid being a manager who relies on coercion? The answer boils down to how comfortable you are with learning and creatively dealing with uncertainty.

When you aren't sure about what will happen next, you can either step in to control the situation (the strategy that blocks creative contribution), or you can try another option: You can engage your own and your team's creativity by making deliberate choices to experimentally develop solutions. This approach expands the intellectual horsepower you have available.

Because you can't command people to be creative, you place trust in your own ability to accept and deal with what happens in the moment rather than directing effort toward a specific, preconceived outcome. You listen and ask questions rather than take the traditional approach of "tell, sell, and — when that doesn't work — yell."

Think of tennis players. They don't know where the ball is heading next, so what do they do? Bounce back and forth on the balls of their feet so that they're ready to respond to anything that comes their way. Think of yourself as a tennis player, able to adjust to wherever the ball goes next. If you dig in your heels, you'll just be stuck and get hit by a fast-moving ball.

Taking steps to support employee engagement

When you work with your team, the role you play determines how the team acts and reacts. The following points outline the things you can do to ensure that your actions support your team.

Provide the team what it needs to get the job done

Provide money, expertise, experience, talent, fun, comic relief — basically whatever is required to take the pressure off the workload.

One way to make the best uses of limited time (a common scenario for managers) is to change how you allocate your top people. Usually, for example, the people who have the most experience and expertise are assigned to projects first. The result? Top talent is often overcommitted. Instead, assign the least experienced first and develop that new talent, while reserving the more experienced staff to go where they're needed. This tactic, called the *Real Options business model,* as described by Chris Matts and Olav Maassen (specialists in risk management, project management, and financial investment), lets you reserve assigning those with high levels of experience and expertise when and where they are needed — to the more important projects.

Find and remove barriers that impede teamwork

Barriers can appear in various forms: interpersonal issues, ineffective processes, and so on. For example, imagine that you work in a company where competition rather than collaboration is the dominant trait, and the project you're working on involves team members from different departments. These team members report to you for the project, but they are also responsible to their own managers, who are accountable for their performance.

Now suppose that your project has encountered a small glitch that would be easy enough to fix, except that the team member with the expertise to fix it tells you that she can't do so in the given time. Her position puts the project schedule in jeopardy, and you may feel that she's just being difficult, that she's not committed to the project, that she's unwilling to help out, and so on. But if you approach the situation with true curiosity, you may discover that, according to the procedures her own manager has put in place to keep track of the workflow, she must follow a labyrinthine process that takes a lot of time.

Often, interpersonal issues, including conflicts between units, are the result of problems with processes. When you approach these issues with curiosity — that is, investigate the problem with an open mind — you're likely to find the cause is some process or procedure that may be in place for no other reason than "that's just the way things are done around here." Therefore, always be hard on the problem but soft on the people. When you replace blame and judgment with curiosity, you increase your chances of discovering and resolving the real issue while improving working relationships.

Anytime you have multiple managers internally and externally tasked with working together, invest time upfront on determining what processes you'll use and how you'll collectively handle glitches or obstacles. Use this agreement during the course of the project to work with surprises during implementation.

Step back when you're tempted to interfere

When you're tempted to jump in with both feet and control a situation, wait and watch. Interfering is hard to resist, but by standing back, you can see how the team sorts itself out. If you feel anxious, take five deep breaths into your belly to allow your brain to stay calm. The stepping-back strategy also helps team members develop their own problem-solving skills, displays your trust in their competency, and underscores that each team member is an integral part of the process.

Companies that focus on telling employees what to do create employees who wait to be told and, as a result, lose their initiative. Clearly, if you're dealing with a safety issue and direction saves lives, provide it. But otherwise, avoid the habit of always stepping in. Otherwise, team members will wait for your direction in any situation. From their viewpoint, this approach is less risky (after all, you're the one making — and therefore are accountable for — all the decisions), but it doesn't help your employees grow and develop their own skills. Instead, ask them what ideas they have and push the initiative back to them. And then don't decide whether their ideas are right or wrong. It defeats the whole idea. If you're concerned that team members don't have enough experience or know-how, discover what you can do to help: find mentors, assume a group coaching role, and so on. The idea is to build the strength of the team, not to rush in and save the day by doing everything yourself.

If you need to be right and in control all the time, you're not ready to help your employees learn to lead themselves. Head to Chapter 13 for ways to overcome your need to be in control and let team members lead. Managers who've made the change report that it takes time, consistency, patience, and encouragement from management and the ranks, but in the end there's a high reward for your commitment.

Oversee the team dynamic

You can put a team of very smart people in the room, and yet they can still somehow make decisions that are less than intelligent. Why? Because the group may not be functioning well together. Here are two common sources of the problem:

- ✔ **The team was put together without a clear sense of purpose or an understanding of why each person was selected.** Clarify the purpose of the group and the contribution of each team member. When they can work out what they can achieve by working together, the purpose of their teamwork is nailed down. With that shared understanding, each team member will understand his or her role in achieving project goals.

- ✔ **The group dynamics may be off.** Observing how team members interact can shed insight on what is impeding the team's success. As you observe, be sure to do so without looking for blame. Your intuition is invaluable in seeing what isn't obvious; head to Chapter 7 for ways to tap into your intuition.

Know when you need to control

Assume control when an emergency dictates it and you can see that people are running around without a clue about what to do next. Assuming you know the proper course of action, stepping in is appropriate to restore order to the chaos. If you don't know any more than your team does, take the time to stop, regroup, and reflect. Before putting together an action plan, identify why people are feeling confused. You also step in when you have a legal responsibility to take control or if safety issues are a concern.

Choosing Your Leadership and Management Styles

Despite the fact that "leadership" and "management" are often mashed up in terms of how someone performs his or her role, the general belief is that managers *can't* be leaders. What those who hold this belief don't say is that managers can't be leaders because they're overloaded with tasks or fighting fires daily. Knowing what styles lie at the intersection of management and leadership enables you to understand the different ways to use authority and exercise your responsibilities. With this information, you can make deliberate decisions about what kind of manager you want to be.

Looking at leadership styles

Business literature classifies many leadership styles, and you may see yourself fitting into one or all of them. Which style you apply to a situation depends on the situation itself, the group dynamics, and what is needed. Gaining awareness and having the flexibility to adapt your style is a strength you bring to your role as manager (this capability also depends on self-knowledge, which I cover in Chapters 5 and 6). Following are some of the different leadership styles.

Visionary

Visionary leaders see ahead. Although they're not quite able to predict the future, they certainly have the foresight to visualize the destination. If the vision is clear and everyone understands it, coworkers and subordinates can use it as a guide as they convert the idea into reality. Foresight guides.

Coaching

In a coaching style, you work short-term, one-on-one with an employee to improve a specific skill, such as the employee's presentation skills or his or her ability to think strategically. If you are engaged in your personal growth, you can credibly coach employees through difficult situations. However, if you aren't committed to your own growth, taking on a coaching role will turn you into a micromanager coach, which isn't effective.

If you are a self-confessed micromanager, don't try to be a coach to your staff. Instead, invest time developing yourself as a leader. In particular, work to increase the trust you have in your own decisions before you attempt to guide someone else's. See Chapter 13 for more on micromanaging.

Team-based (democratic)

In the team-based leadership style, your primary focus is on strengthening team relationships. The central goal of this leadership style is to attain harmony to realize optimum performance. To do it well, however, you must be able to confront conflict tactfully. Otherwise, the emphasis shifts from achieving higher performance to maintaining harmony and giving praise — a scenario that fosters a contrived sense of agreement instead of a real appreciation for the value of disagreement. The result? A team that blows up because the pressure of repressing diverse perspectives impairs functioning or individual contribution. A much healthier approach is to air diverse views so that the points are understood and incorporated.

I once worked with a team in which team members wanted to be nice to each other to be in agreement. To achieve that end, team members suppressed ideas that challenged the norm. New ideas, and the people who came up with them, were dismissed. Resentment silently built up until a day came when the team members sat down to explore why they were stuck. It didn't take long to find out. When one person communicated his experience of being shut out, the group became instantly aware of the problem and was able to adopt a different approach that didn't stifle ideas.

Consensus-building

A consensus-building style draws on the skills and knowledge of employees to fill a void typically created through lack of direction (that is, no visionaries are around). Consensus is one way to use the collective wisdom of a group to identify a shared sense of direction or a shared goal. In this leadership style, you use facilitation skills and the methods I describe in Chapters 10 and 11.

Unless done scrum style (huddle-plan-get it done), this leadership approach isn't useful in an emergency. That said, the mutual trust and understanding achieved through consistent use of consensus can strengthen collective capacity to respond in situations where no authority exists, things are changing rapidly, and coordinated action is needed.

Consensus is vulnerable to vocal, domineering individuals who get their way by hijacking the discussion and intimidating or pressuring others to align to their view. As a leader, your skills in observing and gently but firmly calling for equity are invaluable. You can also use dot voting (Chapter 11) and the structured round table approach (Chapter 17). Head to Chapter 3 for details on how managers can shape workplace cultures to support decision-making.

Using authority effectively: Different styles for different situations

You've no doubt heard the old saying, "With great power comes great responsibility." Well, holding the power to make decisions that impact other people's lives is a great responsibility, too. By intentionally deciding how you want to use that power, you deliberately create and monitor the conditions for better decision-making. In this section, I list a few different approaches. Try each one on, as you would a new coat, to see how it fits, and keep trying them until you find a style that suits you. You'll wear that coat until you decide to switch styles. (Yes, an old dog can always learn new tricks!)

Using this information about the different styles helps you do the following:

✔ Decide where to involve staff in the decision-making process, from information gathering to the point of decision. Also be sure to give consideration to the support required for implementation.

✔ Recognize when to make decisions alone and when to engage others. Sometimes, acting alone can produce a negative impact.

✔ Decide how to adapt your personal style for the situation at hand. By being flexible and knowing the alternatives, during any given situation you'll know whether to stick to your personal style or to modify it, either temporarily or permanently.

Command and control: "Do what I tell you to do!"

As you would expect, with this management style, decisions are made unilaterally and employees are closely monitored (see Chapter 13 for information on micromanaging). In this style, employees are often tasked with getting the job done — as long as the method in which they perform the task and the end result meet management's expectations, regardless whether those expectations are clearly communicated.

Although this style can work — and is often the style traditionally used in many businesses — inappropriate use of command and control creates a lot of suffering in the workplace and often leads to poor decisions. It creates stress and is costly on many levels:

✔ In day-to-day management practice, particularly in dynamic environments, command-and-control management disengages employees and impedes implementation.

✔ It doesn't do much for business resilience or leadership. Managers who use coercion spend more time looking for what is wrong instead of recognizing what is right.

✔ Behaviors like intimidation, bullying, and unrealistically high demands stifle initiative and create very passive employees, demotivated environments, and low morale.

✔ It isn't practical from a decision-making point of view — or too many other points of view — because the stress that comes in a command-and-control environment impedes effectiveness. In the worst cases, trauma is a possibility, which I explain further in Chapter 13.

✔ Learning comes to a grinding halt and skilled employees either disengage or leave. Decision-making is slowed down by bureaucracy and onerous levels of approval.

Don't get me wrong; command and control has its place in emergencies, but full-time management by command and control isn't warranted because every day at work isn't a life-threatening situation — at least not in the majority of workplaces.

Despite the fact that using a command-and-control style in today's decision-making environment isn't logical or rational, when uncertainty prevails, many managers revert to a command-and-control style primarily because it offers the illusion of being in control. Other companies use command and control even though they say they don't, but you can bet their employees notice the difference!

You can be in a position of authority and not use a command-and-control style, even in institutions — like those of the U.S. Armed Forces — that seem to be built on a high command-and-control structure. Consider, for example, David Marquet, a former naval officer, who describes how he accomplished sustained leadership and performance in his book *Turn the Ship Around!: A True Story of Turning Followers into Leaders* (Portfolio Hardcover [USA]). Ben Simonton, himself a former naval officer, describes developing self-sustaining leadership, capable of withstanding poor bosses in his book *Leading People to Be Highly Motivated and Committed* (Simonton Associates), which you can find on his website www.bensimonton.com. Both offer lessons in leading and decision-making for business decision-makers.

The unilateral approach: "I'll do it myself"

The unilateral approach stems from the belief that you either have the talent or you don't, so those who act unilaterally believe that their standards set the bar for what's expected. Managers using this style set high standards and expect people to meet or exceed them. Decisions are made without consultation, and employees have plenty of room to deliver . . . unless they fail to meet expectations.

This style works well when employees require little direction and are highly competent, and when cooperation and teamwork aren't required. However, it doesn't allow for professional development and is not flexible enough to adapt to a collaborative working environment.

Authentic approach: "Let's do this together!"

This style relies on effective communication of the vision, giving the team members the flexibility and freedom to accomplish the goal by applying their expertise and skills. Decisions are made using agreed-upon processes, including consensus. (You can read more about consensus in Chapter 11.)

Employees work together to support one another. The mix of experienced members and inexperienced employees is balanced as the members transfer necessary knowledge back and forth. Because this style creates an environment where consistency and trust are key parts of the working relationship, stability is created.

Dealing with unmet expectations

Sooner or later someone will deliver the opposite of what you expected or wanted. At these times, you can take one of two approaches: You can focus on deciding who's to blame, or you can focus on where the communication broke down.

Often, unmet expectations occur when a picture of the outcome you envision isn't showing up on the ScreenShare in the other person's mind. You have two opportunities to communicate expectations effectively: at the point of initial communication and after the miscommunication has taken place. Here are some pointers to 1) get it right the first time, and 2) correct any miscommunication that may have occurred:

✔ **When conveying expectations, explain what is needed and why, and how it will be used.** Here are some pointers:

   • **Provide details:** For example, "We need to make a presentation to a group of ten executives who respond better to visuals than to data. By the end of the presentation, those ten executives need to feel confident that the adjustment we're proposing meets their goals better than the previous version did."

   • **Communicate what you expect the results to look like and explain how this task contributes to the overall direction:** For example, if you're implementing a project and new information arises indicating that the options you've been exploring aren't appropriate, you pitch a change that allows preparation of several approaches simultaneously: "The purpose of the presentation is to gain approval from a client for an adjustment to a project that will cost them slightly more money but offer a better product."

✔ **When a miscommunication has taken place, put the problem in front of all parties.** Here are some suggestions to get the changes you need:

   • **Convey how work done so far meets your expectations and then ask for specific improvements:** For example, "We've met basic requirements. Now what can we do to exceed expectations?"

   • **Be aware of your emotions so that you can avoid an emotional outburst that's disguised as feedback.** Anger won't serve to improve the quality of the product or morale of your team. In fact, it's a way to regain control.

   • **Give all sides a chance to clear up any miscommunication.** Remember, the most important thing in dealing with unmet expectations is to respond and take time to be fair and to listen so that you can hear what lies at the heart of the matter.

These suggestions on how to communicate expectations effectively don't apply exclusively to professional relationships. When you figure this skill out, you'll improve your personal relationships as well. Consider that an added bonus!

Chapter 15

Making Decisions as an Entrepreneur or Small Business Owner

An entrepreneur can be anyone from a newly fledged solopreneur or a small business owner to a founder of a corporation. Some entrepreneurs specialize in start-up companies, leaving when the company moves to its next stage; others are turn-around specialists, taking failing companies and reversing their fortunes. Entrepreneurs who become small business owners work for themselves and accept risk and uncertainty in exchange for the freedom to chart their own and their companies' destinies.

In this chapter, I show you the types of decisions entrepreneurs regularly make. I also show those who've been entrepreneurs for awhile a way to recover the entrepreneurial direction and passion when it has flamed out. Because freedom allows you to reinvent yourself and your business at will, you'll want to revisit the points in this chapter more than once annually and multiple times over the life of your business.

Knowing What Makes You Tick

As an entrepreneur, you rely on yourself, your vision, and your decisions. Not all of your decisions will be good ones, but the mistakes provide invaluable experience and help you make better choices (go to Chapter 6 to find out how to use mistakes to improve). Despite all the support you'll receive (some dependable, some not so much), all the critics you'll hear (some very vocal, some less so), and all the advice you'll get (some lousy, some good), in the end, you have to defer to your own counsel. For that reason, your best allies are your self-knowledge, your team, and your willingness to make mistakes, learn, and move on. In this section, I explain how self-knowledge and reflection direct your choices.

Identifying your entrepreneurial qualities

As work environments fail to engage employees' creative aspirations, the numbers of entrepreneurs and small business owners are growing. If you're one of those moving from a secure position to start your own business, knowing what inner qualities you will rely on is helpful. Following are attributes and mindsets common to entrepreneurs; as you read the list, notice how many of these qualities you possess:

- Are highly self-reliant
- Are self-starters who take initiative, feel in control of their lives, and have a positive outlook
- Have high standards often coupled with a desire to make a difference
- Are visionary and forward-looking, and focus on success
- See opportunities where others see problems and take action
- Accept calculated risk in exchange for high reward and autonomy
- Remove barriers in the way of achieving their goals
- Are committed to success but, if their company is struggling, don't shy away from making hard decisions that enable them to change course
- Are comfortable with uncertainty
- Grow their company by remaining open-minded
- Are creative in taking ideas and applying them to meet a need or niche

In summary, these characteristics mark a "growth mindset" — one in which learning is found in every moment. The more of these attributes that ring regularly true for you, the better! In fact, place a check mark by the attributes you predominantly rely on. The list of your specific entrepreneurial attributes is important, as I explain in the next section.

The entrepreneurial mindset at work: Skype

The founders of Skype offer a good example of the entrepreneurial mindset at work. In 2001–2002, Swedish entrepreneurs Niklas Zennström and Danish Janus Friis were working on their second start-up, developing peer-to-peer technology software. They were working with Estonian engineers Ahti Heinla, Priit Kasesalu, and Jaan Tallinn. Long-distance charges were adding up due to the communication between Stockholm, Copenhagen, and Tallin, Estonia, sparking the thought that perhaps the technology they were developing was a potential solution. The magic "what if" question came: What if you could communicate over long distances between computers, handhelds, and other devices? They connected their need with their peer-to-peer technology software to meet an opportunity and — shazaam! — Skype was born.

The founders of Skype shared these entrepreneurial attributes: One, they were self-starters, and this was their second start-up (their first was Kazaa, a music-sharing platform). Two, they were visionaries; they could foresee a future in which computers were the vehicle for conversations worldwide. And three, they accepted a calculated risk and removed barriers to achieving their goals (investors wouldn't touch the idea).

In the first month of operation, Skype attracted a million users. Then investors began to call.

Gaining clarity on your values and philosophical foundations

Entrepreneurs rushing to get their companies off the ground often don't take the time to understand their values and business philosophy. Yet the entrepreneurs' core values and underlying beliefs form the philosophical foundations of the companies created. They also set up the decision-making environment and the nature of working relationships, as well as guide the development of *business systems,* the processes put in place to structure how work gets done, and the metrics by which outcomes and overall performance are tracked.

Understanding why values matter

Core values, or what is important and nonnegotiable, guide behavior and direct the tenor of relationships internally with employees or externally with customers and community. Knowing your values also provides focus when making decisions because it helps you ensure that what is important gets done. Examples of values include things like accountability to customers, responsibility for the natural resources used, and interaction with stakeholders.

When everyone in an organization knows and pays attention to the core values, the company can more readily adapt to business scenarios and growth in a way that aligns with those values, resulting in good things happening:

- **A company that thoughtfully chooses how things get done and aligns its actions with its values builds trust with employees and customers alike.** Research shows that companies that live by their values and don't abandon them when the going gets tough instill greater customer and employee loyalty and better employee morale. The biggest and most successful companies in the world — Novo Nordisk and Canon, for example — are value-based companies.

- **Being aware and able to intentionally apply values to direct action puts your company ahead of the competition.** Novo Nordisk's total return to investors over the past 20 years has been more than 3,700 percent. To see the performance of other companies operating from vision and core values, visit `http://www.lampindex.com/2011/10/house-of-futures-talk-copenhagen-denmark/`.

Conversely, if these core values are never articulated or are forgotten, then habits based on past beliefs take over decision-making. Bottom line: Core values are the bedrock of any successful company, even more so when employed for decision-making. Integrity builds trustworthiness, and a trustworthy business can attract and keep high-value talent and loyal customers. It is a ripple effect. You can read more about values-based decision-making in Chapter 5.

Taking a closer look at your core beliefs

Beliefs serve to filter new information into two categories: First, does it confirm what I already know? and second, does it challenge what I think I know? Consequently they can work for you or against you, as happens when you reject new information that challenges what's worked in the past. Beliefs also drive behavior in the workplace. They can limit or free performance. Examples of beliefs include the following:

"The sole purpose of a company is to make a profit. Nothing else matters."

"Employees are not to be trusted. They have to be told."

"We trust our employees and expect them to be leaders."

The first two beliefs are limiting, stifle creativity and independent thinking, and foster bad feelings. The third is empowering.

Your core beliefs dictate the kinds of risks you leave yourself vulnerable to. For example, companies that believe in making a profit at any cost often use fear, coercion, and intimidation to reach their goals. Because profit is the key objective, they overlook other important considerations and, as a result, make themselves vulnerable to ethical breaches (opting to not recall cars with faulty ignition switches, for example, because of the cost associated with doing so).

In addition, your beliefs about how to get the results you want also impact which metrics you use to evaluate success, which has its own consequences, both intended and unintended. Companies may end up making decisions that save money in the short term but cost even more in the end. Companies that buy into the "make a profit at any cost" idea create higher numbers of stress-related illness, weaker performance, and poorer relationships with customers. They also make less money, because their penny-pinching decisions end up inadvertently increasing costs.

Infusionsoft, a company specializing in small business marketing, believes in people and their dreams, so it created a Dream Manager position — a dream job, don't you think? The Dream Manager is responsible for personally coaching people who have a dream they want to put into reality. Because Infusionsoft believes in people and their dreams, they help them make their dreams a reality.

From Flying by the Seat of Your Pants to Putting Systems in Place

In the initial stages of getting your company started, you have to juggle a lot of balls: securing financing, designing marketing campaigns, increasing sales, building client relations, taking care of bookkeeping and accounting tasks . . . in short, doing the work of a team, with each task requiring its own expertise. As an entrepreneur in start-up mode, your time is precious, and you can either drown in all the jobs that are required to build a business, or you can take the steps necessary to see your business through its early-stage growth and onto solid footing. In this section, I give you a strategy for putting together your team, explain how to build processes for getting work done, and share why you must always be aware of your decision-making process.

The biggest risk for entrepreneurs? Not being able to switch from working *in* their businesses, totally preoccupied with the day-to-day operations and administration, to working *on their* businesses, making the higher-level, strategic decisions. A key component for making this transition is delegating and outsourcing those tasks that they don't need to do in order to free their time doing what they do best. One book that has helped many an entrepreneur get off the hamster wheel is *The E-Myth Revisited: Why Most Small Businesses Don't Work and What to Do About It,* by Michael Gerber (HarperCollins). By working on your business, seeing it from a higher vantage point, you can achieve more prosperity. In the end, according to Virgin Group's Richard Branson, entrepreneurs at the top of their game make three to four game-changing decisions in a year. The rest are handled by their teams.

Moving from multitasking to building a team

When you go from multitasking — performing most of the functions of the business by yourself — to building a team, you need to decide which functions to delegate or outsource. To gain clarity on what to delegate, begin by separating what you can do from what you *need* to do for the company to succeed. Work through the following steps to discover which functions you want to keep as part of your workflow and which functions you need to outsource or delegate to existing team members:

1. **List the job functions that are required in operating your business and delivering products or services.**

   This list typically includes basic functions such as marketing/sales, customer service, distribution, finance, and legal. The actual tasks associated with each of these functional areas depend on the nature of your business. If your business is in food service or manufacturing, your list will include more areas.

2. **Identify the functions in Step 1 that can be outsourced or automated.**

   Tasks that are good candidates for outsourcing or automation have these characteristics:

   - They distract you from making strategic decisions or delivering the higher value services.

   - Someone else can do them better and cheaper (in terms of the value of your time) than you can.

   - They are tasks you aren't particularly good at or don't want to learn.

At this point, you know which tasks you want to keep doing and which you want to give to others. When you distribute tasks, be sure to match the function to the team member's strength. If, during your assessment of your existing employees' strengths, you discover gaps such that your existing team is unable to perform some of the functions, you have decisions to make: Do you put these tasks back on your plate, train existing staff, or hire or contract to fill the gaps?

Deciding how work gets done

How will work get done in your company? That question is one you need to address throughout the various stages of your company's growth. In answering that question, you also decide what kind of owner/manager you want to be: the one who retains all decision-making power him- or herself; the one who promotes a self-organizing approach, where everyone contributes; or something in between. How do you plan to organize your business as you grow: Will you let your company fall into the traditional hierarchical structure when it reaches 50 employees, or will you look at alternatives more aligned with your values or the need to stay agile?

The first question (how will work get done?) largely depends on the answer to the second question (what kind of organizational structure do you envision?) In the following list, I outline the most common ways work is organized now:

- In family-run or small businesses, the owner makes the strategic decisions, confers one-on-one with key staff to gain input, and then calls the shots alone or with the counsel of a trusted employee or family member. Work is organized by function, but because no formal systems are generally in place, this organizational structure can feel a bit chaotic and dysfunctional. Adding formalized systems brings efficiencies.

- In medium-sized to large companies, roles and responsibilities are standardized and codified. Decision-making is either centralized at the top or distributed throughout the levels of authority. These businesses generally end up somewhat bureaucratic because they tend to adopt the traditional approach to organizing as they grow.

- Flat organizations are characterized by high levels of autonomy and personal responsibility. Centralized administrative functions provide core support, and decision-making is intentionally structured to fit the importance of what is being decided.

- Virtual communities of practice (groups of people who share a craft and/ or a profession) take a few forms: In one version, the entire company is a network of professionals from different specialties who are united by shared values or shared economic interest. These groups team up on specific projects to serve a wider clientele. Building strength through diversity can also be achieved through joint ventures or strategic alliances between two companies, which I discuss in Chapter 18. A third form is cooperative collaboration between two or more professionals working remotely for a specified time to develop and market a product. As tools for remote collaboration become increasingly available, the ways you can work together is limited only by imagination.

Decentralized decision-making is far more agile than centralized decision-making, and companies of any size can adopt decentralized decision-making. To make the decentralized structure work, you must cultivate leadership at every level, creating *intrapreneurs,* employees who embrace an entrepreneurial mindset even as they work within a formal community. In his book *Wiki Management: A Revolutionary New Model for a Rapidly Changing and Collaborative World* (AMACON), Rod Collins describes how progressive companies are applying this knowledge to stay adaptive. Find out more at http://www.optimityadvisors.com/WikiManagement/

Staying aware of your decision-making process

Starting up a company is one challenge. Keeping it going is another. Unfortunately, few entrepreneurs pay attention to how they make decisions. They wing it — and that drives failure. How can you avoid being a failure? Make your decisions conscious and intentional. For instance, instead of thinking you'll succeed when you have more employees, you may decide to limit growth and retain flexibility. A few of the factors that contribute to failure include those I discuss in the next sections (there are many others, however).

Start-up companies have a high failure rate. Over 90 percent of tech start-ups fail; that percentage is slightly less for companies in other industries.

Running out of cash

As I mention in Chapter 10, managing cash flow is pivotal to successfully starting, growing, or running your business. Start-ups invariably focus on generating revenue instead of creating value to the customer; consequently, they can run out of cash too soon.

Sometimes, you have to spend money, and sometimes you have to conserve. When you're in the midst of developing a product and it isn't ready, be frugal. When you're ready to grow, you may find that spending should exceed your revenue. Pedal to the metal to ramp up growth! Treading lightly is best in early-stage development when you still have barriers to overcome and don't have a prototype. After customers confirm that your business model is sound, you can accelerate to achieve growth. If you're used to being conservative, making the shift will be based on an inner sense of timing (gut feel). Head to Chapter 7 for more on how intuition can guide decisions, especially ones that are made in gray areas.

Having loads of money doesn't guarantee success, either. In fact, companies with too much money and not enough management experience can burn through their cash before having their product ready. Often, the companies that are better positioned to scale up growth at a sustainable rate are those that have been forced to bootstrap their finances, using available resources.

Inadequate management skills

Great products alone are not enough to make a business successful. To grow, your company needs great talent and business management skills, too. Companies — even ones with great potential — can sink if they don't start with or are not willing to develop good business skills. Common and costly mistakes that weak teams make include accepting advice from family, underestimating the time and effort required to bring a product to market or to grow a business, expanding too quickly, miscalculating finances, and more.

You can avoid these problems if you have a good team in place, know that you can trust your own instincts, and have taken the time on the front end to plan. You can also seek out a mentor whenever you need advice.

Being too attached to your idea, business model, or company

So what's wrong with being attached to your company or idea? Nothing, provided that you don't fall into these two traps:

- ✔ **You know you have a great idea, so you proceed, assuming that all you have to do is build your product, and your market will materialize.** Well, maybe and maybe not. Your potential customers may not think your idea is as brilliant as you think it is. In fact, they may not be interested at all, they may want it delivered in a format you haven't considered, or they may be just fine with their current solution (even though it doesn't have the bells and whistles yours has). Maybe your great idea really is great, but it may be ahead of its time. If you discover that gaining and keeping customers costs more than you make from their purchases, you'll run into cash-flow problems.

  Doing comprehensive market research can avert a fall. Ask your target market what they'll invest in and why they'd part with their money. How do they make their buying decisions? The core criteria: Focus on your customers. Empathize with your customers so that you can connect your product or service to their needs. The empathy map in Chapter 12 is a useful guide.

- ✔ **You're so attached to your product, business model, or company that you fail to see the signs that the market is changing and hang on to your baby too long.** The result? Your window of opportunity to close the deal or sell your business evaporates, leaving you no other option but to close your doors.

Thinking about closing or selling your business is hard. Perhaps you still feel passionate about what you do. Or maybe you care about and feel loyalty toward your team, which created your company's value. Your decision relies on your intuition — a sense of knowing whether you've achieved what you set out to achieve and whether the time has come to let go — and understanding the market trends for your product or service, as well as the personal and business considerations that are unique to your situation. Keep in mind, however, that selling may not be the only option. Other approaches may help you achieve your longer term goal.

Taking Steps When the Thrill is Gone

Every business has its own life cycle, and every owner has a life. As an entrepreneur, you dedicate your passion, drive, vision, commitment, and hard work to getting your company off the ground and onto solid footing. But suppose that the passion you felt for your company has waned, or suppose that the creativity that was inherent in your decision-making has given way to crisis decision-making that takes so much of your time that you're neglecting the important people in your life.

Being an entrepreneur isn't for everyone. Reaching pivotal points in your life or your business gives you the opportunity to go in new directions, professionally and personally. Maybe you want to revamp or reinvent your company. Maybe you want to reinvent yourself! Reclaiming your passion calls for a detached review on where you are in your life and where you see your business heading. In this section, I tell you how to decide where to head next.

Step 1: Figuring out what you want

What do you want to do: Retire? Take a serious timeout to live life? Start another business or become an employee again? To find out, the first steps is to observe, without coming to any conclusion, what is going on in the world around you and what you want in your life. Sometimes recording your feelings and ideas helps you clear away the chatter so that you can more clearly see your options. Follow these steps:

1. **Reflect on what you want for yourself and the business.**

   This step involves a bit of soul searching and realizing where your priorities lie. You may write down, "Personally, I want to be an involved parent and spouse and to feel that I am contributing meaningfully to my community. I want my business to be able to grow in value but not at the cost of my quality of life."

2. **Ask yourself, "Have I met the goals I set for myself and for the company?"**

   This step takes more than a yes or no answer. List your accomplishments so that you can focus on what you want to move toward rather than what you want to move away from. If you're tired, for example, and you only focus on how to escape fatigue rather than focusing on your accomplishments, you may move to a different location (a beach perhaps), but that change won't illuminate the path to your passion. Direction and energy surface when you acknowledge the value your experience has given you. So celebrate your gains in experience, in accomplishment, and in your decision-making!

3. **List your personal goals and decide whether you've met them.**

   For example, you may list that you've taken the business to the place where it's ready for the next growth stage and have done so while maintaining your personal relationships, health, or fitness. Counting your wins helps you gain perspective on what you've achieved.

Step 2: Ascertaining where your business is

After you determine what you want, the next step is to ascertain where your business is and to figure out what you want for it. This evaluation helps you determine whether you or your business is at a crossroad. Here are a few scenarios to consider:

✔ **Your company is growing fast, and to go to the next level, it needs a cash infusion and expertise that you don't have.** If this scenario describes your business, you have to decide if you want to bring in business partners that have the capital and expertise you lack, sell to a company that can bring in the needed cash and expertise, or hire professional business managers who can take it to the next level. The first two options often mean that you must give up control and some ownership.

   Lay out your options and then reflect, being sure to give yourself enough time to see what makes sense. Also, try looking at the situation from a different perspective. If a CEO from outside your company were to walk through the door or if you hired a new CEO, what decision would that person see and what decision would she likely make?

✔ **Your company is running itself (or it could run itself).** If your company is humming along and you want to do something else, you may decide to transition out of the business. If so, what is the best way? Should you sell the business outright, or should you delegate your responsibilities to others so that you can be an evangelist, promoting your brand from the outside?

When deciding what role you want to play in the company, go back to your earlier reflection about what you want for your life and what gives you energy (refer to the preceding section). If your vision and passion are not aligned with what you are currently doing, then do something different. The beauty of being an entrepreneur is that you are in charge and get to decide.

✔ **Your business is struggling because market conditions have changed and your company's value offered to customers is no longer viable.** If this is the case, you could reinvent it so that, like a phoenix, it can rise from the ashes, or you can shut it down.

MySpace started before Facebook. It's an example of a company that had a great idea — social networking for entertainment and music fans — that went slightly sideways. A combination of strategic errors accompanied by the emergence of Facebook hindered MySpace's ability to adjust features to improve the customer experience, resulting in ultimate failure to meet expectations. After reinventing itself, in 2013, Justin Timberlake, who holds a stake in the new version, announced the new MySpace as a streaming music player, claiming a different niche in the marketplace.

Key questions when you still can't decide

Still not clear on which way to proceed? Don't give up. Ask yourself these questions:

✔ **Do I feel pulled in a hundred directions? Am I constantly reacting to crisis? If so, what am I doing to create that situation?** The answer to these questions helps you change how you lead yourself. Maybe you love crisis. Thriving on crisis is one way to feel alive and vibrant, but it isn't a good way to make sound decisions. Moving from crisis to a more aware state reduces stress and creates a better environment for decision-making. If you really need the adrenaline rush, consider making a swap: Instead of operating from crisis mode, try bungee jumping!

✔ **What business decisions lie ahead? Are the options clear? Do I have clear feelings about them?** Doubt, fear, and confusion are simply signals to pull back and gain altitude (say, high enough to see the planet) so you can recognize what is important to you in the short and long terms. Then decide which road to travel. Otherwise, you'll be tempted to administer to emotional needs without gaining perspective on the consequences. I've worked with lots of business owners who wanted to sell because they were tired and wanted more time to do what mattered to them. The future of these businesses was entangled with their owners' personal desires. Stepping back allows you to sort out what's motivating a decision so that you can gain clarity and see more options.

Part V
Applying Decision-Making Skills to Specific Challenges

Five Insights into Ethical Decision-Making in Business

- ✔ Publicly traded companies that embed care and compassion for life (people and planet) in their cultural DNA far outperform their peers.

- ✔ Companies that offer a great place to work and employ an engaging management style experience fewer to no ethical breaches.

- ✔ Ethical decision-making is about creating shared value for the greater good in the present and future, and values-based decision-making puts companies in the driver's seat, pointed to the future.

- ✔ Companies most vulnerable to ethical breaches directly or indirectly send the message that their primary goal is to make money at any cost. Such a message implies that unethical behavior is permitted or ignored if it increases profit. Remember, people trust in what you do. If your company's actions are unethical, then the message to staff is that unethical behavior is okay.

- ✔ Transparency and open flow of information keep communication honest and open, and support ethical decisions and behaviors. Decentralizing decision-making to employees provides autonomy and creates an environment that supports timely decisions and learning. Loyalty is built into trust.

To discover ways that managers and executives can work together to transform a business's capacity for innovation, head to `http://www.dummies.com/extras/decisionmaking`.

In this part . . .

- ✔ Achieve personal fulfillment as a part of improving your decision-making proficiency

- ✔ Discover how to get people engaged and involved in participatory decision-making

- ✔ Learn the fundamental decision-making criteria for entering a partnership or joint venture

- ✔ Design formal and informal standards to increase the ethical integrity of your company and employees

Chapter 16

Using Change to Achieve Personal Fulfillment

....

In This Chapter

▶ Managing your personal life through unexpected interruptions

▶ Reinventing yourself after things go sideways

▶ Finding your passion and purpose

▶ Moving toward a fulfilling life

....

*J*ust as global changes help businesses step back and take stock of their practices, unexpected interruptions to personal lives — job or financial losses, self-sabotage, and professional decisions you regret, for example — give people opportunities to make decisions that can lead toward more fulfilling lives! This chapter helps you become more self-aware so that you can make better decisions, strengthen your character, and discover how to benefit from all your life experiences, both good and bad. I show you how to gain clarity on your personal direction, introduce some tips on reinventing yourself, and explain how to bounce back and integrate leadership lessons learned through your past mistakes and successes.

Reinventing Yourself after a Setback

People work hard to attain the lifestyle of their choice and to enjoy the luxuries in life. But sometimes the best-laid career plans go awry, and your once-comfortable existence is disrupted. When the rug gets pulled out from under you, when the job you hated — or loved — is gone, when your retirement savings evaporates or you lose your house, you need to bounce forward.

These events, as upsetting as they are, give you the opportunity to reexamine who you are and what you want from life. When Murphy rears his ugly head and lays waste to your career plans, regroup and choose the new life you want. Although you may dread the idea of having change thrust upon you, sometimes losing the security of a job or money or even a relationship may be the best thing that could happen. The challenge is figuring out how you can gain the most from the situation.

Changing your mindset after a setback

Several sparks, such as the following, can ignite a personal reboot. In this list, I explain how some mindsets can thwart your chances of making a fresh start and what you can do about them:

- ✔ **Losing the job you counted on for financial security:** Losing a job can equate to losing your identity. But you are not your job! You have many talents and only exercise a few of them in each situation you're in. Recognize the loss of a job as an opportunity to switch direction and explore new avenues for your talents. To find out how to identify the direction you want to go, head to the next section.

  A professional I volunteered with was a bank manager whose career path was a bit unconventional. Before becoming a bank manager, he'd gone from being a waiter to a taxi driver to a commercial airline pilot. He chose his career path. You can, too.

- ✔ **Losing your savings and investments, your home, or other possessions that give you a sense of security:** Life gets complicated when you have too much stuff. By "too much stuff," I mean too many material possessions. Most people have much more stuff than they actually need to survive and feel happy. Losing it all is a chance to get down to basics, simplify your life, and clear the clutter so that you can feel true happiness. (Of course, you don't have to wait for a personal crisis to simplify; it just speeds up the process.)

- ✔ **Losing a key relationship:** If you rely on someone else for emotional or financial security, that support may evaporate if the relationship ends. But you don't need the dynamic of a relationship to define you or your role; you can define it for yourself. When you lose a key relationship, you have the chance to reconnect to more of what makes you feel inwardly secure. A huge sense of creative freedom results from seizing the moment.

- ✔ **Losing the sense of satisfaction or challenge you used to feel in your current role:** Rather than staying in a position that is unfulfilling (and running the risk of becoming cynical or burned out), consider making a change. People often change jobs or careers because they want to develop themselves and discover what else they are capable of. Some even reinvent themselves.

When the economy is failing and the markets falter, you might stay in a job you hate because you feel you have no other choice and are trapped. Doing so has a cost. When you aren't happy, your personal and professional relationships suffer.

Unexpected change can break routine patterns and toss everything up in the air for reexamination. Stepping beyond your safety net to explore your potential takes courage and self-leadership. As new possibilities emerge, you'll see that there are no real barriers to what is possible, other than your imagination and willingness to take initiative.

Taking the first steps to a new future

So what can you do when your world is turned topsy-turvy and change is imminent? Try the following for starters:

- **Reflect on what gives you joy to find your true passion.** Do you possess some skill or talent you haven't truly developed? Is there an activity you love to do and do well but haven't cultivated? Uncovering the dreams and passions you've set aside over the years helps guide you to the next step. Just remember to keep your options open until the path is clearer.

  If you think that success means accumulating material possessions, reflection gives you a chance to redefine what success means to you. Maybe it isn't having the most expensive car in the neighborhood but spending quality time with people you care about or doing the things you enjoy. Remember, when you reinvent yourself, all aspects of your life are on the table, and you get to decide which ones to pick up again and which ones to leave behind.

- **Pay attention to what excites you.** Doing so is a way to separate the things you routinely do from the things that keep your batteries fully charged. Activities, situations, other people, or inner doubts that deplete your energy aren't helpful. Focus on what makes you feel vibrant and alive: Is it when you're creating new ideas or when you're taking action, for example? Then make sure you incorporate the thing that energizes you as a necessary criterion, whether you create your own work or select a company to work for.

- **Identify what you have to offer: expertise, character, or aptitude, for example.** You posses unique talents that you can use to begin a new career or carve out a new niche in your current profession.

- **Think of reasons, beyond obligation, for why you do what you do.** To insert fun and pleasure back in, take the same activity and adopt a more positive outlook. Try to separate the obligation part ("I have to create this report because my boss says so") from the fun part ("I can use my creativity to graphically represent data").

✔ **Think about what gives you a sense of purpose — what wakes you up every morning feeling excited about the day.** Gain a clear picture of what difference you make through your contribution to the world. I offer a visual tool in the next section. Moving from the fuzzy zone of not knowing what to do next to a more concrete sense of what matters can guide your decisions.

✔ **Monitor doubts or fears you may have.** When you move into an unfamiliar place, accept fear and doubt as part of the process. Think to yourself, "I'm ready to leave the shore to discover what else I am capable of." Just keep ahold of the steering wheel and don't allow panic to take over. If you decide to maintain the status quo, make sure you're not doing so because you're afraid.

Gaining Clarity on Your Passion, Purpose, and Direction

When you're in the area between where you've been and where you want to be, you may feel like you're in the middle of nowhere without a map to guide you. Fortunately, tools are available that can help you access and discover the things that matter for you and your life. Gaining awareness about the things you feel passionate about, the meaning you want your life to have, and the direction you want to go enables you to make your decisions with a renewed sense of clarity. In this section, you discover how to use your innate knowledge to call forth what, in the hustle and bustle of your current situation, you can't see.

Using a vision board to gain clarity

The easiest tool to use for visually and intuitively tapping into hidden desires is a vision board. A vision board holds a variety of images that you select and present as a collage; however, there is a key difference. In typical collages — at least the ones you probably did in school — you know exactly what meaning you want the board to represent, and you carefully select images to represent that meaning. With a vision board, you begin with a very general idea — "What success means to me," for example — that you don't give too much thought to and then you select images, including any image that speaks to you.

What you end up with may be a hodge-podge of images, but therein lies the beauty — and effectiveness — of the image board: You selected those images for a reason, even if the reason wasn't one you were consciously aware of. Uncovering those reasons leads you to self-discovery. You may think, for example, that success is having a big house, a fancy car, and a high-powered position. But if your image board is full of sunny meadows and smiling families, you've just discovered something very important.

In short, images make meaning, meaning informs purpose, and purpose activates energy. Without an inspiring vision, ideas sit there, inactive and unimplemented. The vision board can help you discover and then move toward your real passions.

Creating a vision board

To create a vision board, follow these steps.

1. **Gather the raw material for your personal vision board from the following sources:**

   - At least 15 old magazines, the more variety, the better. (I raid recycling bins.)

   - Scissors and glue

   - A 2-x-3-foot Bristol board or poster

   - A notepad and pen

2. **Find a workspace in which to create your vision board.**

   A flat surface big enough for the Bristol board and other supplies helps. Make sure you have enough room to move freely as you create your board.

3. **Ask a question you don't have a fast answer to.**

   You can do this in your mind, but write it down if necessary. For example, "What is my passion?" or "What is my purpose?"

   Ask only one question. The single question gives focus to your creativity and intuition. If you ask more than one question, you send out mixed signals. After you identify the question, forget about it. Put it in the background and turn to your pile of magazines.

4. **From the magazines, pull out any images that appeal to you and place them in a pile.**

   Collect from 15 to 30 images. Two doesn't cut it. You need enough variety to allow you to filter through and get down to a few images that speak most loudly to you. Just yank the image out and add it to the pile.

   Don't think, don't think, don't think. Don't analyze whether an image answers your question or wonder why you chose one over another. You're just yanking out and piling up images. If you think about every image you select, you'll likely blow a brain fuse or get a headache. Put the analytical mind into neutral. Don't think. Act on impulse.

5. **After you select the images, go through your pile and choose the one core image that says it all; place this image in the center of the Bristol board (but don't glue it down yet).**

6. **Go back through the pile, select other images that speak to you, and place them around the central picture.**

   Basically, you're creating a short list of qualified images that complement the core image you chose in Step 5.

7. **Arrange the images and, when you're happy with the layout, glue them down.**

   Your vision board is created. The core image is the central idea. The other images serve to complement that idea.

8. **Post the vision board on a wall and walk away.**

   Take time out so that you can gain some distance and a fresh perspective before you interpret the result. Taking a break inserts distance between you and what you've done so that when you look at it again, you can better see what the images say or represent. That's the next step.

Interpreting your vision board

The next day, or after you've taken some time away from your vision board, you can interpret what the board means. As you stand back and observe your vision board, follow these steps to gain some insights:

1. **Jot down words that come to mind and see how they answer the original question symbolically.**

   Look at the images to see what the combined visual represents. You'll see a thread surface from the images that addresses your initial question. For example, images showing patterns, colors, and shapes may suggest a predilection for designing spaces to evoke a feeling.

   Images are symbolic; therefore, the interpretation is more intuitive than representative of the actual pictures. For instance, if you have a lot of pictures of fast cars, it doesn't necessarily mean you want a fast car or you like fast cars. Perhaps the cars represent you: One possible interpretation is that you love fast-moving environments or love being mobile.

2. **Connect the impressions gained from the vision board to the original question you asked before starting.**

   Summarize the ideas as they arise. You should be able to identify qualities you value or things you care about that the analytical mind just can't serve up. For example, if you asked about purpose, then you'll gain a picture of how you can contribute to the workplace. If you asked about passion, then use that information to guide your choice of career or to identify your direction. Using the example from earlier, a passion for mobility and fast-paced situations may point to a passion for fast-moving working environments, such as start-up or design, where you can help put things on the ground.

If you find yourself staring blankly, ask your kids (or a friend's kids) for their take. Be ready to receive anything, including wisdom. Kids are often more in touch with their creative side and may see things that adults pay little attention to. Add input from peers, friends, or colleagues, too. You're looking for fresh perspectives that offer a view you may not have seen yourself.

Testing your commitment to a decision: Visualization

The decisions that lead to fulfillment are guided by your heart's intelligence, not your mental will. The rational mind is in charge of getting things done, but the heart provides the energy. Consider the many good ideas that didn't engage your passion or purpose or that had little meaning for you. When your heart is inspired, you become committed to your decisions, and doing so really helps reignite your life.

Suppose, for example, that you're thinking of going back to school. You know the idea makes sense rationally, but you're still not sure whether it's the right decision for you. To test your commitment to a decision, follow these steps:

1. **Visualize the action (or outcome of the decision) as if it were a reality.**

   Picture yourself in the situation. In the going-back-to-school example, picture yourself studying, attending classes, and learning new material.

2. **Observe your reactions to what you visualize.**

   This question isn't about what you think; it's about how you feel, which tells you everything. Do you feel energized, excited, scared, exhausted, or overwhelmed when you picture yourself in a lecture hall, taking notes? If you feel disheartened, it may not be the right decision. Feeling both excited and scared is likely a good thing because it suggests you're heading outside your comfort zone but see doing so as an adventure. You're right. It is!

Assessing commitment doesn't come from the head; it comes from the heart. If your heart isn't into it, nothing will happen. Anything you do will feel like pushing rope uphill.

Going my way? Choosing your path

Desperation leads to poor choices, and poor choices are subject to failure. Leaving a situation, like a career or job, before you understand (or even appreciate) what you've learned and gained from the experience is essentially the same as running from yourself. Unless you realize what made the situation intolerable or why your interest lagged, choosing wisely the next time will be more difficult. Although you may feel compelled to accept any job to meet financial pressures, that approach typically backfires because the job won't last.

To choose what you want rather than what you're used to, you must have a clear vision of where you want to be. Imagine your future as if you have already achieved it. That way, instead of moving away from a bad situation, you will be intentionally choosing to move toward a better one. The distinction lies in knowing what you want rather than focusing on what you don't want.

To gain clarity on what you really want, follow these steps:

1. **Draw a big circle on a piece of paper.**

   Leave some room on the outside of the circle.

2. **Inside the circle, list the things you want in your life.**

   Here, you define the supportive environment you want to create. Include the following:

   • **The kind of people and experiences you want in your life:** You may say, for example, that you want to associate with positive, energetic, affirming, and honest people.

   • **The kind of work you want to do:** Name the kind of work that combines what you know you can do plus invites you into unfamiliar territory — for example, work that marries your love for food with your expertise with chemistry.

   • **How you feel about your work:** You may say, for instance, that you want energizing, creative work where you feel your talents are being used and developed.

   If you don't have a positive and clear sense of what you want, you're less likely to make decisions that will attract a new and fresh reality to you.

3. **Outside of the circle, name the things you want to keep out of your circle or leave behind.**

   The things you want to keep out of your circle, for example, may be negativity and feeling like the life has been sucked out of you at the end of the day. Maybe you want to leave behind work that made you feel safe but unfulfilled.

   Be absolutely ruthless in this exercise. Your goal is to keep within the circle what you want to create and leave outside the circle of your new reality anything that doesn't support it. Then align your decisions with what you want.

4. **Apply what you've learned to decision-making.**

   Apply the new awareness you gained from Step 3 when you make your decision. Clearly, that means having a level of commitment and sometimes courage to, for example, not accept a job that meets the need for financial security but fails on the workplace criteria. It also means taking time to ask questions to find out how well people work together in a company you're considering.

As you make changes, train your mind to stay positive or, if not positive, at least neutral. Clear your emotional issues out, and drop all sarcasm. Forgive those who have wronged you so that you can set yourself free to attract what you want.

Your life is no accident. Many of the choices you make are subconscious, the result of deeper beliefs you may not even be aware of. For example, perhaps you see yourself as a victim and your decisions tend to reinforce the idea that you aren't in control — or responsible. Or maybe you see yourself as invincible (or infallible) and immune from making mistakes, in which case you overlook opportunities to learn. Reclaim the driver's seat for your own life; otherwise, you'll be taken for a ride, with no clear direction or sense of purpose. Choose what you want. Intentionally.

Strengthening Your Resiliency

A lot of things compete for your time, and the many demands can pull you in many directions. In this environment, it's easy to lose balance, feel depleted, or believe that nothing is happening despite your efforts. In this section, I offer a couple of tools that help you identify what you are actually focused on so that you can gain greater confidence, even when you're in the midst of chaos.

Assessing the state of your personal spirit

Mention the word *spirit,* and people assume you're talking about ghosts or religion. Although they are certainly interesting, this section isn't about either of those topics. Here, I discuss the kind of spirit that is the fuel that powers achievement in personal lives and in companies. Spirit in the workplace drives performance and inspires the energy needed to overcome challenges.

Research conducted by Kaizen Solutions (`http://www.kaizensolutions.org/researchdetails.htm-saws`) defines spirit at work as work that is engaging intellectually and emotionally, a sense of connection to something bigger than oneself, a sense of community and connection to shared purpose accompanied by joy or vitality. Companies with a strong workplace spirit benefit from highly engaged employees, higher performing teams, higher overall focus on company goals, and low employee turnover, for example.

In this section, I tell you how to check in on your spirit. A variety of assessment instruments are also available that you can use to take a personal assessment of your spirit. Here are just a few:

- ✔ **OneSmartWorld:** OneSmartWorld (`http://www.OneSmartWorld.com`) provides personal assessment and insight. Check out this blog post for more details: `http://www.onesmartworld.com/content/blog-x-factor-personal-spirit`.

- ✔ **Barrett Values Centre:** The Centre offers both a personal assessment (`http://www.valuescentre.com/pva/`) and more comprehensive assessments designed for companies (`http://www.valuescentre.com`). Using the company assessment, you can discover things like where your company wastes energy in dealing with interpersonal issues; whether it has too many systems, processes, and procedures that act as barriers to getting things done and that stop people from using their creativity; and so on.

Checking in on the three pillars

To run a health check on your spirit, you need to perform regular check-ins on three primary pillars: your *sense of control* (whether you feel free to spend your personal time or have control over how you do your work), *initiative* (whether you feel you can take risk and take charge), and *outlook* (whether your mental attitude and view of life is positive or negative). These three pillars apply not only to your personal life, but they are also mirrored in company performance and workplace health.

You can determine where you stand with each pillar by answering the following questions:

- ✔ **Sense of control — How much control do you feel you have to set direction and make decisions that directly affect your well-being?** Your answers tell you how much freedom you feel you have to direct your working or home life in a way that is fulfilling. If you feel you have no control, chances are your well-being is low. Conversely, feeling you have a high level of control corresponds with high sense of well-being. Moving from low to high may mean removing yourself from a depleting work environment or changing your outlook on the situation.

- ✔ **Initiative — Are you a self-starter, or do you need to be told what to do before you take action?** The answer to this question determines whether you need a push to get going or are comfortable taking action on your own. In a workplace setting, you're more willing to take initiative when you know that failure is considered part of the learning process or when you feel you can take charge and have a high likelihood of success. If you need to be told, chances are the workplace rewards being told, so moving to a "take action" mode requires that you see yourself as bringing value, creative ideas, or a strong contribution to the situation.

> ✔ **Outlook** — Do you see your glass as being perpetually half empty or half full? Does everything seemed doomed to failure, or are negatives just opportunities for action? If you hold a dismal view of everything, change your attitude, and you'll change your life. Outlook, when applied to decision-making, is the difference between seeing risk as an opportunity to innovate or a danger to avoid.

Using the personal spirit self-assessment form

To conduct a self-assessment, use the form in Table 16-1. In each row, choose the description that best fits. At the top of each column, you find a point value. To tabulate your results, note the point values for each of your answers and add them up.

Table 16-1	Personal Spirit Self-Assessment Questionnaire				
Category	*1*	*2*	*3*	*4*	*5*
Sense of Control	Things happen to me; I have zero control.	If only someone would save me!	Hmm . . . no one is coming. I might have to save myself.	My life is improving one decision at a time.	Everything is an opportunity — I have the power to decide.
Initiative	My get up and go got up and went. It's tough to get out of bed in the morning. Give me a reason.	If only someone would tell me what to do next. Although on Tuesday, I did do something that went well.	Good idea. Might lie down to see if the feeling passes . . . unless . . . hey, this could be interesting!	For every door that closes, another one opens, most days. I wonder what's behind that one?	Wahoo! Now I can do what I've always wanted to do. Life is a grand adventure.
Outlook on life	Life sucks. I've been given a bowl of lemons.	It's too big, overwhelming, unmanageable, impossible, hard.	I will give it a shot, but there's a chance the sky might fall on me . . . or maybe not.	Lemons make great lemonade.	Everything I experience has value. I can hardly wait to see what happens next!

After you complete the assessment, tally your total points and refer to the following list for an interpretation:

- ✔ **3–6 points: Your personal spirit needs strengthening!** Work on changing your thinking to focus on what you want rather than what you don't want. Doing so will shift your perspective to a more positive outlook. To bolster your initiative, at the end of each day, give yourself credit for what you've accomplished. If you strengthen your internal foundation, you can create a positive change in your life. Study ways to improve your self-esteem.

- ✔ **7–12 points: Your personal spirit is on the cusp of taking charge.** Make sure you focus on the positive and notice where you're inclined to drift back to old habits. Surround yourself with people who care about you and see you at your best and highest potential. Keep building your inner strength and momentum.

- ✔ **12–15 points: Your personal spirit is strong.** Stay focused on meeting people who share similar values and who challenge you to think differently. Select work or workplaces where you feel you bring value and where you feel valued. You've got a lot of options available to you because you are connected to the greatest fuel of all . . . yourself!

Applying the results in your professional and personal life

Use this assessment to gain insight into where to strengthen your personal spirit to be flexible with what happens unexpectedly or to change how you experience life. Here are some ideas to help you gain insight on how your personal spirit affects your work and what you can do about it:

- ✔ **Monitor your own and workplace talk.** If, after monitoring workplace talk, you discover it to be persistently negative, gossipy, and backstabbing, and you are an active participant, change the pattern. If you feel you need to rebuild workplace relationships, start by extending sincere praise or appreciation to others. Say thank you when someone does a great job. To rebuild your own strength and confidence, acknowledge what you've achieved at the end of each day. Love comes in small, sincere packages.

- ✔ **Notice what your attitude toward work is.** Do you show up to get the job done and get out, or do you wake up excited about going to work? If your work doesn't give you energy or greater fulfillment, perhaps the time has come to move on.

- ✔ **Pay attention to the circumstances that bring out the best or worst in you.** For example, if you find resentment or anger building up or suddenly find yourself snapping, you know that on some level you've lost your sense of control. On the positive side, if you feel joy under certain conditions, pay attention to what those conditions are so you know what environment best supports your work. What you learn from the ups and downs in your professional life and your personal life defines your character and the kind of leader you are, even if the only leadership role you willingly accept is being the leader of your own life.

Viewing your whole life as a lesson in leadership

What can you do to expand your self-knowledge or your ability to lead your life in a fulfilling way? The following list supplies a few suggestions.

- ✔ **Use uncertainty to engage creativity.** Uncertainty provides the edge for growth and flexibility. It invites you to be creative, to think about things differently, to try out new approaches, to discover more possibilities. Because organizations are being asked to engage their creative talent more than ever before, learning to become more flexible and creative is a key to your success.

- ✔ **Notice where and when your ego takes charge.** Ego-based decisions center on feeling secure about basic survival and how valued you feel in the world. Decisions made in the service of achieving fulfillment are, at their core, based on an inner awareness that you are here to achieve a higher purpose, which involves using your life experiences to expand your conscious awareness. Decisions based on meeting the ego's needs are not as effective as those based on achieving a goal. For more on ego, head to Chapter 4.

Eckhart Tolle, author and spiritual teacher, stated that "the ego is the unobserved mind." In other words, by observing your thoughts, you gain the ability to identify when basic needs for security or feeling valued are driving your decisions. Then you can decide whether you believe what you're thinking or choose a different approach.

Your entire life's experiences are replete with leadership lessons. To benefit from these lessons, you must abandon the idea that you exist to suffer. Otherwise, you will move through life in a protective stance, fearful that more bad things will happen. Instead, use the bad experiences to bring out more of yourself so that you can make deliberate decisions and create the life you want to live. Facing adversity also gives you an opportunity to reach deep down inside to retrieve your creative capacity. Go to Chapter 3 to find more on how the workplace environment affects decision-making and Chapter 6 for ways you can use mistakes to expand your self-fulfillment and leadership ability.

Transcendence is the ability to rise above inner limitations or, in business cultures, to rise above barriers to success, such as uncertain market conditions or large uncontrollable issues that may have stopped you in the past. If you can transcend past experiences, you'll look at everything and everyone from a changed perspective. The emotional charge that used to hijack a rational response will no longer be triggered, even when the circumstances are the same. Your reaction will be different. You'll no longer respond to negativity with negativity. You'll live in the present instead of the past.

Meeting up with your deep self: The dark and shiny sides

Each of us has a shiny, bright side and a dark side. The shiny, bright side holds wisdom at the deepest level. It includes love, passion, joy, inner peace, humility, recognition of others, being in service to community or the planet, empathy, access to intuition, and being connected to others and in alignment with your higher purpose. The dark side embraces emotions like fear, anger, frustration, doubt, worry (fear projected into the future), guilt, shame, resentment, aggression, sarcasm, cynicism, judging, and blaming — all intense emotions that result from negative emotional baggage and unhealed emotional wounds that block creativity and trust. You access your inner wisdom by understanding not only the bright and shiny aspects of your character, but the darkest sides, as well.

Like people, companies also have dark and shiny sides. A workplace that relies on fear to control people creates passivity, stress-related illness, and impaired decision-making. In contrast, a workplace that engenders a sense of belonging, leadership at every level, well-being, and personal and professional growth handles change easily by trusting in the collective creative ability of the workforce to adapt and work together.

It would be easy to say that the dark side is bad and the shiny side is good, but that interpretation is too simplistic. The dark side offers multiple gateways to evolving your leadership ability, your health, and your fulfillment with the life you've chosen. The shiny side nurtures healthy personal relationships and healthy workplaces, supports the highest levels of achievement possible, and makes possible quantum leaps in trust and unrealized potential.

Remember, your emotional self-awareness and capacity to regulate your feelings pretty much define your relationship with yourself and dictate the imprint you leave on others. In addition, a direct link exists between what you do to achieve personal fulfillment and how your company evolves and adapts in response to changing business conditions. Leaders that aren't working directly with their dark sides to learn and evolve aren't growing. At all.

Chapter 17

Facilitating Participatory Decision-Making Meetings

Meetings provide a forum for colleagues to contribute, exchange information, implement a project, or strategize. Sooner or later, you'll be assigned to run a meeting. There are some simple things you can do to facilitate equitable and active participation, and that's what I cover in this chapter: steps to make the most out of everyone's time and expertise. You'll also gain tools for participatory decision-making that you can use in traditional meetings and more innovative approaches for in-person, remote, or online meetings. The benefit? You'll gain invaluable engagement and creativity while simultaneously minimizing the chances that your colleagues will doze off!

Ineffective meetings are a time and a money drain. Here are some stats: Overall, 37 percent of an employee's time (estimates say 30 percent of an executive's time) is spent in meetings, and not all of them productive. In fact, a Verizon study revealed that 91 percent of attendees daydreamed, and over 39 percent took a nap! In addition, meetings cost from $700 (an audio conference) to over $5,000 (for on-site meetings) — an amount that excludes the cost of the participants' salaries and other expenses they incur while in attendance.

Clarifying Your Role in a Meeting

Meetings are, at minimum, places where people interact socially to build or strengthen their communication and connection with each other, and to keep tabs on the project(s) they're working on. For team leaders and project managers, meetings are a way to keep track of progress. You can perform the roles of both participant and facilitator simultaneously, but when you do, you have to be careful. The power you have as the person who facilitates the meeting can be misused. In this section, I tell you how to run the process and contribute content without manipulating the results — a surefire way to break trust.

Distinguishing among facilitating, moderating, and chairing

The terms *chair, moderator,* and *facilitator* are used interchangeably, but, although these roles are responsible for managing the process, each uses a different style. When you understand the differences, you'll know what to expect when you take on one of these roles. The following sections explain each role in detail.

Regardless of which role you accept, if you have a stake in the outcome/result, you must avoid directing the group toward the result you expect or want. Try to remain open to the outcome but not attached to it. Showing such restraint requires a great deal of awareness and discipline. To find out how to avoid this common trap, head to the later section "Letting go of attachment to a specific outcome."

Facilitator

As a facilitator, your role is to remove barriers (not forcibly) so that the group can effectively work together. Barriers can result, for example, from differing communication styles, hidden issues that no one wants to talk about, and the use or abuse of authoritative power.

When you facilitate, your task is to achieve a shared or agreed-upon goal within a specified time while strengthening appreciation of differing viewpoints. To perform this role, a facilitator first asks questions to assess the situation, establishes when and where the meeting starts and ends, and then designs a way to accomplish the results step by step.

Suppose, for example, that your unit has a recurring issue that has not been resolved despite every solution that has been tried. As a consequence, work has deteriorated into a blame game. To repair the situation, you design a series of steps that allow the group to identify the systemic reason why the issue returns and to come to agreement on the action to take. Your role is to help the group think together by enabling group members to move away from blaming people (which is too easy to do) to identifying the underlying systemic issue needing to be addressed. In this way, the group can move forward constructively and collectively.

Facilitators are often expected to have subject matter expertise, though being an expert makes staying detached difficult. When egos are involved, there is also a great temptation to manipulate the conversation. In one consultation event I ran, one of the facilitators, who came from academia, skipped the orientation, saying that he already knew what he was doing. Thirty minutes of participant contribution later, he'd recorded zero ideas on the flip chart. Zero. When I asked him why he was ignoring the ideas being offered, his response was, "I haven't heard anything I agree with yet."

Have you ever been to a meeting where your memory of what happened and the record of the meeting events weren't even close? If so, the facilitator or moderator was so attached to her idea of the outcome that the record was manipulated to show it. It's an abuse of power. To avoid breaking trust, notice the mental chatter in your mind. Are you mentally evaluating each idea as it comes forward to see whether it fits your thinking, or are you actually listening to it? If the former, step away from the facilitator role until you can genuinely listen to what is being said.

Moderator

Moderators are usually needed with panel discussions — a meeting format you may use when you are presenting or exchanging information with a community (in a consultation context) or conducting a supplier briefing, for example. As moderator, your role is to ensure that the conversation does what it promised to do to achieve the desired results. Key functions of a moderator include

- ✔ Keeping the conversation on track by avoiding detours and distractions and asking short, clarifying questions
- ✔ Handling introductions and monitoring time
- ✔ Encouraging and managing panel and audience interaction

As a moderator, you are less active as a manager of the process and more active as a manager of how the time is used to benefit the audience.

Chair

The position of chair is a more formal one (consider chairing a task force, for example, or a committee meeting). You receive this position of authority through appointment or election. As a chair, you preside over the meeting's procedures, using a formally prescribed format, like Roberts Rules or your own version of procedural rules.

Just as facilitators who are also subject matter experts must be careful not to steer content or manipulate the outcome, chairs must also be aware of how their opinions guide the direction of the discussion and ensure that they are not unduly directing the outcome to what they consider the right answer.

Letting go of attachment to a specific outcome

When you have a stake in the outcome, there's a natural tendency to steer the group toward your way of thinking. As a facilitator, moderator, or chair, you must let go of controlling the outcome and allow the group to determine how to meet the goal in the best way it can.

If you're a manager who defines your role as maintaining control of others, letting go will be exceptionally challenging, and you may not succeed every time. But over time, with self-discipline, the benefits gained by turning the horses loose toward accomplishing the goal will far exceed your expectations.

You are one of the team, and, as peers, you are pooling your IQs and unique strengths toward achieving a common goal. In the end, sustainable solutions require more heads than one.

Meeting Preparation Basics

Good fortune and productivity favor the prepared, because the more time invested in preparing for the meeting, the higher the perceived value and the greater the productivity. In this section, I outline the basics: identifying the purpose and reason for the meeting, putting together a basic plan, and determining whether a formal or informal meeting format is the better structure. For detailed planning information, head to the later section "Putting Together a Meeting Plan for Complex or High-Stakes Decisions."

Establishing the purpose of the meeting

Preparation starts with identifying the purpose of the meeting. Doing so is an important first step in meeting planning, for these reasons:

- ✔ It guides selection of the processes you'll use to facilitate the result.

- ✔ It makes the focus clear for all participants.

- ✔ It enables you to know when you're stuffing too many meeting tasks into too small a time period.

- ✔ It lets you thoughtfully choose the approach you'll use to achieve each step in the meeting, including time needed for discussion and reflection.

Identifying reasons to meet

Meetings are held all the time. Respondents to a Verizon study, for example, reported attending, in person or over the phone, over 60 meetings a month! Yet many of these meetings aren't needed; other formats could be used to share or gather the desired information. Therefore, when you decide to hold a meeting, make sure the reason is important enough. Meetings are held for the following reasons:

- **To exchange information as part of a briefing or project update:** The purpose could be to bring team members and senior decision-makers up to speed or, in the case of a project update, to verify the status.

- **To make a decision:** The purpose of the meeting states what you'll achieve as a result of the decision.

- **To resolve, once and for all, a recurring issue:** The purpose could be to understand why the issue keeps repeating, with the desired result being to choose proper action. Generating creative options may be one of the steps (you can read more about how to tap into others' creativity to broaden your options in Chapter 9).

- **To conduct a review of a decision post-implementation or at project milestones to learn what went well and what didn't:** A meeting like this is used both to identify areas of improvement and to improve accuracy of decision-making.

- **To plan and allocate resources to get a task, project, or decision implemented:** The purpose could be to arrive at a course of action all participants can support and clearly communicate to others.

Putting together a bare-bones plan

A productive meeting requires preparation and careful planning. You can use the following steps as a guide when planning your next meeting:

1. **Clearly state why the meeting is being held.**

   Gaining clarity on why you are holding a meeting enables you to establish guidelines and prepare meeting participants. For example, you may decide to conduct a project review to bring a troublesome project back on track.

2. **Understand what you hope to accomplish when the meeting is concluded.**

   If you don't know what you want to accomplish, it's a social gathering, not a meeting. Continuing with the project review example in Step 1, the end result of the meeting could be to identify project bottlenecks and come up with solutions to remove them.

3. **Identify what you'll do with the knowledge gained from the meeting.**

   Using the troublesome project example, you could tell upper management what's needed to turn the project around or to implement solutions developed in the meeting.

Whether you are having formal or informal meetings (more on that in the next section), make sure that everyone is clear on why the meeting is being held, what will be talked about, how much time will be allocated for the meeting, what happens with the end results, and how conclusions will be communicated afterward.

In fast-paced environments, it's tempting to avoid basic meeting preparation to save time, but when you do, you risk having to take time to redo what didn't work out. Instead, do what builders do: Measure (plan) twice, cut (meet) once. With thoughtful preparation, you increase the chances of having a productive and effective meeting and earn the right to use your time and other people's in meetings.

Choosing a formal or informal meeting structure

Meetings come in two forms: formal and informal.

- **Formal:** Often, formal meetings have an agenda that is agreed upon when planning the meeting, and advance materials are circulated to participants so that they can prepare. They also have a set structure and are well-planned and documented.

- **Informal:** Informal meetings, such as those held around the water cooler, by the tailgate of a truck, or on the fly in a fast-paced, fun environment, serve as forums in which to exchange ideas, provide project updates, and resolve issues to determine what happens next.

Whether you use a formal or informal style to conduct meetings depends on the working environment in your company.

Putting Together a Meeting Plan for Complex or High-Stakes Decisions

Big decisions — high stakes, high risk, and often strategic decisions — amount to linking a series of smaller decisions until all the pieces converge into the final conclusion. For example, if you are buying a franchise or a company, the final decision — to accept the offer on the table — only occurs after a series of other decisions have been made: how to prepare yourself for the initial bid, whether to move forward after reviewing financial data and evaluating respective strengths and weakness of the business model, how to initiate and participate in the negotiations, and so on. Each meeting builds on work completed and decisions made in prior meetings, and altogether these meetings help you make the decisions today that move you toward the goal or result to be achieved tomorrow.

When a lot is at stake in terms of cost, relationships, or reputation, preparation pays off in terms of productivity and perceived value. In this section, I show you a way of preparing for meetings in which complex decisions are made. By using a planning framework or template (plenty are available on the Internet), you can structure your meetings so that work gets accomplished.

Step 1: Stating the overall goal and metrics

The first thing you need to do is to establish the overall goal and the metrics by which you'll know whether it has been achieved. Knowing the overall context for the decision you're working to attain during the meeting gives the work longer term direction while simultaneously setting out metrics. Metrics aren't easy to get right, so monitor results to see whether you're getting what you aimed for so that you can learn and adjust as consequences surface. The following is an example of metrics:

- **Overall goal:** "Increase employee engagement in learning and development by 50 percent. Bench marks will be established through a peer review process."

- **Measures:** "By the end of the first stage of implementation, we expect 75 percent of employees to have participated in a program in-line with their development objectives. By the end of the first year of implementation, we expect to see team working relationships improve by 50 percent, decision-making speed improve by 20 percent, and organizational strength improve by 30 percent."

Step 2: Putting together a framework for the meeting

After determining the goal, you're ready to set up a framework for the meeting, asking questions such as those outlined in the following list. This sample uses the goal and metrics outlined in the preceding example (increasing employee engagement in self-directed learning):

- ✔ **What is the purpose of the meeting?** Decide the budget allocation for employee-identified learning initiatives.

- ✔ **Who needs to be in the meeting and who has decision-making authority?** Finance and Human Resources need to attend the meeting, and functional managers also need to be involved.

- ✔ **What is the expected outcome of the meeting?** Deciding on the budget allocation for each employee's development.

- ✔ **What advance materials need to be prepared and distributed to meeting participants?** Previous decisions and other information for eligible employees, as well as the total budget allocation for employee self-development and the phases in implementation plan.

Meetings go sideways when you try to do too much simultaneously: exchange or gather information, make decisions, resolve an issue, plan, review, and so on. Meetings also become dysfunctional when they are overly routine, insist on multitasking, or have no agreed-upon way to move from discussion to decision. You use the purpose of the meeting to define the start point and the desired results or goal to anchor the finish line.

Step 3: Assigning tasks in preparation for the meeting

The meeting prework planning is accompanied by an action plan that spells out who is responsible for the logistics (booking a room/venue, communicating to participants, sending out advance materials, and so on) and who contacts the participants to consult on what they should bring to the meeting in support of the work. A typical action plan framework answers the following questions:

- ✔ **What needs to be done?** Identify everything that needs to be done: booking a room, catering refreshments, and coordinating presentations of background information relevant to the meeting, for example.

✔ **Who takes care of each task?** Here, assign an employee or ask for a volunteer for each task.

✔ **What is the deadline for each task?** Assigning deadlines ensures that everyone involved knows what needs to be accomplished and in what time frame.

✔ **What results do I expect?** Tell each employee assigned to a task the end result you desire. If, for example, you're holding a meeting for 85 people, make sure the employee assigned with securing the room knows that. Also be sure to tell each person involved in planning what the budget is, so that overspending is not a factor.

Step 4: Structuring the meeting with a meeting plan

When you plan a meeting, you decide how much time is allocated to each discussion item, what the purpose of each item is, the format in which it is presented, the results you expect, and what is next on the agenda. To do so, systematically walk through the thinking steps one at a time, as I show you here (you can also put this information into a handy table format, as shown in Figure 17-1). This kind of framework, or one like it, keeps discussion on track, allows you to amend the plan when needed, and lets you stay within the time allocated for the meeting:

✔ **Discussion item #1 (10 minutes) — Welcome participants, present the overall goal and how you'll proceed in the time available.** The purpose of this item is to either set up or verify expectations for what will be accomplished in the time available. The format is a short introduction by the chair or facilitator.

✔ **Discussion item #2 (40 minutes) — Presentation of any background information pertinent to the meeting.** The purpose of this item is to make sure everyone's on the same page. This period includes 10-minute presentations by the HR and Finance departments, followed by a 20-minute period for clarifying questions. A whiteboard is used to capture participants' thoughts, ideas, and concerns.

✔ **Discussion item #3 (30 minutes) — Allocations scenarios provided by the Finance department.** The purpose of this item is to present the financial information with input from Human Resources. The format will be a review of two possible scenarios with the desired result being that all parties understand the options and their implications.

✔ **Discussion item #4 (30 minutes) — Group identification of criteria to guide allocation.** The purpose of this item is to make what is important visible to all and to agree on how to select the best option. The item uses the facilitated process for gathering and refining ideas. The desired result is that group members will have determined which criteria will be used.

- **Discussion item #5 (60 minutes) — Weigh the various options.** The purpose of this item is to select the top options, based on how the numbers add up through the weighted criteria in the preceding discussion. This item is facilitated, and the desired result is to determine whether the option works financially, achieves program goals, and works for employees.

- **Discussion item #6 (15-minute break) — Test and confirm.** During this break in the meeting, participants relax, step back, reflect, and gain perspective so that they can look at the final decision with a fresh mind. Participants will decide whether they are making a choice they can support. One way to conduct this part of the meeting is a walkabout, where participants leave the meeting room and, weather permitting, get out in nature.

- **Discussion item #7 (30 minutes) — Reconvene to confirm or to discuss doubts or concerns.** Participants review what has been done so far. Then members combine what they've learned in the meeting along with their gut instinct to arrive at a conclusion.

Figure 17-1:
A meeting framework in table format.

Time	Discussion Item	Purpose	Format	Results	Next Up...
10 min.	Welcome participants, review background material, and explain overall goal of the initiative.	Refresh memories on what has happened so far and explain what happens now.	Short intro by chair or facilitator, accompanied by support materials.	People will know what results are expected from their time (e.g., Stated Outcome: Decide on the budget allocation for employees).	Set up the next step on the agenda.
40 min.	Presentation of background information relevant to the decision, including employee data from HR and financial implications from Finance. Share implementation plan with priority target groups.	Information exchange to put everyone on the same page; specifically, review the material, discuss implications, and confirm priorities.	10-minute presentations by HR and Finance departments, followed by 20 minutes for clarifying questions. Whiteboard to capture thoughts, ideas, concerns.	Shared knowledge of the implications and implementation schedule. Everyone has all the information needed to make a decision.	Review criteria.

© John Wiley & Sons, Inc.

As you can see, I have left out bathroom and care and maintenance breaks (lunch, coffee, and so on), so when you plan your meetings, make sure you leave time for breaks and activities that keep energy up and look after participants' basic needs.

Here are some suggestions to keep participants engaged and energized:

- ✔ **If you want people to stay awake, engage them by adding processes that get people on their feet.** Tasks accomplished in a fun, interactive way tend to be more effective. You'll find some examples in the section "Tools to Help You Facilitate and Manage Meetings," later on in this chapter.

  Many business environments operate under the rigid belief that if you aren't serious 100 percent of the time, you aren't focused or productive. Successful and productive companies like Google have blasted that idea out of the water. You *can* have fun and be focused and productive. For more ideas on how to run meetings that are both fun and productive, check out *Gamestorming: A Playbook for Innovators, Rulebreakers, and Changemakers,* by Dave Gray, Sunni Brown, and James Macanufo (O'Reilly Media). It offers a smorgasbord of techniques, in addition to the ones I share in the upcoming sections.

- ✔ **Even though it's important to stick to a meeting plan, don't be rigid or inflexible.** Leave room for conversation and be prepared to adjust. If you discover that there are details that you haven't anticipated or that haven't been worked out, avoid pushing them through just to stay on time. If you're given no other choice, seek participant ideas to ensure that the important conversations happen. Otherwise, when the results of the meeting are implemented, the effort will be only half-hearted.

- ✔ **Be super attentive to how you're using the time, particularly when you schedule meal breaks.** Bodies and brains need fuel — fresh air, water, food, and breaks — to function. Caring for participants allows you to get more done in less time.

- ✔ **If you're going to push over the end time, then make sure you have permission from the group and let those who need to leave do so without guilt or pressure.** Have fun. Do great work. Simple.

Running a Productive Meeting

The start of any meeting is super important. It sets the tone for the meeting and either invigorates the participants, making them eagerly want to participate, or elicits a series of murmurs from participants when they realize they're attending another boring, ho-hum meeting. If you start a meeting and get the latter response, you won't get the results you expect.

Starting your meeting well is only part of the battle. You then have to keep it on track by making sure that the group stays cohesive, and that's where paying attention to group dynamics comes in. In this section, I tell you how to meet both challenges head on.

Getting on the same page with an overview

The best way to get the meeting started on the right foot is to make sure all participants are on the same page. Providing an overview before starting the actual business portion of the meeting helps everyone know what to expect and offers assurance that they won't be stranded for the duration of the meeting with no food, water, or bathroom breaks. These next three steps provide critical framework for confirming the start point and what you're aiming to achieve by the end:

1. **Provide background information, if appropriate, about what will be discussed during the meeting so that everyone knows what events occurred that necessitated a meeting.**

   This information gets meeting participants up to speed and ensures that everyone has the same information. The following is an example of how to introduce background information in a meeting about employee self-development budget allocation:

   > For as far back as anyone can remember, employees were sent to training programs identified by management. The return on technical skills has been significant, but on leadership and career development, it's missing the mark. To engage employees in their learning and career development, the company is shifting from management-selected training and development to self-identified training and development. A team has been researching all the information required to decide on a course of action to shift to self-managed learning.

   > We are gathered today to map out the series of decisions we need to make and the information required to make them. The final decision for budget allocation has to be made by the end of the month. The program implementation date is at the start of the next quarter, so we don't have a lot of time.

2. **Provide a clear picture of the goal of the meeting, including what is expected from the team and what will happen after the meeting.**

   When you describe the outcome, create an inspiring result that hooks the participants' imagination. Here's an example of what you'd say if you were facilitating the meeting to decide the budget allocation for the employee self-development program:

   > By the time we are done, we'll have mapped out the micro decisions, gathered the information we need, and will know who will take on each area of responsibility. Plus, we'll know how we're going to monitor implementation so we can adjust as needed.

3. **Briefly explain how you expect the meeting to proceed.**

This isn't the Full Meal Deal — just cover what participants can expect during the first two hours. No one will remember details of opening remarks after the first two hours of the meeting, so keep refreshing group clarity on what happens next as you go. Here's an example:

> We'll be using a mix of presentation and interaction. We'll start by using the pile of sticky notes to map out what each of us thinks needs to be done. Then we'll sort out themes (or priorities). Any questions?

Keeping the meeting on track: Dealing with group dynamics

Put a group of people together in a meeting room, and interesting things can happen. There is no question that meetings would go a lot faster if people weren't involved, but they are! In this section, I outline the different kinds of group dynamics and tell you what to watch for so that you can handle any situation in a way that respects everyone's needs and keeps the meeting agenda moving forward.

Handling group dynamic #1: Groupthink

Groupthink refers to the psychological experience in which conformity and the desire for consensus or harmony cause individual opinions or objections to be repressed. It works against effective decision-making because independent thinking is where breakthroughs happen.

When you notice that participants are conforming to one person's viewpoint, you know the group is reverting to groupthink. Groupthink shows up in decision-making behavior when

- ✔ **One option is rationalized without considering others.** One sure sign that groupthink is occurring is when alternative ways of seeing the situation are neglected, or when a person holding an opposing view is judged as wrong and either ostracized or ignored.

- ✔ **The team adopts a sense of self-righteousness thinking.** Another sign of groupthink is when the team thinks it alone has the right answer. It is win-lose thinking common in hierarchies gone badly wrong.

Nip groupthink in the bud so that every participant can share his or her unique viewpoint. Handling groupthink takes practice. Do the following:

1. **Recognize that groupthink is occurring.**

   Observe the group dynamics without blame or judgment and notice when the pressure to conform is switched on. Pay attention to whether you are following the prevailing wind against the direction of your inner feelings. If you find yourself following along, try asking a bold question, explained in Step 2.

   If you're facilitating and you automatically overrule an opposing view, it likely reflects your own desire to preserve harmony. Your role is to bring forward the opposing view so that it can be heard and understood. Project failure or, in the case of health and safety situations, personal injury can be averted simply by spotting what could go wrong *as if it will*.

2. **Ask a bold question to diplomatically check whether others are witnessing the dynamic, too.**

   You can ask bold questions either as a participant or facilitator. For example, say, "I notice we seem to be sticking to a safe path. Does anyone else see that? What ideas haven't we heard yet?" This kind of statement points out a pattern and invites ideas that haven't been heard.

3. **Stress that every participant in the meeting is a unique individual with a unique viewpoint.**

   Making this point is easier when you're the facilitator. Tell participants that there is no need to conform to what others think and that you value everyone's viewpoint, including divergent views.

Group dynamic #2: Power imbalances

Power imbalances occur when one person regularly uses his or her position of authority to undermine or control others. The person in authority can still retain designated power without forcing compliance. If you're the one who always needs to be right or in control, this is a chance to discover how, by letting go of control, you get creative results and the ability to achieve the goal.

If you have a boss or team member who relies on controlling others, then diplomacy is called for. When this scenario occurs, try the following:

1. **Set up a private conversation in advance of the meeting to find out what is important to the power player and why.**

   Gathering this information lets you address his concerns in the process of the meeting, while simultaneously retaining respect for everyone participating.

2. **If you're the facilitator, ask a question in the presence of the group to reveal why the boss or team member has a fixed and firm position.**

   Questions starting with "Why" can be challenging, so aim for a curious rather than confrontational tone. Come from the heart. For example, "You've mentioned this point three times, so it's clearly important to you. Tell us more." Then ask, "Can you tell us how your point connects to what's important to consider." Your intent is to understand the interests underneath the position.

3. **Choose a facilitation process that flattens the power structure so that someone who habitually controls can't because the process doesn't allow it.**

   Having the power player participate as a peer (which requires his agreeing to the arrangement) takes the pressure off him and distributes responsibility for the results to everyone. One such process is Open Space (`www.openspaceworld.org`), which is strong at self-organized discussions, idea generation, and stimulating dialogue across a mix of participants.

Group dynamic #3: The domineering person

This dynamic occurs when someone who dominates airtime tends to drown out or usurp any other views, particularly opposing ones. People like to dominate a situation because it's a way to sell their idea as the winner. As facilitator, your responsibility is to ensure that airtime is divvied up fairly. To stop someone from dominating a meeting, follow these steps:

1. **Start the meeting by letting everyone know you'll be seeking opinions from each person.**

   Say it like you mean it (but without sounding like Attila the Hun). This gives the habitually domineering person the heads-up that you are paying attention. Otherwise, you may just as well meet with the domineering individual in a coffee shop somewhere and save the time and effort of scheduling a meeting with others, who won't be heard anyway.

2. **Leave time throughout the conversation to go to anyone who hasn't contributed.**

   Avoid asking, "Any other ideas?" only to quickly move on in the next second with, "Great! Next!" Some of the best insights come from those who've been thinking internally while others have been thinking out loud. Providing space for silence gives introverts time to realize they have an opening to gather their thoughts and speak. Frequently check with those less vocal during the meeting.

If you know that a domineering person will be at the meeting, you can use the structured round-table method, which I discuss in the later section "Structured round table: A tool for gathering perspectives." This method gives everyone a chance to contribute.

Group dynamic #4: Dealing with emotional tension

Frustration, anger, passion (which can look like anger), and conflicting ideas can generate tension that can derail a discussion unless these emotions are used wisely. When you notice emotional tension in a meeting, try the following:

1. **Think of emotions as data.**

   Emotions, like any other data, need to be processed and understood. They hold information that indicates whether a project will be met with support or resistance.

   Don't ignore feelings, even when you are afraid of your own. When emotions are ignored, projects fail to implement, and meetings get robotic and inflexible. Employee disengagement is high.

2. **Call for a timeout (a 10- to 15-minute break) until things cool down a bit.**

   Use the emotional tension to gain perspective rather than fuel opposing differences. When participants cool down, ask them to privately record and share what they felt. Ask them to reflect on where the tension came from. Was it from a conflict with personal values? A conflict with organizational beliefs? Were two opposing views actually two different perspectives?

   In super-tense situations, the timeout provides a chance for participants to breathe, gain objectivity, and let their emotions simmer down and be processed so that a conversation can then take place. Without a timeout, tensions erupt into conflict, and it's all downhill from there.

3. **Allow five or more minutes to record observations and then go around the table to hear what was observed and can be learned.**

   After gaining perspective and calming down, participants can offer their constructive reflections. Comments that focus on who is right or wrong are destructive and don't contribute to better solutions.

Emotional tension can be a huge stumbling block in any scenario, but when handled properly, it can reveal some interesting perspectives that otherwise may never have surfaced.

Group dynamic #5: The discussion degenerates

One minute things are on track, and the next, ten things are happening at once and the discussion, which seemed to be productive and moving forward, crumbles before your very eyes. This scenario happens to every meeting facilitator at one point or another, so what can you do when a discussion goes south? Try the following:

1. **Notice what kind of thinking was being applied before the discussion disintegrated.**

   A frequent problem is that too many things are being tackled simultaneously. For instance, if one person comes up with a solution only to have it shot down (in flames), the steps of generating and evaluating were happening simultaneously.

    When too many things are being done simultaneously, return to a step-by-step approach to restore order to the chaos; for instance, first identify issues, then generate solutions, then evaluate or select one or more options, and then move to action planning/implementation. You can also bring the discussion back on track by clarifying where you are in the process: evaluating ideas, putting possibilities on the table, and so on.

2. **Identify what instigated the derailment; ask if you aren't sure.**

   Start by understanding where perspectives differ and why, and then ensure that the issues have been discussed sufficiently — but not thrashed so much that the conversation becomes repetitive.

   After some discussion about the source of the conflict (sticking to the issues, not blaming the people), you can ask if they're ready to move on. Then gather value out of what's been discussed by asking, "What point has become clearer from the discussion that needs to be brought forward?" to form the solution.

Tools to Help You Facilitate and Manage Meetings

Every meeting facilitator has a tool kit. Some are skills you develop through experience; others are processes that help structure the conversation into an orderly approach for greater efficiency. In this section, you find process tools you can use Monday morning when working with your colleagues or team. For the inner skill set, see Chapter 4.

Structured round table: A tool for gathering perspectives

Structured round table is a way to gather input, like perspectives on decisions, from participants in meetings. Aside from making sure you've heard from everyone, this approach ensures that those who tend to dominate don't because it gives everybody equal time.

Here's how it works: You assemble a group of people who share a common goal and seek to understand each other's views on a decision or the situation at hand. To do a structured round table, you simply go around the table to each person in turn for his or her opinion.

Sounds simple enough, but before beginning this type of meeting, here are some tips to ensure success:

- ✔ Let participants know how much time they have and explain that no one can interrupt another to ask questions, voice agreement, or put forth a "better" idea.

- ✔ If someone isn't ready to share an idea with the group, he or she can pass, but be sure to go back to that person later. Those who pass on their turns most likely need more time to formulate their thoughts.

- ✔ At the end of the discussion, open the table for questions or clarifying viewpoints.

When facilitating a round-table discussion, your primary task is to establish a climate of respect and curiosity instead of snap judgments. As a chair or facilitator, you also need to safeguard the space for introverts and extroverts. Extroverts like to think out loud. Although they can respond quickly because they don't really know what they think until they hear themselves say it, it takes them awhile to get their points across because they often aren't sure of what it is until they've given a small speech. Introverts, on the other hand, need to process internally first before sharing their views. Allow for both styles.

To read more about the structured round table, check out *A Facilitators Guide to Participatory Decision-Making*, by Sam Kaner (Jossey Bass).

Visual and group collaboration tools for meetings

Statistics from 3M and Zabisco (`http://visual.ly/users/zabisco`) indicate that 90 percent of the information sent to the brain is visual, and visuals are processed 60,000 times faster than print. Therefore, one way to engage meeting participants is to use visual tools to create highly participative environments. In these settings, everyone can see the whole picture at once because the framework for the discussion is put on a wall or whiteboard. Ideas are mapped out graphically where all can see the topic under discussion.

The simplest form of a visual meeting uses different colored sticky notes on a wall. Because they are visual, the information is totally transparent, which means that, assuming there is enough discussion and free exchange of information, fewer assumptions get made. Using visual aides and graphics in meetings speeds up the processing power and enables all to contribute and cooperate. In short, visual tools can be the conduit through which participants create solutions together. Collaboration!

 The beauty of using visual formats is that information is visible to everyone so the entire group can come up with better ways of handling issues like bottlenecks and missing resources. The primary value of a visual format is that the whole team can step back and gain some distance, which enables them to see the situation more clearly and find solutions that they may not have otherwise been able to see.

Teams working in-person or online benefit from participatory methods that combine needed discussion with a simple framework that allows everyone to add ideas and content. Two software solutions for participatory meetings are Lean Café and a visual meeting format used in project management, which I cover in this section.

Lean Café

Lean Café is the name for an agenda-less yet structured meeting format that serves as an alternative to a more formalized agenda structure and works well for getting tasks done creatively within a time limit. Lean Café sprang out of Lean Coffee (`http://www.leancoffee.org`) in Seattle and draws from Lean/Agile practices in software development. Participants come together, form the agenda, and then move through it quickly.

To use Lean Café, provide each participant with sticky notes, 2 to 3 dots, and a pen, and then create a Lean Café template. To create the Lean Café template, make four columns across the top of a whiteboard or wall, using the following headers(Figure 17-2 shows a Lean Café template):

✔ **To Discuss:** Using sticky notes, participants propose topics for discussion — one topic per sticky note — and then post them in this column. Each topic gets a one or two sentence explanation so that people know how to pick their priorities. Then, using the dots, participants indicate which topics have priority, given the time available. For instance, in a project management meeting a topic could be, "Budget overrun" or "Review options."

✔ **Up Next:** Top priority topics move from To Discuss to this column, which gives you the agenda for the meeting. Then, one topic is moved to the Discussing column.

- ✔ **Discussing:** This column holds the current topic being discussed, making it easy for everyone to see exactly what the topic is. After the topic has been discussed and completed, the sticky note moves to the Done column.

- ✔ **Done:** This column shows which topics and tasks have been completed.

  Once a topic moves into the Done category, you go back to the Up Next column for the next topic and move it through the process until you have addressed the priorities. If time is still available, you can go back to the To Discuss column and bring forward other topics.

You can also add a rough estimate of how much time you'll need for each topic just to make sure you get the job done in the allowable time. A modified version of the Lean Café format for online and remote meetings also exists. Check out http://www.trello.com.

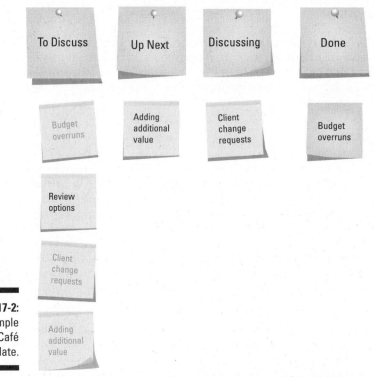

Figure 17-2:
A sample
Lean Café
template.

© John Wiley & Sons, Inc.

Using visualization boards for project meetings

Using nothing more than sticky notes and a wall, you have all the ingredients you need to run a collaborative meeting with your project team. To conduct a project meeting with a visualization board, just follow these steps:

1. **Decide on the headers you'll use and place the headers horizontally across one wall in the room so that people can put their points underneath.**

   Each header is specific to the kind of project you're working on. Software development projects have at least 12 checkpoints (headers), for instance. Each header is the umbrella for topics that will be discussed during the meeting.

   After you decide on the headers, either on your own or after consulting with your team, you can use them again in subsequent meetings. Call it a framework if you like.

2. **Provide each team member with sticky notes and a black felt-tip pen.**

   The black felt-tip pen makes the points readable from a distance, provided no illegible pharmaceutical handwriting is involved.

   Use different colored sticky notes to visually signal different things. For instance, use red notes to flag bottlenecks in a project or yellow to indicate warnings. At minimum, trouble areas need to be flagged so they can be addressed sooner rather than later, when the cost of fixing them is much higher.

3. **Ask each person to put his or her updates on the sticky notes and line them up vertically under the appropriate headings.**

   Ask for full sentences or key words so that the writer's intent is clear.

4. **Ask team members to indicate problem areas by placing a different colored sticky on top of the status update described in Step 3.**

   You'll get a lot of postings down and across that will show the project status, what is working, and what needs attention. Figure 17-3, shows a visualization board used in project management (this image was adapted from www.Commitment-thebook.com, in which a more detailed software development sample exists). You can see, at a glance, where work is distributed and where either bottlenecks or issues must be resolved to be on target — information that can inform the decision about what to do next.

5. **Openly discuss what the visualization board reveals.**

   For example, you may want to discuss the distribution of the work, the timing and budget, client satisfaction, product quality, and delivery. Ask participants to explain what the concern is and why it needs to be addressed. Also ask what needs to be addressed by the whole team and how team members can assist in removing bottlenecks. You may need a flip chart to record the issues to be resolved and the solutions that arise from the discussion.

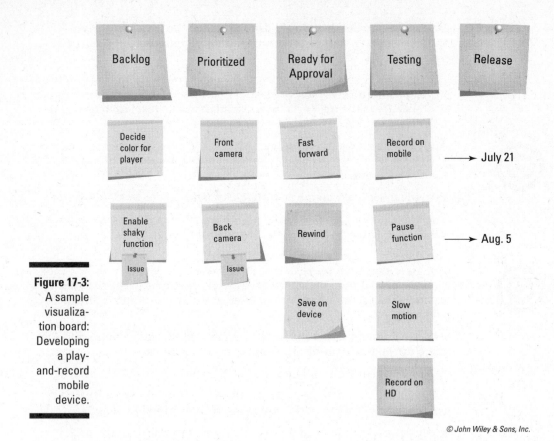

Figure 17-3:
A sample visualization board: Developing a play-and-record mobile device.

A visualization board brings all the pieces of the project into one place so you and your team can collectively determine what to do next. If people need to be reallocated or a totally different approach needs to be explored, then you have plenty of creative talent in your team who can come up with ideas. You don't have to carry the big issues alone.

In demanding, fast-paced environments, it's really easy to think you don't have time to step back to gain perspective. It's equally easy to rush into taking action, especially in companies where being busy is valued over working smart. Yet you can't afford not to gain perspective. Otherwise, you may find that you waste a lot of energy racing down an all-too-familiar path. Watch what pressures you're reacting to. Before you leap into action, spend time observing and being curious. You'll find your decision-making more effective.

Chapter 18

Making Decisions about Partnerships and Joint Ventures

Someday — maybe today — you may come to believe that your company would benefit from establishing a relationship with another company. Maybe you're considering entering into a joint venture to gain exposure to a new market. Perhaps a strategic alliance would be more beneficial. Maybe you're thinking of some other arrangement. The key point here is that, before you enter into any sort of relationship with another company, you want to make sure that the relationship will be beneficial and help you achieve your goals. In short, you need the confidence that comes from knowing you've chosen the right partner. In this chapter, I discuss the different structures available, the factors that drive decisions, and what to do when things go wrong.

Bigger companies like joint ventures or strategic alliances because they are more successful than buying a company. A study by KPMG (an audit, tax and advisory services firm that operates worldwide) states that more than half of joint ventures met or exceeded expectations whereas less than 27 percent of acquisitions created value. Small companies love joint ventures because they can leverage their resources and achieve more with less time and money.

Understanding the Different Partnership Structures

In the context of business, the term *partnerships* can refer to a number of different structures: joint ventures, partnerships, and strategic alliances, to name a few. Each of these arrangements describes a particular way in which companies combine their strengths to accomplish a mutually beneficial goal. In this section, I cover the two most common structural options: partnerships and joint ventures.

Looking at partnerships

Partnerships fall into two categories: one, a legal designation in which two or more people team up to start a business, and two, a cooperative working relationship. A few better known and successful business partnerships include Warner Bros. Entertainment (brothers Albert, Sam, Harry, and Jack), Ben & Jerry's (Ben Cohen and Jerry Greenfield), Hewlett-Packard (Dave Packard and Bill Hewlett), and Google (Larry Page and Sergey Brin).

The business partnership lasts until either the partnership or company falls apart. A partnership agreement specifies details such as how decisions are made; how much money is invested and by whom; what each party brings to the table in terms of sweat equity, product, or expertise; when and how money and vested interest are calculated and paid back; what happens in the event of a death (or divorce, for married partners) of one of the partners; and other important legal considerations.

Partnerships that take the form of working relationships have the goal of, for example, improving the health of the community, or are cooperative ventures of collective benefit. For example, Muhammad Yunus of the Grameen Bank met with Franck Riboud of Danone Foods. Both shared a concern for malnutrition and poverty and a common vision for social business. They cofounded Grameen Danone Foods, Ltd., in India. The company repackaged Danone's products to fit village economies of scale and then worked with a network of woman entrepreneurs to distribute the products.

Examining joint ventures

In a joint venture, two companies team up to achieve a task. They either start a new company to produce a product, or they work together on a specific project with a start and finish date. For example, Ford Motor Company teamed up with Toyota Motor Corporation. The goal, motivated by new regulations on fuel economy that impacted SUVs and pickup trucks, was to develop a hybrid system (Toyota's expertise) that could be used in Ford's full-sized pickups.

On a smaller scale, plenty of entrepreneurs partner with either a competitor or with a client to gain valuable expertise. Following are ways companies can use joint ventures to deliver more services or products to an existing client:

- ✔ **Marketing joint ventures:** Ideal for small and medium-sized companies, these joint ventures bring a product or service of one company to the market of the other. Both companies gain through shared revenue from sales and because customers gain access to additional value. For example, a marketer who has a big list may team up with someone whose product he or she respects. Together they introduce the product and then share a percentage of sales.

- ✔ **Product or project development:** Two or more companies combine expertise and develop a new product to fill a market niche. For instance, master marketer Tom Antion teamed up with Magic 4 Speaker's Steve Hart, a professional magician, to create a video product. Steve flew to Tom's location at his own expense; Tom shot the video and packaged the product at his own expense. Both sell the product without paying royalties to each other.

- ✔ **Licensing:** Licensing is one of the most lucrative of all the joint venture opportunities. After you develop a product or service that has high value to customers, you license it for use by other companies. Then, every time the product is used or sold, you get paid your licensing fee — definitely a sweet deal for all involved! Entrepreneur Sohail Khan, a joint venture and marketing expert, entered a joint venture with a direct mail company that had a huge mailing list but needed a new product. After producing and licensing the product, Khan walked away with a healthy seven-figure joint venture deal in less than 30 days, and the mailing-list company delivered a valued product to the 4.2 million customers on its list!

Depending on the risk and stakes, joint ventures can be formalized by legal agreement, memorandum of understanding (MOU), or a more informal letter of agreement (LOA), which details how profits and costs are distributed and how the agreement can be terminated by either party.

Determining Mutual Benefit

Carl Jung said, "The meeting of two personalities is like the contact of two chemical substances: if there is any reaction, both are transformed." This is as true for companies working together as it is for individuals. For the chemistry to work, the core questions can be boiled down to these: What is the glue that holds the whole venture together? What value does each party gain?

When determining the mutual benefit, look at both the reason for teaming up in the first place and the reason for working together. In this section, I look at the strategic thinking that goes into your decision to partner with another company, as well as the values that impact whether the relationship, even a temporary one, will succeed.

Thinking through partnership potential

Partnerships are about as close to getting married as it gets in business. If you're considering teaming up with a friend or colleague to turn an idea into a viable business, you need to dig deep to give the partnership the best chance for success. Yes, partnerships are legal entities, but that can feel irrelevant when they fall apart. Don't let your partnership begin with goodwill but end with ill feelings. By asking the difficult questions during negotiations, both you and your potential partner will find out what to expect. The following list outlines the details you need to work out:

- ✔ **How decisions will be made:** Will decisions be made by consensus? What values and principles will serve as a guide when making decisions? One partnership I was in, for example, used the principle of what we called "felt fairness." If a decision wasn't felt to be fair to all parties, we didn't proceed.

- ✔ **What each party brings to the table:** This item specifies the money and sweat equity that each party will invest. You, for example, may bring the idea and expertise in running a business; your potential partner may have cash to invest. Therefore, you contribute the labor, and she contributes the capital.

- ✔ **What you expect as a return for your investment or effort and how profits will be calculated and shared:** Here, you determine what each party expects out of the venture and the return for time and dollars invested, as well as how long you'll wait for results or profit. Are expenses from both parties subtracted from profits? Will you split the profits down the middle, for example, or divide them some other way, depending on contribution? (In the case of joint ventures, which I discuss more in the next section, make sure you account for your costs so you don't sacrifice net profit.) You also need to determine what happens if you need more money — where will you turn for funding if an investor decides to withdraw, for example.

✔ **The governance, ownership, and management structure:** Who will call the shots? How will the partnership's day-to-day operations be managed? How will responsibilities be divided, and how do you ensure that objectives are well defined?

✔ **What happens when unexpected events threaten the partnership:** If one of the partners dies or becomes ill, will you deal with the spouse instead? If a partner divorces his spouse, will the spouse still have legal rights in the partnership? How will you handle succession? Knowing the answers to these questions ahead of time looks after everyone's interests in the event that the partnership faces a crisis.

✔ **What the exit strategy will be in the event that the partnership doesn't work:** Addressing this issue sets the ground rules on the exit strategy for each partner or group if things don't work out. It also determines how the partnership is dissolved and how the remaining assets are divided. You also need to determine options for buying a partner out. Creating a plan that specifies each party's responsibilities provides clarity and reduces both parties' exposure to the unpredictable.

✔ **The frequency and timing of communication:** By specifying the frequency and timing of communication, you ensure that time-sensitive activities, such as making key decisions that require owner or employee input, will be agreed to.

Trust is built from open, honest, and transparent communication, and it isn't something you use a legal document to protect. It is embedded in the relationship. In the course of negotiating the preceding points, you'll see just how sturdy the foundation for trust, *the* nonnegotiable element, is in your relationship. Trust is truly put to the test when differences in values or interests appear, as they will during negotiation. Make sure each partner in your negotiation is deemed trustworthy; otherwise, it's better to walk away from the deal.

Mapping out gains and value in joint ventures

In partnerships, what brings two or more people together is complementary expertise and passion for an idea. In joint ventures, there are multiple reasons to team up for a short period of time or a specified purpose. Joint ventures are on the rise because the financial return on mergers and acquisitions has been underwhelming. Plus, joint ventures are more flexible and present opportunities to companies of all sizes.

Reasons for pursuing a joint venture

When you consider participating in a joint venture, you need to decide what you'll gain from your involvement, and what added value you and your company will attain. In other words, you need to answer the age old question: What's in it for me? Following are three common reasons companies enter into joint ventures:

✔ **To gain access to new markets:** Joint ventures can expand your company's reach, nationally and/or internationally. It may be a way to enter foreign markets in countries with growing economies, for example.

Consider the successful joint venture between Volkswagen Group and Chinese car maker FAW Group to make Audi and Volkswagens. Volkswagen successfully gained access to the Chinese market, and FAW gained access to Toyota's expertise, making Volkswagen one of the top two foreign carmakers in China. In 2013, China became the first market to report 20 million in sales in one year. On a different scale, Internet marketer Tom Antion, who has the largest list of public and professional speakers in the world (100,000), and Joan Stewart, "The Publicity Hound," collaborated on producing a $97.00 e-book entitled *How to Be a KickButt Publicity Hound.* Each sold the product and kept the revenue.

✔ **To reduce costs of developing services and products:** Suppose your company has a product that serves the clientele of a competitor. Your competitor has a large list of clients but doesn't offer the product or expertise you have. You are both missing out on sales (you, because you don't have access to the competitor's clients, and the competitor, because he doesn't have a product to sell), so you work out an arrangement to work together. Your competitor gains access to your product (or expertise), and you make your product available in exchange for profit-sharing and new clients.

Internet marketer Tom Antion builds and leverages his 100,000-person list by doing a joint venture where he sells a teleseminar featuring an expert speaker (Tom keeps that money); the expert speakers deliver the high value content, selling their products during and after the program and keeping the revenue.

✔ **To gain access to financing or intellectual know-how:** Many joint ventures combine know-how from one company and specific strengths from another, particularly when entering a foreign market. A company may also bolster its access to research and development (R&D) without having to establish its own R&D department internally by entering a joint venture with a company that is strong on R&D yet lacks access to a market. The first company provides access to the market while the second company offers R&D expertise — and everyone gains.

- ✔ **To profit from selling someone else's product, called *affiliate marketing*:** Affiliate programs are part of the marketing strategy for companies of all sizes. With affiliate marketing, one person has a high-value product and will pay you a commission for selling the product. Joint ventures form when you, as a marketer or fan of the product, sign up as an affiliate so you get paid when you share or directly market the product, and someone buys as a result of your referral. Amazon's affiliate program is probably the best known example, but lesser known but reputable companies such as JVZoo. com offer high-quality products for affiliates. Each affiliate marketing program is structured differently, so research the compensation plan and the product carefully.

Regardless of the reason why you want to get involved in a joint venture, be sure to talk through what is in it for everyone. Doing so minimizes surprises and maximizes the benefits.

Asking key questions at the outset

If you are considering a joint venture, doing your homework on the front end puts you in a better position when the time comes for the initial conversation. When you approach a joint venture from an informed viewpoint, you're less likely to get involved in something that either won't benefit you or will fail. When you're exploring a joint venture, be sure to answer the following questions:

- ✔ **What does our company bring that the other company needs?** Examine how your core strengths bring value to your potential partner's strengths and weaknesses to discover what you can offer in a joint venture. Perhaps it's a product, service, or a list of clients.

- ✔ **What does the other company bring to the joint venture that we need?** In addition to considering the strengths of the other company, examine your company's weaknesses. Perhaps the potential partner has a better product or a product that you can add to your current offerings. Or perhaps the prospective partner offers a service you don't or has a valuable list of clients.

- ✔ **What can both companies achieve together that neither can accomplish by working alone?** When you create a joint venture, the sum is often greater than the parts. By marrying two separate entities into one, you augment each other's strengths, and both parties benefit.

Gaining clarity and a common understanding of how a joint venture can benefit both parties gives you a solid, rational foundation to decide whether a joint venture will benefit everyone.

Assessing the fit

Going on a date is one thing; moving in together is quite another. You want to know ahead of time what skeletons are hidden inside your potential partner's closet and how you'll handle things when unexpected events happen. A successful joint venture, or any other collaborative structure, really depends on the level of trust in the relationship, the quality of communication (can you have the uncomfortable conversations?), and the quality of interaction — frankly, the same qualities that serve as the foundation of any high-performance relationship.

Reviewing the characteristics of successful joint ventures

When assessing whether the joint venture will be a marriage made in heaven or a partnership destined to fail miserably, be sure to explore the following points:

✔ **A good relationship:** Parties are willing to cooperate and face conflicting views and perspectives with honesty and respect. The relationship is one in which parties can openly state what isn't working so that the working relationship can be improved.

A good relationship is not one that is necessarily in harmony on all things all the time; a good relationship is one that deals with conflict, problems, and differing opinions openly, honestly, and respectfully.

✔ **An environment of trust:** Some conversations are difficult because something has gone badly wrong or because the chance for misunderstanding is high. In these situations, trust is key and includes these two components:

- **Being genuine and honest:** Put information on the table, talk about what is sacred, and be forthright about company or team strengths and weaknesses. Doing so helps all parties know what they are getting into with eyes wide open. You can read more about honest communication in the next item on this list.

- **Being reliable and dependable:** When the going gets rough, will the other parties bail out and wave good-bye as the ship sinks? Or will they show up, own up to their responsibilities, and dig creatively for a solution? In a nutshell: Can you count on your partner and can your partner count on you?

✔ **Honest communication:** The willingness to put the truth on the table without a lot of dramatic flare is the true test of solid communication. How willing are both parties to tell the truth? You'll know when you explore what could go wrong.

To assess the quality of the communication between you and your potential partner, listen for blaming. Blame-finding always signals avoidance of responsibility. And as you listen for this in your potential partner, be sure to look in the mirror as well. If your company engages in blame-finding, it probably isn't mature enough to enter into a joint venture. More emotional intelligence is required to avoid letting blame drive decision-making.

✔ **Interactions between partners characterized by sincerity and genuine care:** Collaborations of any kind demand a "we all gain or grow" mindset rather than one that focuses purely on self-interest. Through the course of working together on the project, it is character that largely determines whether the working relationship succeeds or fails. The quality of project management decisions hangs on good character in both parties.

It isn't what people say that counts. It's what people do, especially when tension or conflict are part of the picture. According to Russ Whitney, entrepreneur, veteran of many joint ventures, and author of *Inner Voice: Unlock Your Purpose and Passion* (Hay House Inc.), the deciding factor in any deal (after establishing that the deal makes logical sense, of course) is character. You can find more on character in Chapter 13.

✔ **A solid reason to start a joint venture:** A solid reason to work together is the glue for the relationship, so when you consider a joint venture, be sure that combining forces serves both parties, while also providing value to the clientele or customers. Otherwise, the joint venture is at risk of failure if (or when) things don't go as planned.

✔ **Shared motivation:** Understand the motivation of both parties when contemplating a joint venture. To put it another way, how strong (or flaky) is the commitment? Is the venture intended to achieve a fast profit? If so, and if the fat (and fast) profit doesn't materialize, is the partnership still on, or will one partner walk? Does either party have hidden motivations? When you know the motivation, you can both work toward achieving the goal. For example, some joint ventures are used to test-drive the merits of an acquisition. Two companies entering into collaboration with that knowledge can keep a sharper eye on the quality of the interaction between the two cultures.

Joint ventures between two companies who already have knowledge of one another through reputation or direct experience tend to work out better than ones formed through a "blind date." A good fit is the result of asking a lot of questions, verifying understanding, and allowing time for the companies to get to know one another. When two companies combine forces, the result is bigger than the sum of the individual parts, and everyone, including customers, benefits exponentially.

In assessing whether the venture is a good fit, you may be tempted to focus on all the ways the two companies are a good match. However, a better strategy is to explore the differences, especially where values are concerned. Doing so enables you to see how synergies will emerge.

A step-by-step guide for vetting a joint venture partner

Assess the pluses and minuses of a potential partnership before any formal agreement is created. Use the following steps to determine whether you fit well together:

1. **Determine whether your potential partner is as committed as you are to achieving something that works for everyone.**

   Part of respect and commitment is conveyed by who starts and ends the process of negotiating a joint venture. So pay attention to who you are working with throughout the project and process: Are they the key decision-makers or just the spokespeople or middlemen? If key decision-makers start and stay throughout the process, you have a pretty good idea that the organization is taking the venture seriously.

2. **Put key information — information needed to make decisions — out in the open so that it is accessible to all.**

   Expect the same transparency from your prospective partner. If the other party refuses to share information or keeps things close to the vest, expect unpleasant surprises further along in the relationship. By testing the willingness to be open before starting the joint venture, you can find out whether you're at risk of being blindsided by a hidden agenda.

3. **Watch for indications that your potential partner's strategic intention or motivation is out of sync with your goals.**

   Hidden agendas are a red flag. If you detect a hidden agenda, ask for full disclosure so you know whether it supports your goals — and perhaps find out what else is being hidden!

   Make sure you know all your potential partner's goals; otherwise, you risk a nasty surprise. Owners of one company, for example, accepted an investor, believing he would help the company move revenues to the next level. But once the investor gained majority ownership, he closed the company down. It turned out the investor's goal was to gain control of a company so he could use it as a write-off. Both of the company founders found themselves on the street.

You can share values and vision with a potential business partner, but if the reasons for entering the venture don't respect the needs of all, then discuss the issue until all parties can agree on what is fair.

4. **Have all parties name their strengths and weaknesses**.

   After your potential partner discloses both his assets and potential drawbacks, you can determine whether (and how) his company's strengths and weaknesses can help or hinder the goals of the partnership. For example, is one party (perhaps a bank) strong in finances or venture capital? If the strengths of your potential business partner complement your weaknesses, synergies between you two can propel you both.

5. **Talk about what you'll do when misunderstandings arise or your ideas don't mesh with your potential partner's.**

   The best way to reach agreement on how the partnership will handle such situations is to list the things that could go wrong in the project and then work through the scenarios as though they really happened. As a bonus, you'll gain insight into how your potential partner handled past experiences with similar situations and produce a process for resolving future issues.

6. **Discuss how past joint ventures (or projects similar to the one you're taking on now) unfolded for you and for your potential partner.**

   It's unrealistic to expect a track record of nothing but success. Instead, you want to understand how former project(s) went, how breakdowns were handled, how the relationship evolved, and what the results were. Don't hesitate to ask your potential business partner about a situation that raises questions in your mind. He should be willing to talk about what he learned through the process. So should you. Be prepared to share your own wins and failures.

7. **Ask yourself, "Can I work with this person?"**

   Things are a lot easier when you feel at ease with the people you work with. Character predicts how things will go when things go wrong, so take the time for informal conversation and get to know someone personally so that you can be confident that you have respect for who the other person is.

The chances for a successful venture are much greater if you enjoy working with the members or your partner's team. A key indicator that you have this connection? If you feel comfortable consummating the deal the old-fashioned way, with a handshake.

Finalizing the Agreement

After you work out the practicalities of the deal, the time has come to sign the agreement. At this stage, the trust between you and the rest of the team, and an awareness by all parties of what is going on will see the agreement through to a successful conclusion. Here are some things to think about:

✔ **Double-check that you've addressed all important issues.** Before signing on the dotted line, make sure you've asked the hard questions of each other and have worked out what needs to be in place so that you can jointly achieve the desired results. In the case of larger projects, you need to agree how to handle mistakes, misunderstandings, or disagreement. You also need to agree on who makes the decisions at each level and who to involve when disputes can't be resolved.

✔ **Document your discussion.** The goal of the agreement is to finalize and document understanding. One party can take responsibility for putting the agreement together, or representatives from both parties can work together to draft the agreement. You can also produce a memorandum of understanding (MOU), which outlines what was agreed to, areas of responsibility, and any communication or implementation protocols.

Another option, one I have used in construction projects, is to have the entire group participate in articulating the vision, goals, and conflict and communication protocols. Called a *charter,* this information all fits on one page — a long page mind you — poster size! As a special touch, we include a photo of all who helped craft the agreement and their signatures. This signed charter confirms the personal commitment of each participant to the agreement, and a duplicate is posted in every office as a reminder of the commitment. A charter is a way to confirm everyone's commitment to cooperatively managing the project.

A legal document won't guarantee anything except high legal fees. If you decide to have lawyers write up your agreement, remember that they focus on protecting your interests over achieving mutual gain, and if you enter into an agreement focusing on the probability of failure, failure will likely occur. So look for an attorney who will use the legal agreement to work out a fairer deal for all. Even though a legal document is a must in larger-risk projects, in the end, the relationship between the partners is what will make the project work.

Communicating Productively during the Venture

At one point or another, you've probably thought that reasonable people think like you do and the rest are idiots. Yet diversity is the thing that makes teams tick. Put the same kind of thinkers on a team or in an organization, and they'll stick to familiar patterns and miss opportunities to take innovative approaches or make performance breakthroughs. In fact, a breakdown is more likely.

Furthermore, in cross-cultural environments — the very environments companies seeking to enter new markets find themselves in — cultural norms regarding conflict, negotiations, and partnerships may differ among the different participants. Being aware of these differences helps you avoid assumptions and prompts you to ask questions that can improve the probability for success. In this section, I explore what makes and breaks trust and how facing and addressing conflicts can strengthen the relationship.

Focusing on trust

Joint ventures or partnerships that lack trust are costly to project goals, working relationships, and productivity. Experts estimate that over 50 percent of collaborations fail because of meltdowns in working relationships. Imagine the consequences when your business partner discovers you can't be trusted! In this section, I explain how to establish trust and, if something happens to damage trust, how to regain it.

Establishing trust

It's very important to establish trust with your business partner very early on. Unfortunately, many people fail to realize that they may be undermining trust. Rebuilding trust is a lot harder than consistently behaving in a trustworthy way. Table 18-1 shows some trust makers and breakers.

Table 18-1	Trust Makers and Trust Breakers
Trust Maker	*Trust Breaker*
Courageously confronting a problem when things don't go according to plan, particularly where a lot is at stake	Covering up mistakes; blaming employees or subordinates
Meaning what you say; if things change, explaining what happened, why it happened, and what it means to the project	Changing what you say, depending on the circumstances and who is listening

(continued)

Table 18-1 *(continued)*

Trust Maker	Trust Breaker
Asking questions to elicit assumptions	Making assumptions and then being angry when they turn out to be wrong
Sharing information openly with your partner, suppliers, and customers	Withholding information, presumably to gain greater influence or manipulate results
Having integrity and knowing your values, what you stand for, and what you won't put up with	Changing what you stand for, depending on the situation you're in; behaving in a way that undermines integrity

Regaining trust after it's lost

You may have heard the maxim that it takes one act to break trust and seven repeatedly successful actions to rebuild it. Clearly, gaining and keeping trust is a lot easier than recovering it after it's broken. Still, bad things can happen to good people, and you may find yourself in a situation where you've broken trust with a business partner, or he has broken trust with you. In these situations, regaining the trust of all parties is important. To recover trust, do the following:

- **Explore perceptions.** Find out what happened: Was it a miscommunication (as in failure to express yourself clearly) or misunderstanding (a misinterpretation of what you said). Getting to the heart of the matter lets you address the issue, thus leading to better understanding and a stronger relationship.

- **Invite all affected parties to a meeting to find out what happened and what can be learned from the situation.** I recommend having this meeting professionally facilitated, using a facilitator that both parties accept. Regardless whether the relationship survives the crisis in confidence, the experience leads to learning and has value.

- **Review what you take for granted or presume to be true.** Viewed through a different mindset, what you believe to be true may not be true at all. Reviewing assumptions that may have led to mistrust is particularly relevant in foreign countries where you have cultural differences as an overlay. For example, in China, harmony is valued and grounded in dignity and self-respect. In South America, conflict is an important part of the process. See Chapter 7 for information on how to strengthen your own competency in working with divergent views.

Companies that ignore relationship meltdowns as overly emotional and unprofessional are at a disadvantage. Higher levels of emotional and social intelligence can save a company a lot of time and money while reducing risk.

The process of rebuilding trust is made one tentative step at a time. The good news is that a working relationships that breaks down can serve as the catalyst to reboot the relationship, thus making it stronger, or to terminate the deal, which, although disappointing, may be better in the long run.

Using conflict to advantage

Working relationship meltdowns, combined with poorly thought through business models, cause the majority of failed collaborations. When conflicts arise, communication is needed. When things go wrong in joint ventures and strategic alliances, the culprit is usually a disconnection between what's expected and what's delivered. Being clear about expectations so that everyone shares the same understanding is a simple way to eliminate confusion.

You can address this issue by taking these actions:

✔ **Walk through the agreement so team members from both parties can clarify expectations and the risks before starting the project.** For cooperation to take place, both parties must be aware of what to expect. Doing so lets them rely on the relationships they've established, rather than the legalities of the deal, to work through issues.

Risks are sometimes off-loaded onto one party in a contractual agreement — a typical situation in contracts between the public service and private contractors, for example (when government dumps the risk onto the contractor so the contractor has to absorb the cost). When private contractors are asked to carry the load, they raise their fee, which, in the end, costs the taxpayers more. Walking through the contractual agreement to clarify risk-laden language before the deal is inked, or after if there's no other option, allows both parties to cooperatively manage risk regardless of what the contract says.

✔ **Map out how operational decisions will be made, what procedures will be followed for project updates or difficult conversations, and how conflict will be handled.** When you take care of this chore up front, everyone will have the same guidelines to work with.

A core element in the agreement should clearly establish the decision chain, from the ground up to higher levels, to avoid any confusion. Identify and record the trigger that either moves the decision to the next higher authority (in the case of hierarchies) or brings together people with the expertise or vision to work out what happens next.

✔ **As necessary, work through operational decisions during the project.** As soon as expectations aren't met, put people into a room (physical or virtual) to discover what happened and why. Then agree on how you'll get things back on track.

The key ingredient for reestablishing trust is to communicate, communicate, communicate. Communicating is a lot smarter and cheaper than speculating, accusing, or blaming. Communication happens most often in meetings, and most companies designate a specific schedule and purpose for each meeting. Weekly, monthly, or impromptu meetings are used to bring issues forward, check status, and resolve concerns. Check out Chapter 17 for how to run an effective meeting for making decisions.

An effective way to resolve issues is to have someone follow the issue from the point it is raised through to the point where it is resolved. In small-scale projects, it's easier to know who to talk to, and decision-makers are more accessible. In large, complex projects, however, you may need to designate someone to shadow the issue from decision-making to resolution. Doing so provides continuity — and reduces the tendency for a good cover-up story to get better as it gets further away from what really happened.

Testing Trust, Courage, and Cooperation When the Going Gets Tough

Communicating when things are going well is easy. When things go completely sideways, true leadership steps forward, and all the mechanisms you put in place can guide action. Redeeming value from an embarrassing situation requires leadership qualities and the creative courage to face the mistakes that were made. When things don't go according to plan, the key is to do the following:

- ✔ **Accept responsibility.** After admitting there is a problem, move directly to find a solution that will work.

- ✔ **Avoid the blame-game.** The blame-game looks to identify the responsible person so he can be blamed instead of identifying what can be done to handle the current situation. Learning from the past has enormous value; blaming someone for what has happened does not do anything to advance decision-making skills. So look ahead and be creative.

 If you find yourself thinking that "he (or she) should have . . . " or "he (or she) could have . . . ," recognize that you've fallen into the blame trap.

- ✔ **Recognize that the success of the project is based on the success of *all* the people involved.** Everyone wins when the going gets rough and all pitch in to bail out the situation.

Whether you enter into a partnership, a joint venture, or a strategic alliance, the qualities of trust, leadership, and the capacity to see from another perspective help you create functional working relationships.

Chapter 19

Setting Ethical Standards

. . . .

In This Chapter

▶ Understanding what constitutes ethical business conduct

▶ Uncovering pressures that lead to unethical decisions

▶ Establishing formal ethical guidelines

▶ Creating an ethical business culture

▶ Addressing ethics in health and safety and in your supply chain

. . . .

*E*thics are a hot topic — and for good reason. Breaches of ethics can harm people's livelihoods, quality of life, and health; they can increase the cost of goods to consumers while reducing financial prosperity for all; and they can damage reputations and close companies. Making matters worse, the ramifications can wash over the entire sector and can go far beyond the companies, industries, or employees involved.

From an investor's perspective, companies that engage in unethical behavior are high risk, made even more so because the risk rises with each unethical decision. Fortunately, as a decision-maker, you can decide to go a different route. In this chapter, I show you how to set ethical standards, tell you how you can reduce the likelihood of making unethical decisions, and explain how you can upgrade your company's ethical culture to reduce your risk of exposure. This may all seem like a lot of work, but remember this: Ethical companies make more money, last longer, and are better places to work.

Defining Business Ethics

The term *ethics* refers to the principles that govern a person's or group's behavior. A simple way of understanding ethical behavior is to think of it as a way of relating to others that enhances individual and collective well-being. In this section, I discuss the characteristics of ethical business decisions and outline unethical practices that businesses succumb to.

Looking at ethics in business

Ethics are important in business. Businesses like to work with ethical companies, and clients like to purchase goods and services from ethical businesses. Business ethics incorporate the following principles:

- ✔ **Doing the most good or least harm, with the overall aim being to balance good over harm:** This is a practical view of ethics. Within the context of business, it means that companies operate in a way that achieves the greatest good and least harm to employees, communities, the environment, shareholders, and customers.

- ✔ **Protecting and respecting individual and collective rights:** To do so, ethical businesses exhibit behaviors such as those outlined in Table 19-1.

Not surprisingly, determining what constitutes a right and how and to whom such a right applies is a never-ending area of controversy. You can find some interesting information on rights at this website: http://www.scu.edu/ethics/practicing/focusareas/business/introduction.html.

- ✔ **Treating people fairly:** Fair treatment includes treating everyone equally unless a compelling reason justifies unequal treatment — accommodating people with disabilities by removing barriers, for example. *Note:* Workplace conditions are an important force behind whether employees make ethical or unethical decisions. To find out more about how you can ensure that your company promotes ethical decision-making, head to the later section "Setting Formal and Informal Standards."

What's a compelling reason? Well, it's not age, gender, body shape, race, religion, how well you like (or dislike) a person, and any other such reasons. In fact, a whole body of case law wrestles with this very issue, and the U.S. Supreme Court has weighed in a number of times.

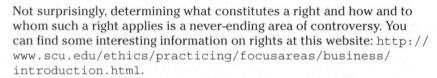

Table 19-1	Examples of Ethical and Unethical Behaviors	
Right	*Ethical Behavior*	*Unethical Behavior*
The right to informed consent	Telling the truth and providing information that enables people to make informed choices and to not be put at risk of injury without their consent	Keeping vital information secret or knowingly engaging in practices that jeopardize a person's health and safety
The right to be treated with dignity	Respecting human dignity and valuing all life, not just human	Establishing unhealthy working conditions, using child labor, or engaging in or tolerating demeaning workplace environments

Right	Ethical Behavior	Unethical Behavior
The right to privacy	Respecting customers' or clients' privacy and protecting personal information	Monitoring private information without authorization or gossiping about confidential patient information
The right to self-determination	Acting in a way that promotes quality of life for both individuals and communities and safeguarding environmental and social well-being by engaging in behaviors that are socially responsible and enhance, rather than harm, communities	Engaging in irresponsible environmental practices; suppressing a community's right to better itself

Falling from grace: Unethical business practices

You can probably name at least one unethical company. Chances are it's been in the news or has provoked outrage because it engaged in one of the practices I outline in this section.

Ethics, morals, laws: Why they aren't the same

Now that you have a good idea of what constitutes ethics and ethical behavior, take a minute to explore what ethics are not. Ethics are not the same as

✔ **Feelings or emotions:** Someone can do bad things and feel good about it, and many times, doing the right thing can be uncomfortable. Ask any whistleblower or truth teller who has had to go against the prevailing winds of deception.

✔ **Religious beliefs:** Ethics are the principles that govern behavior. Although they may incorporate moral or religious principles, they are not the same as religious beliefs. Ethics apply equally to all.

✔ **Following the law:** Some laws make little sense and can depart from what is right or wrong. Outsourcing garment manufacturing to foreign companies where workplace conditions are deplorable is legal, but is it ethical? Paying minimum wage is legal, but when full-time employees can't meet basic living expenses, is it ethical?

To see a list of the world's most unethical multinational companies, go to http://www.huffingtonpost.com/2010/01/28/the-least-ethical-compani_n_440073.html. From a wide range of sectors, the companies on this year's list are willing to increase risk in the short-, medium- and long-term to gain instant gratification.

Misusing funds

The misappropriation of funds occurs when an employee (anyone from the executive down to the bookkeeper) misuses or embezzles funds or steals merchandise or supplies. Greed or rationalization ("They owe me," "No one will get hurt," or "It's good for the company because it lets us meet sales targets") underpins the decision.

Not disclosing information related to public health and safety

Some companies deliberately withhold information pertinent to public health and safety. Drug companies that manipulate studies to downplay risks is one familiar example, but companies that fail to provide adequate training for new hires, particularly youth, who operate risky machinery are also guilty. Greed (seeking to maximize profits or avoid costly changes), dishonesty (altering the truth to support the spurious motivation), and shortsighted decision-making (failing to look past the immediate goal to weigh the consequences) underpin these decisions.

Lying to the public

Some companies provide misleading information. There are so many examples of this behavior that it's hard to narrow down a list. Here are two examples, one highlighting an entire industry that misled customers and the other highlighting a former CEO who lied on his resume:

✔ For years, the tobacco industry hired medical experts to promote the idea that cigarettes were safe, despite internal documents showing the link between tobacco use and lung cancer and other adverse health outcomes.

✔ Former Yahoo CEO Scott Thompson was booted from the job after it was revealed he'd lied on his resume (he claimed a computer science degree he hadn't actually earned).

Taking dangerous or ill-advised shortcuts

Shortcuts, often the result of excessive pressure to meet profit or production targets, invariably lead to increased risk of unethical decision-making. Although convenient, shortcuts are costly when meeting short-term financial or production quotas replaces sound judgment. To avoid this trap, you must be alert to the stress: What are you being pressured to achieve and at what cost?

Stress instigates poor decision-making. Unethical decisions that result from pressure to meet targets are often the result of the poorly thought-out metrics, unreasonable performance appraisal contract goals, and short-term thinking — all of which come at the expense of higher performance. To discover how you can ensure that you're using the right metrics, head to Chapter 9.

Failing to consider the impact of their operations on communities, society, or the environment

Ignoring social and environmental impacts constitutes a fundamental ethical breach of public trust, particularly in the communities where companies do business. Environmental and social damages caused by unethical business decisions are the by-products of a historical belief that humanity is separate from nature (a very costly assumption!), the idea that resources are unlimited (they aren't), and businesses' preference for simple calculations (if the business decision and its consequences aren't easy to count, they don't count it at all).

An unpublished 2010 United Nations report shows that corporations cause an estimated \$2.2 trillion in environmental damage each year. So far, companies have not been held financially accountable for the damage. Instead, taxpayers — and on a wider scale, civilization itself — pay for the unethical decisions that damage the environment and hurt communities.

Expectations are changing about how companies should behave as the effects of global climate change and a shift in social entrepreneurship put outmoded practices in the crosshairs. Companies that don't behave in socially and environmentally responsible ways will fail as progressive companies that embed respect and care for natural resources and people into their cultural DNA continue to outperform them.

Understanding Pressures That Lead to Unethical Decisions

As a rule, unethical decisions are not the result of individuals intentionally planning to commit fraud. Generally, people don't wake up in the morning, look in the mirror, and declare, "I am going to be unethical today!" Instead, other forces impact behavior and drive unethical decisions. Pressures — societal, personal, and professional — can tilt conduct toward or away from ethical behavior. In this section, I show you what those pressures are and what you and your company can do to avoid them.

External pressures: The changing nature of business

The world is changing, and so must business. Business is no longer viewed as simply the engine of economic growth; it is expected to embrace the values of social and environmental responsibility. Companies today are judged not only by their bottom lines but also by how well they respect the integrity of all people, assume stewardship of the environment, and give back in meaningful ways.

Companies are under pressure to adapt to these changing business conditions, yet most don't know how. Adapting is especially difficult for companies in which decision-makers feel confident they are in control, have a low tolerance for uncertainty, or rely on familiar strategies to get work done. The primary indicator that pressures are going unrecognized is the ridiculously high levels of employee disengagement and emotional disengagement. Pushing beyond the traditional business role as an economic engine and embracing the higher leadership role creates tension. This tension can be handled two ways: by resisting it or by using it to come up with better solutions.

Companies that fail to recognize that the business decision-making environment has changed tend to resist and, in doing so, relay pressure directly onto employees, which creates the conditions for unethical decision-making. (It also increases the costs of stress-related illness and disengages employees.) Companies can pass the pressure of changing market conditions onto employees in a number of ways:

- **Focusing on making money at any cost, regardless of the consequences to employee well-being:** The repercussion is that dishonest employees reason that they can also make money at any cost to the company. From the employees' point of view, why not? The company is modeling behavior it tolerates. Consider that one-third of business failures are due to internal theft.

- **Setting up metrics or performance contracts that put on pressure to take shortcuts without gaining efficiency or integrity:** Risky shortcuts occur when attention goes to meeting internal goals and away from supporting employee performance or strengthening customer and community relationships. Consider the employee who is encouraged to lie so that the boss can get his performance bonus. Or the manager who ignores the company's long-term goals and customer service so that she can meet arbitrary internal goals.

- **Cutting costs instead of seizing opportunities:** Rather than being creative during tough economic times, business decision-makers often resort to cutting costs as the sole solution: They jettison staff, eliminate training, or cut back on customer service. Yet cutting costs without considering the consequences can actually result in increased costs. The downside of cutting customer service in retail, for example, is that customers serve themselves, helping themselves to products when no one is around to notice, or take their business to a company that provides better service. Meanwhile, creative solutions that could lead to potential savings are left on the table.

Managers are taught to delegate, which is a good idea, but delegating without questioning the consequences increases stress. Delegating without assessing the situation is a practice guided by two faulty assumptions: one, that working harder will make the pressure go away (it doesn't) and two, that employees can handle the additional work (they often can't). To address the source of the problem, you must notice how changing market conditions, social values, and other factors (all of which I describe in Chapter 1) directly and indirectly impact your employees. Armed with that knowledge, you can implement strategies to adapt to the changes instead of unwittingly intensifying the conditions for failure.

Internal pressures: Working conditions and relationships

Poor working conditions, lack of respect, lack of trust in coworkers, and lack of trust in management — especially when mixed together in a potent brew — can lead to unethical behavior. The potential for unethical behavior is heightened in work environments that exhibit the following conditions:

- ✓ **Employees feel unfairly treated.** When opportunity and temptation collide, employees will rationalize how their unethical behavior compensates for having been treated unfairly, and they're not likely to accept personal culpability for their actions.

  Bosses who take credit for employees' ideas create the conditions for unethical decisions at worst, and low morale, at best.

- ✓ **Disrespectful or demeaning treatment is the norm in the work environment.** Demeaning conditions, where managers ridicule employees for mistakes or where the work itself is demeaning, contribute to theft and other unethical actions.

  You may be rewarding unethical behavior without realizing it. You say — and your policies and procedures manual states — for example, that bullying will not be tolerated, but you look the other way when a valued employee engages in the behavior. This kind of double standard sends the message that some employees are more valuable than others, and the more valued ones are allowed to play by different rules.

- ✓ **Individual needs are not being met by the work or home environment or by conditions of employment.** Needs include acquiring money, social status, and recognition, or resolving a stressful personal problem.

My pre-frontal cortex was malfunctioning!

High-pressure working conditions result in exhausted employees. Tired workers are more likely to make unethical decisions for one simple biological reason: They need sleep! Self-control is a function of your brain's pre-frontal cortex. The pre-frontal cortex uses glucose (sugar) as fuel. When you are tired and try to exercise self-control, you deplete already limited levels of glucose (think of it as withdrawing from a limited credit line). That's why, when you don't get sleep, your temper is short, you can't concentrate, and you're likely more uncoordinated. (Ever experienced a surprise face plant when walking on flat ground? It's disconcerting.) Your capacity for self-control is also compromised. Imagine using this as an excuse: "My pre-frontal cortex made me do it!"

Having unmet needs alone isn't a predictor of unethical decisions. Some of the poorest people in society struggle to meet basic needs but don't act unethically. Some of the richest people do.

Eliminating conditions that lead to ethics breaches

Working conditions and relationships between employees and management that lead to unethical behavior can wreak havoc with your business. Here are some ways to avoid creating these conditions:

- **Model the behavior you want to see.** If your company selects a cause, such as alleviating local poverty, and then actively works with the community to help youth, for example, you're modeling the kind of behavior you'd like to see. Identify core values that employees share and use them as the basis for decision-making.

- **Be consistent.** If you say you care about the environment but toss out garbage rather than finding ways to reuse or exchange it, you're sending mixed messages. If you say you care about employees — as long as they don't ask questions and don't challenge your decisions, that is — then you're reinforcing that saying one thing and doing another is all right.

- **Find a higher purpose, a contribution your company can make that goes beyond profit.** The Conscious Capitalism Credo says, "We believe that business is good because it creates value, it is ethical because it is based on voluntary exchange, it is noble because it can elevate our existence, and it is heroic because it lifts people out of poverty and creates prosperity."

- **Examine the consequences of your metrics.** Metrics that focus on the short term and don't contribute directly or indirectly to overall company goals are problematic. Be sure the metrics you use keep your company's long-term view in mind and go beyond the next quarter's results.

A lot of manipulation and unethical behavior is conducted to meet poorly constructed metrics. For instance, tying personal performance goals to team accomplishment sounds like a good idea, but it fails when the company overloads the unit and expects superhuman results. The metrics in this case are completely disconnected from what is happening on a systems-wide level. Instead, tie metrics to the achievement of larger business goals so that employees can see the relationship between their contribution and the company's success.

Metrics take steady work and commitment to get right because they are loaded with unintended consequences. It is important to monitor how metrics create behaviors and results that you may (or may not) want. You can find more on metrics in Chapter 9.

✓ **Use performance contracts wisely.** If you need them at all, make sure they track an employee's contribution toward achieving the company's mission. Increasingly, companies focus on performance to achieve business goals rather than monitoring individual performance. In other words, the focus is on collective performance (trust-based) instead of overseeing individual performance (control-based). When you reward individual performance over collective achievement, self-interest is rewarded, and you're less likely to see a unit without much to do step up to help one that is overloaded. When performance focuses on achieving the business goals, teamwork is rewarded.

✓ **Ask employees to identify opportunities to improve efficiency and then recognize and credit them for their contribution.** Companies that ask employees for help but then give all credit to management model unethical behavior. Companies that truly value their employees can get help when they need it because employees know they are contributing to something bigger than themselves.

Efficiencies can be gained through reducing costs while maintaining or gaining productivity. Instituting safety measures (that have a cost) while decreasing project time is an example. Novo Nordisk, a global pharmaceutical company, engaged its employees in finding cost savings in energy use. The savings financed implementation of the company's zero footprint goal.

✓ **Relieve stress by implementing a way to handle the workload as a team.** By managing the situation collectively, employees have control over how they get their work done and can come up with ways to meet their personal needs and the company's goals.

✓ **Support healthy working relationships.** Centering work relationships on shared values, like service to the customer, is a way to effectively concentrate a collective effort toward achieving a higher goal.

✓ **Recognize fellow employees for their efforts and ideas.** Try doing so informally, in personal day-to-day interaction.

✔ **Treat people fairly and with respect.** What constitutes fairness varies from one working environment to the next, but generally it means applying the same rules to all, holding everyone to the same standards, not playing favorites (doling out good jobs to those you like and bad jobs to everyone else, for example), and not tolerating bullying behavior from *anyone*.

Both company character and personal character play a big role in an ethical workplace. Is the company trustworthy and supportive? Does it inspire loyalty? Are any employees struggling personally, and if so, are the company and coworkers there to help? If you answer "No" to these questions, your workplace suffers from the absence of a loyal and supportive community — it's a breeding ground for self-serving or self-protective behavior. (For a story on the important role a boss plays to remedy this kind of situation, read Andy Allen's approach to helping staff, which I describe in Chapter 12.)

Setting Formal and Informal Standards

Although companies in specific sectors (those, like retail, that tend to rely on part-time and transient workers who don't see the job as a career and therefore often lack loyalty to the business) must put in place formal standards to address ethics within their businesses, most companies can improve the quality of the workplace conditions by setting up informal yet effective ways to support ethical choices. In the following sections, I show you how you can reinforce ethical decision-making and behaviors both formally and informally.

These solutions — like creating a healthy workplace and installing checks and balances — address individual and group behaviors within your company. Some ethical breaches, however, are much larger — they threaten an industry (such as the fraudulent actions of financial institutions that lead to the 2008 economic crisis), or they violate state and federal laws (insider trading, for example) — and should be handled by regulatory agencies and the U.S. courts.

According to the 25th Annual Retail Theft Survey, conducted by Hayes International (http://hayesinternational.com/news/annual-retail-theft-survey/), over 1.2 million shoplifters and dishonest employees were caught and over \$199 million in goods recovered in 2013. Further, dishonest employees steal about 5.5 times more than dishonest customers.

Developing a formal code of ethics

Until workplace conditions, management skills, and self-responsibility improve, businesses of all kinds and sizes are susceptible to employee theft and other unethical decisions. Establishing formal measures can help solve the problem.

Creating guidelines for your company

Having a formal code in place reminds employees that ethical behavior is expected of everyone in the company. To install a formal code of ethics, follow these steps:

1. **Gather a list of issues on which employees would like guidance.**

   Enlist the help of your team or employees to compile this list, which can include anything from Internet use to interpersonal communication.

2. **For each issue that was identified in Step 1, write out guidelines that address expectations and consequences of potential misconduct.**

   Here are some common issues and the kind of information your guidelines will most likely include:

   - **Internet use:** This guideline specifies what kind of Internet use is permitted on company computers — prohibiting using company computers to troll porn sites or download illegal information, for example.

   - **Anti-bribery policies:** This guideline prohibits employees from offering something of value to public officials, for example, in exchange for a favor.

   - **Gift-receiving policies:** This guideline would prohibit accepting gifts from vendors and suppliers intended to bias the recipient toward their products or services. This applies to gifts intended to influence the decision-making process as distinct from gifts intended to express gratitude or customer appreciation for the business relationship or loyalty.

   - **Health and safety:** This guideline sets company standards regarding health and safety, and outlines what behaviors constitutes a violation of those standards.

   - **Company policies regarding employee benefits and compensation.** Make sure your company has a guideline in place for this important issue. Violations, such as denying wages or ignoring overtime rules, is illegal.

   Preparing these guidelines will likely involve both the company's formal leaders (people who hold the designated levels of authority) and informal leaders (employees who have high levels of respect and/or influence on coworkers).

3. **Communicate the rules and live by them.**

   Ensure that your staff are aware of the company guidelines and can live by them — without exception. Public firms in the U.S. are required under the Sarbanes-Oxley Act to make communicating the code of ethics a priority, and companies, public or not, who encourage dialogue over ethical issues reinforce an ethical culture, and misconduct goes down.

Reinforcing your commitment to your guidelines

Having the rules codified isn't all you can do to promote a culture of ethical behavior. Follow these suggestions to underscore your commitment to the guidelines:

- ✔ **Institute checks and balances.** Having a system of checks and balances in place eliminates any one person having unmonitored control over vital functions. You may have both a bookkeeper and an accountant, each from different firms. It's one way to make sure funds are being handled appropriately as each can cross check the work of the other.

- ✔ **Make it safe to report misconduct.** Provide whistleblowers in the workplace with protection. They are saving you and your company's reputation and viability. Ensure that supervisors act on reports of wrongdoing and that they report their findings privately to the whistleblower and to employees as a whole. Doing so strengthens employee confidence that your company takes unethical misconduct seriously.

When you support truth-telling, you instill higher levels of trust in the workplace. You want your company's actions regarding whistleblowing to be transparent and to encourage truth-telling, not punish it. Without this protection, your code is purely decorative.

The U.S. National Occupational Health and Safety Council reports that providing workers with whistleblower protection helps prevent injury and death. Yet a 2013 National Business Ethics Survey of the U.S. Workforce reports that one out of three people who observe misconduct in action fail to report it. Why? Sadly, 21 percent of workers — six million workers in American private sector companies — who reported misconduct experienced some form of retaliation from superiors. To make matters worse, 60 percent of the misconduct charges were leveled at those in managerial positions (supervisor to the top executives). Until whistleblower protection is in place, unethical companies use threats and intimidation to avoid addressing safety risks.

- ✔ **Back up your formal codes of ethics with an informal code.** Head to the next section to discover how to foster ethics and create a great workplace culture.

Establishing an informal code

You establish an informal code of conduct and ethics through your company's culture, which ideally supports professionalism and ethical behavior, builds strong working relationships, and fosters an environment of trust. A culture that fits that definition has a high level of integrity and is a better place to work.

Failure to warn

The proprietor of a commercial painting company submitted a proposal to paint the roof of a large factory building. The property was about 40 years old and largely constructed of corrugated, galvanized sheet steel. The roof was in poor condition, and it's semi-clear fiberglass roof panels were covered in lichen and dust, making it difficult to clearly see the fiberglass panels.

When preparing the bid, the proprietor took the owner's word that the roof was shabby and needed to be painted. He performed only a cursory inspection of the site: He made a visual inspection of the roof from the ground and did not enter the building or examine whether the roof had skylights, despite knowing from experience how such buildings were customarily constructed.

Upon winning the bid, the owner assembled a crew of unskilled labor. When he sent his crew to work on the roof, he did not raise the possibility of skylights, mention that they become brittle over time, or warn that the skylights must not be stood upon under any circumstances. Within 15 minutes of starting work, a 17-year-old worker fell through a skylight to his death.

This true story illustrates how assumptions and communication failures put employees at risk. Here, it cost one young man his life, and the owner lost his company (he's lucky he didn't end up in jail). The owner failed to consider the risk and potential consequences inherent to the situation or to take steps to inform his employees of the potential danger. In court, he stated that he assumed employees would see the skylights. Yet inexperienced or unskilled workers don't know what questions to ask to prevent personal risk. And most experienced workers lack the confidence or are afraid of losing their jobs if they report safety risks in the workplace. Bottom line: Through reckless decision-making, this owner stage-managed a preventable death.

In this section, I outline some ways you can build a culture that promotes ethical decision-making and behavior. (To read more about the influence of workplace culture on decision-making, head to Chapter 3; Chapters 4 and 5 cover the relationship between better decision-making and personal and organizational growth.)

Fostering open and honest communication

Difficult conversations or decisions arise when doing what is right isn't what is easy. Reporting on health and safety risks is one example of a difficult conversation; honestly discussing a failed decision or poor results is another.

When management communicates openly and honestly and is transparent about what is going on, a stronger impetus to accept personal responsibility and accountability for decisions develops, leading to more ethical operations. Similarly, employees who feel that they can influence the company's direction and contribute to a meaningful purpose have a greater sense of loyalty and are more committed to operating ethically. The result is that actions of the company, which are a collective expression of each employee's decisions, earn trust from customers, investors, and the community.

Diversity of perspective is an asset to a company, yet the inability to embrace different views can result in unproductive conflict. Overcoming bias and prejudice toward differences is best handled by having people work together so that their focus is on achieving a goal. That way everyone learns. If bullying is an issue, head to Chapter 13 to find out how to strengthen leadership skills by confronting bullying behavior.

Reducing pressure to compromise standards

Work pressures and other sources of stress can lead people to compromise standards and make unethical decisions.. These compromises and decisions — like cutting corners on health and safety, choosing substandard parts to keep expenses down, or taking dangerous shortcuts to meet a production quota — all boil down to believing that the end justifies the means.

Has your company fallen prey to this kind of thinking? If "I don't care how you do it — just do it!" is a common refrain, it has. Following are some ways you can reduce these kinds of pressures:

✔ **With the help of staff, identify areas where improving conditions will help remove workplace stress.** These are simple things, like allowing people to go to the toilet without permission or not requiring a note from the doctor saying you're sick. Cooperatively distributing workload within the unit and between units of the company is another way to offset stress. Stress isn't reduced by taking action. It's reduced by stepping back to observe what actions are being taken and then choosing a different approach to how work gets done and by whom.

✔ **Provide support for coping with daily life pressures.** Providing on-site services such as yoga, massage, exercise, meditation, mindfulness, and day care can reduce stress and improve decision-making.

✔ **Make *how* things gets done as important as the result.** Companies often reward achieving results but don't pay attention to how well the work gets done. Shortcuts, like compromising environmental standards, or workplace health and safety, are a consequence. Aligning decision-making to values is one way to ensure that the process used and the relationships built are considered part of the result instead of a "do whatever it takes at any cost" type of approach.

✔ **Conduct a survey of values to isolate where the company is making decisions out of fear.** The Barrett Values Centre has done some outstanding work in helping companies align their cultures with their core values. To identify whether your company is using its energy well or wasting it on pointless conflict, go to the Centre's website to find cultural transformation tools: `http://www.valuescentre.com/products_ services/?sec=cultural_transformation_tools_(ctt)`. A survey can pinpoint action and guide decisions.

Eradicating coercive management styles

When top management relies on coercion, it sets the tone for the entire organization. The coercive style involves telling people what to do and then criticizing their every move. People feel minimized or demeaned, trust is low, and productivity and creativity suffer or disappear. Staying safe forms the basis for decision-making, consequently restricting growth, and ethical breaches are fostered because employees look after their own interests knowing that the company won't.

To address the fundamental sources of intimidating and coercive behavior in individual managers and executives, consider the following suggestions:

✔ **Provide leadership, personal development, or life-coaching opportunities.** Career stagnation at any level, including the management tier, can be remedied through opportunities for growth and development. Everyone benefits, especially the person involved.

✔ **Apply the rules consistently throughout the organization.** From the frontline worker to the highest levels of management, what is fairly applied will be fairly followed.

✔ **Provide guidance for handling those situations in which doing the right thing is harder than turning the other way.** Talk about ethical situations you've faced and provide real-life examples. Explore ways you can collectively improve responses to the situations your employees are observing.

✔ **Give managers a window into the employees' world.** Rotate management into frontline and other positions for a day so that the managers can learn and gain insight from what their employees face day to day. Being aware of the typical situations employees face when serving the public, customers, or internal clients can illuminate the underlying pressures behind any issues.

Focusing team talent on achieving a goal while reinforcing confidence is likely to be more productive than telling employees they suck at what you are paying them to do.

Common Concerns: Dealing with Supply Chains and Health and Safety

Improving workplace conditions and reducing risk exposure throughout the supply chain are two priority areas for companies to strengthen their reputation, reduce operational costs, retain skilled employees, and gain customers. As consumers and clients increasingly base their buying decisions on open transparency in the supply chain and caring about people doing the work, companies that pay attention to ethics gain the advantage. In this section, I show you how to make better decisions about health and safety in the workplace, given competing priorities, and how companies are raising standards through their supply chain.

Reducing workplace hazards

Decision-makers in companies where the health and safety of their workforce are everyday concerns — construction, industries that operate heavy machinery, manufacturing, chemical or hazardous waste removal services, the transportation sector businesses, and so on — can do their part to promote decisions that safeguard both employee safety and the bottom line. So can workers.

As a business owner, you can do the following:

- ✔ **Ensure that safety equipment is kept up to standard and emergency preparedness plans are in place.** Keeping safety equipment up to date lets you reduce both costs and the risk of injury or death. Companies that ignore regular maintenance end up paying higher insurance costs, paying compensation, and possibly defending themselves from a law suit.

  To see how you really feel about the quality of workplace conditions and your company's standards for health and safety, ask yourself, would you let your son or daughter work in your company?

- ✔ **Eliminate procedures that are inherently unsafe.** In 2010, six workers were killed cleaning natural gas pipes in an energy plant in the U.S. The practice was later deemed unsafe. If a procedure is inherently unsafe, find another, safer way to accomplish the same task, before people get killed or injured.

- ✔ **Consider the consequences of risk ahead of time.** Here are the ethical question to ask beforehand: Will withholding information concerning safety or health risk do more harm than good? Will taking the shortcut increase risk to employee safety? Asking questions to reveal what isn't being taken into account helps you avoid risk of permanent injury and fatalities.

As an employee, you can ask questions related to safety risks so you don't go in unprepared. Many injuries or fatalities result when an employee is afraid to question a decision for fear of losing his or her job. In the end, you must be clear on what's important to you: your job, or potential death or loss of limb. Here are some suggestions:

- ✔ **If you're looking for a job, seek out companies that are committed to employee health and safety:** Research the safety record of a company as part of your job search process. Although no protection exists for whistleblowers, most of the worst companies do have marks against them for safety infractions, making them easy to eliminate from your list of prospects. Others may take more research.

✔ **Select a company that has a track record of caring for its employees.** Use websites such as `http://www.greatplacetowork.com`, which lists companies around the world where workers are fairly and respectfully treated, feel pride in their work, and like who they work with.

Bringing the supply chain up to ethical standards

A firm's reputation and its exposure to risk are directly linked to the ethical health of its suppliers. Your business's success is dependent on the success of the entire community of relationships associated with producing your product or service, and you can use your company's buying power and its relationship with suppliers to build value throughout your procurement chain and to clean up unethical practices in your suppliers' operations.

The reputations of a number of big companies were damaged when their labels were found in the charred ruins of a 2013 factory collapse in Bangladesh that was caused by unsafe working conditions. After the fire, over 100 companies signed the Accord on Fire and Building Safety in Bangladesh. Some of the largest garment companies in the world — Britain's Primark, Spain's Inditex (Zara), Dutch company C&A, Swedish company H&M, and U.S. companies Tommy Hilfiger and Calvin Klein — signed on to cover costs of improving safety and working conditions, and they retained the option to stop doing business with company owners who refuse to cooperate with these efforts. (See the Accord at `http://www.bangladeshaccord.org`.) In short, they've used the influence behind their own buying power to initiate ethical practices in the companies that supply them. Suppliers who follow sound labor, environmental, and safety practices reduce their exposure to risk and increase their chances of being on the procurement list.

Working with the supply chain to upgrade efficiencies and promote ethical integrity is a way you can make decisions that are good for the planet, good for people, and good for business. Here is a short list of some other ways companies are upgrading efficiencies and ethics in their supply chain:

✔ **Finding efficiencies:** Companies are looking for cost efficiencies through energy use and use of water and other resources. These companies seek to incorporate sustainability into their brand reputations, and they engage their employees in finding energy cost savings.

By offering carbon neutral shipping and using new routing technology, UPS saves 6.3 million gallons of fuel. The company is cutting its carbon footprint while saving money.

✔ **Participating in collaborative initiatives:** Companies that participate in collaborative initiatives gain leadership skills and update internal decision-making processes in order to work collaboratively.

The Sustainable Food Lab (`http://www.sustainablefoodlab.org`) is a partnership of mostly large companies and nonprofits. Its role is to incubate and sometimes manage sustainable sourcing projects. The Sustainable Food Lab team provides tailored services for organizations, supply chain initiatives, and multi-stakeholders convening around specific challenges for sustainable sourcing. For example, the Sustainable Food Lab helps Unilever measure impact on small farmers in developing countries around the world, coordinates a Corn/Soy Belt collaboration of many organizations improving water quality in the United States Midwest, and manages the development of the Cool Farm Alliance to reduce greenhouse gas emissions and other impacts from agriculture.

✔ **Buying directly from the supplier and streamlining the distribution system:** In some industries, the supply chain has become cluttered with too many handlers, adding cost to the price without adding value. Sometimes, as in the case of food, buying local puts money directly in the pocket of the grower.

No single solution applies across every situation. In some instances, for example, the wholesaler adds a premium for little more than handling the goods; in other instances, wholesalers protect the buyer from volatile markets and thereby add value. So take a close look at your supply chain, their sources, and the effect of your purchase on the producer before determining how you can gain efficiencies while still benefiting the producers in a fair exchange for all.

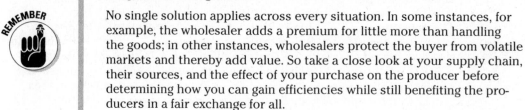

Take coffee, for instance, and the Third Wave (`http://imbibemagazine.com/Coffee-s-Third-Wave`). The Third Wave movement's vision is to treat coffee as an artisanal craft rather than a commodity. Small coffee companies — like Wrecking Gall Roasters (`http://www.wreckingball-coffee.com/index.shtml`) in the U.S. and Drop Coffee (`http://www.dropcoffee.com`) in Sweden — are dedicated to delivering a high-quality product to consumers. By inserting improvements into every aspect of production to help growers provide the highest quality beans (promoting environmentally sound growing conditions and developing direct working relationships with growers, for example), these companies produce a product that has more of what is good for you and less of what isn't. In addition, because these companies buy directly from the grower — an ethic that appeals to many coffee connoisseurs — more money ends up in the growers' pockets.

Part VI
The Part of Tens

For a bonus Part of Tens chapter on decision-making, head to http://www.dummies.com/extras/decisionmaking.

In this part . . .

- ✔ Learn how to work with uncertainty to improve decision-making
- ✔ Discover ways to use the unexpected to your company's advantage
- ✔ Dig deeper into the secrets behind ethical decision-making

Chapter 20

Ten Tips for Decision-Making in Uncertain Situations

Concrete thinkers in today's world are under pressure. As I show throughout this book, viewing the world through a black-and-white lens is deceptive, and your decision-making suffers, especially in a world where market conditions change quickly and you have to navigate ambiguous situations. Here are ten tips to help you make the jump from black-and-white thinking and guide you in your decision-making.

Check Assumptions

Assumptions and unexamined beliefs can limit your understanding of a situation. Unchecked assumptions increase uncertainty because they lead to false conclusions and limit your options. You're probably making assumptions if you tend to think in terms of absolutes — "Business exists *purely* to be the economic engine," "Our product is *only* applicable to Customer A," "That change works great for Company B, but it would *never* work here," for example — and if you think you already know whatever it is you need to know.

Therefore, you want to check your assumptions every now and then. Ask questions before arriving at conclusions or leaping into action. Ask things like "Why are we doing this?"; "What are we taking for granted?"; "Why do I believe this to be true?"; and "Is this the only way?" Doing so helps you see what's blurring your view of the situation.

Stretch Out of Your Comfort Zone

People are like elastic bands — they only grow when they stretch. If you don't invest in your personal and professional growth, you put yourself under a lot more pressure. Decisions made without pushing the envelope or trying something new create the same repetitive results, even when you want something different to occur. The beauty of being an elastic band is that you can play with how much you stretch your thinking, your imagination, or your vulnerability — all of which lead to better decision-making.

Fixed thinking messes up decision-making for a couple of reasons. First, if you're a fixed thinker, you make all your projects confirm to the skills you already have — a surefire way to stunt growth and kill innovation. Second, you try to keep reality under your control and influence, which a) is impossible, and b) creates all sorts of pressure not only on you but also on your employees.

Expanding your comfort zone is a valuable skill for decision-makers and, in fact, any human being. So stretch your thinking: Expand what you see and what you do to gain flexibility. Build trust in yourself by stretching out of your comfort zone, one step at a time until it becomes effortless. Chapter 4 has details on helping you grow as a decision-maker.

Ask Profound Questions

The quality of the decisions you make reflects the quality of the questions you ask. Profound questions illuminate the underlying unseen dynamics that can inspire a new way of working or thinking about the situation. Great questions don't seem profound in the moment, but they inspire illuminating answers.

How many times have you walked into an uncertain situation and sensed that there was more to the situation than met the eye? When you're not sure what happened in a situation and need to conduct a short, reflective debriefing, use exploratory questions characteristic of journalism: What? How? When? Where? By asking these questions, you discover what is going on under the surface and tap into creative ideas. Consider these examples:

- ✔ **"How do I/you feel?"** If you don't air out emotions, the facts will be clouded. This question gives everyone involved a chance to discover what effect the situation is having.

- ✔ **"What happened?"** The answers to this question air out the information, along with the perceptions on what took place.
- ✔ **"What did (or can) I or my company learn?"** This question shifts your perspective into observation and reflection, which lets you pluck value out of the experience.

Profound questions can also spark team breakthroughs in thinking, company reinventions, and so on. To discover the impossible, you have to ask a question that your mind can't answer, such as, "How can we transport people without using cars?" That's when the inconceivable turns into a creative leap.

Learn from the Past

Some people fear uncertainty. At the heart of this fear is the belief that, as along as they keep doing what they've done in the past, everything will go well. But times change, and so does everything else, especially as markets go global, business goes online, and customers expect more than an affordable product. So rather than cling to the past, learn from it. Past experiences can teach you a lot; they can also confirm that you have the creativity, the confidence, and the character to walk into the unknown and thrive.

Resistance pops up when confidence is missing or when the issues are daunting — how to prepare for climate change, for example. But if you look back on human history, you discover that much has been accomplished despite fears of what may happen. When the car was first invented, for instance, people feared that the human body couldn't handle speeds of 30 mph (or 60 kph); they worried that riders' faces would peel back and their lips would flap around like a dog's with its head out the window. To overcome this resistance, remember that what's been done in the past doesn't add up to even a fraction of what humans are capable of achieving. So when resistance pops up because you don't know what may happen next, use that energy to take bigger steps for positive and real change.

Creating new solutions to large challenges requires both certainty and uncertainty. Uncertainty opens the door to exploring new frontiers of achievement, and certainty provides a sense of security and stability.

Listen Deeply

Listening deeply is harder than it sounds because of the tendency to not really pay attention to what the other person is saying. Many people, even when they appear to be listening, are actually jumping ahead in their minds to what they'll say in response, and many others just cut in to redirect the conversation or interject their own opinions.

You gain insight and flex your empathic muscles when you listen deeply to what has heart and meaning to someone, without overlaying your own ideas about whether they're right or wrong, weak or strong, or dumb or smart — or whether you even agree. To listen deeply, do the following:

- ✔ **Say and think nothing.** I mean nothing. Quiet your mind, keep it open, and offer no comment. Just listen.

- ✔ **Don't rush it.** Listen intently for 10 minutes, or 30 if you can make it. If you hit a silent patch, wait. Don't fill in the silence.

When someone gets over the shock of having your undivided attention, you'll experience what listening deeply means. Words don't convey the meaning. Connection to what matters to the person across from you is what listening deeply is all about.

If it feels right, ask how the other person experienced the conversation. Use the questions I offer in the earlier section "Ask Profound Questions" to find out how he or she felt and to discover what you both learned. This approach is one you can apply in many scenarios. You can even try it on yourself when you feel confused.

Shift Perspectives

Perception defines what you see in a situation, and the ability to shift perspective gives you access to better solutions in more situations. Why? Because decisions are better when diverse views converge into approaches or solutions that can be cooperatively held by more people.

To develop the capacity to shift perspective, try this exercise: Picture your backyard. Now picture it through the eyes of a mouse, a creature that lives on the ground and sees details — like the spider web tucked low in the shrubbery — that you tend to miss. Now switch to the point of view of a hawk or eagle flying overhead. As you walk around your neighborhood, try to see items from different vantage points: from the roots of a tree, from your dog's eyes, your cat's mind, from the top of the tree, and from the far reaches of the cosmos. Fun, right? Now repeat the exercise, but this time think of a perplexing problem you're facing or a tough decision you're making. Then think of it from the perspective of the line worker, the customer, the maintenance staff, and so on. How does the problem look from each of these perspectives?

Anytime you're faced with making a difficult decision, explore different perspectives. You will make better decisions if you're flexible about how you see, think, and approach the decision.

Move From Inertia to Action

Moving from inertia to action refers to taking what you've learned or the ideas swimming around in your brain and putting them into action. After you put an idea or understanding into action, you can reflect on what you've learned. By integrating what you know and experience into your future decisions, you improve those decisions.

The unfamiliar looks scary to most people at first. But don't let that stop you from taking action.

Pay Attention to What Your Heart Tells You

Trying to do something without having your heart in it is like pushing rope uphill. It's hard, if not impossible. Paying attention to whether your heart is in a decision is the simplest way to test your commitment to a course of action and to finalize which option you will ultimately choose. You can try, if you insist, to use your mental will to override your feelings about a decision. You can get away with it for a while, but sooner or later, you'll experience burnout or feel disheartened.

Because your heart brings a powerful form of intelligence to decision-making, you may as well use it. So test options or decisions you're making by listening to your heart. Do you feel fully engaged, half-hearted, or numb? As I explain in Chapter 5, your heart is smart; you should listen to it.

Embrace the Unpredictable

The future of the world is uncertain and unpredictable. So why not embrace this inherent uncertainty as an opportunity to be creative? Rather than hunker down in fear over what isn't known, focus your energies and your decision-making on discovering creative possibilities. Even die-hard linear and analytical thinkers can be creative and fast on their feet.

Work with Risk Differently

Humans tend to discount the probability of future events. If a risk isn't immediate, we tend to ignore it. The result? We end up unprepared. Therefore, take a different approach to risk. Instead of viewing it as a future possibility that's not likely to happen, look at the possible risk as though you are dealing with it today. Make it real. Then plan for it.

As you run these scenarios, think of the probable impacts or consequences of your decisions, and plan for them, too. Move a fluffy, may-or-may-not happen risk out of the clouds and into your decision-making process.

Chapter 21

Ten Ways to Improve Decision-Making

*Y*ou know what you want to achieve, yet the results aren't showing. Why? Maybe you're not getting the results you're after because your decisions aren't taking you to where you want to go. In this chapter, I offer ten suggestions that can help you make better decisions.

Find Your Inner Calm

Emotional stress interferes with how you process the information in your surroundings; if you're panicking or stressed, your intellectual and intuitive intelligences are impaired. Your emotions overthrow your decision-making, and you end up in damage-control mode, trying to repair the negative consequences of poorly conceived decisions. Therefore, the number-one way to improve your decision-making is to regulate your emotions.

To restore your inner calm, you need to find your happy place. You can use deep breathing techniques or other methods, such as the Quick Coherence Technique from the HeartMath Institute, which I describe in Chapter 5. Such techniques help you attain the calm necessary for your mind and your heart to work together.

Deep breathing calms your entire nervous system down and clears your mind so that you can hear yourself think. In this state, your heart and mind can work in concert, and the result will be a better decision. Use this method when you're in the midst of chaos, your world is falling apart around you, or any other time during the day.

Know When to Follow Plans and When to Co-create

In emergencies, plans are essential to coordinate expertise and effort so that everyone knows what to do within the chaos. But when work is constantly chaotic, plans can be hazardous. Why? Quite simply because, in those conditions, you need to be creative rather than fixed.

Plans work in situations where the circumstances are predictable. For instance, during a natural disaster like a Category 4 hurricane, what's required is fairly predictable. People need clean water, shelter, and food. But try to follow a fixed plan when things are running amuck, and well, you're hamstringing your ability to react as needed to constantly changing information.

In business, the key is to apply the right approach to the circumstance. Predictable market conditions favor plans. Unpredictable market conditions favor co-creation. Here are some guidelines:

- When you're in new territory, you want to co-create fresh approaches for how things get done. You also want to co-create if management or excessive control measures impede getting things done or when turmoil prevails. Co-creation lets you and your team invent original approaches to solve familiar problems.
- Stick to a plan when you must restore order before anything else can happen.

Keep Your Mind Nimble

How you think informs the actions you take. Concrete thinkers prefer to deal with the tangibles and consider ideas and concepts impractical. Conceptual thinkers work with ideas and concepts but tend to overlook the details. Blend the two, and you've got a lovely combination. Which way(s) of thinking do you rely on? Are you using the same thinking to make every decision? Different kinds of thinking apply to differ kinds of circumstances, and you can't successfully move from operational to strategic or senior-level decision-making without adjusting your thought and decision-making processes.

The next time you're faced with a decision-making task, try some flexible thinking to arrive at a workable solution. Being flexible allows you to draw from the diverse strengths of team members and to expand your own thinking so that you can selectively choose the appropriate action and get better results.

Focus on the Mission

In decision-making, focus dictates where your attention goes. If you pay attention to the wrong things, you make poor decisions. For example, if you focus on meeting the budget solely by instituting cost-cutting measures and ignoring your customers, pretty soon you won't have any revenue at all (customers are optional, after all!). Therefore, be alert to what you're paying attention to. Doing so helps you stay centered on what's important in achieving your overall goals and ensures that you've thought through the consequences of your decisions.

Innovate through Disruption

Use surprises to reinvent the company. For example, when revenues are falling, employee disengagement is high, and nothing you're doing or have previously relied on works, don't resist change or deny inconvenient truths — a strategy that can take you out of the game completely. Instead, acknowledge that an impending shift to market or business conditions is occurring and use the gap between what you think should be happening and what actually is happening to do things differently.

Disruptions can be radical, such as when your company is about to fail because of a sudden, unforeseen event, or they can sneak up over time as conditions change but your approach to them doesn't. At these times, do things differently: Take an idea that doesn't conform to the norm or engage in a risky decision that can be beneficial. The risk of doing nothing is higher than the risk of making a bold move.

It takes only one idea to inject newness into routine attitudes and raise results to a higher level of achievement. Act on the simmering sense that it's time to take a radically different approach.

Tap into Your Intuition

Instant decision-making takes place in milliseconds and draws, without your conscious awareness, on the vast stash of solutions, decisions, and experiences you've built up over time. The best way to strengthen the range of solutions your brain subconsciously taps into is to make a lot of decisions. If you feel confident in your current setting, great! Then change to a dissimilar environment so that you can develop experiences in a new setting.

Everyone has intuitive intelligence, but not everyone trusts it or knows how it works. You can improve access to your intuition by regulating your emotions (see the earlier section "Find Your Inner Calm ") , gaining experience (both successes and failures) with your decision-making, and paying attention to your inner voice (it's the one that sometimes argues with your rational mind). Making more decisions, whether they all work or not, strengthens your subconscious library of possible and probable solutions. To find out more about how intuition works, see Chapter 7.

Learn from Mistakes

Check the newspapers, and you'll find stories that show many ways companies can make mistakes. It's the best way to see, without incurring the expense of making the mistake yourself, how decisions can fail to consider consequences or assess risk.

Ryanair, an Irish air carrier, is well known for its cheap fares, rude treatment of customers, and exorbitant fines levied on baggage. To keep costs down, Ryanair cut customer service and fined its customers for baggage infractions beyond what was perceived to be fair. Customers began to avoid the airline, believing that low fares didn't justify the disrespectful treatment. The company's mistake? Putting internal goals (keeping costs low) ahead of its own reputation and maintaining customer loyalty. In response, in 2014, Ryanair acknowledged that its "abrupt culture" had hurt its reputation, and it decided to communicate more respectfully to customers and be more lenient about fines over bags.

In studying mistakes, try to learn what happened: Where in the decision-making process did the error occur, and why did it occur? Study other companies' successes and failures to observe what they missed in the decision-making process. When you learn from mistakes — whether they involve your own, your company's, or others' misfortunes — you can apply the lessons to your own decision-making.

Keep an Open Mind

Keeping an open mind allows you to incorporate instead of reject new information because it's unfamiliar or seems irrelevant. Being open to new information allows you to stay current and make better decisions because you're not ignoring how your customers or employees feel or what they need.

I know, I know. Having a closed mind is so much easier. If you really want to stay in the dark, here are a few tongue-in-cheek ways to keep your mind locked tight as a drum:

- Accept only information you already know and label anything you don't understand — quantum physics, self-organizing companies, the popularity of Justin Bieber — as pseudoscience, esoteric, or woo-woo.

- Reject the idea that the emotions of employees or any one impacted by the decision are relevant to decision-making — until you need to blame them for being resistant when initiatives blow up in your face.

- Refuse to make a decision; if a sandbox is anywhere within the vicinity, stick your head in it.

- Treat everything as absolute — either this or that, black or white — because seeing how all the pieces fit is an overrated skill favored by anarchists.

Balance the Intuitive with the Rational

Intuition is slippery, has been known to fail, and can't be measured. No wonder decision-makers prefer to trust something more specific and precise, like rational thinking. But here's a little secret: Rational decision-making really isn't that rational. Things other than logic play into just about every decision you make, whether you know it or not. (Think of the number of senior decision-makers who make decisions that serve personal gain over company goals.)

Your intuitive intelligence anticipates events before they occur. When you tap into it, you can process volumes of information in a nanosecond, simultaneously holding the short and long term in your mind without blowing any brain fuses. Intuitive and rational processes each bring unique strengths to the decision-making process.

Get to know the language your intuition uses. Differentiate it from mental chatter and emotions. Still the mind so you can hear what your deep intelligence has to say. The answers will be available. You'll be able to discern how well aligned the decision is with your aspirations. Chapter 7 has the details on intuition's role in decision-making.

Pay Attention to the Workplace

Interpersonal relationships and unwritten rules in the workplace combine with the given circumstances to produce the conditions for decision-making. How things get done, the degree of autonomy employees have, their commitment to their peers, the accountability people have for the decisions they make, and so on, all impact the resilience and durability of decision outcomes.

Workplace design is part of the formula for faster response time and more accurate decisions. Removing barriers to real-time information exchange accelerates rapid, more accurate responses. Creating workplaces and working relationships that support employees improves their ability to make sound judgments and good decisions.

Review your workplace to ensure that it supports the health and wellness of your employees. Offering places for rest and reflection can revitalize the workplace, reduce stress, reduce cost, and increase employee retention. Chapter 2 has more information and suggestions for creating a healthy decision-making environment.

Chapter 22

Ten Secrets behind Ethical Decision-Making

Developing a formal code of ethics is an obvious way to communicate clearly what's acceptable and what's not. Yet words are one thing, and actions are another! Management style, character, procedures, and processes all send messages about what will and won't be tolerated. In this chapter, I give you ten subtle signals you can look for to determine whether the unspoken messages in your workplace are leading decision-makers toward ethical or unethical decisions.

Employees Feel Respected and Happy

Never underestimate the power of respect, happiness, and high personal worth as predictors of ethical behavior. Employees who feel respected, valued, and happy tend to select ethics over self-interest. The power of peer-to-peer acknowledgement builds shared accountability and responsibility. Informal appreciation expressed as part of everyday working relationships conveys how valued someone is to the team and to the company, and happiness is made of meaningful work — feeling that you're having a positive impact and contributing to a higher mission.

Regardless of the role they play, all who work with the company are people first, then employees. A workplace that fosters respect plays an important part in supporting people's well-being. Well-being and a sense of shared responsibility between coworkers and management instills a code of ethics that operates naturally.

Relationships Are Built on Trust

When the going gets tough, what happens in your company? Are you hard on employees, or do you focus on solutions? If you answered that you focus on solutions, you're on the right track. When tough circumstances are faced by focusing on solutions rather than placing blame, you develop more trustworthy relationships. Such relationships foster creativity and encourage employees to take chances on finding solutions.

When employees don't know what to trust, they look after their own self-interest, essentially denying you the benefit of their insight and creativity because sharing these things is too risky. Low-trust environments present a high risk to emotional and social safety. Taking the initiative or being creative is quite likely to be career-limiting move. Conforming is rewarded.

When the relationships are built on trust, the focus shifts from relying on process and procedures to get things done to trusting in the talent of the team, which, when the purpose of the decision is clear, will focus its efforts accordingly. Rather than management being responsible for results, responsibility and accountability for decisions and implementation are shared. Greater autonomy and trust equate to stronger engagement.

The Focus Is on Collective Achievement

Ethical decision-making is profoundly connected to accepting total responsibility for decisions, actions, and consequences. So if you want to know what a company truly values, pay attention to whether decision-making focuses on self-interest — profit at the expense of employees, customers, the local community, the environment, and so on — or on adding value in a long-term and broader sense. In an ethical company, the company's contribution extends to the well-being of its employees, its customers, and the communities it serves or operates in. It also includes care for the natural resources it relies on to create its product or service. When all are successful or cared for, no logical or emotional temptation exists to compromise ethics.

The Right Things are Rewarded

More often than not, a company creates its own ethical breaches by rewarding the wrong things. Companies that pressure employees to get things done at any cost, punish whistleblowers or anyone who reports misconduct or illegal behavior, and ignore the value of people and the planet is just asking for ethical breaches.

My guess is that you want loyal, paying customers plus engaged and happy employees. To find out whether you're measuring the things that promote loyal and happy customers and employees — presumably the ultimate measure of success for your company — ask, "What is the mission of the company?" and "How will we know we've accomplished it?" After you identify the ways you measure whether you've achieve your mission, evaluate whether happiness is taken into account, or whether customer loyalty is a factor. If not, you're not measuring the things that will bring you closer to achieving those goals.

Minimum Compliance Isn't Enough

Doing just enough to get by in the eyes of the regulators implies indifference. Being indifferent toward issues of an ethical nature can invade thinking until doing as little as possible replaces bold action. Leadership, done well, requires courage to boldly go where most companies dare not tread. Companies that courageously venture into original methods of managing and conducting themselves without being told what to do by regulatory or societal demands are natural leaders, and their results are highly rewarded. They meet and exceed regulations.

Change the internal conversation from what a company or an employee must do to what is the right or smart thing to do. Applied to decision-making, the ethical decision might not be the easy path, but it will be the best one in the long run.

Good Character is Important

The question that you should ask with every high-stakes decision is, "Who do I become as a result of this decision?" When the answer teeters between a person of good character and someone who's leaning toward the dark side, the choice is career-defining. Character and integrity work hand-in-hand. When you add up the personal character of each employee, the sum indicates the overall character of a company.

Superman has super powers, and with great power comes great responsibility (along with a cape). Each person has superpowers (though not everyone was issued a cape — I have a T-shirt instead!). When it comes to making ethical decisions, the path of least resistance rarely builds the character needed for high levels of leadership. Choosing to build good character requires that you be able to take the higher, bolder path, the one that leads to higher levels of respect and wisdom.

Everyone Leads

In companies where everyone leads, everyone is held individually and collectively responsible and accountable for achieving results. There is no separation between superior and inferior or between boss, leader, and employee, although the labels may still be used.

Command-and-control management styles have a tendency, except in emergencies, to defer accountability to those in authority. Where autonomy is infused throughout the company's cultural DNA, however, peers are accountable and responsible to peers, as well as to managers. An overall commitment to a code of ethics, written or implied, is ingrained in the company's integrity.

Whether you subscribe to a self-organizing structure or one that is more conventional, when peers are responsible and accountable to their peers for decisions, expectations are clear.

Principles and Values Guide Action

Principles and values can guide ethical decision-making when they are stated and shared. What principles and values do you use to guide and direct decisions in your company? Putting ethics into action demonstrates the company's commitment to its principles and values. (*Principles* are portable, serving to clarify confusion wherever it may exist or help a confused decision-maker regain clarity. *Values* specify what is important to the company — what it stands for and won't stand for.)

Take the Agile Manifesto developed in 2001 by practitioners of the Agile software programming methodology, for example. These principles can inform and influence workplace and company culture as well as indicate priorities:

- ✔ Individuals and interactions over processes and tools
- ✔ Working software over comprehensive documentation
- ✔ Customer collaboration over contract negotiation
- ✔ Responding to change over following a plan

Attention Is Given to Workplace Culture

As is often the case, you can learn about one thing by studying something else. Business cultures are like that. If you want to know what deeply entrenched, underlying beliefs guide your company, pay attention to the actions and behavior of your employees. Studying routine patterns on the surface gives you insight into your company's core beliefs, a topic I delve more deeply into in Chapters 2 and 3.

From a detached, objective viewpoint, look at the activities, actions, and the decisions your employees make. Particularly notice decisions that cycle back, showing up like a bad penny. Eventually, you'll see repeating patterns. Ask "Why?" often enough, and you'll identify the originating belief. Then you can decide whether it's useful or not. The health of the workplace depends on a culture made up of up-to-date and useful beliefs.

Trust Is the Underlying Value

Trust is the context for highly ethical decision-making. Trust gives employees the confidence to step back, see the big picture, make bold leaps of creativity, and work effectively with conflict. When trust is endemic, your employees don't spend their energy and concentration on protecting themselves from risk of danger.

Use every crisis, every decision, and every failure to extend trust, compassion, and care into the decision-making environment. Ultimately, you'll wind up building trust and an innately ethical decision-making environment.

Index

• *W* •

• *X* •

• *Z* •

About the Author

Dawna Jones believes business can be better for the people it serves and employs and for the planet that sustains us all. When not exploring the world or enjoying the great outdoors, she can be found on her website: www. FromInsightToAction.com. Her business podcast, *Evolutionary Provocateur,* is on http://www.Management-Issues.com and on iTunes. She regularly hosts business innovation webinars, exchanging ideas worldwide toward healthier workplaces and restoring care for Nature.

Dedication

To my daughter, Lindsay Henwood, with gratitude for her steady support and unwavering encouragement and to all change agents boldly staying true to their hearts.

Author's Acknowledgments

Writing *Decision-Making For Dummies* has been a cooperative venture with the management and business innovation community bringing together experience and stories that make the concepts in this book tangible. In addition, countless others have provided expertise and inspiration, but I would particularly like to acknowledge Dr. Rollin McCraty, research scientist; Joseph Bragdon, author of *Profit for Life;* Andy Haydon, specialist in occupational health and safety; and Andy Allen, CEO of RJ Allen, Inc. A special mention goes to Jack Barnard who unfailingly offered counsel.

Thanks also to Bill Gladstone and Margot Hutchison of Waterside Literary Agency; Wiley's acquisition editor Stacy Kennedy and the invaluable contribution of project editor Tracy Barr, who steered direction and provided invaluable guidance. Finally, my deepest thanks to close friends and family for their patience.

Publisher's Acknowledgments

Acquisitions Editor: Stacy Kennedy

Project Editor: Tracy L. Barr

Technical Editor: Tracy E. Barnes

Project Coordinator: Sheree Montgomery

Cover Image: ©iStockphoto.com/shawn_hempel